A GUIDEBOOK LIKE NO OTHER!

A unique, comprehensive budget guide to Chicago, *Know More, Spend Less: A Native's Guide To Chicago* gives readers an insider's take on hundreds of free, inexpensive, and unusual things to do around town. Packed with useful information on every page, it's the perfect resource for tourists, business travelers, resident Chicagoans, and anyone on a budget. With this third edition, we are proud to announce expanded coverage of Chicago's South Side. Every chapter contains both mainstream and offbeat suggestions:

⇒ **TOURING** Antique Row, Architecture, Art, Cemeteries, Gardens, Landmark Districts, Holiday Madness, Museums, Natural Spaces, Ringside Politics, Talk Shows, Waterfalls...

⇒ **RECREATION** Arcades, Archery, Bingo, Bowling, Canoeing, Chess, Dog Walking, Euchre, Fencing, Golf, Playgrounds, Pool, Stargazing, Swimming, Trivia, Virtual Reality, Volleyball...

⇒ **FOOD** Ethnic, Inexpensive, and Unusual Favorites: Airport Grub, Beefs, Bratwurst Pizza, Brunch, Cactus Tacos, Cafes, Cajun, Chili, Croatian, Ethiopian, Lakeside Dining, Laotian, Noodles, Pastries, Pierogi, Ribs, Serbian, Subs, Tapas...

⇒ **ENTERTAINMENT** Affordable Clubs, Movies, and Theater, Best Bars for Beer, Blues, Improv Comedy, Jazz, Music Fests, Poetry Slams, Polka, Punk, Reggae ...

⇒ **WALKING** City Parks, Downtown Architecture, Ethnic Enclaves, Historic Districts, Luxury Hotel Lobbies, Neighborhood Treks, Public Art Tours ...

⇒ **LODGING** Bed and Breakfasts, Best Downtown Deals, Boutique Hotels, No-Frills Neighborhood Motels, Room Discount Services, Youth Hostels, Dorm Rooms...

⇒ **SHOPPING** Auctions, Markets, Outlet Stores (clothing, fabric, housewares, liquor, sporting goods...), Resale Shopping (appliances, books, clothes, computers, music...), Unique Browsing (art, cookie jars, costumes, posters, surplus...)...

⇒ **KEEPING INFORMED** Free Publications, Internet Addresses, Key Phone Numbers and Hotlines, Radio and TV Programming...

For those who want to venture into the nooks and crannies of everyday Chicago, **From** someone who knows and loves the city inside and out... **YOU WILL NOT FIND A MORE INDISPENSABLE HANDBOOK TO AMERICA'S SECOND CITY.**

OTHER BOOKS BY LAKE CLAREMONT PRESS

Chicago Haunts: Ghostlore of the Windy City
by Ursula Bielski

Hollywood on Lake Michigan:
100 Years of Chicago and the Movies
by Arnie Bernstein

COMING IN 1999

Graveyards of Chicago
by Matt Hucke

A Native's Guide To Chicago's South Suburbs
by Christina Bultinck and Christy Johnston-Czarnecki

A Native's Guide To Chicago's Northern Suburbs
by Jason Fargo

A Native's Guide To Chicago's Western Suburbs
by Laura Mazzuca Toops and John Toops

A Native's Guide To Chicago's Northwestern Suburbs
by Martin Bartels

Chicago Resource Guide for the Chronically Ill and Disabled
by Susan McNulty

Great Chicago Fires
by David Cowan

Enthusiasm for Previous Editions of

A NATIVE'S GUIDE TO CHICAGO

"Chicago is a big city..., so if you want some help finding what to
do and where to do it, the updated *A Native's Guide To Chicago*
may be the ticket. ...it looks at the Windy City beyond the run-of-
the-mill tourist attractions. ...[*A Native's Guide To Chicago*]
gives readers lots of ideas to help them do what it promises:
Know more, spend less."
—*Milwaukee Journal Sentinel*

"[Sharon Woodhouse] went digging and she put it
all together ...all kinds of wild and wacky things to do.
...This is a Chicago you've never known before."
—Abby Polonsky, Entertainment Reporter,
WCIU-TV, *Today's Chicago Woman*, and *Home & Away*

"How many times have you visited a big city only to wish you knew
those tried-and-true places where the natives hang out? Sharon
Woodhouse has solved that problem for those visiting Chicago
with her new book..."
—*Cedar Rapids Gazette*

"It's a pleasant, easy-to-read approach to this 'city of
neighborhoods.'...The author really knows her Chicago."
—Shirley Davis, *Quad-City Times*

"It's a perfect gift book. You'll be really surprised if you lived
in Chicago...your whole life. ...You may think you know your
neighborhood, and then you'll read about something: 'I didn't
know that was there.' This is the whole idea of the book...that
we get to know the whole city, get to know the neighborhoods."
—Lucyna Migala, WCEV Radio

Also featured on:

⇒ WGN radio's *Dean Richards Show*
⇒ WBEZ radio's *Mara Tapp Show*

And seen in:

*Inside Newspaper, Lerner Booster, New City, River North News,
Chicago Books In Review, Chicago Women's Journal, Vital Times,*
and *The New World.*

See the back cover for more endorsements of
A Native's Guide To Chicago.

KNOW MORE, SPEND LESS:

A NATIVE'S GUIDE TO CHICAGO

Updated and Revised Third Edition

By Sharon Woodhouse

With expanded South Side coverage by Mary McNulty

Lake Claremont Press
4805 North Claremont Avenue
Chicago, Illinois 60625
http://members.aol.com/LakeClarPr

Know More, Spend Less:
A Native's Guide To Chicago

by Sharon Woodhouse,
with expanded South Side coverage
by Mary McNulty

Published January 1999, by:

Lake Claremont Press
4805 N. Claremont Ave.
Chicago, IL 60625
773/784-7517
LakeClarPr@aol.com
http://members.aol.com/LakeClarPr

ISBN: 0-9642426-0-5: $12.95 Softcover
Library of Congress Catalog Card Number: 98-66234

Library of Congress Cataloging in Publication Data
(Provided by Quality Books, Inc.)

Woodhouse, Sharon.
        Know more, spend less : a native's guide to Chicago / by
Sharon Woodhouse ; with expanded South Side coverage by Mary
McNulty. — 3rd ed.
        p. cm.
        Includes index.
        Preassigned LCCN: 98-66234
        ISBN: 0-9642426-0-5

        1. Chicago (Ill.)—Guidebooks.   I. McNulty, Mary (Mary
F.) II. Title.   III. Title: Native's guide to Chicago

F548.18.W66 1998   917.73'110443
                                       QBI98-664

Printed in the United States of America
by McNaughton & Gunn, Inc. of Saline, Michigan.

*For three generations of native Chicagoans
in the Woodhouse and Noesen families, especially
Patricia and Kenneth Woodhouse, my parents
and
Leonard Noesen, my grandfather*
—SW

*To Richard, for leaving the golden sun of Colorado
to indulge my love for Chicago.*

*To Rachel and AnneRenee,
the true South Side natives in the family.*
—MM

CONTENTS

⇒ Airports, Animals, Antiques, Architecture, Architecture (Religious), Art (Indoors), Art (Outdoors), Boat Rides, Cemeteries, Elevator Rides, Factory Tours, Fountains, Gardens, Holiday Madness, Lawn Frenzy, Museums, Natural Spaces, Navy Pier, Newspapers, Politics, Public Transportation, Skyscrapers, Talk Shows, Trades and Exchanges, Waterfalls

⇒ Adaptive Sports, Adult Education, Aerobics, Arcades, Archery, Badminton, Baseball, Basketball, Bicycling, Bingo, Birding, Board Games, Boccie Ball, Bowling, Boxing, Bridge, Canoeing, Chess, Climbing, Croquet, Darts, Dogwalking, Euchre, Fencing, Football, Go, Golf, Handball, Hi-ball, Ice Skating, In-line Skating, Laser Tag, Massage, Nintendo, Trivia, and Horseracing, Origami, Playgrounds, Pool, Racquetball, Roller Skating, Running, Sailing, Shuffleboard, Skiing (Cross Country), Skiing (Downhill), Soccer, Stargazing, Swimming, Table Tennis, Tennis, Tobogganing, Ultimate Frisbee, Volleyball, Walking, Chicago Park District Information

4 FOOD...117

⇒ **Restaurants**

African, Airport Food, Argentinean, Armenian, Asian, Breakfast, Breakfast (All Day), Breakfast (Buffets in Hotels), Breakfast (Downtown and Dirt Cheap), Brunch, Bulgarian, Burgers, Cafeterias, Cajun, Caribbean, Chilean, Chili, Chinese, Coffeehouses, Columbian, Costa Rican, Croatian, Cuban, Dinner (Other Bargains), Do-It-Yourself Stir Fry, Doughnuts, English, Ethiopian, Ethnic Hybrids, Ethiopian, Filipino, Fish Fry, French, French Fries, Game, German, Greek, Guatemalan, Honduran, Hot Dogs, Hungarian, Ice Cream, Indian/Pakistani, Indonesian, Irish, Israeli, Italian, Italian Beefs/ Sausages, Jamaican, Korean, Korean Buddhist Vegetarian, Kosher, Lakeside Dining, Laotian, Late-night Wonders, Lithuanian, Lunch, Lunch in Bars, Lunch (Downtown), Lunch (Downtown Quick Gourmet), Mexican, Moroccan, Nigerian, Peruvian, Pizza, Polish, Polish Sausage, Pub Grub, Puerto Rican, Ribs, Romanian, Russian, Salvadoran, Scones, Scottish, Seafood (Take Out Joints on the River), Seafood (Take Out—Not on the River, Serbian, Serbian With a Gimmick, Smoke-Free Restaurants, Soul Food, Soup, Southern Eclectic, Spanish, Submarine Sandwiches, Swedish, Thai, Tibetan, Tropical Drinks, Vegetarian, Vietnamese

⇒ **Dining Discounts**
⇒ **Internet Resources**
⇒ **Outlet Stores**
⇒ **Farmer's Markets**

5 ENTERTAINMENT...209

⇒ **Live Music**

Blues, Classical, Coffee Houses, Country, Eclectic, Ethnic Tunes, Folk, Irish, Jazz, Piano Bars, Punk, Reggae, Rock/Alternative,

⇒ **Clubs**

Big Band, Dance Clubs, Folk, Gay and Lesbian, German, Latin Dance, Polish, Polka, Stepping, Swing

⇒ **Drink**

Bars for Beer Education, Bars for Beer Selection, Bloody Marys, Bars for Games, Bars with Unique Features, Bars for a Wide Variety of Fine and Unusual Spirits in a Funky Setting, Southwest Side Bar Recommendations, Coffee at Night

⇒ **Theater**
Inexpensive Options, Theaters that Use Ushers, Discount Tickets
⇒ **Comedy and Improv**
⇒ **Poetry and Performance Art**
⇒ **Dance**
⇒ **Movies**
Matinees, The Cheap Movie Theaters, Alternative Movie Houses, Other
Free and Inexpensive Film Options
⇒ **Downtown and Free**
⇒ **Public Celebrations**
The Big Grant Park/Lakefront Summer Events, Music Festivals, Art Fairs,
Neighborhood Fests, Parades

6   WALKING...275

⇒ **Neighborhoods, Historic Districts, and Ethnic Enclaves for**
  Roaming and Exploring
Andersonville, Argyle Street, Beverly Hills/Morgan Park, Boystown,
Bridgeport, Bronzeville, Burnham Park/Printers Row, Chinatown, Clybourn
Corridor, Devon Avenue, Downtown/The Loop, Downtown at Night,
Edgewater/Bryn Mawr Avenue, Gold Coast, Greek Town, Hegewisch, Hyde
Park, Kenwood Mansions, The Lakefront, Lincoln Park, Lincoln Square,
Little Italy/Taylor Street, Little Village/La Villita, Logan Square,
Magnificent Mile, Old Edgebrook, Old Town, Pill Hill, Pilsen, Pullman,
River North, Rogers Park, Roscoe Village, South Chicago, South Shore,
Streeterville, Tri-Taylor, Villa Park, Wicker Park/Bucktown, Wrigleyville
⇒ **Good Parks for Walking**
Columbus Park, Grant and Burnham Parks, Jackson Park, Lincoln Park,
Marquette Park, River Park, and Washington Park
⇒ **Walking Tours**
Downtown Buildings (Classic), Downtown Buildings (Modern), Luxury
Hotel Lobbies, Public Art (Classic), Public Art (Modern), Indoor Public Art

7   LODGING...327

⇒ **Downtown Hotels, Hotels in Other Areas, Neighborhood**
  Inns of Chicago, Room Link-up Services, Hostels, Dorms
  and Dorm-like, No-frills Neighborhood Motels

ACKNOWLEDGMENTS

Instead of getting simpler, each successive edition of *A Native's Guide To Chicago* becomes more involved and draws more people into its creation. For this third edition, that meant the invaluable help of Mary McNulty who took on the project of expanding the book's South Side coverage. It also meant painstaking fact-checking by Susan McNulty, Brandon Zamora, and Kenneth Woodhouse. Additionally, Brandon Zamora did a wonderful job pitching in with some research, writing, and a great deal of proofreading and indexing. Susan McNulty and Kimberly Watkins also applied their flair with details to the tasks of proofreading and indexing. David Cowan and Darlene Noesen gently worked out the manuscript's kinks with their editing magic. Graphic designer Timothy Kocher again performed his artistic wizardry to update the cover. The addition of maps and photos to this edition are due to Rames Shrestha and Bill Arroyo. Rames did a beautiful job poking his camera into the corners of Chicago and Bill spent untold hours designing the intricate walking tour maps. "I couldn't have done it without you" is hardly sufficient to recognize your individual contributions. A million thanks!

My family and friends can't be remembered enough for their continual support of this and other Lake Claremont Press projects. I love you all immensely.

Finally, my tremendous appreciation to all those at the other ends of letters, phone calls, and surprise visits, who supplied either suggestions or information to help make this the best version of *A Native's Guide to Chicago* yet! You've each provided an important piece of the final product and I'm truly grateful for your participation.   -SW

Throughout this project, I have been continually impressed by the enthusiasm that people have for Chicago and their eagerness to spread this enthusiasm far and wide. Everyone I spoke with not only shared their special knowledge, but also referred me to other people and places. Friends and strangers alike strengthened my belief that Chicago is a city of peerless qualities.

In particular, I would like to thank Karen Hudy for her input on polka groups; Neenie Cepenas for information on the Lithuanian community; Neenie and Dee Dee Connor for Southwest-side eating and nightlife suggestions; John and Terrie Winters for Beverly updates; Yvonne Zipter, Judith Wright, and Mark Johnson for tips on Hyde Park. A special thank you to Mike Aniol and Bob Wisz for the vintage Buick Riviera-guided-tour of Hegewisch. Also of great help were David Betlejewski of the Greater Southwest Development Corporation, and Bathsheba Draper and Mark Payne of the Mid-South Planning and Development Commission.

I must recognize my husband Dick Spinelli for letting me drag him all over the South and Southwest sides of the city (although I suspect that he had as much fun as I did). And certainly I would not be writing this if not for Sharon Woodhouse. Thanks, Sharon, for giving me the chance to work on the third edition.

Finally, a big hug to my family and friends for their unfailing love and encouragement.   -MM

PUBLISHER'S CREDITS

COVER DESIGN by Timothy Kocher.

INTERIOR DESIGN by Sharon Woodhouse.

PHOTOGRAPHS by Rames Shrestha and William Arroyo.

MAPS by William Arroyo (walking tour maps) and Sharon Woodhouse (regional maps).

FACT CHECKING by Susan McNulty, Kenneth Woodhouse, and Brandon Zamora.

EDITING by David Cowan and Darlene Noesen.

PROOFREADING by Brandon Zamora, Susan McNulty, Kimberly Watkins, Kenneth Woodhouse, and Mary McNulty.

LAYOUT by Sharon Woodhouse and Kenneth Woodhouse.

INDEXING by Brandon Zamora, with Kimberly Watkins, Susan McNulty, and Sharon Woodhouse.

The text of *A Native's Guide To Chicago* was set in Times New Roman, with headings in Imprest Caps and subheadings in Arial.

NOTICE

Although Lake Claremont Press, the authors, and fact checkers have exhaustively researched all sources to ensure the accuracy and completeness of the information contained in this book, we assume no responsibility for errors, inaccuracies, omissions, or any inconsistency herein.

KNOWING MORE, SPENDING LESS

Chicago's landmark Water Tower on North Michigan Avenue.
(*Photo by Rames Shrestha.*)

KNOWING MORE, SPENDING LESS

O nce, when feeling particularly like a generic American, I listed my ethnicity on an application as "third-generation Chicagoan." Although at the time I was merely amusing myself, upon further reflection, I realized that my affection for Chicago and my rootedness here make it as apt a description as any. A lifelong Chicagoan and an avid traveler, I spend a lot of time exploring and enjoying my hometown, which, even to a native, can be as foreign as it is familiar. I decided to write a guidebook for our friendly village that I would want to use. This book joins the information I've slowly accumulated over a lifetime with the more intensive investigations I've made since starting the first edition.

KNOW MORE

Many guidebooks purportedly show you *the* Chicago. Once you dig through all the padding, however, you often have a list of stuff that won't distinguish your experience of Chicago from that of any of the billions of uninitiated tourists that have passed this way before. You might wonder what we Chicagoans were doing when all these guests were having their "unique" encounter with the town we live in. (We may have been wondering how anyone could so readily discern what makes a visit genuinely *Chicago*.)

Those guidebooks do have a good excuse—the majority were written by non-Chicagoans. Many involve plugging Chicago data into a formulaic outline—just one more volume in a large publishing house's travel series. I wrote and published this guide as an antidote to those corporate guides, constructing a comprehensive budget guide that offers inside information and offbeat suggestions alongside more traditional guidebook fare. I hope it also conveys the love and enthusiasm that I, like many native and transplanted Chicagoans, have for our hometown.

For tourists, business travelers, and other guests, this guide furnishes you with lots of possibilities and suggestions, but does not endorse a specific plan of attack. Use these low-expense suggestions as your point of entry into a complex town. Wherever you start, however much you cover, it will be authentically *Chicago*. For Chi-town inhabitants, this book can be a handy reference for getting out and doing more without doling out any more than you're used to spending. It can gently ease you into neighborhoods you're unaccustomed to, provide fresh perspectives on your neighbors and surroundings, and refine your image of the immense stretch of land that Chicago covers.

SPEND LESS

A low-cost manual is certainly desirable for those with fixed or limited incomes. However, there are reasons beyond necessity that make spending less money attractive. First, spending less makes however many discretionary dollars you do have go farther. You can go out more often if you don't drop it all in one spot. Secondly, many trendy places and pricey joints that suck up your cash are fairly alike. As they often attract similar crowds and project similar images, pouring money in their direction will not give you a clue as to what the rest of Chicago is about. Finally, certain free activities are the best ways to know any place better. They are walking, biking, browsing, people watching, people meeting, etc.

NEW THIS EDITION

Several new elements help make the third edition of *A Native's Guide To Chicago* the best yet:

⇒ Extended coverage of the South Side provided by virtual native Mary McNulty. Mary's contributions helped me to present a fuller picture of this often overlooked half of the city and are most evident in the wonderful entries she wrote on South Side neighborhoods for the *Walking* chapter.

⇒ Nearly 125 more pages than the 2nd edition. By supplying more information for each entry and adding hundreds of new entries, we've been able to give you more of the useful information on Chicago neighborhoods that you appreciated in the earlier editions. (And, because the font is smaller than past versions, you're actually getting a lot more than that!)

⇒ Photographs. Sure they're worth more than 1,000 words, but the photos are hardly enough to give you a graphical representation of the Windy City. However, I hope they do help spur you to get out and see the city for yourself.

⇒ Maps. *A Native's Guide To Chicago* breaks the city into nine regions—each of which has its own map in this edition. (See pp. 411-419). We've also added a map to go with each of the six downtown walking tours in the *Walking* chapter.

⇒ Fact Checking. Susan McNulty, Brandon Zamora, and Kenneth Woodhouse helped insure that the information within these pages was as accurate as possible through various research tasks and checking facts twice and sometimes, three times.

FINDING YOUR WAY

Curious? Ready to actively explore the city? *A Native's Guide To Chicago* does not give you street by street directions to the places listed. Don't panic. A little map reading and learning the simple grid layout of our streets (explained shortly) will quickly increase your familiarity with our geography.

Every entry in this book is coded with a geographic abbreviation: **C** (Central), **W** (West), **N** (North), **NW** (Northwest), **FN** (Far North), **S** (South), **SW** (Southwest), **FSE** (Far Southeast), and **FSW** (Far Southwest). This scheme was designed to give you a rough idea of where a place is located and to help you find things that are convenient for you. Hopefully, you will also use it to find points of interest, restaurants, entertainment spots, recreational facilities, stores, and festivals in neighborhoods that are unfamiliar to you. Doing more of this will quickly expand and clarify your picture of Chicago, its inhabitants, and the things that go on here.

Following are the boundaries of the different regions. Consult the map on page 7, for a visual representation of these areas.

Central: Bounded by North (*1600 N*), Lake Michigan, Cermak (*2200 S*), and Ashland (*1600 W*).

West: Bounded by North (*1600 N*), Ashland (*1600 W*), Cermak (*2200 S*), and the Chicago city limits (*between 4600 W and 6000 W*).

North: Bounded by Lawrence (*4800 N*), Lake Michigan, North (*1600 N*), and Kedzie (*3200 W*).

NorthWest: Bounded by Lawrence (*4800 N*), Kedzie (*3200 W*), North (*1600 N*), and the Chicago city limits (*between 7200 and 9200 W*).

Far North: Bounded by Lawrence (*4800 N*), Lake Michigan, and the Chicago city limits on the north (*between 6400 and 7600 N*) and the west (*between 7800 and 9200 W*).

South: Bounded by Cermak (*2200 S*), Lake Michigan, Marquette/67th (*6700 S*), and Halsted (*800 W*).

SouthWest: Bounded by Cermak (*2200 S*), Halsted (*800 W*), Marquette/ 67th (*6700 S*), and the Chicago city limits (*between 4600 and 7200 W*).

Far SouthEast: Bounded by Marquette/67th (*6700 S*), Lake Michigan, the Chicago city limits (*between 13000 and 13800 S*), and Halsted (*800 W*).

Far SouthWest: Bounded by Marquette/67th (*6700 S*), Halsted (*800 W*), and the Chicago city limits on the south (*between 11500 and 13000 S*) and on the west (*between 2400 and 4800 W*) .

At least 90% of Chicago's streets fall neatly into a "grid system" that originates at State and Madison streets downtown. Street indexes and common knowledge tag these streets by their distance either north or south of Madison, or east or west of State. (Many Chicagoans pride themselves on the amount of these numbers they can remember.) Eight city blocks constitute one mile. 1/8 of a mile is "100," thus, Chicago Avenue, at one mile (8 blocks) north of Madison, is considered "800 North." Ashland, being 2 miles or 16 blocks west of State, is "1600 West." 1600 W. Chicago would be at the corner of Chicago and Ashland.

Major streets come every four blocks. A helpful reminder when orienting yourself: The lake is always east, unless you are so far southeast that you can see Indiana. Many of the diagonal streets that defy this easy blueprint were once trails of the Native Americans that previously lived here. The main ones are Archer, Clark, Clybourn, Elston, Grand, Higgins, Lincoln, Milwaukee, Ogden, Ridge, South Chicago, and Vincennes.

Map of Coded Regions

SOME INDISPENSABLE RESOURCES

To help you move fluidly through the city, I suggest acquiring the following:

⇒ A Chicago street map, available at drugstores and gas stations for $2-$4, will help you with all the smaller streets we couldn't fit on our maps.

⇒ A street index, which tells how far north, south, east, or west a street is located. This information matched with a street address serve as coordinates, giving you a place's precise location in Chicago's grid system. An index can be found in the white pages in the beginning of the Chicago Yellow Pages or can be purchased at drugstores and gas stations for $2.95.

⇒ A CTA transit map, which has detailed information on all bus and train routes. They are available free from the CTA's Main Offices in the Merchandise Mart at *350 N. Wells*, 7th Floor; from *181 W. Madison*; and from certain el stations; or by calling CTA customer assistance at 664-7200, x 3316.

In addition to arming yourself with the important cold, hard facts these geographic resources provide, you might want to stockpile a few attitudinal assets. Things like an open mind, a spirit of adventure, senses attuned to the outside world, and a desire to learn, see, and do more will carry you further in this city than a pocketful of cash.

SECURITY

The relative safety/danger of establishments, neighborhoods, etc. is understandably difficult for newcomers to gauge, especially if they are generally unacquainted with ebb and flow of big city living. Even city dwellers sharply disagree on how harmless or hazardous specific areas of the city are. Let good sense rather than fear dictate your movements.

If you tend towards the cautious side, just keep in mind that the neighborhoods and establishments in this book are frequented by real people every day, the overwhelming majority of which never encounter a single difficulty in these places. 95% of the places in this book, I have visited alone on foot, bike, or by public transportation—often at night.

WHAT'S NOT IN THIS BOOK

Due to both my municipal pride and the unwieldy amount of territory the Chicago suburbs take up, I've limited all entries to places located within the city bounds. (If you want suburbs, Lake Claremont Press is releasing *Native's Guides* for four different Chicago suburban regions in 1999.) While it saddened me to have to exclude a few suburbanites, I was generally content to ignore the outlying metro area. Evanston is not Chicago, Park Ridge is not Chicago, and Wheaton—to disagree with someone I once met— is definitely not Chicago.

Similarly, many worthwhile and notable Chicago institutions disqualified for mention in this volume because of the money required to appreciate them. Making exceptions for costly favorites, would only detract from the many fantastic inexpensive options at hand. The Lyric Opera, the Chicago Symphony, Michigan Avenue shopping, four-star restaurants, and other activities of that ilk are great if you've got the money, but hardly required for a full experience of the city. If interested, you can learn more about these places through the Tourist Information Center (312/744-2400), numerous tourist publications (listed in *Chapter 9: Keeping Informed*), other guidebooks, and *Chicago Magazine*.

AN ENDLESS TASK

Like the wise observation that the more you know, the more you realize how much you don't know, the more information I gather while updating this guide every couple of years, the more I realize how many streets and alleys still remain undiscovered after three editions. When writing the first edition, I wanted to cover it all—to tread down every last sidewalk. Like any good fanatic, I wanted to see it all, share it all, and have everyone be as hooked on Chicago as I. Though this streak still exists in my efforts, it is, of course, unrealistic. The line has to be drawn somewhere. Temporarily stopping the research to release a new edition, however, leaves you with by far the most complete budget and insider's guide that exists for Chicago. It leaves me with a long list of leads for the next edition.

DISCLAIMER

It certainly would make the job of writing a guidebook and advising on Chicago easier (though not as exciting), if things stayed the same all the time. As this is not the case, things like times, dates, locations, and prices change frequently. It is always a good idea to call ahead if you need up-to-the-minute information. To the best of my knowledge, all information contained within this book was current at the time it went to press. Also, this is not meant to be the last word on anything in Chicago—its contents were chosen from the native Chicagoan experience and opinion of the authors and a handful of their colleagues, friends, and families.

GO FORTH

Have a great time with the book, but save the real fun for your own city adventures!

AN INTRODUCTION TO CHICAGO'S SOUTH SIDE

by Mary McNulty

Somewhere in our history, Chicago's South Side has come to be regarded as the poor relation of the glitzy lakefront and the trendy north side. The die was cast early. In Edna Ferber's 1924 Pulitzer Price-winning novel, *So Big*, the title character tells his mother, "Chicago'll never grow this way, with all those steel mills and hunkies to the south of us. The North Side is going to be the place to live. It is already." In contrast, it was on the South Side that much of the character of Chicago was developed. In fact, Chicago itself was born on the South Side in 1674 when explorer and trapper Pierre Marquette established his camp on the south branch of the Chicago River, near what is now the intersection of Archer and Damen Avenues.

While some of the city's prominent businessmen, including Marshall Field and George Pullman, once lived in stately mansions south of downtown, it was the influx of immigrants, who came to build the waterways and railroads and to work in the factories, that created the tightly knit ethnic communities where you can still sample the cultures of Eastern Europe, Asia, Africa, Latin America, and the British Isles.

Among the first to arrive were the Irish, escaping the potato famine in their homeland, and lured by work opportunities provided by the construction of the Illinois and Michigan Canal from 1836 to 1848. The canal, which linked the Great Lakes to the Mississippi River, originated from the same spot as Marquette's camp. The Irish workers established a shantytown along the banks of the Illinois River in what would become the Bridgeport neighborhood. The opening of the Union Stock Yards a few miles south in 1865 brought in another group of immigrants, primarily from the Slavic countries of Europe. Soon after the turn of the century, Mexican Americans and African Americans from the south were flocking to Chicago for work.

The population spread in two directions: south along the lakefront and southwest along the diagonal Archer Avenue. Mention "housing" and "south side" in the same breath and most people think of the high-rise projects that line the Dan Ryan expressway. But the south side boasts many lovely residential areas with housing styles ranging from majestic brownstones to brick two- and three-flat apartment buildings to long blocks of immaculately kept bungalows. Happily, much of the public housing is slated for redevelopment.

Three parks have contributed to the history and character of the South Side Jackson Park and Washington Park, which constitute the south and west borders of Hyde Park, were the brainchild of developer Paul Cornell and designed in magnificent fashion by Frederick Law Olmsted. The World's Columbian Exposition of 1893 and the 1933 Century of Progress, events that helped to bring world-class status to Chicago, were held in Jackson Park and Washington Park. To the west, the lesser but equally beloved Marquette Park brought notoriety of a different kind to the city when Martin Luther King Jr. marched through it in the 1960s. Since then the park has often been the focus of a power struggle between races.

We can't escape the fact that the racial and political divisions of Chicago are an integral part of the city's heritage. Much of the story of the South Side is the story of race—white Europeans moving out of neighborhoods because African Americans and Latinos were moving in. It's a pattern that continues and, unfortunately, keeps many people from mining the various pleasures of the South Side.

One of the few places where blacks and whites have come together in Chicago is in the jazz and blues clubs, which have deep roots in the city's South Side. While the bulk of these clubs are now downtown or on the North Side, in the early 1900s Louis Armstrong, Duke Ellington, Scott Joplin, and Nat "King" Cole created their purely American brand of music in the neighborhoods adjacent to the Dan Ryan Expressway. One of these neighborhoods, known alternately as Bronzeville or Black Metropolis, is undergoing intense renovation and deserves to be explored for its rich cultural and historical value, not only to Chicago, but to the United States.

While a few South Side neighborhoods such as Beverly, Hyde Park, and Pill Hill are known for their wealthy residents, the South Side remains the working-person's side of the city. That's what makes it so appealing—it's Chicago stripped to its essence, free from pretension. Yes, you'll hear a lot of "dese, dem, and dose." Yes, you'll see a lot of polyester. Yes, you'll see some heart-wrenching poverty. But, in exchange, you will encounter vibrant and friendly people who are eager to tell you about their neighborhood and how their families came to live there. Here you will find bustling neighborhoods, crammed with sumptuous, low-cost restaurants and affordable fun.

Did you know that the South Side hosts two of the city's largest parades? The South Side St. Patrick's Day Parade on Western Avenue and the Annual Christmas Parade on 63rd Street are two events of infectious frivolity that are free! On 63rd Street alone, you can enjoy a mouth-watering range of ethnic cuisines including soul food, Mexican, Lithuanian, Polish, Italian, Chinese, and Middle Eastern without emptying your wallet. How about Illinois' only state park that lies within the Chicago city limits? The Wolf Lake/William Powers Conservation Area, in the far southeast community of Hegewisch, is an idyllic oasis for boating, picnicking, and biking, plus a chance to see the infamous Monk parrots who escaped from a University of Chicago experiment.

South Siders are a proud bunch, but many have developed something of an inferiority complex about their side of town. This guide should help change their opinion of themselves, as well as that of North Siders who rarely venture south of Madison. Spend time exploring the neighborhoods that fan out from Archer Avenue, South Western Avenue, and South Michigan Avenue, and you will come to better understand the heart and soul of Chicago.

2 TOURING

Art and Architecture: (*Top*) One of the city's many neighborhood murals. (*Bottom*) The one-block stretch of Alta Vista Terrace was the first to be named a Chicago historic district. (*Photos by Rames Shrestha.*)

Chicago's visitors information centers are located in the **Historic Water Tower** (Chicago & Michigan), in the **Chicago Cultural Center** (78 E. Washington), and in Navy Pier's **Illinois Market Place** (700 E. Grand).

TOURING LINKS

Chicago Art Galleries
http://centerstage.net/chicago/art/directory-stuff/art-galleries.html
Chicago Artists
http://www.chicagoartists.net
One-stop Chicago art Web site devoted to artists, galleries, theaters, performers, performances, and openings.
Chicago Department of Cultural Affairs
http://www.ci.chi.il.us/WorksMart/CulturalAffairs
Check out the extensive schedule of free cultural programming.
Directory and Links to Chicago Neighborhood Ethnic and Cultural Centers
http://www.ci.chi.il.us/WorksMart/CulturalAffairs/Cultural Development/Directory.html
Directory and Links to Chicago Museums
http://www.ci.chi.il.us/Tourism/Museums
National Register of Historic Places (Chicago Tour)
http://www.cr.nps.gov/nr/Chicago/chintro.htm
A tour of 25 Chicago sites on the National Register of Historic Places.

2 TOURING

Whether you're a restless native, a frequent visitor, or a guest who wants something old and something new, this collection of places to visit should keep you occupied.

AIRPORTS

For those who dream of flying, for those who dream of escaping, for those who have little money to spend and need an interesting place to walk and watch, we have airports in three sizes: small airstrip, mid-sized and growing, and international jumbo.

Meigs Field
Northerly Island, 16th Street and the lakefront   **C**
Kick back, enjoy the lakefront at Northerly Island Park or 12th Street Beach (just north of the airfield and just south of the Adler Planetarium) and watch small aircraft take off from and land on this strip in the lake. When it's cold and rainy, try the viewing balcony in the two-story terminal, with a snack procured from the lobby's Lakefront Cafe. Northerly Island is a landfill creation dating back to the 1933 Century of Progress and originating in Daniel Burnham's master Chicago plan. Ground was broken for the airport in 1947, and a decade later the first commercial flight occurred. In 1996, **Meigs'** lease was up, resulting in a bitter feud between Chicago's Mayor Richard M. Daley and Jim Edgar, the governor of Illinois. The parks-and-beautification-minded Daley wanted to reclaim the land for an oak savanna, bird sanctuary, and marina. However, state officials, accustomed to using the airports for quick jaunts between Springfield and Chicago, balked. The lease was extended for a brief period.

Midway Airport
5700 S. Cicero   **SW**
Midway Airport was on a fast track to expansion when Midway Airlines

folded in 1991. Many on the southwest side feared for the area's economic future. Then Southwest Airlines, which would definitely qualify as the official airlines of "know more, spend less," moved in. By 1998, the city had embarked on a six-year, $700-million airport expansion project. The 50-year-old Terminal A will be replaced, and a glass pedestrian bridge will provide views of the surrounding neighborhood. For hard-core plane watchers, this is an ideal small airport—free from the crowds, concessions, and architectural distractions of O'Hare. Good places to watch planes take-off and land include gate C5 and the even gate numbers on the B concourse. Better yet, stand on the corner of 63rd and Cicero and wave to the passengers as the planes sail over your head.

O'Hare Airport
About 10400 W and 5600 N   **FN**
Take the O'Hare (blue) line northwest to its end and pull into the space age subway terminal of the world's busiest airport. Similarly psychedelic is the United Airlines Terminal Pedestrian Tunnel, where a jazzy light show on the walls and ceiling combines with piped-in New Age music and a repetitive, electronic voice instructing how to use the moving sidewalks for a bizarre, futuristic effect. Skip plane watching if you want, there's plenty more to do. While benefiting from the fantastic exercise and people-watching opportunities this mammoth complex provides, make sure to hit the United Terminal itself (designed by Helmut Jahn and finished in 1988) and the International Terminal (completed in 1993), which displays an impressive collection of antique and contemporary stained glass windows, including works by Frank Lloyd Wright and Louis Sullivan. Terminal 2 is a virtual theme park. Enjoy memorabilia and clips from the Golden Age of radio and television at an installation of the Museum of Broadcast Communications. Check out the airport's growing collection of art, including hand-painted park benches from **Gallery 37** (see p.33). A musician could be pumping out piano standards on the nearby baby grand. Take the kids to the *Kids on the Fly* play-and-learn area for some hands-on action with the Lego Sears Tower, air traffic control tower, helicopter, and cargo plane. The new People Mover monorail system provides quick access to other terminals. See p.120 for O'Hare **Airport Food** suggestions.

ANIMALS

When your curiosity about our fellow critters goes beyond squirrels and pigeons...

Animal Kingdom
2980 N. Milwaukee, 773/227-4444   **N**
Since the mid-1940s, **Animal Kingdom** pet store has introduced an array of unusual animals to prospective pet owners and the merely curious. Some of the animals—like the tiger my dad took us to see over two decades ago—are only for show. That long-time mascot died about five years ago. Among the broad assortment of animals currently in residence are a 28-year-old white-throated capuchin monkey, an African hornbill, toucans, and macaws.

Indian Boundary Park Zoo
2555 W. Estes, 312/742-7862   **FN**
Chicago's only neighborhood zoo has goats, deer, llamas, pheasants, swans, and more. Add the park's active sprinklers and unique playground and **Indian Boundary Park** becomes a fun summer afternoon field trip for young children. Open daily from dawn until 11pm. Free.

Lincoln Park Zoo
2200 N. Cannon Drive, 312/742-2000   **N**
One of the world's premier zoos, **Lincoln Park Zoo** is also Chicago's largest tourist attraction, the country's most visited zoo, the oldest public zoo in the United States, and one of the last free zoos in the country. Apes, endangered and big cats, flamingos, seals, elephants, and polar bears are some of the more popular attractions of the 2000 animals living here. Other highlights include the penguin pool and the Farm-in-the-Zoo. With the **Rookery** (see p.82), **Lincoln Park Conservatory** (see p.45), **Cafe Brauer** snack shop and ice cream parlor (see p.160), the lake for swimming, a pond for paddle boating, and the park for picnicking all adjacent to the zoo, this whole area is an ideal place for a family to spend the day. Free. Open daily 9am-5pm.

ANTIQUES

Some of the largest places to shop—or browse—for history...

"Antique Row"
Belmont from Western to Ashland   **N**
When construction of the nearby Kennedy Expressway in the 60s changed the flavor of the neighborhood, antique dealers were able to move in during the 70s because of the low rent. Now Chicago's oldest antique district, the eight-block stretch of **"Antique Row"** contains nearly two dozen dealers,

plus three malls: **Phil's Factory Antique Mall** (2040 W. Belmont, 773/528-8549) and the **Belmont Antique Malls** (2039 W. Belmont, 773/549-9270 and 2229 W. Belmont, 773/871-3915). All three are open from 11am to 6pm daily. While most of the wares along this strip tend to be from the later half of the 20th century—and therefore more affordable— **Antique Resources** (1741 W. Belmont, 773/871-4242) is one distinct exception. Their entire stock pre-dates the 1930s and is heavy with items from the 17th through 19th centuries, including exquisite furniture, oil paintings, and chandeliers. Tues.-Sat., 11 am-5 pm.

Armitage Antique Gallery
1529 W. Armitage, 773/227-7727   N
45 dealers, who handle primarily collectibles, comprise "Chicago's most unique antique mall." Open daily 11am-6pm.

Chicago Antique Centre
3045 N. Lincoln, 773/929-0200   N
35 dealers under one roof. Open daily 11am-6pm.

Lincoln Antique Mall
3141 N. Lincoln, 773/244-1440   N
55 dealers. Daily 11am-7pm.

Wrigleyville Antique Mall
3336 N. Clark, 773/868-0285   N
Carrying "an ever-changing selection of the 20th century's very best... ," the 65 merchants in this 10,000-ft.^{2} mall deal particularly in Art Deco, 50s and 60s furniture, housewares, and accessories: art glass and pottery, dinnerware, Bakelite, cocktail shakers, cigarette cases, watches, jewelry, textiles, and more. Mon.-Sat. 11am-6:30pm, Sun. Noon-6pm.

Pick up the *Guide to Antiques on Lincoln Avenue*—a free brochure outlining 33 sources for antiques on Lincoln Avenue between Fullerton and Lawrence—from the **Steve Starr Studios** (2779 N. Lincoln, 773/525-6530). Steve Starr, an antique frames specialist, compiles and regularly updates the guide, which contains addresses, phone numbers, hours, and merchandise descriptions.

Park West Antiques Fair
600 W. Fullerton, 773/477-5100   **N**
Generally the first Saturday and Sunday in June, this annual summerfest provides a background of music and food for a weekend of serious antique shopping.

ARCHITECTURE

Here is a partial (incomplete and subjective) register of single buildings and groups of buildings in a one or two block area that are worth a visit for their architectural, historical, or social value. Following this section is the subdivision **Buildings (Religious)**. Refer also to *Chapter 6: Walking* for the **Downtown Buildings (Classic)**, **Downtown Buildings (Modern)**, and **Luxury Hotel Lobbies** walking tours that will introduce you to numerous noteworthy buildings in the center of the city. And, if your appetite for architecture has yet to be satisfied, *Chapter 6* also provides information on neighborhoods loaded with structures deserving of your admiration.

860-880 Lake Shore Drive   **C**
Referred to as "the glass houses" when first built between 1948 and 1951, these twin, 26-story apartment buildings were a design that architect Mies van der Rohe had had in mind since the 1920s. Not just any old high-rises, these modernist towers became the model for future steel and glass skyscrapers, and in so doing, changed the face of urban architecture worldwide. This contribution to 20th-century cityscapes earned **860-880 Lake Shore Drive** Chicago landmark status at the "young" age of 45 in 1996—the first Miesian building to be thus recognized.

Alta Vista Terrace   **N**
Alta Vista Terrace (1050 W) between Grace (3800 N) and Byron (3900 N)
Designed by Joseph Brompton and built by Samuel Eberly Gross between 1900 and 1904, this block of homes, characteristic of the row houses in London's Mayfair neighborhood, was the first in Chicago to be labeled an historic district in 1971. The 20 houses from Grace to Byron are replicated on the other side of the street from Byron to Grace.

Beverly Frank Lloyd Wright Houses   **FSW**
In the Beverly neighborhood—the country's largest urban historic district—are four Frank Lloyd Wright Prairie School houses. The two on Hoyne are prefabs from a short-term business partnership between Wright and Richard

Brothers of Milwaukee.

- **9326 S. Pleasant** (1900)
- **9914 S. Longwood** (1908)
- **10410 S. Hoyne** (1917)
- **10541 S. Hoyne** (1917)

Beverly Walter Burley Griffin Prairie School Houses   **FSW**
104th Place in Beverly is also called Walter Burley Griffin Place after the student of Frank Lloyd Wright who designed Chicago's greatest concentration of Prairie School houses for this block.

- **The Furneaux House** (1913), 1741 W. 104th
- **The Newland House** (1913), 1737 W. 104th
- **The Salmon House** (1913), 1736 W. 104th
- **The Clarke House** (1913), 1731 W. 104th
- **The Blount House** (1911), 1724 W. 104th
- **The Jenkinson House** (1913), 1727 W. 104th
- **The Garrity House** (1909), 1712 W. 104th
- **The Van Nostrand House** (1911), 1666 W. 104th

The Chicago Bee Building
3647-55 S. State Street   **S**
The facade of this former editorial office for a leading black-owned newspaper of the 1920s features terra cotta decorations. Now a branch of the Chicago Public Library, it is listed on the National Historic Register.

Chicago Daily Defender Building
2400 S. Michigan   **S**
Built in 1936 by Philip Maher for the Illinois Automobile Club, this building has housed the offices of the *Chicago Daily Defender*—a preeminent local black newspaper with a national reputation—since 1960. Since 1975, the building has been recognized as an "historical site in journalism."

Edgewater Beach Apartments
5555 N. Sheridan   **FN**
Pale pink, Art Deco, and Miami-esque, these lakefront apartment towers were created by Benjamin Marshall in 1928 as part of the now defunct, once luxurious and fashionable Edgewater Beach Hotel Complex. The lobby and ground floor shops and cafe are open to the public.

Elks National Memorial Building
2750 N. Lakeview   **N**
Finished in 1926, this extravagant, but little-visited building is dedicated to peace and freedom and memorializes the Elks that died during World War I. Adorned with sculptures, mosaics, murals, and the finest marble, the entire building is a stunner. An allegorical mural spans twelve panels in the 100-foot rotunda. Open weekdays 9am-5pm (year-round) and weekends 10am-5pm (April 15th-Nov. 15th only).

Essanay Studios
1333-45 W. Argyle   **N**
Now part of St. Augustine College, this building's most illustrious days were between 1907 and 1917 when it was used by **Essanay Studios** for the making of silent films. Prominent in both Chicago and the movie industry in general, **Essanay** worked with some of the era's biggest stars, like Charlie Chaplin and Gloria Swanson.

Farrakhan Home
4855 S. Woodlawn   **S**
Designed with Muslim motifs for the Nation of Islam leader, this home-fortress stands among the other mansions of Chicago's Kenwood neighborhood. It was previously the home of the Honorable Elijah Muhammed and is now the residence of Minister Louis Farrakhan.

Hutchinson Street
Hutchinson (4232 N) between Marine Drive (600 W) and Hazel (900 W) **N**
Tiny landmark district contains a handsome variety of homes from the early part of the 20th century: classic, Georgian, Prairie School, and Queen Anne. Five were designed by George Maher between 1894 and 1913: **750 W**, **817 W**, **826 W**, **839 W** and **840 W**.

Ida B. Wells/Ferdinand Lee Barnett Home
3624 S. King Drive   **S**
Wells, the noted social reformer, and Barnett, her husband and founder of the *Conservator*, Chicago's first black-owned newspaper, lived in this three-story rock-faced granite house from 1919 to 1930. A prime example of an urban row house of the late Victorian period, it was designated a National Historic Landmark in 1974.

The "Irish Castle"
10244 S. Longwood Drive   **FSW**
Since the Potter Palmer Castle on Lake Shore Drive was demolished in the

1950s, this model of 13th and 14th century Irish estates apparently is the only "castle" in town. Enduring stories maintain that Robert Givens had the castle built in 1886 for his fiancée, who unfortunately died before they were wed. It is now the Beverly Unitarian Church.

Jackson Boulevard Historic District
(300 S) between Ashland (1600 W) and Laflin (1500 W)   C
In the late 1800s, when the 30 mansions on this block were built, they stood in sharp contrast to neighborhoods—just blocks away—where immigrant populations were struggling in less than ideal conditions. Saved by early preservationists in the 1970s, this strip still stands apart from the decay of surrounding streets, although those blocks are fast in the midst of development efforts.

Jesse Binga Home
5922 S. King Drive   S
Binga established the first black-owned bank at 35th and State in 1908. Although the bank survived the Depression, it ultimately failed in 1930, and Binga was jailed on charges of embezzlement. His stature in the community, however, was such that a group of supporters was able to obtain his release from prison in 1938. At the height of his success, Binga lived in this house, which survived numerous fire bombings between 1918 and 1919 when hostile white residents tried to oust him from the neighborhood.

O'Leary House
726 W. Garfield   S
Designed in 1901 by Zachary Davis, this is the big ol' home of the gamblin', tavern-ownin' son of the woman with the notorious fire-startin' cow. However, it should be noted that most historians have cleared the O'Leary Cow of all blame for that grievous conflagration known as the Great Chicago Fire.

On Leong Chinese Merchant's Association Building
2216 S. Wentworth   S
Since 1928, the home of the On Leong tong has been one of the most prominent Chinese-style buildings on the block. The On Leongs, once involved in organized crime, are now focused on providing business and social services to the community.

Operation Push Building
930 E. 50th Street   S
Jesse Jackson's Operation Push (People United to Save Humanity) makes its

headquarters in this 1923 Greek revival style building that was originally home to the K.A.M. Isaiah Israel Temple. Operation Push is committed to educational and economic equality for all people, focusing especially on the needs of African Americans, Hispanics, and people with low income.

Prairie Avenue Historic District
Prairie Avenue (300 E) between 16th (1600 S) and Cermak (2200 S) **C**
This former mansion strip of Chicago's original elite includes the historically and architecturally significant **Kimball** (1801 S. Prairie—1890-1892), **Coleman** (1811 S. Prairie—1885), **Keith** (1900 S. Prairie—1870s), and **Marshall Field Jr./William H. Murray** (1919 S. Prairie—1884) houses. But the following are its two prize jewels:

- **Clarke House**, 1827 S. Indiana
  Chicago's oldest surviving building dates from its pioneer town days (1836). Instead of building a modest "balloon" house as was common at the time, the Clarkes built a sizable Greek Revival home with a columned porch and broad staircase.

- **Glessner House**, 1800 S. Prairie (1885-1889)
  Within the bulky granite exterior lies one of the city's first modern interiors, decorated with many of the original Arts and Crafts furnishings and the Romanesque flourishes of architect Henry Hobson Richardson.

Prairie Avenue House Museums (1800 S. Prairie, 312/326-1480) is a sophisticated organization established to preserve and promote the history, architecture, and art of the Prairie Avenue historic district. Some of their eclectic programming includes an exhibit on the History of Chicago Home Cooking (1836-1900), candlelit readings of Edgar Allen Poe stories at Halloween, and Sunday afternoon lectures on highly specialized topics. They offer two-hour guided tours of the Clarke and Glessner houses Wed.-Sun. at Noon, 1pm, and 2pm. $8 adults, $6 students, seniors, and children.

Race Avenue and Midway Park Houses
5700-5900 West Blocks of Race (543 N) and Midway Park (500 N) **W**
These grand old homes on large lots in Austin are a remnant of the area's suburban past. Seventeen of them date between 1886 and 1922. Many were

designed by noted architect Frederick Schock, whose own home stands at 5804 W. Midway. The Austin neighborhood was annexed to Chicago in 1899.

Robie House
5757 S. Woodlawn, 708/848-1976   **S**
The internationally famous Frank Lloyd Wright masterpiece is open daily for one-hour tours at 11am, 1pm, and 3pm. Adults $8, students, seniors, and children (ages 7-18) $6.

Union Stock Yards Gate
850 W. Exchange (4100 S)   **SW**
This former archway to the animals' quarters serves as a solitary reminder of Chicago's stockyard past.

University of Chicago Campus Tour
773/702-8374   **S**
Free, one-hour guided tours of the University of Chicago campus are given on Saturdays at 10am from April through September. Meet at the Visitor's Center in Ida Noyes Hall (1212 E. 59th).

Wabash Avenue YMCA
3763 S. Wabash   **S**
It is believed that historian Carter G. Woodson founded the Association for the Study of Afro-American Life and History here in 1915. Woodson was also responsible for establishing Negro History Week, the precursor of today's Black History Month. In the ballroom is a wall mural painted by Chicago artist William Edward Scott in 1936, depicting people of color in various professions.

◆ ◆ ◆ ◆ ◆

AIA Lecture Series
Chicago Cultural Center, 77 E. Randolph   **C**
www.aiachicago.org/ExploreChicago/ExploreChicago.html
The **American Institute of Architects** holds its annual lecture series on local topics in the Claudia Cassidy Theater of the **Chicago Cultural Center**. This year's lectures have covered the new museum campus, rebuilding Chicago Public Schools, improving the public housing mix, and repairing park district buildings. Wed. 5:30pm. Free, no reservations required.

Chicago Architecture Foundation Lectures
224 S. Michigan, 312/922-3432   **C**
The ultimate source of building information in Chicago, **CAF** sponsors a variety of affordable opportunities to learn about local architecture. Bring a lunch for the weekly 12:15pm lectures on architecture and housing topics in its lecture (suggested donation, $2). Various walking tours of downtown, specific buildings, and city neighborhoods take place nearly every day of the year ($3-$7). **CAF** also sponsors numerous architecture tours by bike and bus, plus a summertime river cruise. Call 312/922-TOUR for upcoming tours and events.

> Self-guided, audio-taped walking tours that discuss the architecture of Chicago's Loop are available from the **Chicago Cultural Center**'s gift shop (77 E. Randolph) for a $5 rental fee.

Commission on Chicago Landmarks
320 N. Clark, Suite 516, 312/744-3200   **C**
The city organization responsible for conferring landmark status on city structures has recognized 144 individual landmarks and 30 districts (containing over 4,000 important structures) to date. Pick up the *Chicago Landmarks Map* from various visitor information centers or by calling the commission.

ARCHITECTURE (RELIGIOUS)

In the good old days, before vandals ran rampant, one could retreat to a house of worship any time of day or night for prayer, peace and quiet, or aesthetic browsing. Unfortunately, most places now keep limited hours or only open their doors for services. Call ahead to learn a good visiting hour.

Bultasa Buddhist Temple of Chicago
4358 W. Montrose, 773/286-1551   **NW**
This worship place of Korean Buddhists houses an exquisite "1000 Buddha Temple Altar," not found elsewhere in the American Midwest.

Christ Universal Temple
11901 S. Ashland, 773/568-2282   **FSE**
Evoking a sports stadium, this church is noted not for its age or art, but

merely for its capacity to accommodate thousands of congregators at one time.

First Baptist Congregational Church
60 N. Ashland, 312/243-8047   **W**
Having survived the Great Chicago Fire after its completion in 1871 by architect Gurdon P. Randall, the former Union Park Congregational Church is one of Chicago's oldest. Its Gothic features, circular seating, and enormous, old pipe organ are impressive.

Five Holy Martyrs Church
4301 S. Richmond, 773/254-3636   **SW**
In the heart of Brighton Park, **Five Holy Martyrs** offers mass in Polish four times a week. Pope John Paul II celebrated mass here during his 1979 visit to Chicago and, in typical Chicago fashion, a portion of 43rd Street was renamed Pope John Paul II Drive.

Kehilath Anshe Ma'ariv Isaiah Israel Temple
1110 E. Hyde Park, 773/924-1234   **S**
Built in 1924 by Alfred Alschuler, this splendid old temple with Byzantine flourishes includes a 1973 addition by John Alschuler.

Midwest Buddhist Temple
435 W. Menomonee, 312/943-7801   **N**
Hideaki Arao designed this traditional Japanese temple in 1971.

Nation of Islam
734 W. 79th, 773/602-1230   **FSE**
The church of Minister Louis Farrakhan and the Black Muslims.

Our Lady of Sorrows Basilica
3121 W. Jackson, 773/638-5800   **W**
Unknown to most Chicagoans, the basilica would be a tourist attraction if located in Florence or Rome. The dramatic, barrel-vaulted ceiling is an immediate attention-grabber. This beauty was designed by Henry Engelbert, John Pope, and William Brinkmann (1890-1902).

Pilgrim Baptist Church
3301 S. Indiana, 312/842-5830   **S**
The former synagogue of Chicago's oldest Jewish congregation (K.A.M.) is an Adler and Sullivan classic (1890).

Quinn Chapel, African Methodist Episcopal
2401 S. Wabash, 312/791-1846   **S**
Constructed between 1891 and 1894, **Quinn Chapel** is the worship place of
the city's oldest African-American congregation.

St. Nicholas Ukrainian Catholic Cathedral
2238 W. Rice, 773/276-4537   **W**
Thirteen-domed, mosaic-clad church built in 1915 by Worthmann,
Steinbach, and Piontek. Take Oakley a few blocks south to the newer **St.
Volodymur and Olha Ukrainian Catholic Church** (c.1975) at 739 N.
Oakley for more beautiful exterior mosaic work.

> Nearby, the 60-year-old **St. Stephen King of Hungary Catholic
> Church** (2025 W. Augusta) is the last remaining Hungarian church
> in Chicago. It is the second of only two churches in Chicago history
> to serve the Hungarian community.

St. Paul Roman Catholic Church
2127 W. 22nd Place, 773/847-7622   **SW**
The German immigrants who built this extravagant French Gothic
masterpiece (1897), per the design of Henry Schlacks, used not a single nail
(only bricks) in its construction—a feat recognized by *Ripley's Believe It or
Not*. Its interior contains Italian mosaics and German stained glass. Later, far
beneath the church's towering 245-foot spires, St. Paul Federal Bank was
founded in the basement.

St. Thomas the Apostle
5476 S. Kimbark, 773-324-2626   **S**
The site of Hyde Park's Catholic parish since 1869, this majestic structure at
the corner of 55th and Kimbark was designed by Francis Barry Byrne.
Byrne once studied with Frank Lloyd Wright, and the church's modernist
design reflects Wright's influence. Within the walls lies a tranquil courtyard.
Inside, note the bronze bas-reliefs of the Stations of the Cross created by an
Italian-born American sculptor Alfeo Faggi. The church was added to the
National Register of Historic Places in 1978.

Second Presbyterian Church
1936 S. Michigan, 312/225-4951   **S**
Despite being a Chicago landmark and on the National Register of Historic
Places, the **Second Presbyterian Church** is one of about a dozen

architecturally stunning Chicago churches in dire need of big bucks for major repairs. Once the church of the Chicago's Prairie Avenue upper class, it was designed in 1874 by James Renwick after the 1871 Chicago fire destroyed their previous church. Howard Van Doren Shaw remodeled it with an Arts and Crafts interior in 1900 after another fire. Among this Gothic gem's many dramatic features are 14 Louis Comfort Tiffany stained-glass windows.

ART (INDOORS)

The gentrification of the River North area in the 1980s and the growing West Side arts community have helped boost Chicago's gallery scene to the scale of Manhattan or San Francisco. The sheer number of galleries, the range of art forms and styles displayed, a constantly changing lineup of exhibits, and free admission make gallery-hopping the ideal hobby for any art enthusiast.

Gallery Districts

The majority of Chicago galleries are concentrated in these four areas. River North is the largest district, Michigan Avenue the ritziest, and River West and the West Side are the most experimental.

Michigan Avenue   **C**
Bounded by Oak Street (1000 N) on the north, Lake Shore Drive (600 E) on the east, Congress (500 S) on the south, and Wabash (45 E) on the west, with most galleries lining Michigan Avenue (100 E).

River North   **C**
Core district bounded by Chicago (800 N) on the north, Wells (200 W) on the east, Erie (658 N) on the south, and Sedgwick (400 W) on the west, with boundaries extending to Hubbard (430 N) on the south, State (0 E/W) on the east, and Institute Place (828 N) on the north.

River West   **C**
Bounded by Halsted (800 W) on the east, Jackson (300 S) on the south, Ashland (1600 W) on the west, and Division (1200 N) on the north.

West Side W/N
Core district bounded by Leavitt (2200 W) on the west, Cortland (1900 N) on the north, Paulina (1700 W) on the east, and Division (1200 N) on the south, with boundaries extending to Western (2400 W) on the west, Chicago (800 N) on the south, Ashland (1600 W) on the east, and Fullerton (2400 N) on the north.

Neighborhood Cultural Center Galleries

Various neighborhood arts centers have free galleries.

Beacon Street Gallery and Theatre
1145 W. Wilson, 773/769-4284, *www.beaconst.org* **N**
Located at Truman College in the O'Rourke Center, the **Beacon Street Gallery** showcases multicultural works that reflect the diversity of the Uptown neighborhood. Exhibits are often accompanied by performances. Open Tues.-Sat. 11am-4pm.

Beverly Arts Center
2153 W. 111th, 773/445-3838 **FSW**
Gallery includes a permanent collection of works by James Whistler, Mary Cassatt, and early Chicago artist John Vanderpoel. Open Mon.-Fri. 9am-5pm, Sat. 10am-2pm.

Boulevard Arts Center
6011 S. Justine, 773/476-4900 **SW**
Opened in 1984 to provide cultural education in a neighborhood where such opportunities are scarce, the center offers arts instruction in photography, ceramics, dance, painting, drawing, music, and theater. The building and grounds feature colorful murals and the city's only neighborhood sculpture garden. Exhibits, readings, and recitals are presented throughout the year. Open Mon.-Sat. 9am-9pm.

ETA Creative Arts Foundation
7558 S. South Chicago, 773/752-3955 **FSE**
Created in 1971 as a showcase and training center for African-American visual and performing arts, **ETA** opens its art gallery to the public daily from 10am to 6pm.

Flat Iron Gallery/Near Northwest Arts Council
1579 N. Milwaukee, 773/278-7677 **W**
Located in the historic, white terra cotta Flat Iron Building (1919), the **Flat**

Iron Gallery displays the talents of emerging artists who work outside the mainstream. It is supported by the Near Northwest Arts Council—an activist group committed to cultural self-determination that represents over 150 artists. Thur.-Sat. Noon-5pm.

Hyde Park Art Center
5307 S. Hyde Park, 773/324-5520   S
One of the city's oldest community art centers, the **Hyde Park Art Center** has a reputation for showing the work of emerging artists. Ed Paschke and his Hairy Who cohorts are among the artists who received early backing from the center. Open Mon.-Sat. 11am-5pm.

Little Black Pearl Workshop
4200 S. Drexel, 773/285-1211, *www.blackpearl.org*   S
A non-profit organization that provides arts education for inner-city children to encourage the appreciation of and participation in the world of art, **Little Black Pearl** exhibits local artists and hosts traveling workshops on African-American art and history. Mon.-Fri. 10am-6pm.

North Lakeside Cultural Center
6219 N. Sheridan, 773/743-4477   FN
Housed in a renovated 1910 mansion on the lake, the **NLCC** offers a lovely and intimate parlor setting for enjoying the ten art exhibits that are featured here yearly. Author readings, performance art, concerts, recitals, drama, and dance are also held. Open Tues., Wed., and Fri. 10am-6pm., Thur. 10am-4pm, and Sun. 1pm-5pm.

South Shore Cultural Center
7059 S. South Shore, 312/747-2536   FSE
The gallery in this grand landmark building, dating from 1906, focuses on the work of African-American artists. Except on days when special events are staged, visitors can also wander through the center's opulent ballroom. Open Mon.-Fri. 10am-6pm, Sat. 10am-4pm.

The two free public galleries of the **School of the Art Institute** are additional venues to witness the creative endeavors of both student and established artists. The **Betty Rymer Gallery** (Columbus & Jackson, 312/443-3703) is open Mon.-Sat. 10am-5pm. **Gallery 2** (1040 W. Huron) can be visited Tues.-Sat. 11am-6pm.

Publications

The free weeklies, the *Chicago Reader* (Section 2) and *New City,* have extensive listings of gallery exhibits and goings-on. *Chicago Gallery News* is a triannual brochure filled with information on galleries, openings, artists, and special events. It includes maps and a complete gallery listing. These booklets are distributed from 730 N. Franklin, Chicago, Illinois, 60610, 312/649-0064 and can be found at the tourist information center in the **Chicago Cultural Center** at Washington and Michigan.

ART (OUTDOORS)

Chicago may rank the highest among U.S. cities when it comes to quantity and quality of outdoor art. Our reputation as the nation's architectural capital goes unchallenged. Codes that favor interesting building tops keep our skyline spectacular, and ordinances promoting artistic plaza space keep the ground views fresh as well. The sculpture, murals, mosaics, fountains, and innovative landscaping that beautify downtown are just as prevalent in many neighborhoods. Three walking tours in *Chapter 6: Walking* offer comprehensive introductions to downtown public art: **Public Art (Classic), Public Art (Modern), and Indoor Public Art**.

Gallery 37
Bounded by State Street, Randolph, Dearborn, and Washington, *www.gallery37.org*   **C**
With the arrival of summer, this empty three acres—Block 37—of prime downtown property becomes an outdoor art workshop where young Chicagoans, aged 14-21, receive a minimum wage to apprentice with established artists. This innovative jobs-training program has been replicated in 16 cities around the world and was selected in the "Top 10" for a 1997 Innovations in American Government Award. Apprentices work on commissioned pieces—such as decorations for city events or artwork for public buildings—or on items that are sold at a non-profit retail store that helps support the program (see p.356). Over 600 students a year (more than 7,000 to date) can choose from a staggering array of disciplines, including: music, musical theater, playwriting, choreography, dance, video production, journalism, poetry, architecture, horticulture, wood carving, stone carving, light sculpture, textiles, silkscreening, printmaking, papermaking, book binding, hat sculpture, jewelry, ceramics, drawing, painting, and mural.

Training goes on at various locations throughout the city and continues throughout the year in after-school programs. Open late June to late August, 10am-4pm.

Murals and Mosaics

In the city's open air galleries—neighborhood walls—are murals and mosaics that make bold aesthetic, social, and political statements. Here are some of the better known and more recent murals:

⇒ **FAR SOUTHEAST**

Atlas Center Mosaic, 1767 E. 79th
By Kiela Songhay Smith (1994)

Benu, The Rebirth of South Shore, 71st and Jeffery
By Marcus Akinlana and Jeffery Cook (1990)

Bright Moments—Memories of the Future,
79th and Stony Island at The New Regal Theater
By Mitchell Caton and Calvin Jones (1987)

Builders of the Cultural Present, 71st and Jeffery
By Mitchell Caton and Calvin Jones (1980)

By All Means Necessary, 1800 E. 71st St.
By Olivia Gude and Dorian Sylvain (1992)

"I Welcome Myself to a New Place...," The Roseland/Pullman Mural, 113th Street and Cottage Grove
By Marcus Akinlana, Olivia Gude, and Jon Pounds (1988)

Patterned Plaza, 1801 E. 71st St.
By Caryl Uasko and Olivia Gude

Song of Enlightenment, 1818 E. 71st
By Rene Townsend, Orisegun Olomidun, and Mirtes Zwierzynski (1994)

South Shore Rests at the Bosom of Oshun, 75th and Crandon
By Markus Akinlana (1989)

To Think the World, 1850 W. 71st
By Mirtes Zwierzynski, Phil Schuster, and Orisegun Olomidun (1993)

Untitled Mosaic Columns, 1818 E. 71st
By Nina Cain and Kiela Songhay Smith

Where There is Discord, Harmony: The Power of Art, 1801 E. 71st
By Markus Akinlana and Olivia Gude (1991)

⇒ **SOUTH**

Alewives and Mercury Fish, 55th and Lake Park
By Albert Zeno (1974)

Another Time's Voice Remembers My Passion's Humanity,
40th and Michigan
By Mitchell Caton and Calvin Jones (1979)
Restored by Bernard Williams and Paige Hinson (1993)

Bring It Back Home, 43rd and King Drive
By Bernard Williams and Paige Hinson (1993)

Children of Goodwill, 56th and Lake Park
By William Walker (1979)
Restored by Olivia Gude and Bernard Williams (1993)

Feed Your Child the Truth, 50th and Cottage Grove
By Bernard Williams (1994)

Justice Speaks, 57th and Lake Park
By Bill Walker (1977)

Pioneer Social Work, 57th and Lake Park
By Astrid Fuller (1977)

Pyramids of Power: The Black Family, 23rd and Federal
By Nina Cain and John Yancy (1988)

Save Our Children, 50th and Lake Park
By Astrid Fuller (1980)

The Spirit of Hyde Park, 57th and Lake Park
By Astrid Fuller and Bill Walker (1976)

Tribute to Harold Washington, 47th and Champlain
By Bill Walker

Tutu Egun, 4331 S. Federal
By Turbado Marabou, Julian Aikins, and Aun Mu Ra (1993)

Under City Stone, 55th and Lake Park
By Caryl Yasko (1972)

Wall of Daydreaming, Man's Inhumanity to Man, 47th and Calumet
By Bill Walker, Mitchell Caton, and Santi Isrowuthakul (1974)

Wheels of Time, 51st and Lake Park
By children from Hyde Park (1989)

"Where We Come From, Where We Are Going," 56th and Lake Park
By Olivia Gude (1992)

⇒ **SOUTHWEST**

Maya, 55th and Leavitt
By Mitchell Caton and Siddha Webber

The Mexican neighborhood of **Pilsen** (named after a Czech town by its original inhabitants) is particularly noteworthy for its abundance of outdoor murals. Its boundaries are roughly 16th (1600 S) on the north, Halsted (800 W) on the east, the Chicago River (about 2700 S) on the south, and Damen (2000 W) on the west. The walls of the square at **18th and Paulina**, **Casa Atzlan** community center (1831 S. Racine) and **Calles y Sueños Cultural Center** (19th and Carpenter) make good starting points for your explorations.

⇒ **WEST**

Arbol de Vida (Tree of Life), 2125 W. North
By John Pitman Weber and Catherine Cajandig (1989)

Aren't I a Womyn?, Division and Western
By Olivia Gude and Dzine (1993)

Homage to the Women of Mexico, Paulina and 18th
By Francisco Mendoza (1994)

How To Build A Brighter Future, 1512 S. Pulaski
By Olivia Gude and Dzine (1993)

Lowell School Mosaic, 3320 W. Hirsch
By Olivia Gude

Still Deferred, Still Dreaming, Washington and Sacramento
By Dzine and Olivia Gude (1993)

⇒ **CENTRAL**

Casa Aztlan, 18th and Racine
By Marcos Raya, Ray Patlan, Aurelio Diaz, and others

Hubbard Street Endangered Species Murals, Hubbard, near Halsted
By several artists in the late 1970's

Jackson Language Academy Mosaic Play Sculpture, Harrison at Loomis
*By Nina Cain, Henri Marquet, Cynthia Weiss, and Mirtes Zwierzynski
(1989-1990)*

Large Trompe L'Oeil, Congress and Racine
By Richard Haas

LaSalle Towers Trompe L'Oeil Tribute to Chicago Architects,
Division and State
By Richard Haas

⇒ **NORTHWEST**

Calling Forth the Spirit of Peace, North and Kedzie
By Jeffrey Cook, Phil Schuster, Martin Solo, and Ginger Drobias

Es Tiempo de Recordar (It's Time to Remember), Pulaski and Wabansia
By Markus Akinlana, Sandra Antongirogi, and Rolf Mueller (1992)

Firefighters' Memorial, Kimball and Milwaukee
By Jose Berrios

For the People of the Future, Spaulding and North
By Jose Guerrero, Lynn Takata, and John Pitman Weber (1980)

Shiva: 2021, 6417 W. Irving Park
By Dzine, La Force Alphabetick, and John Pitman Weber (1994)

⇒ **NORTH**

For a New World, 925 W. Diversey
By John Pitman Weber and Oscar Martinez

Great Wall of Women, 4646 N. Rockwell
(Visible from the alley or the Rockwell el platform)
By fifteen women artists

Lakeview High School Mosaics, Sculptures, Door Frames and Columns,
4015 N. Ashland
By Mirtes Zwierzynski, Phil Schuster, Miriam Socoloff, and Esther Charbit (1984-1995)

Lincoln Square Mural, Lincoln and Leland
By Lothar Sanchez-Speer and students from Amundsen, Clemente, and Senn High Schools (1991)

Rompiendo Barreras/Breaking Barriers, 2150 W. North
By Turbado Marabou and Veronica Werckmeister (1994)

TILT (Together Protect the Community), Fullerton & Washtenaw
By John Pitman Weber (1976)

⇒ **FAR NORTH**

Arts For All, 6900 block of North Glenwood
By fourteen local artists (1993)

Chicago Public Art Group
1255 S. Wabash, 773/427-2724   **C**
This 20-year-old organization—the former Chicago Mural Group—produces the majority of new neighborhood public art (mostly murals and mosaics) in Chicago. Their activist approach encourages artists' involvement with a community and neighborhood participation in the production of an artwork. They are the primary source of information on the murals and mosaics that exist throughout the city.

Sculpture

Pier Walk
Navy Pier, 700 E. Grand   **C**
From May through November, at least until the year 2000, Navy Pier will be encompassed by annual large-scale sculpture exhibits. **3-D Chicago**—a non-profit group that oversees the placement of large contemporary outdoor sculptures for public edification—arranges for over 100 singular pieces of artwork to line the pier and its outside gardens.

Two airy, 56-foot steel sculptures of the Puerto Rican flag wave over Division Street these days in the Humboldt Park neighborhood, where nearly 1/4 of the area's residents are of Puerto Rican descent. They span from one side of the street to the other—one at Artesian (2428 W) and one at Mozart (2834 W)—creating what's referred to locally as the *Paseo Boricua*—Puerto Rican walkway. They're the latest effort to employ grand public monuments to the neighborhood's ethnicity as a means of generating cultural pride and stimulating commercial development. The original was, perhaps, the intricate Chinatown arch installed years ago. Much later came the mini-pagoda adorning the Argyle Street el station in "New Chinatown" and two massive Greek columns that solidified the recent facelift of Greektown. When an archway was erected in the Mexican Little Village area not too long ago, the Mexican president at the time, Carlos Salinas de Gotari, even flew in for the dedication ceremony.

BOAT RIDES

With the recent refurbishing of Navy Pier, the ongoing development of the Chicago River banks, and Chicago's lifelong devotion to Lake Michigan, the tour and entertainment boat business in the Windy City is booming. Sightseeing and tour boat rides range anywhere from $6 to $18. Add dinner and/or entertainment to the mix and the prices go from $27 on up. For a quick waterway fix, try this much cheaper alternative:

Wendella Commuter Boats
A mere $1.50 (ten rides for $11) will afford you a swift trip down the Chicago River with commuters during morning and evening rush hours. Board at either Union Station (2 N. Riverside Plaza) or 400 N. Michigan (at the Chicago River). Boats run every 7-10 minutes. Mon.-Fri. 7:48am-8:45am and 4:44pm-5:40pm.

A little taste of Venice...

Shoreline Water Taxis
OK, so cabs are cheaper and more flexible when it comes to routes, but these warm weather touristy water cabs are still fun. There are two routes: Navy Pier to the Shedd Aquarium and Navy Pier to the Sears Tower. Boats leave every half hour between 10am and 6pm. Tickets are $6 one-way and $10 round-trip.

CEMETERIES

For many, cemeteries are a source of fascination. They're very much alive with art, architecture, and history and make great destinations for peaceful, escapist strolls. Listed below are Chicago's three oldest (and perhaps, most magnificent) cemeteries, along with some of their well-known inhabitants.

Graceland Cemetery (1860)
4001 N. Clark, 773/525-1105   **N**

Death-styles of the rich and famous! Every extravagance in funerary art and architecture has been employed for the Chicago luminaries buried here. Chicago businessmen Phillip D. Armour, Marshall Field, Cyrus McCormick, Potter Palmer, and George Pullman; architects Daniel Burnham (check that plot of shady land that juts into the lake), Ludwig Mies van der Rohe, Louis Sullivan, and John Wellborn Root; and detective Allen

Pinkerton all make **Graceland** their final resting place. Under the granite baseball lies the co-founder of the National League, William Hulbert. As you meander through the tombstones and monuments, keep an eye out for the ornate Getty family tomb (created by Louis Sullivan), Loredo Taft's chilling *Eternal Silence* monument, and for the grave markers of these people who gave their names to Chicago streets: Governor John Peter Altgeld, Ernest Robert Graham, Henry and Eliza Honore, William Kimball, John Kinzie, and Timothy Webster. The Chicago Architecture Foundation gives tours of Graceland Cemetery on Sundays in the fall for $5. You can also buy information booklets on the cemetery

Oak Woods Cemetery (1853)
1035 E. 67th, 773/288-3800   **FSE**
Within stone walls in a residential neighborhood is Chicago's oldest cemetery with four lakes, enormous mausoleums, and a large number of tall obelisk monuments. It's the final resting place for a long list of notable citizens, including Chicago's first African-American mayor Harold Washington, civil rights leader Ida B. Wells, federal judge and first baseball commissioner Kenesaw Mountain Landis, bluesman Junior Wells, and architects Solon Beman and George Nimmons. George Fuller, builder of the Rookery and the Monadnock Building, lies in Oak Wood's largest mausoleum, marked by Roman pillars and overlooking Symphony Lake. Olympic gold medalist Jesse Owens' red stone grave marker also overlooks the lake. The grave of "Cap" Anson, National League baseball player and manager of the Chicago White Stockings (precursor of the Cubs), is easily identified by two crossed baseball bats on the headstone. By contract, physicist Enrico Fermi lies beneath a modest marker. Six thousand confederate soldiers who died while imprisoned at Camp Douglas (it once stood near 35th Street) are buried here in what is the largest northern Confederate gravesite. Their resting place is marked with the 46-foot Confederate Mound Monument. Panels list the names of 4,200 of those soldiers who were identified. A dozen Union soldiers who served as guards at the prisoner-of-war camp are also buried on the spot.

Rosehill Cemetery (1859)
5800 N. Ravenswood, 773/561-5940   **FN**
Rosehill's 350 acres comprised the city's first "rural park" cemetery—a Parisian concept that promoted lush, green cemeteries as tranquil, scenic escapes from the day-to-day grit of urban life. Another slate of famous folks lie here: Chicago businessmen Milton Florsheim, James Scott Kemper, Julius Rosenwald, Maurice Rothschild, Ignaz Schwinn, John G. Shedd, and A. Montgomery Ward; Coolidge's vice-president, Charles Gates Dawes;

Charles Hull, who gave a house with his name to Jane Addams; and Frances E. Willard of the Women's Christian Temperance Union. Rosehill is also the final resting place of fifteen Chicago mayors; sixteen Civil War generals, Robert Franks, the fourteen year old victim of the 1924 Leopold/Loeb murder; and a sixteen year old, Lulu Fellows, who died in 1883 and is said to haunt the adjacent woods.

Stephen A. Douglas Tomb and Memorial
636 E 35th St.   S
How ironic that a man known as "The Little Giant" has a 96-foot monument erected for him. The Illinois politician who once vied with Abraham Lincoln for the presidency lies in Chicago at 35th Street and the lake in a landmark tomb, done by Leonard Volk between 1863 and 1881.

For a more in-depth examination of Chicago cemeteries, look for Matt Hucke's *Graveyards of Chicago* (Lake Claremont Press), due for publication in the Spring of 1999. His elaborate, photography-heavy Web site, *www.graveyards.com*, provides a sneak preview.

£L£VAtOR RID£S

In a city of skyscraping structures, Chicagoans are well-acquainted with elevators. Among Chicago's ear-popping rides, a few stand out as memorable:

First, is the nighttime climb to the 96th floor of the **John Hancock Building** (875 N. Michigan). This is not the $7 trip to the 94th floor's observation deck. It's a free glide to the lounge, where you can opt, like oh, so many others, to soak up breathtaking views of the glittering city below without sitting down and buying a drink. (A drink with tax and tip from a window-side table will run about $10.) Next, the old-fashioned, attendant-controlled elevators of the exquisite and musty **Fine Arts Building** (410 S. Michigan) come to mind. The operator pulls a protective iron gate across the door for the ride—just like in the old days. When you reach the top floor, wander into Curtiss Hall for a magnificent view of the lakefront. Walk your way down the ten flights of stairs stopping at any point to roam the historic hallways filled with studios, practice rooms, and music and design classes. Finally, I have a hard time forgetting the days (late 70s/early 80s) when the glass elevators of Michigan Avenue's first enclosed mall, **Water Tower Place** (845 N. Michigan), caused quite a stir. They even caught the attention of the director of the movie *Class* (1983), who used the 7-story ride as the setting for a racy love scene between Jacqueline Bisset and Andrew McCarthy.

FACTORY TOURS

Eli's Cheesecake Company
6701 W. Forest Preserve Drive, 773/736-3417 **NW**
Daily, 20-minute tours are given of the factory/bakery that unleashes **Eli's** "world famous" cheesecake to the insatiable public. Noon, Mon.-Fri. Pick up some "sweet imperfections" from the outlet store afterwards. It *is* lunch time after all.

FOUNTAINS

Buckingham Fountain
Congress and Lake Shore Drive **C**
Buckingham Fountain—one of the world's largest, most magnificent fountains—has remained a popular Chicago attraction since its completion in 1927. Its three-tiered, pink marble exterior; four pairs of bronze sea horses symbolizing the four states that border Lake Michigan; and a dramatic, 165-foot central geyser make it the regal centerpiece of Grant Park. The beaux-arts design was apparently influenced by the Fountain of Latona at Versailles. Kate Buckingham, an arts philanthropist, donated the money to build the fountain in memory of her brother Clarence. She even left an endowment, administered by the Art Institute, to maintain it. Recently, new, more intense lighting was added to help the fountain better compete with Chicago's ever brighter nighttime skyline. Water gushes daily May 1st to October 1st from 10am-11pm, with a spectacular colored lights display from 9pm-11pm.

Nicholas J. Melas Centennial Fountain and Water Arc
McClurg Court and the Chicago River **C**
Centennial Fountain is accompanied by a stream of water that arcs across the Chicago River for the first ten minutes of every hour between 10am and midnight, except for a 3pm-4pm hiatus. It operates daily from May 1st to October 1st.

Newer fountains have sprung up at **Navy Pier** and **McCormick Place** as part of the creative landscaping connected with the renovations and expansions of those sites.

Note: More downtown water fountains can be seen on the public art walking tours found in *Chapter 6: Walking*.

GARDENS

Bergen Garden
5050 S. Lake Shore Drive, 773/288-5050   **S**
On top of this three-story parking garage is a one-acre paradise filled with 30,000 plants and trees, ponds and fountains. It was designed in 1982 by Phil Shipley—a California landscape architect who previously worked on the estates of such Hollywood luminaries as Clark Gable, Jean Harlow, and Walt Disney—to provide an aesthetic view for residents of the apartments above. Walkways meander through lush plantings of petunias, viburnum, daisies, English and Baltic ivy, and marigolds, shaded by Austrian pines, flowering crab apples, and honey locust trees. A waterfall cascades into a small stream that is crossed by a footbridge. A small wild duck population from the Lincoln Park Zoo spends part of the year here. Numerous other birds can also be seen, bathing in the water or eating berries from the shrubbery. Open to the public from May to October. Call to make an appointment for a free self-guided tour.

Chicago Wildflower Works
North end of Grant Park between Randolph and Monroe   **C**
Two gigantic oval gardens burst with the verve and color of wild prairie flowers, amidst the formal, planned precision of Grant Park's hedges, trees, and rose gardens.

The city's two public conservatories are open daily from 9am-5pm. Admission is free.

Garfield Park Conservatory
300 N. Central Park, 312/746-5100   **W**
This is the largest indoor public botanical garden in the world, displaying 5,000 plant species, including one of the best cactus collections in the country.

Lincoln Park Conservatory
Fullerton and Stockton, 312/742-7736   N

> The **Lincoln Park** and **Garfield Conservatories** hold five annual
> flower shows with regular, seasonal themes: the *Christmas Show*
> (Mid-December to the first week in January), *Azalea Show*
> (February), *Spring Show* (late March to early May), *Summer Show*
> (early June to early Sept.) and the *Chrysanthemum Show* (Oct. to
> Nov.). Back in the 1960s, the chrysanthemum was designated the
> official flower of Chicago. All shows are free.

HOLIDAY MADNESS

Far from downtown's architectural splendor, Chicagoans engage in another
form of arts appreciation: marveling at their neighbors' holiday displays.
Please note that the following are private homes. While the displays are
meant for public enjoyment, please respect the owners' privacy and property
and do your viewing quietly from the sidewalk.

Christmas

Just be glad *you're* not paying their electric bills...

"The Logan House"
2656 W. Logan   N
People from all over the north side talk about this particular home on a large
corner lot in Logan Square. Most commonly referred to as **"The Logan
House,"** the more it changes from year to year, the more it stays the same.
Life-size, light-studded wire figures, strands and strands of colored bulbs,
shadowboxes, flags from around the world, animation, and holiday tunes
playing over the speaker engorge the senses.

"Maria Court"
4632 N. Maria Court   NW
Every year after a hearty Christmas dinner, members of our family make a
ritual pilgrimage from our gathering place in the O'Hare neighborhood to
"Maria Court." Ostensibly, the short walk in the bitter cold is to get some
exercise and "make room for dessert," but none of us can resist the annual

gawkfest. From the end of the block, we identify it by its sheer brilliance. We scan the lawn, house, and driveway for new examples of the owner's precision handiwork. How does it all fit? A few avid decorators in our crowd will inevitably contrast the display with the restraint and good taste of their personal decorating, but they could also be taking notes for next year.

Both of these electric extravaganzas are acknowledged in Mary Edsey's book, *The Best Christmas Decorations in Chicagoland* (Tabagio Press). Edsey offers a couple of suggestions to explain why Chicagoans seem to be even more zealous in their outdoor Christmas decorating than other Americans. First, two of the world's largest light manufacturers, Silvestri Corp. and NOMA Christmas, are located here. Secondly, from 1962 to 1966, Polk Brothers gave away 250,000 five-foot, lighted Santas with appliance and furniture purchases, surely having an impact on external holiday displays. You can still see many of these pioneering decorations on lawns, porches, and roof tops around the city. Edsey gives very merry Yuletide bus tours (773/404-9402) of mind-blowing holiday displays. She recommends **Cornelia's Restaurant** (748 W. Cornelia, 773/248-8333) for Christmas time dining because of its attractive display of antique decorations.

Apart from gaping at light displays in residential areas, Chicago has a number of Christmas time traditions. Certain ones—like seeing *The Nutcracker Ballet* at McCormick Place's **Arie Crown Theater** or *A Christmas Carol* at the **Goodman Theater**, eating lunch under the giant Christmas tree in **Marshall Field's** 7th-floor Walnut Room, and seeing the international collection of Christmas trees at the **Museum of Science and Industry**—can be costly for the budget-minded. However, there are plenty of free and low-cost options as well. For decades, Chi-town residents have hopped on the el to downtown to see the super-tall city Christmas tree in **Daley Plaza** and the animated holiday window displays of the State Street department stores. You can purchase a cup of hot chocolate or roasted chestnuts from street vendors. Head to the **Lincoln Park** or **Garfield Park Conservatory** (see pp.44-45) for the seasonal poinsettia show or to the **Adler Planetarium** (see p.52) for their *Star of Wonder* sky show.

Halloween

Outdoor decorating is not just for Christmas anymore. Elaborate Halloween displays are appearing with greater frequency on neighborhood side streets.

1052 W. Wrightwood   **N**
Hundreds of lighted jack-o-lanterns grin and grimace from the front lawn of
this Wrightwood residence.

7025 W. Berwyn   **FN**
A bounty of headstones, ghosts, witches, monsters, and coffin-bound
mummies are barely contained by the spider web fence of this house's lawn.
Visit at night to experience the full force of the light and sound effects.

LAWN FRENZY

If you miss the seasonal shows, here is another extreme manifestation of
unique exterior home decorating:

House of Crosses
1544 W. Chestnut   **C**
Straight from a fantastical dream (or nightmare, for some) is the eccentric
"House of Crosses"—referred to as the "It's What I Do" House by the
American Institute of Architects Guide To Chicago. For almost 25 years,
the owners have been covering the house, lawn, and coach house with
hundreds of wooden crosses, plaques, and shields. This isn't a grotesque
fixation on death but an artistic tribute...primarily, *to the movies!* The names
of movie stars, movie characters, and movie titles appear on these colorful
structures: Ingrid Bergman, Bing Crosby, Bette Davis, Mickey Rooney, Zsa
Zsa Gabor, Tarzan, Buckwheat, the Cisco Kid. Camelot, the Pope, Joan of
Arc, and former mayor Jane Byrne are also acknowledged.

MUSEUMS

Foundations, associations, philanthropists, and volunteers present us with
museums of all stripes, from one-room exhibits to world class institutions.
Most of Chicago's thriving museum culture can be yours at no charge; the
rest you can have for under a few bucks.

Never an Admission Charge

ABA Museum of Law
750 N. Lake Shore Drive, 312/988-6222   **C**
The American Bar Association pays tribute to the legal profession with their

modest museum. The recent *America's Advocate: The Story of the ABA* and *Famous Trials in American History: Cases that Shaped and Shocked the Nation* are typical of their exhibits. Mon.-Fri. 11am-2pm, Sat. 11am-5pm.

Chicago Cultural Center

78 E. Washington, 312/346-3278 (FINE-ART) for events listing,   **C**
Known as "The People's Palace" when it first opened in 1897 as the city's original public library, this national landmark still deserves every implication of that affectionate name. It remained the Chicago's central library until 1977 and has been the **Cultural Center** since an extensive renovation was completed in 1991. Although Chicagoans, in true second city fashion, often brag about being number one, in the case of this cultural treasure—it really is true. As an architectural masterpiece, this beaux-art spectacle wows on every repeated visit. The Grand Staircase, Preston Bradley Hall, and G.A.R. Rotunda *are* the type of things usually associated with palaces. Try eating your lunch under the $35 million Tiffany dome (the world's largest) in Preston Bradley Hall during a **Dame Myra Hess Memorial** concert Wednesdays at 12:15pm. You will feel like royalty. When it comes to the 1,000 free cultural events a year—exhibits, concerts, dance and dramatic performances, films, classes, lectures, and workshops— it is peerless. The first floor also houses a visitors information center, the Museum of Broadcast Communications, a photo exhibit of Chicago landmarks, a gift shop, and cafe. Guided architectural tours begin in the Randolph Street lobby Tues.-Sat. at 1:45 pm. Open Mon.-Wed. 10am-7pm, Thur. 10am-8pm, Fri. 10am-6pm, Sat. 10am-5pm, Sun. Noon-5pm. You'll need to pick up the monthly schedule of events to keep track of everything.

David and Alfred Smart Museum of Art

5550 S. Greenwood, 773/702-0200   **S**
Although opened in 1974, this fine art museum of the University of Chicago houses a permanent collection that began in the 1890s, the decade of the University's founding. Its 7,000-piece collection spans five centuries of Western and Eastern civilizations and includes Chinese, Neolithic, and current American art. It was named for the founders of *Esquire* magazine. Tues., Wed., Fri. 10am-4pm, Thur. 10am-9pm, Sat.-Sun. Noon-6pm.

Dr. Pedro Albizu Campos Museum of Puerto Rican History & Culture

1457 N. California, 773/342-4880   **W**
Devoted to Puerto Rican art and history, this small museum features temporary shows, along with a permanent exhibit focusing on Puerto Rican national hero and martyr Albizu Campos. Sat.-Sun. Noon-4pm.

Federal Reserve Bank of Chicago
230 S. LaSalle, lobby level, 312/322-5111 **C**
The bank's visitors' center contains a small museum that takes guests through the machinations of the **Federal Reserve**. 70-minute tours of the bank and its inner chambers are given through advance scheduling only. Groups (ages 14 and older) should make reservations at least two weeks in advance in general and at least a month in advance during the busy spring and fall seasons. Individuals can join Tues. tours at 1pm by calling a minimum of one day in advance.

Harold Washington Library Center
400 S. State, 312/747-4300 **C**
The main branch of the Chicago Public Library (in a stunning new building) offers numerous services (sign up to use pianos, computers, and AV equipment), performances, films, lectures, workshops, art exhibits, and children's programming free of charge. While touring the **HWLC**—the second largest public library in the world—don't miss the Winter Garden on the ninth floor; the Jazz, Blues, and Gospel Hall of Fame on the eighth floor; or the permanent art collection scattered throughout the building. Look for monthly schedule of events. Guided tours Mon.-Sat. at noon and 2pm. Open Mon. 9am-7pm, Tues. and Thur. 11am-7pm, Wed., Fri., and Sat. 9am-5pm, Sun. 1-5pm.

Hyde Park Historical Society
5529 S. Lake Park, 773/493-1893 **S**
Housed in an 1893 cable station, this museum documents and displays the history of the long-flourishing Hyde Park neighborhood. Sat.-Sun. 2pm-4pm.

Intuit: The Center for Intuitive and Outsider Art
1926 N. Halsted, 773/929-7122 **N**
This unique, not-for-profit group recently organized to promote the art of those who are rejected, ignored, marginalized, or unimpressed by the institutions of the mainstream art world. The galleries of **Intuit**'s headquarters showcase the creative efforts of these intuitive and outsider artists.

Jane Addams' Hull House
800 S. Halsted, 312/413-5353 **C**
Visit a historic building where Nobel Peace Prize winner Jane Addams and crew began their settlement house and social work projects to improve the lives of immigrants in the surrounding neighborhood. Accompanying

exhibits focus on Addams, other women who lived and worked at Hull House, their social endeavors, and Chicago immigration history. Mon.- Fri. 10am-4pm, Sun. Noon-5pm.

The Martin D'Arcy Gallery of Art
Loyola University, 6525 N. Sheridan, 773/274-3000   **FN**
Loyola University gallery rotates the various art works from its impressive array of European art. The pieces, which date from 1150 to 1700, include sculpture, decorative arts, and paintings by Bellini, Bassano, and Tintoretto. Open to the public when school is in session, Mon.-Fri. Noon-4pm,

Mexican Fine Arts Center Museum
1852 W. 19th, 312/738-1503   **W**
The Midwest's only Mexican museum has developed an international reputation for itself and its first-rate exhibits of local, national, and international artists. Its extensive permanent collection contains original pieces from such Mexican greats as Diego Rivera, José Orozco, and David Siqueiros. The museum also sponsors performances, lectures, classes, and community events. Tues.-Sun. 10am-5pm.

Museum of Broadcast Communications
Chicago Cultural Center, Michigan & Washington, 312/629-6000   **C**
Entertaining and educational survey of the world of broadcasting centers on the Golden Age of radio and TV, the realm of advertising, and broadcast personalities. Watch award-winning commercials and learn how to make one. View clips from Oprah's early days, then appear in your own videotaped newscast. Read about Edgar Bergen and his contemporaries, then check out the real Charlie McCarthy or Mortimer Snerd. The archives contain 60,000+ hours of recorded newscasts and other programming. Mon.-Sat. 10am-4:30pm, Sun. Noon-5pm.

Museum of Contemporary Photography
600 S. Michigan, 312/663-5554   **C**
Columbia College gallery features changing exhibits of contemporary photography. Mon.-Fri. 10am-5pm, Thur. 10am-8pm, Sat. Noon-5pm.

National Vietnam Veterans Art Museum
1801 S. Indiana, 312/326-0270   **C**
Housed in a renovated old warehouse donated by the city of Chicago, this new three-story museum is unique in its specialization in art produced by Vietnam war veterans. Artists from the U.S. and Southeast Asia have contributed over 600 powerful and, sometimes, disturbing paintings,

drawings, sculptures, and photographic pieces to a collection that also contains North Vietnamese and Viet Cong artifacts. The museum includes a theater, library, and archives. Tues.-Sun. 11am-6pm, Wed. 11am-9pm. Closed Mondays.

Newberry Library
60 W. Walton, 312/943-9090   **C**
Independent history and humanities research library boasts a world-class collection of rare books, maps, graphics, and manuscripts—such items as a leaf from the Gutenberg Bible and original drawings for *Alice in Wonderland*. Tours are given Thursdays at 3pm and Saturdays at 10:30am. Tues.-Thur. 10am-6pm, Fri.-Sat. 9am-5pm.

Oriental Institute
1155 E. 58th, 773/702-9521   **S**
Since the early part of the 20th century, the University of Chicago has been collecting and displaying artifacts from the ancient Near East and teaching Chicagoans about the history, art, archeology, and anthropology of that region's civilizations. Now nearing the completion of a major renovation and extension project, the institute will reopen in late 1998. Tues.-Sat. 10am-4pm, Wed. 10am-8:30pm, Sun. and holidays Noon-4pm.

Renaissance Society at the University of Chicago
5811 S. Ellis, 773/702-8670   **S**
Contemporary art exhibits at the University of Chicago. Tues.-Fri. 10am-5pm, Sat.-Sun. Noon-5pm.

Rogers Park/West Ridge Historical Society
6424 N. Western, 773/764-4078   **FN**
The **RPWR Historical Society** aspires to encourage and perpetuate an interest in the history of those neighborhoods through education, preservation, and research. Their storefront museum displays numerous photographs and memorabilia depicting the rich history of the area. An on-site reference library includes a large collection of historical photos, maps, deeds, and other documents. Wed. & Fri. 10am-5pm, Thur. 7am-9pm.

Scholl College of Podiatric Medicine
1001 N. Dearborn, 312/280-2880   **C**
Truly the only such museum in the United States! The hands-on features educate on the human foot, its relationship to the rest of the body, proper foot care, and Dr. Scholl's contributions to foot health and comfort. Mon., Tues., Fri. 9am-4pm, Wed. -Thur. 9am-7pm.

Vietnam Museum
954 W. Carmen, 773/728-6111 **FN**
Military, civilian, and multi-cultural displays cover the years 1954-1975 and focus on Vietnam, the "Vietnam Conflict," and that period of American history in hopes of helping visitors better understand the personal experiences of those who fought in the war. Museum has archives and a library. Sat.-Sun. 11am-3pm.

Free One Day A Week

The following museums are free to the public one day weekly. Prices listed are admission charges for the other days of the week.

⇒ **MONDAYS**

Chicago Historical Society
1601 N. Clark, 312/642-4600, *www.chicagohistory.org* **N**
Founded in 1856, the **CHS** is Chicago's oldest cultural institution. Its wonderful exhibits chronicle the city's history from its days as a wilderness outpost to current times, plus throws in some regional and national history for good measure. Don't miss the "Hands-On History Gallery," recent explorations of Chicago neighborhoods, the permanent "Pioneer Life" display, and the examination of the era of Abraham Lincoln. Mon.-Sat. 9:30am-4:30pm, Sun. Noon-5pm. Suggested donation $5, $3 students & seniors, $1 kids, 6-12.

⇒ **TUESDAYS**

Adler Planetarium
1300 S. Lake Shore Drive, 312/322-0300 **C**
The country's original planetarium and the Midwest's leading museum of astronomy and space exploration features three floors of exhibits and regular sky shows in its domed theater, which is accessed by a 77-foot escalator straight from a sci-fi fantasy. These thematic sky shows combine visual effects, narration, and music to teach about comets, constellations, the solar system, or related topics. Throughout the museum, you'll encounter a remarkable assortment of antique astronomical instruments from around the world—a collection rivaled only by those in Florence and Oxford. Other favorites include the hands-on experiments with lenses and prisms and devices that tell you how much you would weigh on different planets. Mon.-Thur. 9am-5pm, Fri. 9am-9pm, Sat.-Sun. 9am-6pm. Adults $3, children (ages 4-17) and seniors $2. Sky shows cost an extra $3. Use the

observatory's telescope to peer into outer space after the 8pm sky show on Fridays.

Art Institute of Chicago
111 S. Michigan, 312/443-3600   **C**
Built for the 1893 World's Fair, this internationally renowned museum boasts a consummate collection that features various genres of fine and decorative art and spans 5,000 years and six continents. Along with Seurat's famed "Sunday in Park with George" are recognizable paintings by Monet, Renoir, Caillebotte, Picasso, Hopper, O'Keefe, and Warhol. Those looking for something more three-dimensional will appreciate the paperweight collection, textiles, architectural works, suits of armor, Thorne miniature rooms, and folk art and antiquities from far away lands. Mon., Wed.-Fri. 10:30am-4:30pm, Tues. 10:30am-8pm, Sat. 10am-5pm, Sun. & holidays Noon-5pm. Suggested admission is $7, $3.50 for students, seniors, and children (ages 6-14).

In an effort to hook the 25-35-year-old set on arts patronage, Chicago's two major art institutions have devised monthly cocktail party type gatherings aimed at savvy, young professionals (but open to all adults over 21). The **Museum of Contemporary Art**'s (220 E. Chicago, 312/280-2660) "First Fridays" and the **Art Institute**'s (Michigan & Adams, 312/443-3600) Thursday evening "After Hours" offer guided tours, gallery hopping, live music, appetizers, cash bar, lively conversation, and mingling with very eligible singles. Call for specific dates. The **MCA** affair runs 6pm-9pm and the **Art Institute**'s 5:30pm-8pm. Each has a $10 cover charge, $5 for members. Hint. Hint.

Terra Museum of American Art
666 N. Michigan, 312/664-3939   **C**
Explore American art from 1763 to the present with this museum's permanent collection—which includes Homer, Wyeth, Whistler, and Cassatt—and their first-rate temporary exhibits. Tues. Noon-8pm, Wed.-Sat. 10am-5pm, Sun. Noon-5pm. Closed Mondays $5, $2.50 teachers & seniors, $1 students. Always free for kids.

Free only the first Tuesday of every month:

Museum of Contemporary Art
220 E. Chicago, 312/280-2660   C
Enjoy the work of established and emerging contemporary artists (post-1945) in this spectacular new building designed by German museum architect Josef Paul Kleihaus. At 151,000 ft.^{2}, the MCA is now the largest single building devoted to contemporary art in the country. Calder, Johns, Kline, Magritte, Nauman, Paschke, Sherman, and Warhol are among the artists featured in the museum's permanent collection, but the majority of space is left for constantly changing exhibits. Striking views of the city and lakefront, a theater for film and live performance, an education center for workshops and artist discussions, video and electronic galleries, and an outdoor sculpture garden are other notable features. Tues., Thur., Fri. 11am-6pm, Wed. 11am-8pm, Sat.-Sun. 10am-6pm. Closed Mondays. $6.50, $4 students and seniors.

⇒ **WEDNESDAYS**

Charnley-Persky House
1365 N. Astor, 312/915-0105   C
The Society of Architectural Historians recently began offering tours of its national headquarters, which is located in what Frank Lloyd Wright referred to as "the first modern house in America." Wright helped Louis Sullivan design the building for lumber merchant James Charnley when Wright was a young architect in Adler and Sullivan's firm. One-hour tours are given Wed. at noon for free and Sat. at 10am for $5. The Saturday tour can be extended one hour (for $4) for a walk of historic Astor Street and a tour of Madlener House, a Prairie School residence designed by Schmidt and Garden in 1901-1902.

Field Museum of Natural History
Roosevelt Rd. and Lake Shore Drive, 312/922-9410, *www.fmnh.org* C
Opened as the depository for the 1893 Columbian Exposition's natural history artifacts, this grand old museum now has a collection of 20 million pieces, nine acres of exhibits, and few peers on the world's museum circuit. Just for starters, take note of the 75-ft. mounted Brachiosaurus in the lobby and visit the popular exhibits on ancient Egypt, peoples of the Pacific Northwest, and "DNA to Dinosaurs." Competing for your attention will be the fascinating special exhibits; topics of the recent past include the artifacts of voodoo, art of American Indian women of the Great Lakes region, photographs of Jews hiding in the Netherlands during WWII, tribal peoples

discovering videotaping technology, and butterfly gardens. And, if that's not enough, the **Field Museum** is also the setting for the 1996 sci-fi horror movie *The Relic*. Open daily 9am-5pm. $7, $4 students, seniors, and kids (ages 3-17), $16 family admission.

⇒ **THURSDAYS**

Chicago Children's Museum (evenings 5pm-8pm)
Navy Pier at 700 E. Grand, 312/527-1000
www.chichildrensmuseum.org   **C**
Since moving from its Cultural Center origins to its new Navy Pier location, the **Chicago Children's Museum** has become the second most visited children's museum in the country and one of Chicago's top cultural attractions. Its exhibits, workshops, and performances are designed to activate the creative and intellectual potential of children under 12. Inventing Lab, Waterways, PlayMaze, Treehouse Trails, Face to Face: Dealing with Prejudice and Discrimination, Info Tech Arcade, and the Kraft Artabounds Gallery are among the delightful, permanent hands-on exhibits. The recent blockbuster "Seuss!" and the "Junior Jams" interactive jazz concert series are typical of the extraordinary lineup of special performances and traveling exhibits. Tues.-Sun. 10am-5pm, Thur. 5pm-8pm is free family night. $6 per person for an all-day pass, children less than a year old are free.

DuSable Museum
740 E. 56th Place, 773/947-0600   **S**
Named for Chicago's first permanent settler, a Haitian man named Jean Baptiste Pointe du Sable, this major Chicago cultural institution is devoted to the preservation and interpretation of the history and culture of African-Americans. The recent "Amistad" exhibit and the new display devoted to Chicago's first black mayor, Harold Washington, exemplify their commitment to timely and relevant programming. Mon.-Sat. 10am-4pm, Sun. Noon-4pm. $3, $2 students & seniors, $1 kids.

Museum of Science and Industry
57th St. and Lake Shore Drive, 773/684-1414
www.msichicago.org   **S**
Science for Dummies! Anyone can learn about science at the **MSI**, and they're bound to have a grand old time of it too. Housed in the Fine Arts Building from the 1893 Columbian Exhibition, the **MSI**'s 14 acres hold countless offerings, including over 800 interactive exhibits. Attractions focus on space, manufacturing, the human body, communications, transportation, current science topics, and more and are not at all boring like

this list might imply. Although nearly half of the museum's exhibits have been newly created or refurbished over the past few years, the classics will never disappear. The coal mine, the captured German WWII submarine, a 16-foot walk-through heart, the miniature Fairy Castle, and the annual Christmas Around the World tree display are but a few of the historical favorites. It's hard to believe that until a few years ago, this museum was always free of charge. Alas, as the busiest tourist attraction in the Midwest, the museum needed to begin charging admission fees to ensure its continued greatness. Mon.-Fri. 9:30am-4pm (5:30pm in summer), Sat.-Sun. 9:30am-5:30pm. $7, $6 seniors, $3.50 kids. A combo ticket that grants admittance to the current 5-story Omnimax movie are $12, $10, and $7.50. (On Thursday, Omnimax tickets are $7, $6, and $5.)

Shedd Aquarium
1200 S. Lake Shore Drive, 312/939-2438, *www.sheddnet.org*   **C**
Among the more than 8,000 aquatic animals—representing over 700 species from all parts of the world—at this, the world's largest indoor aquarium, you'll discover flashlight fish, bobbing iguanas, electric eels, venomous anemones, and hungry piranhas. Don't miss feeding time at the humongous, 90,000-gallon Caribbean coral reef tank in the museum's center. Divers hand-feed sharks, sea turtles, moray eels, and many others at 11am and 2pm. The recently added oceanarium—with winding nature trails—houses beluga whales, dolphins, sea otters, and harbor seals in a recreation of a rugged Pacific Northwest coastline. A separate area reproduces a Falkland Islands environment for a colony of penguins. Mon.-Fri. 9am-5pm, Sat.-Sun. 9am-6pm. $11, $9 seniors and children (ages 3-11). On Thursday, admission to the aquarium is free, but you must pay extra for the Oceanarium: $6, $5 seniors and children.

> Neighborhood libraries have a limited number of free passes to many of Chicago's museums and other cultural institutions that can be checked out like books. If you don't already have one, get a library card today!

⇒ **FRIDAYS**

Spertus Museum of Judaica
618 S. Michigan, 312/922-9012   **C**
Discover Jewish history and culture through an extensive collection of art and artifacts. Adults will appreciate the temporary exhibits on relevant

subjects, and kids will enjoy the Artifact Center that allows them to play archaeologist in the ancient Middle East. Sun.-Thur. 10am-5pm, Fri. 10am-3pm. Artifact center open Sun.-Thur. 1pm-4:30pm. $5, $3 students, seniors, and children, $10 family maximum.

Donations Appreciated

The Chicago Athenaeum: The Museum of Architecture and Design
6 N. Michigan, 312/251-0175, *www.chi-athenaeum.org*   **C**
The nation's only independent museum of architecture and design hopes to educate the public about the value of good design and how it can positively impact the human environment. It covers all aspects of design from architecture and urban planning to graphic arts and industrial design. Its permanent collection includes over 5,000 objects that were designed and manufactured in Chicago between 1910 and 1960; some Frank Lloyd Wright chairs; and large models, sketches, and photos of some of the city's more design intensive buildings. Tues.-Sat. 11am-6pm, Sun. Noon-5pm. Suggested donation is $3, $2 for students and seniors.

International Museum of Surgical Science
1524 N. Lake Shore Drive, 312/642-6502, *www.imss.org*   **C**
Learn the gory and glorious history of surgery and related sciences. Tues.-Sat. 10am-4pm. Suggested admission is $3 for adults, $2 for seniors and students.

Latvian Folk Art Museum
4146 N. Elston, 773/588-2085   **NW**
Latvian folk art exhibits include a large textile collection and audio tapes of folk music. The museum is opened with a key from the Latvian community Center next door. Someone is generally there Thur.-Sat. 11am-3pm. Donations appreciated.

Peace Museum
314 W. Institute Place, 312/440-1860   **C**
This one-room museum presents changing exhibits on the peace movement, conflict resolution, and related topics, often through various artistic media. Tues.-Sat. 11am-5pm. Requested donation is $3.50, $2 for students, seniors, and children.

Polish Museum of America
984 N. Milwaukee, 773/384-3352   **C**
Founded in 1935 and housed in a former ballroom, this is one of the largest

and oldest ethnic museums in the U.S.! Among the abundant and varied Polish cultural, religious, and historical artifacts, you'll find a Picasso and a Chagall donated by prominent Polish Chicagoans. Included in the collection is an 18th-century Royal Sleigh, carved from a single log as a gift to Princess Maria—daughter of the Polish king, Stanislaw Leszaynski—and pre-historic objects found in Poland. 60,000 volume lending library. Open daily 11am-4pm. Requested donations are $2 adults and $1 seniors/students.

Ukrainian Institute of Modern Art
2320 W. Chicago, 773/227-5522   **W**
Ukrainian Village gallery features several major exhibitions by independent artists yearly. Tues.-Thur. and Sat.-Sun., Noon-4pm. Donations requested.

Ukrainian National Museum
721 N. Oakley, 312/421-8020   **W**
Also located in the Ukrainian Village neighborhood, this museum has a large stash of cultural and historical artifacts, including a collection of the famous Ukrainian Easter eggs, beaded jewelry, and folk costumes from 26 different regions of the Ukraine. Thur.-Sun. 11am-4pm. $2 suggested donation.

Low Entrance Fees

American Police Center and Museum
1717 S. State, 312/431-0005   **C**
Where the Eliot Nesses are glorified more than the Al Capones... Chicago cop and criminal memorabilia at this museum of law and order includes a real electric chair, a display of seized weapons that would make Al Pacino's *Scarface* drool, and an assemblage of not-so-pretty photos depicting crime scenes and victims. A current, ongoing exhibit covers the history of women in law enforcement. Weekdays 9:30 am-4:30pm. $4, $3 seniors, $2.50 kids 3-11.

A. Philip Randolph Pullman Porter Museum Gallery
10406 S. Maryland, 773/928-3935   **FSE**
Located in Chicago's Pullman Historic District, this new museum fills in a pivotal piece of Pullman history and makes an important contribution to Chicago's cultural scene. The only African-American Labor History Museum in Chicago, the museum gallery focuses on A. Philip Randolph, chief organizer of the Brotherhood of the Sleeping Car Porters (the first African-American labor union in the U.S.), members of the BSCP, African-American railroad attendants in general, and George Pullman, owner of the

Pullman Rail Car Company and founder of the planned town of Pullman. Phillip Randolph and the Pullman Porters' struggle for equality within the Pullman Rail Car Company led the way for future advancements in labor history and civil rights. The story is told through the permanent collection of historical photos and well-preserved memorabilia. Open Tues.-Fri. 11am-4:30 pm and on alternate Saturdays. Call for Sat. hours. $2 admission.

Balzekas Museum of Lithuanian Culture
6500 S. Pulaski, 773/582-6500   **SW**
Founded in 1968 by southwest-side car dealer Stanley Balzekas Jr., the **Balzekas Museum of Lithuanian Culture** is housed in a former animal hospital. In the various rooms, one can view traditional Lithuanian woodcarvings—many crafted by war refugees held in displaced person camps; a rare book collection that includes the first book printed in Lithuanian—a 1547 catechism; woven tapestries; and an extensive collection of amber, the translucent fossil resin that is found in abundance in Lithuania. The children's section is fun, even without high-tech gadgets. It includes a miniature farmhouse with accompanying animals and people, traditional Lithuanian costumes for dress-up, an enormous jigsaw puzzle depicting a suit of armor, and blocks for building replicas of the medieval castles of Lithuania. Open daily 10am-4pm. Adults $4, students and seniors $3, children $1.

Hellenic Museum and Cultural Center
168 N. Michigan, 4th floor, 312/726-1234   **C**
Located in the National Bank of Greece building, this one-room museum presents rotating exhibits on various elements of Greek culture and history. Tues.-Fri. 11am-3pm. $3.

Museum of Holography
1134 W. Washington, 312/226-1007   **C**
This small tribute to the holographic image distinguishes itself as the nation's only all holography museum. And with a range of images so vast as to include a whirling Michael Jordan and a bladder/prostate combo, there's sure to be something to capture everyone's imagination. Open Wed.-Sun. 12:30pm-5pm. $2.50, free for children under six.

Swedish American Museum Center
5211 N. Clark, 773/728-8111   **FN**
Stop in this storefront museum after breakfast at one of the Swedish restaurants on the block. Besides regular exhibits on Swedish culture, history, and immigration experiences, the center offers a diverse line-up of

cultural events. Tues.-Fri. 10am-4pm, Sat.-Sun. 10am-3pm. $4, $2 students & seniors, $1 children.

NATURAL SPACES

From a swampy land filled with wild smelly onions grew Chicago, whose motto since its 1833 inception has been *Urbs in Horto* (City in a Garden). Daniel Burnham's legendary, large-scale 1909 "Chicago Plan" has left us a liberal inheritance of green spaces: a lakefront preserved for culture and recreation and "The Emerald Necklace"—an extensive boulevard system that joins some of our biggest and oldest city parks. This precedence for making greenery a priority has helped put Chicago at the forefront of the current urban greening trend. The present Mayor Daley is a well-known tree fanatic (being born on Arbor Day and all) who has boosted the withering forestry department and instituted *Green Streets* programs, designed to maintain the 500,000 city-owned trees, while planting thousands of new ones annually. For the record, Chicago has close to 30 miles of lakefront, with 29 beaches, about 560 parks, covering nearly 6,800 acres, and is surrounded by 67,000 acres of Cook County Forest Preserve. It's not quite a jungle out there but a sizable, flourishing, and expanding garden. See also **Gardens** (pp.44-45) in this chapter and **Birding** (p.82) in *Chapter 3: Recreation* and **Parks** (pp.298-300) in *Chapter 6: Walking*.

North Park Village Nature Center
5801 N. Pulaski, 312/744-5472   **FN**
Formerly the city's tuberculosis sanitarium (1915-1974), **NPVNC** has increased its annual attendance—from 6,500 in the early 1990s to over 60,000 currently—through a hearty commitment to education, conservation, restoration, and unique programming. On its 61-acre parcel is a 46-acre preserve with four distinct eco-systems teeming with native plants and wildlife: wetlands, woodlands, oak savanna, and prairie. Call/write to be put on the mailing list for a quarterly schedule of events for children, families, and adults. Bird watching, nature walks, star-gazing sessions, and an array of classes are all popular activities, as are the annual festivals. The Maple Sugar Festival is in March, the Harvest Festival in October, and the Winter Solstice Celebration in December. Open daily from 10am-4pm. Free.

North Pond Wildlife Preserve
In Lincoln Park, between Fullerton and Diversey   **N**
The 10-acre North Pond and surrounding region are undergoing an

ecological restoration to improve water quality and preserve the area's biological diversity. Currently a refuge for fish, small mammals, and over 40 types of migratory and nesting birds, restoration efforts hope to increase the amount of wildlife by bringing more indigenous plant species back to the water's shore.

Wolf Lake/William Powers Conservation Area

Approx. 118th to 134th streets, Avenue 0 to Calumet   **FSE**

This, the only state park within the city limits, boasts fields of native grasses, wildflowers, and plenty of wildlife, with accompanying picnic tables, jogging paths, and bike trails to enjoy the surrounding nature. As a main feeder to the Mississippi flyway, **Wolf Lake** is heavily traveled by migratory waterfowl. A colony of swans and the descendants of several Monk parrots—which escaped from an experimental project at the University of Chicago in the 1950s—have taken up permanent residence in the area. Plaques at the bases of the trees on the drive into the park commemorate each of Chicago's veterans organizations.

Wooded Island and Lagoon/Osaka Japanese Garden

In Jackson Park, just east of Cornell, about 5900-6200   **S**

The Wooded Island, a nature refuge protecting native Midwestern plants, was the site of the Japanese pavilions of the 1893 Columbian Exposition. Various Japanese gardens have come and gone since then. The current Osaka Garden is named for Chicago's Japanese sister city, which donated a traditional cedar entrance gate and money for restoration and landscaping in 1995. An ideal, tranquil escape, the garden's path winds meditatively past changing mini-environments.

In addition to Osaka, Japan, Chicago has several other sister cities: Accra, Ghana; Birmingham, England; Casablanca, Morocco; Durban, South Africa; Galway, Ireland; Goteborg, Sweden; Hamburg, Germany; Kiev, Ukraine; Milan, Italy; Moscow, Russia; Paris, France; Petach Tikva, Israel; Prague, Czech Republic; Shenyang, China; Toronto, Canada; Warsaw, Poland; and Athens, Greece. **Chicago Sister Cities** began in 1960 with an arrangement with Warsaw. The purpose of these relationships are to promote understanding between the two cities and to encourage business, artistic, diplomatic, and educational exchanges.

NAVY PIER

Constantly bustling with activity and attractions, it's hard to be a Chicagoan—or even a Chicago visitor—and escape acquaintance with **Navy Pier**.

Navy Pier
600 E. Grand, 312/595-PIER, 800/595-PIER (outside Chicago)
www.navypier.com   **C**
"Municipal Pier #2," constructed in 1916, has functioned as a freight center, navy training base, University of Illinois branch, and entertainment grounds (a use which continues to this day). Since its latest renovation was completed in 1995, the pier's indoor portion houses an Imax Theatre (using the latest in 3D technology), the **Chicago Children's Museum** (see p.55), shops, restaurants, a six-story glass enclosed botanical garden, WBEZ radio station, convention facilities, and an historic ballroom with an 80-foot domed ceiling. Outside, there are picnicking areas, a beer garden, dinner and tour boats, a sculpture walk, an open-air stage, a winter skating rink, and a giant Ferris wheel (150 ft.). All in all—50 acres of fun. The ferris wheel—which is open year-round, weather permitting—offers a spectacular view of the city, especially at nightfall. Open daily from 6am-11pm, the exterior region of Navy Pier is a great spot for strolling, picnicking, and skyline gazing. The building is open Sun.-Thur. 10am-10pm, Fri.-Sat. 10am-Midnight. The restaurants and bars stay open longer. Be sure to pick up a brochure that details the many year-round events that happen here.

NEWSPAPERS

See how the facts get reported and printed in this town.

Chicago Sun-Times
401 N. Wabash, 312/321-3251   **C**
Free, one-hour tours of the newspaper facilities are given Tues., Wed., and Thur. at 10:30am to groups of 10-25. Phone several weeks in advance to reserve time for a group or call a couple of weeks in advance if you're an individual who would like to join in on another group's reservation.

Chicago Tribune Freedom Center
777 W. Chicago, 312/222-2116   **C**
Make advance reservations (one day is often enough for small groups) for a

free tour of the *Trib*'s printing facility. Tues.-Fri. 9:30am, 10:30am, 11:30am, and 1:30pm.

POLITICS

City Council Sessions
City Hall, 121 N. LaSalle, 312/744-5000   **C**
Watch the mayor and council members in action from the council chambers' public viewing area on the 2nd floor. They usually meet in the morning, so call early in the day to find out if the council will be session. City Hall is very accessible. Walk right in and wander around, popping into those offices that interest you. City jobs listings are on the first floor, Special Events and Streets and Sanitation on the 7th, and the Board of Elections on the 3rd. Stop in and see the mayor on five.

Watch Chicago election politics first hand...

Chicago Board of Elections
City Hall, 121 N. LaSalle, 312/269-7984   **C**
Serving as an election judge is the best, easiest way to glimpse the Chicago political network in action (and you get paid about $100 to do it). From 5am-9pm, you'll be overseeing the voting process—a role that will privy you to a non-stop barrage of gossip, opinions, insights, and instructions from voters, precinct captains, police officers, poll watchers, state's attorneys, and sometimes even candidates. You'll see it's all about people...and pull.

PUBLIC TRANSPORTATION TOURING

The Loop's el marked its 100th anniversary in 1997, spurring the Landmarks Preservation Council to name four of its stations—State/Lake, Randolph/Wabash, Madison/Wabash, and LaSalle/Van Buren— "endangered historic places." They're advocating a refurbishing of these stations with a spiffier 19th-century look. The Quincy/Wells station, which was restored nearly ten years ago for a nostalgic movie set, continues to be one of the system's best-looking stations.

Loop Tour Train
Randolph & Washington el station, 312/744-2400   **C**
Every Saturday from mid-June to mid-October, tour guides from the

Chicago Architecture Foundation (see above) give 40-minute tours on the history of "The Loop," its architecture, and the elevated train system, from an el train that encircles downtown. The free tickets can be picked up any day of the week, but at least 1/2 an hour before departure from the Visitor Information Center in the **Chicago Cultural Center** (77 E. Randolph). Times: 12:15pm, 12:55pm, 1:35pm, and 2:15pm.

Hop aboard a CTA el or Metra train for an inexpensive ride through the city's neighborhoods...

Chicago Transit Authority (CTA)

The CTA recently switched to magnetic fare cards which must be purchased from automated machines in the stations. One ride costs $1.50 and transfers (good for two transfers over a two-hour period) are $.30. Get ten rides for $13.50. Children and students and seniors with passes are half price.

PHONE NUMBER/URL TO KNOW:

* 312/836-7000, for questions on fares, routes, and how to reach any destination. Visit *http://www.transitchicago.com* on the Internet.

PUBLICATION TO OWN:

* *CTA System Map*, available free from CTA Main Offices in the **Merchandise Mart** at 350 N. Wells, 7th Floor; from 181 W. Madison; and from certain el stations.

ROUTES:

* **Howard-Dan Ryan (Red) Line**
  Runs north/south between Howard Street Station (about 1600W) and State/95th St.

* **O'Hare-Congress/Douglas (Blue) Line**
  Runs northwest from downtown to O'Hare Airport and west from downtown to DesPlaines Avenue in Forest Park and 54th/Cermak in Cicero.

* **Midway (Orange) Line**
  Runs southwest from downtown to Midway Airport at 55th and Cicero.

Inaugurated in 1994, the orange transit line connecting downtown to the southwest side is as much fun as visiting Midway Airport itself. If you've got $1.50 and an hour, you can ride the elevated train above the southwest side, get a bird's eye view of the residential development around Chinatown and the South Loop, and land back at Midway. As the train snakes around the loop of track that gives downtown Chicago its nickname, you can check out intricate architectural features that you can't see from the street and spy on office workers. Look east as the train parallels Wabash Avenue and you will catch glimpses of Lake Michigan, Grant Park, and Buckingham Fountain. (MM)

- **Ravenswood (Brown) Line**
  Runs north/northwest from downtown to Kimball/Lawrence

- **Lake-Jackson Park/Englewood (Green) Line**
  Runs west from downtown to Harlem in Oak Park and south from downtown to University/63rd and Ashland/63rd.

TOURING TIPS:

Riders can transfer downtown (and at certain other large stations) from one line to another without a transfer. If you have lots of time and want to see the most city with the least energy and money expenditure, you might like to try riding every line to its end and back on a single fare (perfectly legal). Nearly every station permits changing directions without paying again.

Metra

Metra bills itself as the finest commuter rail system in the country. Its multitude of trains and tracks connect suburbanites—and those even farther out—with the city. Their bi-level, comfortable, and large-windowed trains are perfect for sitting and sight-seeing. While their weekday rates aren't the cheapest for train-hopping, a $5 weekend pass will give you unlimited rides all day Saturday and Sunday (except, unfortunately, on the South Shore train going to Indiana Dunes State Park). The Metra stations at Union Station (Jackson and Canal) and at Randolph and Michigan can provide maps and information about their lines and city and suburban destinations.

PHONE NUMBERS/URL TO KNOW:

- 312/322-6777, weekdays 8am-5pm
- 312/836-7000, all other times for information on fares, routes, etc.
- *http://www.metrarail.com* for online information.

SKYSCRAPERS

John Hancock Building Observatory
875 N. Michigan, 888/875-VIEW, *www.hancock-observatory.com*   **C**
Apparently, looking out over our great Midwestern metropolis from 94 floors above the street just wasn't enough for the tourists anymore. The **Hancock Observatory** just finished a $2.5 million rehab project in 1997 that turned this classic attraction into a tall-building theme park experience. The price tag of that renovation is 2-1/2 times what it cost to *build* the entire structure between 1965 and 1970! The interactive, multi-media adventure begins in the ground-floor ticketing area that's designed to look like the original "Big John" construction site. Once the "world's fastest" elevators have whisked you to the observation area in 39 seconds, you can now step outdoors onto the Skywalk and experience the *windy city* first hand. Windows on Chicago virtual reality "kiosks" allow guests to navigate the cityscape and hone in on 80 major attractions for close-up virtual tours. 3-D Soundscope telescopes speak in four languages and provide sound effects to enhance the view: cheering baseball fans at Comiskey Park, crashing waves at Navy Pier. For the more somber, 60 feet of History Walls detail the city's past. Open daily 9am-midnight. Adults $8, seniors and children (ages 6-17) $6.

Sears Tower Skydeck
233 S. Wacker, 312/875-9696 (Enter on Jackson)   **C**
What a fright we Chicagoans had back in 1996. It appeared that the twin Petronas Towers of Kuala Lumpur, Malaysia were about to nab the **Sears Tower**'s "World's Tallest Building" status with their exaggerated spires. The international body that confers such lofty titles, the Council on Tall Buildings and Urban Habitat, met to discuss the essence of a skyscraper and pose such tricky questions as whether or not uninhabitable towers, spires, and antennae should be factored into a building's height. The **Sears** would lose out if its top floor were compared with the spired towers as originally figured (1450 ft. vs. 1483 ft.). However, if the **Sears Tower**'s antennae counted (1518 ft. vs. 1483 ft.) or any spiny attachment discounted (1450 ft.

vs. 1241 ft.), we would prevail. You be the judge. From the 103rd floor **Skydeck**, seven floors *below* our highest floor, one could look snootily down on Petronas' 86th floor—it's highest occupied level. Open daily March-September 9am-11pm and October-February 9am-10pm. Adults $6.50, seniors $4.75, children (ages 5-12) $4, family passes $18.50.

National skyscraper criteria allow a structure to lean up to one foot! This built-in "sway" helps buildings withstand fierce winds, earthquakes, and other intemperances. The **Sears Tower**'s tilt can be 6-7 inches and the **John Hancock**'s tilt about 5-8 inches.

TALK SHOWS

You may have to call several weeks in advance to book your free seat as an audience member, but that should give you plenty of time to practice your applause and heckling and develop a self-righteous opinion.

Jenny Jones
NBC Tower, 454 N. Columbus Drive, 312/836-9485   C

Jerry Springer
NBC Tower, 454 N. Columbus Drive, 312/321-5365   C

Oprah Winfrey
Harpo Studios at 1058 W. Washington,   312/591-9222   C

TRADES AND EXCHANGES

Trading floor after trading floor, notice how Chicago smoothly moves from its solid, earthbound reputation to the abstract world of stocks, bonds, commodities, and futures.

Chicago Board Options Exchange
400 S. LaSalle, 312/786-5600   C
Watch the world's largest options market in action from its spacious 4th floor visitors' gallery. A 20-minute video explains the intricate world of options. You can experiment with your new-found knowledge at one of the

hands-on computer exhibits. Mon.-Fri. 8:30am-3:30pm. Free.

Chicago Board of Trade
141 W. Jackson, 312/435-3590   **C**
Gape at the trading floor of the world's oldest and largest commodities
futures trading market from the 5th floor visitors' center Mon.-Fri. 9am-
1:15pm. 1/2-hour lecture/video presentations begin at 9:15, 10, 10:30, and
11am, 11:30, Noon, and 12:30pm. The visitors' center includes a mini-
museum with historical artifacts. Free.

Chicago Mercantile Exchange
30 S. Wacker, 312/930-8249   **C**
Watch the swapping at the world's largest (in square footage) financial
futures exchange on its two trading floors from the 4th and 8th floor
galleries. Videos and other educational displays in the 4th floor gallery
provide a clue to what's happening. The upper one is open 7:15am-2pm, the
lower from 8am-3:15pm, Mon.-Fri. Free.

Chicago Stock Exchange
440 S. LaSalle, 312/663-2980   **C**
From the 5th floor gallery, watch the largest exchange of stocks in the
Midwest. All trading is done here electronically, without the shouting and
gesturing antics of the other exchanges. Explanatory videos are also in
operation. Call in advance to make reservations for guided tours. Mon.-Fri.
8:30am.-3pm. Free.

WATERFALLS

Chicago may have become great by its connection to the Great Lakes
System and the Mississippi River, but cascading water is no part of that
windfall. By most stretches of the imagination, waterfalls do not exist within
the city limits. For purposes of touring and trivia, however, I include these:

Columbus Park Waterfalls
In Columbus Park at Adams and Central   **W**
Not large, but trickling since the 1920s when architect Jens Jensen created a
small-scale replica of the Illinois river bluffs for Columbus Park.

Chicago River/River Park Waterfall
In River Park, near Argyle and Whipple   **FN**
An adventure only for fanatics... Where the north branch of the Chicago

River splits from the main branch, there gushes a mysterious little "fall," quite distinct in its energy and noise from the typically languid river. Walk 1/2 block north into River Park from Argyle Street, just east of Whipple and west of the River. Though you once had to listen for the tumbling current and climb through a small hole in the fence to find this waterway treasure, the city has since removed some obstructing trees and some neighbors have widened that hole into a makeshift entrance. Once on the "forbidden" side of the fence, follow the riverside trails, maybe picking up some of the garbage along the way.

Osaka Japanese Garden Rock Waterfall
In Jackson Park, just east of Cornell, about 5900-6200 S.   **S**
A rock waterfall was added during a 1981 restoration of the historic Japanese Gardens that have appeared, declined, and reappeared in various guises since the Columbian exposition of 1893. See **Natural Spaces** (p.61) above for more details about the garden.

3 RECREATION

Overgrown with plants every summer, Caldwell Woods' Jensen Slides are cleared for inexpensive tobogganing every winter.
(*Photo by Rames Shrestha.*)

ADDITIONAL RECREATION LINKS

Chicago Area Paddling & Fishing Page
http://pages.ripco.com:8080/~jwn/
A site devoted to sailing, kayaking, canoeing, whitewater, pedalboats, fishing, and all forms of water relaxation and recreation in the Chicago area. Maps; photos; and information on events, races, instruction, clubs, rentals, and water quality. Updated regularly.

Adventures in Scuba
http://www.advscuba.com

Chicago Area Adult & Junior Volleyball Leagues
http://volleyball.org/chicago/

Lincoln Park Lacrosse Club
http://www.ez-shop.net/lplc

Chicago Motorcyle Rider's Guide
http://miso.wwa.com/~cgobiker
Information on rides, dealers, clubs, news, rallies, traffic, weather, scenic rides, and "Saloons & Greasy Spoons" known for their friendly service to the motorcycling community.

FOR THOSE WHO RECREATE IN STADIUMS

The latest stats, scores, and news on Chicgo teams and players.

Cubs *http://www.cubs.com*
Wrigley Field *http://www.wwcd.com/stadiums/il/cubs.html*
White Sox *http://www.chisox.com*
Comiskey Park *http://www.wwcd.com/stadiums/il/wsox.html*
Bears *http://www2.nando.net/SportServer/football/nfl/chi.html*
Soldier Field *http://www.wwcd.com/stadiums/il/bears.html*
Blackhawks *http://www.chiblackhawks.com*
Bulls *http://www.nba.com/bulls/*
Rockers (CBA—basketball)
http://www.sportsline.com/u/basketball/cba/teams/Chicago.html
Wheelchair Bulls (NBA wheelchair team)
http://www.elnet_com/wheelchair_bulls/
Fire (MLS—soccer) *http://www.chicago-fire.com*
Wolves (IHA—hockey)
http://www.theihl.com/teams/Chicago/chicago.htm
Chicago Sports Teams Schedule For Coming Week
http://www.windy-city.com/sports/index.html

3 RECREATION

Surrounded by a bustling city and still wondering what to do? Whether you recreate passively or actively, physically or mentally, something on this list will get you going. Not only will kicking the couch potato habit reactivate your muscles and introduce you to new facets of city life, most of the time it will cost you next to nothing to do so.

Thanks to millions of taxpayers pooling their money, the visions of past and present leaders, vast land resources, including an exceptional 30 miles of shoreline (including 18 miles of bike paths and 15 miles of beaches), Chicagoans and their guests can enjoy the dynamic programming and impressive resources of a thriving park system. Recent surveys show that however much we Chicagoans love our parks, we still greatly under use everything they have to offer!

Many of the entries in this chapter refer to this park district bounty. For the sake of brevity, addresses and phone numbers were omitted from activities featured at a large number of parks. This information can be found at the end of the chapter in a comprehensive Chicago Park District listing.

ADAPTIVE SPORTS FOR PEOPLE WITH DISABILITIES

Rehabilitation Institute of Chicago
Virginia Wadsworth Wirtz Sports Program
710 N. Lake Shore Drive, 312/908-4292   **C**
RIC's Wirtz Sports Program offers an incredible array of sports activities at both recreational and competitive levels for people with a variety of physical disabilities: men's, women's, and juniors' wheelchair basketball, quad rugby, swimming, tennis, wheelchair softball, aerobics, strength training and conditioning, track and roadracing, field events, powerlifting, skiing, sitting volleyball, fencing, golf, and outdoor education. Besides

having access to state-of-the-art equipment, many Wirtz athletes have gone on to compete internationally and even to set world records. The crowning feature is that it's all free.

McFetridge Sports Center
3845 N. California, 312/742-7585   **N**
Wed. nights (7:30-8:45pm winter, 7-8:15pm summer) at **McFetridge** are slated for ice sports instruction and practice for those with physical disabilities. Whether you use a wheelchair, walker, braces, or crutches, the program has adaptive equipment for ice skating, speed skating, and hockey. Competitive hockey players can join the **Chicago Blizzard** sledge hockey team which competes against primarily Canadian teams. Again, the entire program is free of charge.

To learn more about ice sports and other Chicago Park District programs for people with disabilities, call the **Therapeutic Recreation Office** at 312/747-1467. The park district also offers special golf lessons (312/747-2483) and the elaborate **Judd Goldman Adaptive Sailing Program** (312/747-7684). Offering three levels of instruction in specially modified sailboats, this program can lead to Crew, Skipper, or Advanced Racing Certification. The sailing lessons do have a fee, but scholarships are available.

ADULT EDUCATION

Discovery Center
2940 N. Lincoln, 773/348-8120   **N**
Learn how to flirt, tango, or fly an airplane. Delve into yoga, stunt fighting, kick boxing, the art of stained glass, and silk screening techniques. Chicago's largest adult education center offers over 200 different classes and puts out a new course catalog every two months. Many of **Discovery Center**'s offerings such as wine tastings, ethnic dining adventures, limo mystery tours, and all day rafting trips are popular events for meeting new people.

The Latin School of Chicago's "Live and Learn" Adult Education Classes
59 W. North Avenue, 312/573-4698   **C**
The prestigious **Latin School** offers an exciting list of adult education courses on a quarterly basis. Many of these introduce attendees to new

hobbies and recreational pursuits like foot reflexology, Zen meditation, pool, pet shamanism, knitting, portrait photography, flamenco dancing, fly fishing, or cardio-boxing.

Other classes allow participants rare glimpses into the kitchens of fine restaurants like Charlie Trotter's, Spruce, Trio, Grapes, Kiki's Bistro, or Coco Pazzo where you'll meet the chefs, learn new cooking techniques, and perhaps sample items from the menu.

A favorite is the $5 **Joke Exchange**, a two-hour, once-a-month gathering where participants bring one joke to share and leave with a treasury of fresh humor and a side split from laughter.

Old Town School of Folk Music
4544 N. Lincoln, 773/525-7793   **N**
As part of their mission to encourage the folk music of all cultures, the **Old Town School of Folk Music** teaches over a hundred different classes quarterly that explore the vast range of international music, both vocal and instrumental, as well as dance. Some recent offerings: yodeling, bluegrass mandolin, clog dancing, jazz scat singing, blues harmonica, funk guitar, Celtic Canadian fiddle, Tahitian drumming, and Irish stepdancing.

AEROBICS

Sure to beat any health club's prices...

Daley Bicentennial Plaza
337 E. Randolph, 312/742-7648   **C**
Head to the field house at the northern end of Grant Park for "walk-in," pay-as-you-go aerobics. Classes run Mon.-Fri. at 12:05pm and Mon., Tues., and Thur. at 5:30pm. The cost is $2 per 45-60 minute session. Stay for $2 line dancing classes, Tues. and Thur. at 1pm.

Aerobics, weight-training, yoga, and other fitness classes can be found at most city parks. Contact your regional office for nearby options and schedules. Some parks maintain fitness centers, with aerobic machines and weight-lifting equipment. Though some are free, passes for these facilities typically run $20 for 20 visits.

ARCADES

Fun Zone
3641 N. Western, 773/528-3032   **N**
A shabby, but clean, well-lit, and safe game room caters to the electronic gaming tastes of various generations with its nearly 50 games. Hockey, basketball, pinball, and a wide range of early video games including Galaga, Tron, Centipede, and various Pac-Man incarnations cost only one token. The latest sporting, driving, and fighting video games go for 2-3 tokens. Tokens are 5 for $1, 30/$5. Unlimited games Sun. 10am-12:30pm, $4.

Time-Out
North Pier, 435 E. Illinois, 312/527-2947   **C**
Enormous game room nibbles your quarters at old favorites like skeeball, pinball, basketball, and early video games ($.25), then gobbles them ($1+) for all the cutting-edge games, including virtual biking and skiing and those with holographic characters.

Pinball wizards may consult Chicago Pinball (*www.chicagopinball.com*) for current reviews of local places to play pinball. **Excalibur** (632 N. Dearborn, 312/266-1944) and **Dave & Buster's** (1024 N. Clark, 312/943-5151) recently received high marks. Those under 21 can enjoy pinball action at the arcades described above.

When Chicagoan David Gottlieb created the coin-operated "Baffle Ball" in 1931, he raised pin games to a commercially viable amusement. Chicago has been the nucleus of the pinball industry ever since. To keep up with the demand for these games, Baffle Ball's distributor released "Ballyhoo," which eventually gave its name to the pinball empire of Bally Manufacturing. Bally Manufacturing Corp. is now located near Chicago's O'Hare airport.

ARCHERY

Saracan Archery Range
4050 N. Milwaukee, 773/545-3043   **NW**
Mon. through Sat., practice your bows and arrows all night from 6:30-10pm for $8.50. Fee includes equipment rental.

If you have your own archery equipment, practice for free on one of the park district's seven ranges.

Park District Indoor Archery Ranges

Gage Park   Pulaski Park

Park District Outdoor Archery Ranges

Columbus Park   Marquette Park
Lincoln Park   Riis Park

BADMINTON

McKinley Park Badminton Club
2210 W. Pershing Road, 312/747-6527   **SW**
The only non-suburban, non-university affiliated badminton club in Chicago meets at the McKinley Park fieldhouse. Players of all ages and skill levels can drop in Tues. and Fri. 6pm-9pm and Sun. 11am-3pm. The annual fee is $20, but prospective members are allowed three free visits before deciding if they want to join.

For more regional badminton club and tournament information, contact Paras Shah at 312/951-9450.

BASEBALL

Some 213 Chicago parks have facilities for baseball and 167 are equipped for softball. To find the diamonds nearest you or to join a local park district league, contact your regional park district office.

Batting Cages

Sluggers World Class Sports Bar's Indoor Sports Facility
3540 N. Clark, 773/472-9696   **N**
Baseball and softball batting cages are located upstairs and separate from the bar (kids allowed). Batting tokens run 1/$1, 6/$5, and 13/$10. Unlimited batting for $5 per person Mon. and Thur. 5pm-10pm and Sun. 6pm-10pm. This affordable gaming complex, located a half block from Wrigley Field,

also offers hi-ball (see description later in the chapter), air hockey, skeeball, pinball, video games, and more.

Winning Edge Baseball Academy
4445 N. Milwaukee, 773/545-6100   **NW**
Batting practice for casual or serious players runs 16 pitches for $1.
Mon.-Fri. 3pm-9pm., Sat. 11am-6pm., Sun. 11am-9pm.

BASKETBALL

Chicago has 264 parks outfitted with outdoor basketball courts, and almost as many have gymnasiums with hoops. To hook up with a team or league, find a nearby court, or learn open gym days and times, call your regional park district office.

BICYCLING

Community groups and the mayor's office have taken active steps over the last several years to make Chicago a bike friendly city. One major component of the mayor's Bike 2000 Plan, to encourage bicycle use, is the establishment of a 300-mile network of bikeways in the city. Other elements include adding more bike racks and improving the Lakefront Path.

Much of this progress is due to the work of the **Chicagoland Bicycle Federation**. In addition to advocating on behalf of cyclists, **CBF** sponsors recreational activities and dispenses useful bicycle information on local trails, urban bike safety, how to be a successful bike commuter, and more. A $20 yearly membership entitles you to a monthly newsletter, periodic ride calendars, and discounts at bike shops. Contact them at 417 S. Dearborn, Suite 1000, Chicago, IL 60605 (312/42-PEDAL).

Bike Trail Maps

The *Chicago Bicycling Map* is available free from the Chicago Department of Transportation, 30 N. LaSalle, Suite 400, Chicago, IL 60602 (312/744-4686). A more detailed *Chicagoland Bicycle Map* which covers Chicago and the surrounding seven counties can be purchased for $6.95 from **CBF** (see above). For any of the eight free **Cook County Forest Preserve** trail maps, call 773/261-8400.

Bike Rentals

Biking is a great way to traverse the city, especially during the summer months. If you're without wheels, here are the best bets for rental:

Bike Stop Cycle (1034 W. Belmont, 773/868-6800) rents 21-speed mountain bikes for $7/hour, $25/day and tandem bikes $10/hour, $40/day. They're closed Wednesdays. Farther north, **Edgebrook Cycle and Sport** (5404 W. Devon, 773/792-1669) rents 10-speeds for $5/hour, $35/day, mountain bikes for $5/hour, $25/day, and tandem bikes for $9/hour, $45/day. Credit card deposit required. For tourists and lakefront biking, **Bike Chicago**'s (800/915-BIKE) lakefront locations (Navy Pier, Oak St. Beach, Lincoln Park Zoo, Buckingham Fountain) are the most convenient. They rent mountain bikes, classic cruisers, and tandems for $8/hour, $30/day, $49/two days, and $79/five days. They also provide maps, helmets, and locks upon request and offer free bike delivery to hotels for daily rentals.

Bike Tours

Bike Chicago
312/944-2337 and 1-800-915-BIKE   **C**
This bike rental outfit sponsors a free, easy-riding, 2-hour/6-mile bike tour that introduces riders to Chicago history, architecture, and night life. Bring your own two-wheeler or rent one from **Bike Chicago**'s Navy Pier stand, where the tour originates Mon.-Fri. at 1:30pm. Reservations are accepted and recommended because tours are limited to fifteen riders.

Chicago Architecture Foundation
312/922-3432
The **Chicago Architecture Foundation** gives periodic historic and architectural bike tours of different Chicago neighborhoods for $5 (CAF members free). Call the above event hotline to learn about future rides.

Chicago Cycling Club
773/509-8093, *http://www.suba.com/~ccc*
The **Chicago Cycling Club** takes a 15-50 mile ride every Saturday and Sunday morning and Tuesday evenings in summer. They meet at Waveland and the clock tower in Lincoln Park, and head for a city, suburban, or outlying destination. (Good food stops are usually involved.) Ride with them once for free, afterwards pay a $15 annual membership fee. Call the ride line for upcoming events and more information.

Whether it's dawn, day, dusk, or evening; winter, spring, summer, or fall; quiet or crowded; in any and all conditions, it's always an appropriate time to experience the 18½ miles of Chicago's lakefront from Kathy Osterman Beach (5800 N) to the South Shore Cultural Center (7100 S) on bicycle. Besides winding through Lincoln, Grant, Burnham, and Jackson Parks, the path will take you past sculptures, gardens, golf courses, museums, cultural institutions, the "Totem Pole," the Chess Pavilion, Soldier Field, and McCormick Place. Any of the beaches or outdoor cafes make great resting spots. The free park district *Lakefront Trail Map* outlines these and other shoreline delights. Pick up a copy at Tourist Information Centers or by calling 312/747-2474.

Other scenic off-street pedaling can be found on the dedicated bike trails of these city parks:

Bessemer Park	**Legion Park**	**Portage Park**
Calumet Park	**Marquette Park**	**Riis Park**
Douglas Park	**McKinley Park**	**River Park**
Garfield Park	**Oriole Park**	**Sherman Park**
Humboldt Park	**Oz Park**	**Warren Park**

The **Chicago Area Bike Rides** page (*http://miso.wwa.com/~jvitous/ 1998/index.htm*) provides information on organized rides in Chicagoland. Those with recumbents and other unique bikes can check out the **Chicago Recumbent Riders'** website (*http://www.mcs.net/~gkpsol*) for local recreational opportunities. Information on rides, trails, and trail conditions for mountain bikers can be found at the **TURF** website (*http:// members.aol.com/turfinfo/index.html*).

BINGO

The various games at these major bingo centers benefit different community organizations. Spend a few bucks on some cards and you could walk away with tens or even hundreds of dollars. N-43, forty-three under the N...

Bingo City
6800 N. Western, 773/338-6298   **FN**
A bonus of this grand poobah of bingo halls: complementary rides home for players living from Addison north to Howard and Lake Shore Drive west to Pulaski. Games begin Sat.-Sun. noon and 7pm, Mon. 7pm, Tues. 11am and 7pm, Wed. 7pm, Fri. 11:30am and 7pm.

Golden Tiara
3231 N. Cicero, 773/736-5350   **NW**
Game times are Sun. 1pm and 7pm, Mon. 11am, Fri. 7pm, Sat. 7pm and
midnight. Doors open 2-3 hours before the games begin. Wheelchair access,
extensive concessions, and a non-smoking section are available.

Northwest Community Center
4883 W. Diversey, 773/622-2070   **NW**
Games begin Sat.-Sun. 7pm, Wed. 11am and 7pm, Thur. 7pm, Fri. 11am
and 7pm.

The legendary Bingo and Catholic Church connection is alive and well in
Chicago. As the largest Roman Catholic Archdiocese in the nation, Chicago
is teeming with neighborhood churches and schools (72 of them!) that have
a weekly bingo fundraiser. Compare this with the eight fraternal lodges, six
community centers, and five churches of other denominations that hold
weekly games. Phone local parishes for information and pack your chips,
markers, and good luck charms.

Hard-core enthusiasts will appreciate Rosalie Edelstein's *Rosie's Bingo
Directory Chicago* from **Boo Boo Press**, which gives the location for every
Chicago bingo game, as well as addresses for games in the suburbs, outlying
areas, and northwest Indiana.

If the campy nature of bingo means something to you, you might try...

Annoyance Theatre's "Dick O'Day's Big Lovely Bingo"
3737 N. Clark, 773/929-6200   **N**
How about playing bingo with 35-100 others during this interactive,
theatrical bingo event? Once a month, usually the last Tuesday, join host
"Dick O'Day" at 8:30pm for a night of comedy, entertainment, food, and
fun. $5 gains you admission and a bingo card. Extra cards sell for $1. Win
prizes such as CDs, gift certificates for stores and restaurants, or real
treasures like a Donny and Marie scrapbook. You're really playing bingo
and winning real prizes but pretending you're at a fictional bingo parlor. Get
it?

Daisy Mae's Disco Bingo
Spin, 800 W. Belmont, 773/327-7711   **N**
Well-known local drag queen Daisy Mae hosts and calls Bingo amidst a
background of disco music for 100+ crowds at this spacious gay dance club.
Mon. 9pm-Midnight. Free, with prizes on the order of squirting sunglasses.

Adults over 21 welcome.

BIRDING

For early birds...

Chicago Audubon Society's Bird Walks   **S**
Doug Anderson leads two free bird walks weekly (as he has for 23 years) through Jackson Park. Meet at the Clarence Darrow Bridge (the lawyer's ashes were scattered in this lagoon) behind the Museum of Science and Industry. Walks take place Wed. 7am-8:30am and Sat. 8am-10am, beginning the end of March and running through December. Call Doug Anderson (773/493-7058) or the **Chicago Audubon Society** (773/539-6793) for more information.

Lincoln Park Rookery
Fullerton between Stockton and Cannon Drives, 312/742-2000   **N**
Birders and non-birders alike will understand what draws over 200 species of birds to the **Lincoln Park Rookery** and its lily pond. This lush and tranquil wooded sanctuary still retains the Japanese and Prairie School influences of its original 1936 landscaping and provides a sublime escape from urban chaos. Besides its normally limited hours (to prevent overuse), maintenance and weather problems cause the **Rookery** to be closed quite often. Call ahead for hours.

The first wetlands restoration project in Chicago, though still underway, has already received the approval of the area's native waterfowl. The indigenous grasses, reeds, and wildflowers of **North Park Village Nature Center**'s (See *Chapter 2: Touring*, p.60) wetlands lure egrets, herons, pied-billed grebe, kingfishers, blue-winged teal, and, of course, avid bird watchers.

BOARD GAMES

American Bridge and Social Club
6199 N. Lincoln, 773/588-8196   **FN**
While the 1,500 ft.^{2} **American Bridge and Social Club** (tucked between Fannie May and The Dress Barn in the Lincoln Village Shopping Center)

focuses on bridge six days of the week, it does "social" on Friday evenings with its singles only (all ages, but mostly 30s-40s, some 50s) board game nights. Fourteen game stations are prepared, but the patrons tend to favor Scrabble, Trivial Pursuit, Boggle, and Balderdash. There's also a pool table and a TV lounge. Munchies are provided and pop (a supermarket assortment) is 50 cents. No alcoholic beverages. 8pm-midnight, $7.

For bars with closets full of board games, see *Chapter 5: Entertainment* (p.236).

BOCCIE BALL

For those with their own set of boccie balls, refine your game on courts located at one of these parks. If you're without equipment, phone the park office to learn how you can team up with local players.

Calumet Park	**McGuane Park**	**Veteran's Mem. Plg.**
Hiawatha Park	**Smith Park**	**Wolfe Playground**
Jackson Park		

In the 'round-midnight hours at **Welles Park** (Lincoln Avenue side between Montrose and Sunnyside) on fair weather weekends, a group of Europeans (40s-50s and older) like to gather for some rousing boccie ball as if it were the middle of the afternoon. At times there's various degrees of picnicking and partying involved. It doesn't look like they'd mind the company of kindred spirits.

BOWLING

Here's 11 of the most, uh...striking of the over 30 bowling alleys that dot Chicago's neighborhoods.

College Campus Bowling

U of I at Chicago Lanes
750 S. Halsted, 312/413-5170   **C**
Guests can bowl alongside UIC students for $1.45 per game, $.75 for shoe rental. Open seven days a week after 2pm for non-students. Throw in their seventeen regulation pool tables, forty video games, and dinner at the

cafeteria or in nearby Greektown and you've got an affordable night on the town.

Downtown Bowling

Spencer Marina City Bowl
300 N. State, 312/527-0747   **C**
The only bowling alley in downtown Chicago, located in the architecturally curious Marina City Towers. Weekday games, $2. Weekends, $2.50. Shoe rental $1.50.

Glow In the Dark Bowling

Turner Bowl
6625 W. Belmont, 773/637-6654   **NW**
Fridays after 10:30pm and Saturdays after 8pm, the house lights go off, the black lights go on, and the bowling alley is aglow. Add some music and disco lights and it's party time. Lanes rent for $15/hour for up to five people, shoe rental $1.75. Reservations necessary.

Hand-set Pin Bowling

Southport Lanes & Billiards
3325 N. Southport, 773/472-1601   **N**
Built in 1922 by the Schlitz Brewing Company, 3325 N. Southport served, among other things, as a speakeasy and brothel before becoming a neighborhood bar/bowling alley. **Southport Lanes & Billiards** is one of only a handful of bowling alleys left in the United States where the pins are still set by hand and the rest of the refurbished tavern retains much of this vintage charm. Call ahead to reserve one of the four hand-set bowling lanes. Bowling runs $14/hour per lane, and pool $12/hour per table, Fri. and Sat., and $9/hour per table, Sun.-Thur.

Lawn Bowling

The Chicago Park District has bowling greens at these two locations:

Columbus Park   **Jackson Park**

Neo-Art Deco Lounge Bowling

Lucky Strike
2747 N. Lincoln, 773/549-2695   **N**
Bowling, billiards, and the "Art Deco Fantasy" atmosphere serve as one more cool backdrop for adults just hanging out. The swank may be fake but much of the decor is authentic, from the vintage posters and Art Deco artifacts to some antique bowling benches, tables, and lanes. Food and, of course, martinis are available. Bowling costs $12/hour per lane, billiards, $9/hour per table. Prices rise weekends after 7pm to $14 and $12. Shoe rental $1.50.

Rock 'n' Roll Bowling

Diversey-River Bowl
2211 W. Diversey, 773/227-5800   **N**
"Rock 'n' Bowl" alley ministers to bowlers with jukebox music weekdays and DJs and light shows on the league-free weekends. Lanes run $12/hour Sun.-Thur., weekends $16/hour. Shoe rental $1.75.

Second-Floor Neighborhood Bowling

Great places to disappear for a night...

North Center Bowl
4017 N. Lincoln, 773/549-2360   **N**
Small, long-standing neighborhood bowling alley sits above a similarly noisy TV and stereo store. $2.25 games, $.75 shoe rental.

Lincoln Square Lanes
4874 N. Lincoln, 773/561-8191   **FN**
Climb the worn staircase to a compact facility above a hardware store. $2 games, $.75 shoe rental.

24-Hour Bowling

Marigold Bowl
828 W. Grace, 773/935-8183   **N**
When the neighborhood bars and clubs have closed, the local pancake house and Marigold Bowl still have open doors. 32 lanes, $1.75 games weekday, $2.80 weekends, $1.50 shoe rental. My mom and dad met here while

bowling in a company league!

Marzano's Miami Bowl
5023 S. Archer, 773/585-8787   **SW**
Don't miss the city's (and the world's?) largest bowling alley with 80 lanes.
Games run $2.50-$3, $2 on Sunday; shoe rental is $2 adults, $1 children.

Waveland Bowl
3700 N. Western, 773/472-5900   **N**
Folks of all ages pack its 40 lanes, snack shop, bar, and video games at all
hours. $3 weekday games, $3.25 weekends. $2 shoe rental.

BOXING

Self-defense. Aerobic exercise. Stress reduction. Legal aggression. Boxing
offers something for everyone and the park district teaches it to them—male
or female, young or old. Besides holding classes, these boxing rings are the
sights of numerous local shows and tournaments.

Armour Square Park	Fuller Park	Lawler Park
Bessemer Park	Garfield Park	Loyola Park
Calumet Park	Hamlin Park	Scottsdale Plg.
Clarendon Cmty. Ctr.	Harrison Park	Stateway Park
Davis Square Park	Humboldt Park	West Pullman Park

If you prefer to watch others slug it out, try St. Andrew's Gym (1658 W.
Addison)—the center for an intensive lineup of amateur and local boxing
matches and tournaments.

BRIDGE

American Bridge & Social Club
6199 N. Lincoln, 773/588-8196   **FN**
Lincoln Village Shopping Center, between Fannie May and The Dress Barn
Duplicate games Tues.-Thur. 7pm, Sat. 6:30pm, and Sun. 7pm. Mondays
7pm-10pm are for beginners who already know the rules. Cost is $5 for
members, $6 for non-members. Price includes snacks, except for pop ($.50
extra).

Bridge Chicago, Inc.
655 W. Irving Park, 2nd Floor, 773/935-3032   **N**
Chicago's largest and oldest dedicated bridge club holds open games, Mon.-Fri. at 7pm and Sun. 1pm and 6pm. All levels play together here, meaning you can realistically expect to find yourself going head to head with a world class player every now and then. Barometer game every Monday, handicapped Swiss team games on Fridays. Beginner and intermediate lessons available Monday and Wednesday evenings. All games are non-smoking. Fee $3-$7, college students pay no more than $3.

Vanderbilt Bridge Club of Downtown Chicago
Chicago Cultural Center, 78 E. Washington, 312/744-4554   **C**
Duplicate games for ages 55 and older, Mon. 1pm, $2.

Among the 70 organized bridge games held in the Chicago area on a weekly basis are these: **Imperial Towers Bridge Club** (4250 Marine Drive, 773/248-0133) plays Mondays at 7pm from April through December. The **International Bridge Club** (5050 S. South Shore Drive, 773/684-7116) meets Saturdays at 1pm. Join the **Lawson Bridge Club** (929 W. Belmont, 773/274-7512) at Ann Sather's Restaurant for Monday games at 6:45pm. **Mid-City Bridge Club** plays downtown (180 N. Wabash, 3rd floor, 773/262-7279) Fridays at 6:30pm. Those on the far north side can head to **Pottawattomie Park** (7340 N. Rogers, 773/583-0650 or 312/742-7878 during game times) on Fridays and Saturdays at noon.

CANOEING

Chicagoland Canoe Base
4019 N. Narragansett, 773/777-1489   **NW**
Rent a canoe for $35 for the 1st day, $15 the 2nd day, $15 the 3rd day, and $10 for any additional days. A $25 cash deposit is required. A special $55 weekend rate lets you pick up a canoe Friday after 3pm and return it Monday before noon. The **Canoe Base** can offer suggestions about canoeing the North Branch of the Chicago River and other local waterways. However, since it is landlocked, you will need a vehicle to transport any rentals to a waterway.

CHESS

Two popular outdoor spots lure chess players of all ages and levels:

Chess Pavilion at North Avenue Beach
North Avenue and Lake Michigan   C
In this open shelter on the lake, gamesters have been dueling since the 1960s
over the chess/checker boards built into cement benches.

Harper Court
Harper between 52nd and 53rd   S
The tiled chess boards in the public courtyard of **Harper Court** shopping
center had been a popular draw for neighbors of all ages and skill levels.
Recent remodeling, however, sent half of the benches to nearby Nichols
Park (54th and Kenwood), thereby splitting up the former flurry and bustle
into two camps.

Players of all levels can drop by **The Chicago Chess Club** (1149 W. Lunt,
773/761-5050) Wed.-Sun. 6pm-11pm and play for $1/hour. **The Wild
Onion Chess Club** (6136 N. Clark) is a newer club that's still getting off the
ground. They're open until midnight during the week and later on the
weekends.

CLIMBING

Tired of moving on horizontal planes?

Fitplex Extreme Fitness Club
1235 N. LaSalle, 312/640-1235   C
After you become certified on your first visit, non-members are welcome to
use the 1,200 ft.^{2}club. The first visit runs $15, afterwards, day passes are $12
and a 10-visit card is $90. Admission includes access to the entire facility
and its amenities.

Gravity Climbing Gym
1935 S. Halsted, 312/733-5006   C
After one $10 orientation session, you should have enough know-how to
brave the climbing walls. Thereafter, a $10 entry fee and $8 equipment
rental fee entitle you to hours of gravity-defying stunts.

Hidden Peak Climbing Gym
937 W. Chestnut, 312/563-9400   C
A \$35, 2-hour class introduces neophytes to the techniques and glories of
vertical challenges. After that, you can join other climbers at the following
rates: \$10/day, \$7/lunchtime visit, \$70/for ten visits, \$45/monthly pass, and
\$295/annually. Rent equipment for \$5 per visit. More classes for everyone
from beginners to pros are available.

CROQUET

Chicago's only park with a croquet court...

Warren Park
6601 N. Western, 773/742-7888   FN

DARTS

Windy City Darters
4340 W. Montrose, 773/286-3848   NW
This clearinghouse for dart activities administers league play at
neighborhood bars around the city for players of all skill levels. For a
ten-week season your team pays \$25 (for 4 people) or \$30 (for 6-10
players). Additionally, individuals pay \$15 annual dues and a \$10 seasonal
fee.

Di's Den
5100 W. Irving Park, 773/736-7170   NW
Di's Den hosts one of the largest weekly blind draw tournaments on the
North Side on Fridays at 9pm. Partners are picked from a hat and may go a
few rounds together. Rounds consist of one game of 301, 501, and Cricket
and are played "Chicago Format." \$5 entrance fee and cash prizes. All skill
levels welcome.

DOGWALKING

"Bark Park"
Just north of Belmont Harbor along Lake Michigan   N
Unleash your hound on this quarter-mile strip of beach where pet owners

come year round to let their pooches romp in the surf and run free in the sand.

If your dog and you make some new friends during the day, maybe you should continue a good thing later that night at **Lemming's** (1850 N. Damen, 773/862-1688). Clean, well-behaved dogs on leashes are welcome at this Wicker Park bar (fewer grooming restrictions for their owners) when it's less crowded, typically Sun.-Thur. Sunday seems to be the busiest of those days, with some regulars referring to it as "Dog Night."

£UCHR£

The Euchre Club of Chicago
312/458-9010, *jardins@alexia.lis.uiuc.edu*
Although the Euchre Club has a primarily gay and lesbian membership and plays at gay bars, it is an all-orientations, all-ages group that opens its games to the non-member public. Games are held 7:30pm Wednesdays at **Big Chicks** (5024 N. Sheridan, 773/728-5511) and 7pm Saturdays at **Lost & Found** (3058 W. Irving Park Road, 773/463-9617). Donation is $2 for members, $3 for non-members. Each person plays five games with five different partners on a typical night, keeping track of their own score. The high scorer for the evening wins cash, a bar tab, or another prize. Instruction in this trick and trump card game of Pennsylvania Dutch origin begins 30 minutes before the scheduled start time on every play date.

F£NCING

Fencing 2000 Academy
328 S. Jefferson, 312/879-0430   C
Run by three distinguished fencing pros, **Fencing 2000** is the only full line fencing academy in the Chicago area. Many of its members are highly competitive, but the facility is open to all levels for recreation, training, and lessons. Daily floor fee is $10. Call for monthly and yearly rates. Mon.-Fri. 6pm-10pm, Sat. 10am-1pm, and Sun.10am-11am.

FOOTBALL

Contact your regional park district office to discover which of the city's 156 public football fields is most convenient for you. They can also link you with a neighborhood team and league.

GO

No Exit Cafe

6790 N. Greenwood, 773/743-3355   **FN**

Although there appear to be no organized Go events in town, Go players regularly congregate at the **No Exit Cafe**, particularly on Mondays and Tuesdays. Before finding yourself an opponent for this ancient Japanese strategy game, buy a cup of coffee or something else to support the house. Note: Nights with entertainment will require a small cover charge.

GOLF

You won't golf anywhere much cheaper than on the well-kept greens of the Chicago Park District, which maintains one 18-hole course, five 9-hole courses, two driving ranges, and one miniature golf course. Courses are open daily from dawn to dusk, with lower prices during the off season (Nov.1st-March 31st). All golf questions can be answered by administrators, **Kemper Golf Management** (312/755-3500), or obtained from its automated **Golf Information Line** (312/245-0909). This phone message even gives a description of each course's unique features and offers 24-hour tee time reservations. Visit **Golf Chicago!** (*http://www.golfchicago.com*) for more local information.

Great courses at great prices accessible to all citizens may be one reason *Golf Digest* recently named Chicago as "a likely candidate for best golf city in America." Not bad for a *Hog Butcher, Tool Maker, and Stacker of Wheat...*

Robert A. Black Course

Pratt between Western and Ridge   **FN**

9 holes, par 33. Chicago residents pay $8.50 weekdays/$9.50 weekends, non-residents $10.50/$11.50. Club rental $6-$8. Good for all skill levels.

Columbus Park

500 S. Central   **W**

9 holes, par 34. Chicago residents pay $7.50 weekdays/$8.50 weekends,

non-residents $9.50/$10.50. Club rental $5. Ideal for beginners.

Jackson Park
63rd & Lake Shore Drive, 312/245-0909   S
The city's only 18-hole course costs residents $10.50 weekdays/$11.50
weekends, and non-residents $12.50/$13.50. Club rental $8.50. "Best 18-
hole golf value in Chicago."

Marquette Park
6734 S. Kedzie   FSW
9 holes, par 36. Chicago residents pay $8.50 weekdays/$9.50 weekends,
non-residents $10.50/$11.50. Club rental $6-$8. Perhaps the system's most
challenging course with water surrounding seven of the nine holes.

Sydney R. Marovitz Course
Waveland & the Lake, 312/245-0909   N
Its 9 holes mimic some of the nation's most challenging holes, par 36.
Chicago residents pay $9.50 weekdays/$10.50 weekends, non-residents
$11.50/$12.50. Club rental $6-$8. One of the more difficult courses, but
perhaps the most scenic. Try it just after sunrise and finish with breakfast at
the adjacent cafe.

South Shore Cultural Center
71st & South Shore Drive, 312/245-0909   FSE
9 holes, par 33. Chicago residents pay $7.50 weekdays/$8.50 weekends,
non-residents $9.50/$10.50. Club rental $6-$8. Another scenic lakefront
course.

More affordable golfing can be found within the **Cook County Forest
Preserve System**. At the **Edgebrook Golf Course** (5900 N. Central,
312/763-8320) and **Indian Boundary Golf Course** (8600 W. Forest
Preserve Drive, 312/625-9630) green fees are $16 weekdays before 4pm
and $10 after 4pm, $19 weekends and holidays and $12 for seniors and
children. Prices are $4 less for residents. The **Billy Caldwell Golf Course**
(6200 N. Caldwell, 773/792-1930) runs $11 weekdays before 4pm and $8
after 4pm, $13 weekends and holidays, and $8 for seniors and children.
Resident receive a $3 discount. For die-hards, the **Caldwell** course is
modified so that golfers can play in the snow.

Driving Ranges

Diversey Driving Range
141 W. Diversey, 773/281-5722   **N**
$5.50 for a bucket of balls. You can also putter around on their miniature golf course. New heated stalls for the winter months! Open daily 7am-10pm.

Jackson Park Driving Range
63rd & Lake Shore Drive, 312/288-6104   **S**
$6 per bucket. Open daily 7am-10pm.

A used sporting goods dealer—**Play It Again Sports** (2101 W. Irving Park Road, 773/463-9900)—has a good-sized driving range, primarily for customers to test prospective clubs, but is available to the public at $3 for a bucket of balls.

Miniature Golf

City Golf
435 E. Illinois, 312/836-5936   **C**
18 holes with city themes. Adults $4.95, children $3.95.

South Side YMCA
6330 S. Stony Island, 773/947-0700   **S**
A 20,000 ft.^{2}, 18-hole mini-golf course with trees, flowers, and waterfalls. $2-$4 per game, $4 for a family of four on Fridays. Open daily 7am-9pm.

HANDBALL

Park District courts:

Armour Square Park	**McGuane Park**	**Sheridan Park**
Bessemer Park	**McKinley Park**	**Sherman Park**
Gage Park	**Palmer Park**	**Washington Park**
Hamilton Park	**Rainbow Beach & Pk.**	**West Lawn Park**

HI-BALL

For the uninitiated, hi-ball is a game of shooting baskets with a sponge ball while jumping on a trampoline. Optimally played by four people, the cylindrical court is divided into four sections by 8-ft. high walls of netting with a basket built into each quadrant of the "cylinder." Though you still may be confused about the looks of this game, the rules aren't tough. Each seven-minute game (which lasts quite long when your aerobic stamina is being pushed to its limit) costs $2 per person. While it's not economical to play all night, this brief not-to-be-missed athletic experience is well worth a couple bucks. If you and your friends get hooked, the Tuesday ($25/hour for the court) and Friday ($30/hour for the court) night specials are a bargain. I've been playing this addictive little game for fifteen years at **Sluggers World Class Sports Bar's Indoor Sports Facility** (upstairs and separate from the bar—kids are allowed) at 3540 N. Clark (773/472-9696) and have seen it nowhere else in the city.

HORSESHOES

They built the pits, you bring the horseshoes...

Archer Park	**Grand Crossing Park**	**Norwood Park**
Armour Square Park	**Harrison Park**	**O'Hallaren Park**
Ashe Park	**Hiawatha Park**	**Portage Park**
Beverly Park	**Hoyne Plg. Park**	**Riis Park**
Bosley Plg. Park	**Independence Park**	**Russell Square Park**
Brooks Park	**Kelvyn Park**	**Rutherford-Sayre**
Calumet Park	**Kennedy Park**	**Senka Park**
Chopin Park	**LaFollette Park**	**Shabbona Park**
Cooper Park	**Lawler Park**	**Smith Park**
Dunbar Park	**Marquette Park**	**Strohacker Park**
Dunham Park	**Mather Park**	**Valley Forge Park**
Dvorak Park	**McGuane Park**	**Vittum Park**
Foster Park	**Merrimac Park**	**Warren Park**
Galewood Park	**Munroe Park**	**West Pullman Park**
Gompers Park	**Nat King Cole Park**	**Williams Park**

ICE SKATING

Inexpensive recreation for those who refuse to hibernate...

Daley Bicentennial Plaza
337 E. Randolph, 312/742-7648   C
Outdoor ice skating during winter months in Grant Park, just a breeze away
from the lake. Open weekdays 10am-10pm, weekends 10am-5pm.
Admission is $2/adults, $1/children under 14, and rental is $2/adults,
$1/children. Free admission and rental for seniors.

McFetridge Sports Center
3843 N. California, 312/742-7585   N
Year-round, indoor ice skating with a variety of day and evening open skate
sessions for different ages. Call for times or pick up a current schedule.
Adults $2.50, teens $2.25, kids $2, skate rental $2.

Navy Pier
600 E. Grand, 312/595-7437   C
Outdoor, seasonal skating on the renovated Navy Pier offers fabulous vistas
of Lake Michigan and the skyline. Free skating sessions Mon.-Sat. 11am-
8pm, Sun. 11am-7pm. Skate rental $3. For a unique experience, watch the
skaters from the adjacent ferris wheel which runs in the winter...weather
permitting!

Skate on State/Block 37 Ice Rink
State St. between Washington and Randolph, 312/744-2883   C
Free outdoor ice skating from late November through mid-March. Skate
rental available: adults $3, children $2. Great view at dusk.

The Park District and Cook County recently joined forces to build new
neighborhood skating rinks. These new rinks will offer occasional lessons,
clinics, and competitions. Some will double as in-line skating rinks in the
summer. Typical skating sessions run Mon.-Fri. 3pm-5pm and 5:30pm-7pm;
Sat.-Sun. 12:30pm-7:30pm. Skating is free Mon.-Thur. and $3 all other
times. Skate rental, $3.

⟹ **Avalon Park**
83rd and Woodlawn, 312/747-7201   FSE
⟹ **Caldwell Woods**
6200 W. Devon, 312/742-6200   FN

⇒ **Garfield Park**
100 N. Central Park, 312/746-4380   C
⇒ **McKinley Park**
2210 W. Pershing, 312/747-5992   SW
⇒ **Midway Plaisance**
59th and Woodlawn, 312/747-0233   S
⇒ **Mt. Greenwood Park**
3721 W. 111th, 312/747-3690   FSW
⇒ **Riis Park**
6100 W. Fullerton, 312/746-5735   NW
⇒ **Rowan Park**
115th and Ave O., 312/747-8880   FSE
⇒ **West Lawn Park**
65th St. and Kildare, 312/747-6342   FSW

More figure skating and speedskating resources can be found at the **Chicago Ice** Web site (*http://www.chicagoice.com*).

IN-LINE SKATING

The lakefront in-line skating faction is becoming as formidable as the running and biking contingents. To participate in their glory without your own in-line skates, visit one of these rental sites:

The best rates can be found at **Air Time** (3315 N. Clark, 773/248-4970) at $10/day during the week and $20/day on weekends. **Bike Chicago** (800/915-BIKE) offers lakefront convenience with its four stands at Lincoln Park Zoo, Oak Street Beach, Navy Pier, and Buckingham Fountain. $7/hour, $24/day, $34/two days, $49/five days. **Bike Stop Cycle** (1034 W. Belmont, 773/868-6800), **City Sweats** (2467 N. Clark, 773/348-2489), and **Londo Mondo** (1100 N. Dearborn, 312/751-2794) rent their in-line skates for $6-$7/hour and $19-$20/day. **Kozy's Cyclery and Fitness** (3712 N. Halsted, 773/281-2263; 1451 W. Webster, 773/528-2700; and 601 S. LaSalle, 312/360-0020) allow their rental prices to be applied toward the purchase of a pair of skates.

If you try it and like it, it may be wise to invest in a used pair of skates from the well-stocked **Sports Exchange** or **Play It Again Sports** (p.381).

Londo Mondo organizes two free group skates weekly during warm weather and leads anywhere from 35 to 200 bladers up the lakefront path to the Adler Planetarium and back. The communal thirst is quenched afterwards by a group trip to a neighborhood tap. Meet at **Londo Mondo** (1100 N. Dearborn) at 6:30pm Tuesdays for a relaxed skate and 6:30pm Wednesdays for the aggressive skate. More in-line skating activities in Chicago and the midwest can be found at *http://www.skaters.com.*

LASER TAG

All incarnations of laser tag basically involve two teams of individuals, equipped with power packs and laser guns, accruing points by hitting opponents' power sources and temporarily disengaging them from the game. Darkened, futuristic landscapes—with plenty of structures that allow one to dodge antagonistic laser streams and creep up on unsuspecting enemies— are created for the playing field. Laser tag was more popular in Chicago in the 80s (some former sites have resurfaced in the 'burbs), and now **Cyberia** at North Pier (435 E. Illinois, 312/527-3002) is the city's sole option for laser warfare. As long as you put your self-consciousness aside, get into a space age cops and robbers mode, and don't make a hobby out of laser tag, the $6 for an intense ten-minute battle session is an enjoyable and affordable encounter with high-tech recreation. Mon.-Thur. 11am-8pm, Fri.-Sat. 11am -12am, Sun. 11am-8pm.

MASSAGE

Not for those who give massages as recreation, but for those who need massages—at a discount—after recreation...

Chicago School of Massage Therapy
1300 W. Belmont, 773/477-9444 or 773/528-3398 during clinic hours   N
Book yourself some relaxation time amidst all this activity with a student massage at the **Chicago School of Massage Therapy**. The student clinic sets aside 2-4 hours for massages Wednesdays through Sundays, with an average of six students available for each time slot. Generally, reservations must be made two weeks in advance. No requests for particular gender or level of student masseuses can be made, although all students have successfully completed their first semester. $32 per hour-long massage.

NINTENDO, TRIVIA, AND HORSE RACING, OH MY

The Boom Town Saloon
7607 W. Addison, 773/625-4116   **NW**
All twenty tables at this nice, clean neighborhood bar are equipped with a
television set which is the foundation for some of the unique recreation **The
Boom Town Saloon** offers its customers. First, there's **Nintendo** at all
hours (7am-2am). Take a game console back to your table (no cost), hook it
up to your TV, and rent one of the 30 cartridges ($2 for unlimited playtime).
Then, on Wednesday nights, **Video Trivia** begins at 9pm. Customers
answer multiple choice questions that appear on the screen. After a short
break, they correct their own papers, with the bartender holding a carbon
copy to keep everyone honest. The first prize winner takes home $100; the
runner-up collects $50. There are more cash prizes on Mondays when
customers pick horses beginning at 9:30pm (free, no betting) for **Video
Horse Racing.**

ORIGAMI

CHAOS (CHicago Area Origami Society)
Magic, Inc., 5082 N. Lincoln (left rear gate), 773/334-2855   **FN**
Join other paper folders the second Wednesday of the month from 6:30pm-
10pm to fold, create, swap ideas, and socialize. Meetings are open to all
ages and all levels, and parents are encouraged to bring their children. If you
want to become a regular, membership is $10 annually. A special wrinkle in
the evening is the locale: the back room of Jay Marshall's 35-year-old
Magic, Inc., which, among other things, is one of the country's busiest
mail-order magic trick businesses. The octogenarian Marshall is a former
Vaudeville performer, ventriloquist, puppeteer, and internationally
recognized magician and illusionist. Memorabilia from his lengthy career
decorate the back room, from the pictures of old-time magicians to a Punch
and Judy stage.

PLAYGROUNDS

For tykes who have seen it all...

Harold's Playlot
53rd and Lake Shore Drive   **S**
Designed to accommodate children with disabilities, this large playground with sandbox and sprinkler is dedicated to the late mayor, Harold Washington.

Indian Boundary Park
2500 W. Lunt, 312/742-7887   **FN**
Just steps away from a zoo and a sprinkler, an award-winning playground palace sprawls, bedecked with towers, tires, bridges, slides, and more.

Oz Park
601-733 W. Webster, 312/787-3274   **N**
Designs created by local children were used to create this wooden kingdom.

POOL

The current surge of pool playing has filled up tables in bars and pool halls across the city. When you want your game unencumbered with trendsters and alcohol, climb the stairs to the pool room where scenes from *The Color of Money* were filmed:

Chris's Billiards
4637 N. Milwaukee, 773/286-4714   **NW**
$5.75/hour weekdays before 6pm, $7/hour after 6pm, $7.25/hour weekends for two players, every extra person pays $1-$1.20/hour. Individuals practicing alone pay $2.30, $2.70, or $2.95. 45 tables available, 9:30am-1am daily. Snack bar, but no alcohol.

See **Southport Lanes & Billiards** and **Lucky Strike** above under *Bowling* (p.84) for pool in upscale and unique surroundings.

RACQUETBALL

Reserve a racquetball court at one of these three parks at the lowest price in town.

Pottawattomie Park
7340 N. Rogers, 312/742-7878   **FN**
$6/hour, open 10am-9pm weekdays, 10am-3pm weekends.

Warren Park
6601 N. Western, 312/742-7888   **FN**
$5/hour weekdays 10am-3pm, $6/hour weekdays 3pm-8pm and weekends
10am-3pm.

Washington Park
5531 S. Martin Luther King, 312/747-6823   **S**
$6/hour, open 7am-9:30pm weekdays, 7am-3pm weekends.

West Lawn Park
4232 W. 65th, 312/747-7029   **FSW**
$5/hour weekdays 10am-10pm, $6/hour weekends 9am-3pm.

ROLLER SKATING

Though slick and speedy, in-line skating will never entirely replace the
four-wheeled old-timer and the charm of a wooden rink.

The Rink Fitness Factory
1122 E. 87th, 773/221-2600   **FSE**
Adults aged 21+, adults aged 27+, families, teens, and children all have
designated skating sessions throughout the week at **The Rink**. Saturday
nights are saved for teen disco and Saturday after midnight for persons over
21. Prices for sessions vary from $5-$8 for 3-4 hours of skating. Skate
rental is $1 but is not available at adult sessions. Recorded message gives
every last important detail you could want.

United Skates of America Rainbo Roller Rink
4836 N. Clark, 773/271-6200   **FN**
Rainbo, well known for its children's birthday parties and teen skating
sessions, actually has a larger lineup of activities for adults. The adult
sessions lure different ages by variously restricting sessions to those 18+,
21+, and 25+. Their after-midnight sessions on Fri. and Sat. draw a mellow
and funky crowd. Skating runs $2-$7 for 2-5 hours. Music varies with time
and day, but gospel, R&B, dusties, jazz, soul, and top 40 are all covered in
a typical week. Pick up a quarterly schedule or phone for the automated
schedule. In-line skates are welcome, but $2.50 skate rental is required at

most adult skates.

RUNNING

These 32 parks have either oval or straight away tracks for the disciplined or casual runner.

Avalon Park	**Grand Crossing Pk.**	**Nat King Cole Park**
Bessemer Park	**Hamilton Park**	**Norwood Park**
California Park	**Hayes Park**	**Ogden Park**
Calumet Park	**Kilbourn Park**	**Orr School Park**
Chase Park	**LaFollette Park**	**Riis Park**
Douglas Park	**Lake Shore Park**	**Rowan Park**
Dunbar Park	**Lincoln Park**	**Sherman Park**
Ellis Park	**Loyola Park**	**Trumbull Park**
Foster Park	**Marquette Park**	**Union Park**
Fuller Park	**McKinley Park**	**Wrightwood Plg.**
Gage Park	**Munroe Park**	

For Chicago area race and event information, look for *Chicago Runner Magazine* (p.409), the quarterly publication of the Chicago Area Runners Association.

SAILING

Rent a boat from the **Chicago Park District's Rainbow Fleet**. Sailboats rent for $15/hour and $25 for two hours. Catamarans run $25/hour and $40 for two hours.

⇒ **South Shore Beach**
7100 S. Lake Shore Drive, 312/747-1900   **FSE**
⇒ **Burnham Harbor**
1500 Linn White Drive, 312/747-7684   **C**
⇒ **Montrose Beach**
601 W. Montrose, 312/742-0600   **N**

For more park district harbor and boating activities, including well-developed sailing instruction programs for children, adults, and people with disabilities, call 312/747-7684.

Sail Chicago, affiliated with American Youth Hostels and other hosteling organizations, has offered Chicagoans an extensive, low-cost sailing program since 1959. In addition to their affordable lessons and boat rentals, they also offer some fun boat rides. Take a lakefront cruise or a "pleasure sail" in the afternoon, evening, or moonlight. Many enjoy the unique chance to watch city fireworks shows from one of their boats out on the lake. Call 773/327-8114 or e-mail *hiayhcigo@aol.com.*

Women interested in pursuing their sailing avocation have the **Chicago Women's Sailing Network** (773/935-1347, *sailcwsn@aol.com*) as a resource. Suggested donation, $15/year.

If you're in the market for a sailboat, **Darfin Yachts, Ltd.** (6003 S. Archer, 773/582-8113) and **Sailboat Sales Co.** (2500 S. Corbett, 312/225-2046) are good bets for used vessels.

SHUFFLEBOARD

While shuffleboard courts are found at the following parks, park district equipment may be unreliable. Call ahead to see what the park nearest you offers.

Avalon Park	**McGuane Park**	**Sr. Citizens Park**
Columbus Park	**Orr School Park**	**Union Park**
LaFollette Park	**Piotrowski Park**	**Valley Forge Park**
Lake Meadows Park	**Rosenblum Park**	**Warren Park**
Loyola Park	**Schreiber Park**	

SKIING (CROSS COUNTRY)

Cross country skiing is permitted in the forest preserves—except its golf courses—and the city parks. Try braving the lakefront! The following city parks are best equipped for cross country skiers:

Burnham Park	**Gage Park**	**Hamilton Park**
Douglas Park	**Garfield Park**	**Hayes Park**
Dyett Rec. Center	**Grant Park**	**Horner Park**
Eugene Field Park	**Hale Park**	**Humboldt Park**

Jackson Park	Mt. Greenwood Park	Peterson Park
Lincoln Park	Norwood Park	River Park
Loyola Park	Ogden Park	Shabbona Park
Mann Park	O'Hallaren Park	Washington Park
Marquette Park	Olympia Park	Wentworth Park
McKinley Park	Oriole Park	

SKIING (DOWNHILL)

Before you leave the city for the precipitous slopes of suburban Chicago and Wisconsin, save money by renting your skis in town.

Viking Ski Shop
3422 W. Fullerton, 773/276-1222   **NW**
An inclusive package of skis, poles, and boots rents for $30/day and $49/2 days, with each successive day costing less.

The **Chicago Metropolitan Ski Council** (*http://www.skicmsc.com*)—an umbrella organization for over 100 local ski clubs—is a great place to find fellow skiers and skiing outings. (Maybe skiing is such a social activity around here because the slopes are kind of lame?)

SOCCER

Having played host to World Cup games in 1994, Chicago, a softball and basketball kind of town, can now boast its soccer credentials to the world. Residents, however, have been taking advantage of the soccer fields at 157 city parks for years. Call your regional park district office to join a league near you or scout local parks for pick up games.

STARGAZING

For information on what's presently going on in the heavens and what we can see in our little corner of the night sky, call the **Adler Planetarium** information line (312/922-STAR) and select the "Summary of the Current Sky" option from its recorded message. We all know, however, that the urban atmosphere permits us access to only a small portion of our sky niche.

Astronomy buffs can turn next to the **Chicago Astronomical Society**—America's oldest astronomical society, founded in 1862—which prints up a quarterly schedule of events that lists many opportunities for free telescopic stargazing at the **Adler Planetarium** (1300 S. Lake Shore Drive) and **North Park Village Nature Center** (5801 N. Pulaski, 312/744-5472). Contact them at 773/725-5618 to find out where you can pick up a schedule.

SWIMMING

With 15 miles of beaches lining a 22-mile stretch of Chicago's shoreline and the Park District's 50 outdoor and 29 indoor pools, every Chicagoan and visitor is just minutes away from a cool—and free—dip.

Lakefront Beaches

Lakefront beaches open officially (with lifeguards on duty) the Friday of Memorial Day weekend and close the Monday of Labor Day weekend, staying open daily, weather permitting, 9am-9:30pm. **The Beaches and Pool Unit** (312/747-0832) can answer further questions.

Ashe Park	**Juneway Terr. Beach**	**Oak Street Beach**
Burnham Park	**Lane Beach & Park**	**Pratt Beach & Park**
Calumet Park	**Leone Park & Beach**	**Promontory Pt. Pk.**
Columbia Ave. Beach	**Lincoln Park**	**Rainbow Beach**
Fargo Avenue Beach	**Loyola Park**	**Rogers Ave. Beach**
Hartigan Bch. & Park	**Montrose Beach**	**South Shore**
Howard St. Beach	**North Avenue Beach**	**31st Street Beach**
Jackson Park	**North Shore Beach**	**12th Street Beach**
Jarvis Ave. Bch. & Pk.	**Northerly Island Park**	

The first North Avenue Beach house was built in 1938 by the Federal Works in Progress Administration. Constructed to resemble a ship, the blue and white Art Deco building with its portholes, smoke stacks, towers, and railings had been an endearing and memorable icon of summer for generations of Chicagoans. Unfortunately, it is being replaced for the summer of 1999. Its successor, however, will apparently retain many of the beloved features of the original.

Outdoor Pools

The Park District's outdoor pools begin their season in mid-June and close the Monday of Labor Day weekend.

Abbott Park	Gill Park	Palmer Park
Ada Park	Gompers Park	Portage Park
Altgeld Park	Grand Crossing Park	Pulaski Park
Avalon Park	Hale Park	Ridge Park
Avondale Park	Hamlin Park	Riis Park
Beilfuss Park	Holstein Park	River Park
Bessemer Park	Humboldt Park	Russell Square Pk.
Bogan Park	Independence Park	Shabbona Park
Brown Memorial Pk.	Jefferson Park	Smith Park
California Park	Kennedy Park	Stateway Park
Carver Park	Madden Park	Taylor Park
Chase Park	Mather Park	Trumbull Park
Columbus Park	Meyering Plg.	Tuley Park
Curie Park	Mt. Greenwood Park	Union Park
Dyett Rec. Center	Don Nash Cmty. Ctr.	Washington Park
Foster Park	Norwood Park	West Pullman Park
Gage Park	Oakdale Park	

Indoor Pools

Free swimming time is scheduled for everyone at the park district's indoor pools: children, teens, families, women and men (together and separate), and lap swimmers. Contact your neighborhood park for a seasonal time table. Swim clubs, swim teams, swimming lessons for all ages, aquafitness classes, or water polo are also available at many of these parks for no cost or a very low fee.

Austin Town Hall	Griffith Natatorium	Orr School Park
Beilfuss Park	Harrison Park	Portage Park
Blackhawk Park	Independence Park	Ridge Park
Bogan Park	Kelly Park	Shabbona Park
Carver Park	Kosciuszko Park	Sheridan Park
Clemente Park	LaFollette Park	Stanton Park
Curie Park	Mann Park	Welles Park
Eckhart Park	Mather Park	Wentworth Park
Foster Park	McGuane Park	Young Park
Gill Park	Don Nash Cmty. Ctr.	

> Portage Park's Olympic-size outdoor swimming pool was built for the 1954 Pan-American Games.

Water Slides

Two city parks have noteworthy waterslides for their pools—a perfect refreshment for Chicago's inevitable scorching summer afternoons: **Washington Park Aquatic Center** (5531 S. Russell Drive, 312/747-7613) has a 36-footer and **Norwood Park** (5801 N. Natoma, 312/742-7847) boasts one 22-feet high and 110-feet long with 4-5 ample curves.

TABLE TENNIS

Net & Paddle Club
4754 N. Leavitt, 773/271-8580   N
Some of the city's best players join table tennis enthusiasts of all skill levels at the **Net & Paddle Club**, which meets at Berry Memorial Church six nights a week. Open play Mon.-Fri. 7:30pm-11pm and Sun. 4pm-7pm, $5 fee.

TENNIS

143 park sites around the city have free outdoor courts, many of which are lit for nighttime play. A phone call to your regional park district office will match you with a nearby court.

The Park District's better tennis courts sit along the lakefront and are lit for night play. They run $5/hour. Reservations are advisable for weekends and after-work slots. Call 312/742-7650 for the **Grant Park** courts, 312/742-7674 for the **Waveland** courts, and 773/348-9533 for the **Diversey** courts.

Mid-Town Tennis Club
2020 W. Fullerton, 773/235-2300   N
Improve your game without expensive lessons at **Mid-Town**'s matinee drill and open play session for $22. A certified tennis pro runs the four-hour programs, Mon.-Fri. noon-4pm.

TOBOGGANING

When there are four inches of snow on the ground and the temperature is holding steady under 20 degrees, one good way to spend time outdoors in Chicago is to go tobogganing! The Forest Preserve District has slides in two locations that operate from 10am-10pm under the conditions mentioned above. Rent toboggans that hold 2-4 people for $3/hour (leave an Illinois Driver's license or $40 as a deposit). If you own your own toboggan, pay only $1 for a daily chute pass.

⇒ **Dan Ryan Woods**
87th and Western, 773/233-3766   **FSW**
⇒ **Jensen Slides**
Devon and Milwaukee, 773/631-7657   **FN**

Both of these forest preserve locations also have some hills for regular sledding. Within the park district, **Cricket Hill** (approx. Montrose and the Lake) and the **Horner Park** hill (California between Irving and Montrose) are favorite sledding sites. Incidentally, **Cricket Hill** is also known as the site of "Weedfest" and other occasional marijuana legalization rallies.

ULTIMATE FRISBEE

Chicago Ultimate, Inc. (773/989-2642, *http://members.aol.com/ ChUltimate*) is a new group organized to promote ultimate frisbee in the Chicago area. Through them you can find out about the long-standing **Chicago Ultimate Summer League (CUSL)** that plays Mondays and Wednesdays June through mid-August at the Midway Plaisance in Hyde Park and the newer **Spring Chicago Ultimate League (SCUL)** that plays in the Schiller Woods Forest Preserve.

For something less committal, there are always these weekly coed pickup games: Thursdays at 5:30pm at Jackson and Michigan, by the Art Institute (game moves to **Grant Park**); Thursdays at 8pm at **Brands Park** (3285 N. Elston); and Sundays at 2pm at **Welles Park** (this is a year-round, all-weather event). Regular holiday pickup games include the New Year's Day game at noon at **Welles Park** (2333 W. Sunnyside) and the Oct. 31 Halloween game played at 9pm-11pm at **Oz Park** (2021 N. Burling).

VOLLEYBALL

Beach Volleyball

Without question, **North Avenue Beach** (North Ave. and the lake) is Chicago's spot for beach volleyball. Reserve a court for the weekends up to six days in advance—they go fast. Courts can be reserved for a maximum of two hours and cost $5/hour. Nets ($5) and balls ($5) are also rented if you need them. I.D. required as a deposit. Free courts are available on a first come first serve basis. If you'd rather spectate, look for the various high-action amateur and professional tournaments going on throughout the summer. **Montrose Beach** (Montrose and the lake) also has some beach volleyball facilities for the same fees, but you're less likely to need a reservation here. If you have your own net, poles are set up at **Foster Beach** (Foster and the lake) and **Hollywood Beach** (Ardmore and the lake) during the summer months. Call 312/74-BEACH for more info.

Outdoor Park District Courts

160 Chicago Park Districts have either indoor or outdoor facilities for volleyball. Call your regional office for the location nearest you. Four of those parks also have outdoor sand courts:

⇒ **Hayes Park**
2936 W. 85th, 312/747-6177   **FSW**
⇒ **Kennedy Park**
11320 S. Western, 312/747-6198   **FSW**
⇒ **Munroe Park**
2617 W. 105th, 312/747-6561   **FSW**
⇒ **Rainey Park**
4350 W. 79th, 312/747-6630   **FSW**

Indoor Volleyball

Almost every city park that has a gymnasium has indoor volleyball facilities. Their open gym periods offer you and your set-and-spike cohorts free court time. Several parks also have designated volleyball nights for casual play and leagues for more organized play. Contact your regional office for more information.

Lincoln-Belmont YMCA
3333 N. Marshfield, 773/248-3333   N
Adult open volleyball Wed. 7pm-11pm, Fri. 8pm-11pm, and Sun. 5pm-7pm.
$8 for non-members.

New City YMCA
1515 N. Halsted, 312-266-1242   C
Adult open volleyball Tues. and Thur. 7pm-9pm and Sun. 4pm-6pm. $5 for
non-members.

Indoor Sand Courts

Where volleyball and trendy nightlife meet...

Bamboo Bernie's
2247 N. Lincoln, 773/549-3900   N
Tropical theme bar has free indoor sand volleyball on a mini-court. (Just
one step removed from the oyster shot chute.)

North Beach Chicago
1551 N. Sheffield, 312/266-7842   C
Immense sports bar draws serious and casual athletes to its indoor sand
courts that go for $54/hour for the regulation court and $38/hour for the two
smaller courts ($38 and $22/hour before 5pm weekdays).

WALKING

Chicago Walkers
773/525-4492   N
Join the **Chicago Walkers** Saturdays at 9am on Cannon Drive (South of
Fullerton in Lincoln Park) for fitness and race walking clinics and a
three-mile group walk. They meet year-round but draw the bigger crowds
(35-60) in the summer. All ages welcome. No fee.

Chapter 6: Walking devotes 51 pages to suggested recreational and
informative walking through the streets, neighborhoods, and parks of
Chicago.

See the free, monthly *Windy City Sports* magazine (p.409) and the *Chicago Tribune's Friday Section* for regular listings of active endeavors, new opportunities, and current events in Chicago recreation.

CHICAGO PARK DISTRICT INFORMATION

Recently the park district divided the city into six regions: North, Near North, Central, South, Southwest, and Lakefront in order to better promote and develop neighborhood parks. Your region's office or a nearby park are the best places to pick up a seasonal schedule of regional park offerings or to get information on park district programs, classes, facilities, etc. Don't overlook their extensive non-athletic programming in arts and crafts, music, dance, drama, lapidary, woodshop, GED, ESL, and more. A general directory of the entire park system and its resources is available from the **Chicago Park District's Department of Marketing and Program Support**, (425 E. McFetridge Drive; Chicago, IL 60605). The parks mentioned in this chapter, along with their addresses and phone numbers, are listed below alphabetically, within their new region.

North Region

Regional Office:
Warren Park 6621 N. Western, 312/742-7888   FN

Avondale Park 3516 W. School, 312/742-7581   NW
Brands Park 3285 N. Elston, 312/742-7582   N
Broadway Armory Park 5917 N. Broadway, 312/742-7503   FN
Brooks Park 7100 N. Harlem, 312/742-7855   FN
California Park 3843 N. California, 312/742-7585   N
Chase Park 4725 N. Ashland, 312/742-7518   N
Chopin Park 3420 N. Long, 312/742-7607   NW
Dunham Park 4638 N. Melvina, 312/742-7606   NW
Emmerson Playground 1820 W. Granville, 312/742-7877   FN
Eugene Field Park 5100 N. Ridgeway, 312/742-7591   FN

Gill Park 825 W. Sheridan, 312/742-7802   N
Gompers Park 4224 W. Foster, 312/742-7628   FN
Gross Playground 2708 W. Lawrence, 312/742-7528   FN
Hamlin Park 3035 N. Hoyne, 312/742-7785   N
Hiawatha Park 8029 W. Forest Preserve, 312/746-5559   FN
Hollywood Park 3312 W. Thorndale, 312/742-7578   FN
Horner Park 2741 W. Montrose, 312/742-7572   N
Independence Park 3945 N. Springfield, 312/742-7590   NW
Indian Boundary Park 2500 W. Lunt, 312/742-7887   FN
Jefferson Park 4822 N. Long, 312/742-7609   FN
Jenson Playground 4600 N. Lawndale, 312/742-7580   NW
Kilbourn Park 3501 N. Kilbourn, 312/742-7624   NW
Kiwanis Playground 7631 N. Ashland, 312/742-7884   FN
Legion Park Peterson-Foster @Chicago River, 312/742-7516 FN
Mather Park 5841 N. Richmond, 312/742-7501   FN
Mayfair Park 4550 W. Sunnyside, 312/742-7610   NW
McFetridge Sports Center 3845 N. California, 312/742-7585 N
Merrimac Park 6343 W. Irving Park, 312/742-7626   NW
Norwood Park 5801 N. Natoma, 312/742-7847   FN
Olympia Park 6566 N. Avondale, 312/742-7851   FN
Oriole Park 5430 N. Olcott, 312/742-7852   FN
Paschen Playground 1932 W. Lunt, 312/742-7865   FN
Peterson Park 5601 N. Pulaski, 312/742-7584   FN
Portage Park 4100 N. Long, 312/742-7634   NW
Pottawattomie Park 7340 N. Rogers, 312/742-7878   FN
Revere Park 2509 W. Irving Park, 312/742-7594   N
River Park 5100 N. Francisco, 312/742-7516   FN
Rogers Park 7345 N. Washtenaw, 312/742-7859   FN
Sauganash Park 5861 N. Kostner, 312/742-7618   FN
Schreiber Playground 1552 W. Schreiber, 312/742-7876   FN
Shabbona Park 6935 W. Addison, 312/742-7608   NW
Welles Park 2333 W. Sunnyside, 312/742-7511   N
Wildwood Park 6950 N. Hiawatha, 312/742-7848   NW
Wrightwood Playground 2534 N. Greenview, 312/742-7816 N

Near North Region

Regional Office:
Riis Park 6100 W. Fullerton, 312/746-5363   NW

Altgeld Park 515 S. Washtenaw, 312/746-5001   W

Amundsen Park   6200 W. Bloomingdale, 312/746-5003   NW
Augusta Playground   4431 W. Augusta, 312/742-7544   W
Austin Town Hall Park   5610 W. Lake, 312/746-5006   W
Bell Park   3020 N. Oak Park, 312/746-5008   NW
Blackhawk Park   2318 N. Lavergne, 312/746-5014   NW
Clark Playground   4615 W. Jackson, 312/746-5043   W
Clemente Park   2334 W. Division, 312/742-7538   W
Columbus Park   500 S. Central, 312/746-5046   W
Cragin Playground   2611 N. Longwood, 312/746-5065   NW
Eckhart Park   1330 W. Chicago, 312/746-5490   C
Galewood Playground   5729 W. Bloomingdale, 312/746-5089   NW
Garfield Park   100 N. Central Park, 312/746-5092   W
Haas Playground Park   2402 N. Washtenaw, 312/742-7552   N
Holstein Park   2200 N. Oakley, 312/742-7554   N
Humboldt Park   1400 N. Sacramento, 312/742-7549   W
Kelvyn Park   4438 W. Wrightwood, 312/742-7547   NW
Kosciuszko Park   2732 N. Avers, 312/742-7546   NW
LaFollette Park   1333 N. Laramie, 312/746-5316   W
Mozart Park   2036 N. Avers, 312/742-7535   NW
Orr Park   730 N. Pulaski, 312/746-5354   W
Oz Park   2021 N. Burling, 312/742-7898   N
Pulaski Park   1419 W. Blackhawk, 312/742-7559   C
Rutherford-Sayre Park   6851 W. Belden, 312/746-5368   NW
Senior Citizens Park   2228-48 N. Oakley, 312/742-7554   N
Seward Park   375 W. Elm, 312/742-7895   C
Smith Park   2526 W. Grand, 312/742-7534   W
Stanton Park   618 W. Scott, 312/742-7896   C
Tilton Playground Park   305 N. Kostner, 312/746-5399   W
Union Park   1501 W. Randolph, 312/746-5494   C
Wicker Park   1425 N. Wicker Park, 312/742-7553   C

Central Region

Regional Office:
Hamilton Park   513 W. 72nd, 312/747-6174   FSE

Addams Park   1301 W. 14th, 312/746-5487   C
Armour Square Park   3309 S. Shields, 312/747-6012   S
Barrett Playground Park   2022 W. Cermak, 312/747-6016   W
Bosley Playground Park   3044 S. Bonfield, 312/747-6026   SW
Cornell Square Park   1809 W. 50th, 312/747-6097   SW

Davis Square Park   4430 S. Marshfield, 312/747-6107   SW
Dearborn Park   865 South Park Terrace, 312/747-7640   C
Donovan Playground Park   3620 S. Lituanica, 312/747-6111   SW
Douglas Park   1401 S. Sacramento, 312/747-7670   W
Dvorak Park   1119 W. Cullerton, 312/746-5083   C
Franklin Park   4320 W. 15th, 312/747-7676   W
Fuller Park   331 W. 45th, 312/747-6144   S
Harrison Park   1824 S. Wood, 312/746-5491   W
Hoyne Playground   3417 S. Hamilton, 312/747-6184   SW
Kelly Park   2725 W. 41st, 312/747-6197   SW
Lindbloom Park   6054 S. Damen, 312/747-6443   SW
McGuane Park   2901 S. Poplar, 312/747-6497   SW
McKinley Park   2210 W. Pershing, 312/747-6540   SW
Memorial Playlot Park   149 W. 73rd, 312/747-7640   FSE
Moran Playground   5727 S. Racine, 312/747-6560   SW
Ogden Park   6500 S. Racine, 312/747-6572   SW
Piotrowski Park   4247 W. 31st, 312/747-6608   SW
Sheridan Park   910 S. Aberdeen, 312/747-5369   C
Sherman Park   1301 W. 52nd, 312/747-6672   SW
Sherwood Park   5705 S. Shields, 312/747-6688   S
Skinner Park   1331 W. Adams, 312/746-5560   S
Throop Playground   4920 S. Throop, 312/747-6740   SW
Taylor-Lauridsen Playground   647 W. Root, 312/747-6729   S
Wentworth Gardens   3770 S. Wentworth, 312/747-6996   S
Wilson Community Center   3225 S. Racine, 312/747-7001   SW
Wilson Playground   1122 W. 34th, 312/747-7002   SW
Young Park   210 S. Loomis, 312/746-5478   C

South Region

Regional Office:
Kennicott Park   4434 S. Lake Park, 312/747-7138   S

Abbott Park   49 E. 95th, 312/747-6001   FSE
Anderson Playground Park   3748 S. Prairie, 312/747-6007   S
Avalon Park   1215 E. 83rd, 312/747-6015   FSE
Bessemer Park   8930 S. Muskegon, 312/747-6023   FSE
Bradley Park   9729 S. Yates, 312/747-6022   FSE
Carver Park   939 E. 132nd, 312/747-6047   FSE
Cooper Park   1323 W. 117th, 312/747-6096   FSW
Dunbar Park   300 E. 31st, 312/747-7661   S

Dyett Recreational Center 513 E. 51st, 312/747-6118	S
Ellis Park 648 E. 37th, 312/747-6122	S
Griffith Natatorium 346 W. 104th, 312/767-7661	FSE
Haines School Park 274 W. 23rd, 312/747-7661	S
Lake Meadows Park 3113 S. Rhodes, 312/747-6287	S
Madden Park 3800 S. Rhodes, 312/747-6446	S
Mann Park 13000 S. Carondolt, 312/747-6457	FSE
Meyering Playground 7140 S. Martin Luther King, 312/747-6545	FSE
Midway Plaisance Park 59th & Stony Island, 312/747-7661	S
Don Nash Community Center 1833 E. 71st, 312/747-1831	FSE
Owens Park 2032 E. 88th, 312/747-6709	FSE
Palmer Park 11100 S. Indiana, 312/747-6576	FSE
Rosenblum Park 1936 E. 76th, 312/747-664	FSE
Rowan Park 3611 E. 114th, 312/747-6650	FSE
Russell Square Park 3045 E. 83rd, 312/747-6651	FSE
Stateway Park 3658 S. State, 312/747-6707	S
Taylor Park 41 W. 47th, 312/747-6728	S
Trumbull Park 2400 E. 105th, 312/747-6759	FSE
Veteran's Memorial Playground 2820 E. 98th, 312/747-6812	FSE
Washington Park 5531 S. Martin Luther King, 312/747-6823	S
West Pullman Park 401 W. 123rd, 312/747-7080	FSE
Williams Park 2710 S. Dearborn, 312/747-7554	S
Wolfe Playground 3325 E. 108th, 312/747-7005	FSE
Woodhull Playground 7340 S. East End, 312/742-7006	FSE

Southwest Region

Regional Office:

Foster Park 1440 W. 84th, 312/747-6135	FSW

Ada Park 11250 S. Ada, 312/747-6002	FSW
Archer Park 4901 S. Kilbourn, 312/747-6009	SW
Auburn Park 406 W. Winneconna, 312/747-6135	FSE
Beverly Park 2460 W. 102nd, 312/747-6024	FSW
Bogan Park 3939 W. 79th, 312/747-6025	FSW
Brainerd Park 1246 W. 92nd, 312/747-6027	FSW
Brown Memorial Park 634 E. 86th, 312/747-6063	FSE
Curie Park 4959 S. Archer, 312/747-6098	SW
Dawes Park 8052 S. Damen, 312/747-6108	FSW
Durkin Park 8445 S. Kolin, 312/747-6115	FSW
Gage Park 2415 W. 55th, 312/747-6147	SW

Grand Crossing Park 7655 S. Ingleside, 312/747-6158	**FSE**
Hale Park 6258 W. 62nd, 312/747-6168	**SW**
Hayes Park 2936 W. 85th, 312/747-6177	**FSW**
Kennedy Park 11320 S. Western, 312/747-6198	**FSW**
Lawler Park 5210 W. 64th, 312/747-6435	**SW**
Marquette Park 6700 S. Kedzie, 312/747-6469	**SW**
Minuteman Park 5940 S. Central, 312/747-6559	**SW**
Mt. Greenwood Park 3721 W. 111th, 312/747-6564	**FSW**
Mt. Vernon Park 10540 S. Morgan, 312/747-6566	**FSW**
Munroe Park 2617 W. 105th, 312/747-6561	**FSW**
Nat King Cole Park 301 E. 85th, 312/747-6063	**FSE**
Normandy Playground 6660 W. 52nd, 312/747-6568	**SW**
Oakdale Park 965 W. 95th, 312/747-6569	**FSW**
O'Hallaren 8335 S. Honore, 312/747-6573	**FSW**
Pasteur Park 5825 S. Kostner, 312/747-6597	**SW**
Rainey Park 4350 W. 79th, 312/747-6630	**FSW**
Ridge Park 9625 S. Longwood, 312/747-6630	**FSW**
Scottsdale Playground 4637 W. 83rd, 312/747-6668	**FSW**
Senka Park 5656 S. St. Louis, 312/747-7632	**SW**
Strohacker Park 4347 W. 54th, 312/747-6723	**SW**
Tuley Park 501 E. 90th, 312/747-6763	**FSE**
Valley Forge Park 7001-7131 W. 59th, 312/747-6810	**SW**
Vittum Park 5014 W. 50th, 312/747-6815	**SW**
Wentworth Park 5625 S. Mobile, 312/747-6993	**SW**
West Lawn Park 4232 W. 65th, 312/747-7032	**SW**

Lakefront Region

Regional Office:
South Shore Cultural Center
7059 S. South Shore Drive, 312/747-2536   **FSE**

Ashe Park 2701 E. 74th, 312/747-6625	**FSE**
Berger Park 6205-47 N. Sheridan, 312/742-7871	**FN**
Burnham Park Roosevelt (1200 S) and the lake, 312/747-6620	**C**
Calumet Park 9801 S. Ave. "G", 312/747-6039	**FSE**
Clarendon Community Center 4501 N. Clarendon, 312/742-7512	**N**
Columbia Park and Beach 1039 W. Columbia, 312/742-7857	**FN**
Daley Bicentennial Plaza 337 E. Randolph, 312/742-7648	**C**
Fargo Avenue Beach Fargo (7432 N) and the lake, 312/742-7864	**FN**
Foster Beach Foster (5200 N) and the lake, 312/742-7726	**FN**

Grant Park Randolph to Roosevelt along the lake, 312/747-6620 C
Hartigan Park and Beach 1031 W. Albion, 312/742-7857 FN
Howard St. Beach and Park 7519 N. Eastlake, 312/742-7864 FN
Jackson Park 6401 S. Stony Island, 312/747-6187 S
Jarvis Ave. Beach and Park 1208 W. Jarvis, 312/742-7857 FN
Juneway Terr. Beach and Park 7751 N. Eastlake, 312/742-7857 FN
Lake Shore Park 808 N. Lake Shore Drive, 312/742-7891 C
Lane Beach and Park 5915 N. Sheridan, 312/742-7857 FN
Leone Park and Beach 1222 W. Touhy, 312/742-7864 FN
Lincoln Park 2045 Lincoln Park West, 312/742-7726 N
Loyola Park and Beach 1230 W. Greenleaf, 312/742-7857 FN
Margate Park 4921 N. Marine Drive, 312/742-7522 FN
Montrose Beach Montrose (4400 N) and the lake, 312/742-7226 N
North Avenue Beach North (1600 N) and the lake, 312/742-7226 C
North Shore Bch North Shore (6700 N) and the lake, 312/742-7857 FN
Northerly Island Park 1400 S. Linn White Drive, 312/747-2471 C
Oak Street Beach Oak (1000 N) and the lake, 312/742-7891 C
Kathy Osterman Bch Ardmore (5800 N) & the lake, 312/742-7226 FN
Pratt Blvd. Beach and Park 1050 W. Pratt, 312/742-7857 FN
Promontory Point Park 5491 S. South Shore Drive, 312/747-6620 S
Rainbow Park and Beach 2873 E. 76th, 312/747-6625 FSE
Rogers Ave. Beach and Park 7705 N. Eastlake, 312/742-7864 FN

Keep in touch with park district happenings:

Chicago Park District
http://www.ci.chi.il.us/WorksMart/Parks

4 FOOD

It's hard to go wrong on Devon. Delicious *and* affordable dining
abounds at this strip's many Indian restaurants and buffets.
(*Photo by Rames Shrestha.*)

Windy City fast food classics: Jim's Hot Dog Stand (*above*) in the old Maxwell Street neighborhood for 24-hour Polish sausages and pork chop sandwiches, and Superdawg (*below*) on the far Northwest Side for pure beef dogs, crinkle cut fries, and all-American kitsch. (*Photos by Rames Shrestha.*)

FOOD

Not surprisingly, this is the only chapter in the book where you won't find a glut of free possibilities. However, if you're going to spend money on anything in Chicago, it might as well be food!

RESTAURANTS

Whether you're craving something in particular or eager to try something new, check out this bill of fare. You won't find a more complete list of quality budget dining anywhere.

African See also: **Ethiopian**, **Moroccan**, and **Nigerian**.

Vee-Vee's African Restaurant and Cocktails
6243 N. Broadway, 773/465-2424 **FN**
This spacious restaurant with African folk touches is where native Africans dine for home cooking. Extensive menu is organized by Bean Plates, Stews and Soups, Yam and Plantain Specials, and Rice Entrees. Vee-Vee's special *Ofe Imo* soup contains fish, shrimp, meat, pumpkin, and red pepper and comes with semolina on the side. Entrees $5.25-$12.99, most under $8. Sunday buffet (Noon-6pm), $9.99.

For other variations on traditional African dishes, head to **African Heritage Restaurant** (2333 S. Michigan, 312/842-0964), where the servers are clad in traditional African attire. Your wallet will appreciate the weekend and happy hour specials (3pm-6pm). Also try **Bolat** (4834 N. Sheridan, 773/769-6189) for their *jollof* rice and *fufu*.

Airport Food

These two home-grown eateries stand out among O'Hare's high-priced, junk food franchises and chain concessionaires.

Butch's Grill
O'Hare Airport, Terminal 3, 773/686-6114   **NW**
Named for Edward "Butch" O'Hare, this 50s-style grill, complete with
music and soda jerks, is a much-needed oddball in the sterile airport world.
For $4-$5 enjoy a gourmet burger, meatloaf sandwich, or a Chicago
specialty sandwich: a Maxwell Street grilled Polish sausage, grilled pork
chop, or Chicago-style hot dog. Black cows, shakes, sodas, and sundaes
from the fountain run $1.80-$2.95. Great chili, soup, and daily hot dinner
specials.

Lou Mitchell's Express
O'Hare Airport, Terminal 5, 773/601-8989   **NW**
Though relatively new to the international terminal's food court, **Lou
Mitchell's** has a long history in Chicago (See **Breakfasts**, p. 124). Make
this your first stop for homemade and affordable baked goods at the airport:
jumbo cookies loaded with chunks of chocolate and nuts, thick pound cake
slices, and monstrous muffins cost $1.25-$1.40. Fresh deli sandwiches go
for $3.95-$4.25. Salads and ice cream also available.

Argentinean See also: **Chilean.**

El Nandu Restaurant
2731 W. Fullerton, 773/278-0900   **N**
Exposed brick walls provide a nice backdrop for colorful artwork and an
ongoing slide show of Argentina. Start with the menu's highlight—
empanadas (turnovers filled with shrimp, corn, spinach, cheese, ground
beef, or steak) that cost only $1.95-$2 each. Salads ($2.50-$5.95), chicken
($8.95-$10.95), and steak ($9.95-$13.45) complete the menu. Open mic on
Thursdays begins a line-up of weekend entertainment.

Tango Sur
3763 N. Southport, 773/477-5466   **N**
The dance of love at this newer Argentinean restaurant is beef coupled with
more beef. Start with, say, a fried beef empanada, *chinchulin* (fried cow's
intestine), or *matambre* (cold veal roll stuffed with vegetables and egg).
Follow with one of the *parilla* (barbecue) steaks or *milanesa a caballo*
(fried breaded steak crowned with fried eggs). For variety, the *parrillada*
samplers are the house specialty. The $15 platter feeds 1-2 and contains
grilled short ribs, chorizo, *morcilla* (blood sausage), and sweetbreads; the

$25 platter feeds 2-4 and throws in one of the *vacio* steaks besides. Entrees $8-$25. Outdoor seating in summer. BYOB.

Armenian

Sayat-Nova
157 E. Ohio, 312/644-9159   **C**
Middle Eastern appetizers, kebabs, couscous, and Armenian lamb, seafood, and vegetarian classics have pleased customers for 25 years at this downtown staple off Michigan Avenue. Raw *Kibbee*—Armenian steak tartare ($9)—and *Lamajoun*—Armenian ground lamb "pizza" ($3.50)—join standards like hummus, baba ghannouj, and stuffed eggplant on the *mezza* (appetizer) list. Charbroiled kebabs ($10.95-$14.95), couscous plates ($10.95-$11.95), and Armenian dinners ($9.95-$12.95, $16.95 for the famous lamb chops) include red lentil soup or salad with mint vinaigrette. Lunches $6.95-$10.95.

Asian   See also: **Chinese, Indonesian, Japanese, Korean, Laotian, Thai,** and **Vietnamese.**

Asia Bowl
1160 N. State, 312/587-8667   **C**
1001 W. Webster, 773/348-3060   **N**
3411 N. Broadway, 773/529-2600   **N**
Sleek, new fast food chain serves fresh and healthy pan-Asian bowls, rolls, and wraps. Bowls contain rice or noodle dishes, ranging from Lemon Grass Chicken to Shanghai Noodles. Rolls include Vietnamese spring rolls, Chinese pot stickers, and Japanese sushi rolls. Meals, like Thai or Java BBQ, enfolded in whole-wheat or spinach tortillas are referred to as wraps. Also, soups, salads, and an impressive tea collection. Bowls and wraps, $3.95-$5.95; rolls, $1.50-$5.25.

Hi Ricky
941 W. Randolph, 312/491-9100   **C**
1851 W. North, 773/276-8300   **W**
3730 N. Southport, 773/388-0000   **N**
This trio of "Asian Noodle Shops and Satay Bars," located in hiply rehabbed buildings, inspires repeat business with its friendly service, fun atmosphere, low prices, extensive menu, and good cooking. Bring a crowd and nibble your way through the flavors of Southeast Asia. There's

Indonesian lamb satay, Vietnamese beef salad, Chinese-style greens with garlic oyster sauce, Burmese curried fried rice, Thai green curry with eggplant and basil, and Malaysian Hokkien noodles. BYOB. Dishes $2.95-$6.45, most $5-$6.

Lulu's
1333 E. 57th, 773/288-2988   S
Pan-Asian, luncheonette-style restaurant divides its menu into Small Eats ($2.50-$4.25 for such items as Chinese hot & sour cabbage soup and steamed blue mussels in a spicy chili, garlic, and scallion broth) and Big Eats ($6.50-$7.25 for favorites like Pad Thai and barbecued pork with thin Chinese noodles). The $10.95 all-you-can-eat Saturday and Sunday brunch (11am-3pm) allows customers to order anything from the menu...and to keep ordering, until satisfied. Plenty of vegetarian entrees.

Pan Asia Cafe
3443 N. Sheffield, 773/880-0008   N
Fresh and natural ingredients along with thoughtful preparation insure that anything on the varied and extensive menu of Chinese, Japanese, Korean, Thai, and Vietnamese dishes will please. Man Doo Korean dumplings, Vietnamese spring rolls, Thai Tom Yum soup, Cashew Chicken, and Tofu Bi Bim Bop are just a few of the menu choices marked with a picture of chopsticks to indicate a customer favorite. Fortune ice cream for dessert comes in a green tea flavor. Separate Vegetable Lovers menu for vegetarians. Appetizers $1.95-$3.95. Entrees $4.25-$6.95. Closed Tuesdays.

Penny's Noodle Shop
950 W. Diversey, 773/281-8448   N
3400 N. Sheffield, 773/281-8222   N
Renowned cheap-eats cafe prepares Thai, Vietnamese, and Japanese noodle specialties not far from your table's view. Delectable spring rolls, perfectly seasoned soups, and big bowls of Pad Thai, ramen, or udon noodles will leave you blissful. Beware of big crowds at the tiny original location on Sheffield. All dishes $3-$6. Closed Mondays.

Breakfast

The Bongo Room
1470 N. Milwaukee, 773/489-0690   C
The Bongo Room's imaginative, eclectic decor is matched and surpassed

only by its creative and tantalizing menu that changes with the seasons. Short-lived dishes like raspberry cheesecake pancakes, chocolate chunk brioche French toast, and shrimp Benedict with mustard and dill hollandaise are as delicious as they sound and worth prices that exceed a "cheap" breakfast. The breakfast burrito and fresh squeezed orange juice are perennial favorites. Entrees $5-$10, most around $7. Open 8am weekdays, 9:30am weekends.

Classic Desserts
2921 N. Sheffield, 773/929-9970   N
Evoking a Victorian tea room, the cafe attached to the **Classic Desserts'** bakery offers an elegant start to any day for a very reasonable price. Enjoy the complimentary basket of mini baked goods (muffins, croissants, scones, danish, and brioche) while narrowing down the selection of inviting entrees to a single choice. Some house favorites include the cinnamon bread French toast, chorizo omelette, and breakfast tacos. Entrees $3.25-$5.95. Open 7am Tues.-Sun.

Golden House
4744 N. Broadway, 773/334-0406   N
Old paneling, a maze of sparkling, red-vinyl booths, and Uptown's mixed bag of neighbors provide an oddly relaxing environment to start the day. This diner/pancake house serves quite an array of good food at unbeatable rates. Top pancakes and waffles with apple, blueberry, strawberry, peach, cherry, or pineapple compote; pecans; chocolate chips; cinnamon; and, of course, plenty of whipped cream. Match your eggs with hash, pork chops, French toast, chopped ham, and more. Breakfast items $2-$5. Opens 6am.

Joanne & Sons
1775 W. Sunnyside, 773/334-0101   N
There's not a time when I'm at this corner of Ravenswood and Sunnyside that I don't feel for a moment as if I've been transported to the deserted intersection of a small, careworn town, far, far away. Stepping into the cheerful and idiosyncratic **Joanne & Sons** in that frame of mind seals the surreal experience. A sleepy corner place bedecked with license plates, Pepsi paraphernalia, Elvis memorabilia, movie collectibles, and other nostalgic treasures, **Joanne**'s is a world entirely unto itself and 100% down-to-earth. Prices peak at $4.75 for rib eye steak and eggs and $4.50 for the baked apple pancake. Two-egg omelettes with toast and hash browns start at $2.75 (additional ingredients $.30-$.75) and are just the right size. Swedish and Mexican influences creep in among the ample

menu of standard and unusual offerings. Open 8am Mon.-Sat., 9am Sun. Most breakfasts run under $4.

The Lincoln Restaurant
4008 N. Lincoln, 773/248-1820 **N**
Honest Abe and the Civil War are the pervasive themes at this Greek-owned, country-decorated family restaurant. Recommended omelettes and egg combos are served in pewter skillets and take the names of Civil War generals. The General Sheridan, for example, is a three-cheese omelette. Try the unique granola-laced pancakes or shun breakfast conventions altogether with a fancy ice-cream sundae (named after the earliest American presidents). Dishes $3-$6. Take home chocolate-covered Oreos or marshmallows from the pastry case. Opens 5:30am.

Lou Mitchell's Restaurant
565 W. Jackson, 312/939-3111 **C**
Classic coffee shop (1923) efficiently and expertly serves the food that has earned recurring endorsements. (Those waiting for tables are compensated with free Milk Duds.) Notable omelettes, waffles, thick Greek toast (with homemade orange marmalade), and homemade baked goods (brownies, muffins, cinnamon-raisin bread...) hover near the top of a list of affordable favorites ($3-$6). Opens 5:30am Mon.-Fri., 7am Sat.-Sun.

Original Pancake House
22 E. Bellevue Place, 312/642-7917	**C**
1517 E. Hyde Park Blvd., 773/288-2322	**S**
2020 N. Lincoln Park West, 773/929-8130	**N**
700 E. 87th, 773/874-0010	**FSE**
10437 S. Western, 773/445-6100	**FSW**

Diners can find breakfast bliss in all corners of the city thanks to this chain of legendary pancake houses. Long waits for tables and long waits for certain menu items are almost inevitable, but the unanimous chorus of past patrons is: "It's worth every stomach-growling minute." The oven-baked German and apple pancakes are 20-30 minute masterpieces. One variation, the Dutch Baby Treat, is a German pancake stuffed with bananas and strawberries. Crêpes also head the list of requested items; spinach, mandarin orange, and cherry kiafa are top fillings. Entrees $3.75-$7.75.

Breakfast, All Day

Clarke's Pancake House and Restaurant
2441 N. Lincoln, 773/472-3505 **N**
Healthy and innovative pancake house fare 24 hours a day. Carrot &
zucchini pancakes, German pancakes, chocolate chip pancakes, spinach
burritos... Meals $4-$8, most under $6.

The Original Mitchell's
101 W. North, 312/642-5246 (Opens 6am, 24 hours Fri.-Sat.) **C**
1953 N. Clybourn, 773/883-1157 (Opens 8am) **N**
The Mitchells have been operating family restaurants in Chicago since the
1940s—their North Avenue location has been around for 35 years. They
pride themselves on their omelettes (try 'em pizza-style), their fresh,
natural ingredients, and a wide selection of heart-healthy and vegetarian
items (including "sausage" patties). Breakfasts $3.50-$6.50, more for steak
and lox.

Tempo Restaurant
1 E. Chestnut, 312/943-4373 **C**
If you tend to crave breakfast at unconventional hours and your nightlife
often takes you to the center of town, add **Tempo** to your little black book.
The people watching is good at all hours (the outdoor cafe is open until
11pm) and the food is even better. Eggs Florentine, chicken liver and eggs
("The Continental"), raspberry pancakes, and egg-white French toast are
but a few of the menu's highlights. Entrees $2.95-$8.95, most $4-$6. Open
24 hours.

Memorable Chicago Pancakes

- Apple Pancakes from the **Original Pancake House** (p.124)
- Swedish Pancakes from **Ann Sather's** (p.198)
- Granola-laced Pancakes from the **Lincoln Restaurant** (p.124)
- Carrot & Zucchini Pancakes from **Clarke's** (p.125)
- Oat Bran & Buckwheat Pancakes from **Healthy Food** (p.161)

Breakfast Buffets In Hotels

30 East American Bistro (Courtyard By Marriott)
30 E. Hubbard, 312/329-2500   C
Eat your heart out at one of three breakfast buffets. The European Continental buffet ($6.53) offers juices, coffee, and an assortment of breakfast breads. The American Continental buffet ($7.63) includes all of that, plus hot and cold cereals, fruit, and yogurt. The complete buffet ($8.73) offers eggs, omelettes, waffles, meats, and other hot dishes along with the items from the other two buffets. Weekdays 6:30am-10:30am, Sat. 7am-12pm, and Sun. 7am-1pm.

Plaza Cafe (Quality Inn)
One S. Halsted, 312/829-5000   C
Fortify yourself for hours to come with multiple trips to the hot breakfast buffet ($7.95). Scrambled eggs, pancakes, corned beef hash, hash browns, grits, oatmeal, cold cereals, danish, fruit, juice, coffee, and more. The cold breakfast buffet is $5.50. Opens 6:30am.

Breakfast, Downtown and Dirt-cheap

Billy Goat Tavern
430 N. Michigan, 312/222-1525   C
309 W. Washington, 312/899-1873   C
Legendary tavern has cheap breakfasts, too. See lunch time entry below (p.168) for the details. Closed Sundays.

Fast Track
629 W. Lake, 312/993-9300   C
Hot dog stand with train theme has inexpensive breakfasts.   Closed Sundays.

Flamingo Bar and Grill
440 E. Grand, 312/222-0901   C
Neon in the morning. Breakfast 6am-10:30am.

Little Louie's
24 E. Congress, 312/939-3181   C
Sandwich place with all breakfast stuff under $2: eggs, French toast or pancakes with meat, Mexican eggs, breakfast sandwiches. Cappuccino and

hot chocolate $.75. Closed Sundays.

Mallers Building Deli
5 S. Wabash, 3rd Fl., 312/263-7696   C
Long-standing coffee shop caters to downtown office workers. Closed
Sundays.

Ronny's Steak House
340 S. Wabash, 312/939-6010   C
16 W. Randolph, 312/346-6488   C
Steak, eggs, potatoes, and toast bonanza for $2.19.

332 Deli & Metro Espresso
334 S. Michigan, 312/427-4046   C
Stay upstairs to fulfill your caffeine and sweet tooth needs. Downstairs at
the deli, bagels, egg dishes, and breakfast sandwiches ($.75-$1.79) furnish
a more substantial first meal. Closed Sundays.

Brunch

Hotel Florence
11111 S. Forrestville, 773/785-8900   FSE
You haven't "done everything" in Chicago until you've trekked down (it's
a trek for the vast majority of Chicagoans) to the historic Pullman district
for an intriguing tour (see p.293) and a magnificent brunch. Sunday brunch
is held in the sprawling, restored **Hotel Florence** (1881), where $12.95
($3.95 for kids under 12 and $3.50 for seniors) buys multiple trips to an
overflowing buffet of breakfast and lunch items. Omelettes, pancakes,
bacon, sausage, eggs, coffee cake, juice, roast beef, chicken, salad, soup,
potatoes, vegetables, and desserts can all be walked off by exploring the
remnants of Pullman's planned community. Sunday, 10am-3pm.

Stanley's Kitchen & Tap
1970 N. Lincoln, 773/642-0007   N
Lincoln Park bar (known for its whiskey selection) and restaurant (known
for its low-priced American home cooking) has a brunch buffet that can't
be beat. For $7.95, fill up on fried chicken, macaroni & cheese, potatoes &
gravy, biscuits & sausage gravy, bacon, home fries, fruit, muffins, biscuits,
bread, bagels, and cinnamon rolls. Oh, and don't forget trips to the
omelette and Belgian waffle stations! Complete with bowling trophies,
family photos, antique appliances, and a contemporary flair, Stanley's

dimly-lit backroom re-creates a mid-century roadside kitchen. For an additional $6.95, visit the build-your-own Bloody Mary bar. They start you with three shots of vodka—you add the rest. Hint: Come on Saturday to avoid the Sunday mob. Sat.-Sun. 11am-4pm.

Classic pubs that provide a distinctive backdrop and an appealing menu for brunch include **John Barleycorn Memorial Pub** (658 W. Belden, 773/348-8899), **Four Farthings Tavern** (2060 N. Cleveland, 773/935-2060), and **Red Lion Pub** (2446 N. Lincoln, 773/348-2695).

The **Original 50 Yard Line** (69 E. 75th, 773/846-0005) is a popular Chatham sports bar, serving a hard-to-pass-up $4 brunch, Saturdays from 1pm to 5pm. The rotating buffet menu may include baked chicken, pepper steak, meatloaf, macaroni salad, potatoes, rice, corn, string beans, greens, salad, and corn bread.

Bulgarian

Mario's Cafe
5241 N. Harlem, 773/594-9742 **FN**
The only Bulgarian restaurant in the Midwest, the 2-1/2-year-old **Mario's Cafe** was recently named on *Chicago Tribune*'s list of "Top 10 Ethnic Restaurants in Chicago." Bulgarian cookery bears much resemblance to Greek cooking, as is apparent in **Mario's** appetizers like the yogurt dip, eggplant spread, feta cheese, and fried cheese. It also is meat-intensive, with pork predominating. Try the meatballs, sausages, and Bulgarian salami. For dessert, there's *baklava*, *tolumba* (fried dough with syrup), or cheese and chocolate filled pastries. Entrees hover near $10; appetizers near $4. Closed Mondays.

Burgers

A hot-dog-stand-with-umbrella-tables burger...

Yo-Joe's Red Hots
6401 W. Addison, 773/286-0131 **NW**
Carry-out their "Tummy Buster"—a 1/2 lb. of ground beef ($3), loaded with trimmings (including sauerkraut, if you so choose)—or, in warm weather, take it to the picnic tables out back. Pair it with the unique fried cheddar cheese cubes or one of their notable hot dogs for a chaser. Closed

Sundays.

These three dark neighborhood taverns—popular, yet somewhat dated or even careworn—all have something else in common: burgers that Chicagoans rave about.

Boston Blackie's
164 E. Grand, 312/938-8700   **C**
Dim, bustling, and strangely like a hotel banquet hall, this stalwart neighborhood bar and grill, just a stone's throw from the sheen of ritzy North Michigan Avenue, crams folks in at lunch, dinner, and in-between for their cherished beef patties ($5.15).

Howard's Bar and Grill
152 E. Ontario, 312/787-5269   **C**
Entering this space-challenged Streeterville bar instantly removes you from any bustle or glitz of nearby Michigan Avenue. If you've already tried the much-lauded 1/2 lb. burgers ($4.25) and cheeseburgers ($4.50) from its bare-bones menu, there are also Wisconsin brats, BBQ beefs, and pork tenderloin sandwiches ($3.95-$4.95). Prices include slaw, chips, and peanut M & Ms. Tiny beer garden in back.

Moody's Pub
5910 N. Broadway, 773/275-2696   **FN**
The award-winning 1/2 lb. Moodyburger ($5.75) is the center of **Moody's** limited pub menu. The dark, charming, heavy wood, and fire-lit interior is perfect for winter, while the large, atmospheric beer garden makes an ideal summer retreat.

Cafeterias

Manny's Coffee Shop and Deli
1141 S. Jefferson, 312/939-2855   **C**
Patrons show up by all modes possible (Lincolns, cop cars, delivery vans, messenger bikes...) for the American deli, Eastern European, and Jewish classics served at this spacious 56-year-old Maxwell Street- area fixture. Grab a tray and stand in line. It's full service—someone even pours the sodas and juices—and no money is exchanged until you've finished eating. Most dishes on the vast and changing menu are priced between $3 and $7, whether they're potato pancakes and knishes; corned beef, pastrami, and lox sandwiches; or hot entrees like meatloaf and liver. Buy your cigars at

the cashier's counter on the way out. Open Mon.-Sat. 5am-4pm. Closed Sunday.

Valois Cafeteria
1518 E. 53rd, 773/667-0647   **S**
The **Valois** invites diners to "see your food." Folks come from every corner of Hyde Park for chicken pot pies, cheap hot sandwiches, and a changing line-up of hearty dinners. Everything falls under $6, most dishes between $1.50 and $4. This place is such a neighborhood institution that in the early 1990s, U of C student Mitchell Duneier conducted a sociological study of the black working-class men who regularly meet at the **Valois**, eventually publishing his dissertation as a book entitled *Slim's Table*.

Cajun/Creole See also: **Southern Eclectic**.

Heaven on Seven
111 N. Wabash, 7th Floor, 312/263-6443   **C**
Crowded luncheonette (7am-5pm weekdays) packs in office workers for the noontime meal, particularly its complete Louisiana menu and deluxe hot sauce collection. Excellent gumbos, jambalayas, etouffee, po-boys, crayfish tamales, crab cakes, and such, along with the lively crowd (that often stretches down the hall to the building's elevator), make this a Chicago favorite. Dishes $4.25-$9.95, Cajun entrees $7.50-$9.95. Closed Sundays. Where the original evokes a bayou-town kitchen, the new **Heaven on Seven on Rush** (600 N. Michigan, 312/280-7774) resembles a sleek Bourbon Street tourist restaurant. Although the new location has later hours, it also comes with more upscale cooking and downtown prices. Most entrees are priced between $12 and $18.

Caribbean See also: **Cuban, Honduran, Jamaican,** and **Puerto Rican**.

El Dinamico Dallas
1545 W. Howard, 773/465-3320   **FN**
On Chicago's periphery lies this quirky, "undiscovered," pan-Caribbean hideaway that dishes out Jamaican, Cuban, and Haitian specialties. Jerk chicken, curried chicken, and curried goat are favorites ($7.75-$8.50) but there's oh, so much more to choose from. Try beef liver "Italian style" (served with black beans and rice, fried plantains, and plantain bread), catfish with spaghetti, beef tongue, cod fish with creole-style yams, or

oxtail soup. Regulars recommend the carrot cake (!) for dessert. Live music once a month. Closed Tuesdays.

Chilean See also: **Argentinean.**

Empanadas Unlimited
2046 N. Damen, 773/772-1335   N
Lively and artsy storefront focuses on empanadas to showcase the flavors of Chile. These baked turnovers are filled with seafood, chicken, vegetables, or the traditional mix of seasoned ground beef, onions, raisins, hard-boiled egg, and an olive. Black bean soup makes the perfect accompaniment to any combination of empanadas. *Mate*, an herbal South American tea, is the recommended beverage. Dishes $2-$9. Live Chilean music on Saturday nights.

Chili

Bishop's Chili
1958 W. 18th, 312/829-6345   W
"Chicago's Original" chili/chili mac dates back to 1925 and comes in three sizes: 8 oz. for $2.49, 16 oz. for $4.49 and 32 oz. for $7.59. Top that chili with cheese, onions, spicy tomatoes, jalapeños, sour cream, or pickled cactus. For variety, try a chili dog, chili cheese dog, or chili tamale. Wash it down with Filbert's Old Time Draft Root Beer, which has been made on the southwest side from the Filbert secret family recipe for almost as long as Bishop's has been doing chili.

Lindy's Chili
3689 S. Archer, 773/927-7807   SW
A popular stop for White Sox fans after the game, this original **Lindy's** location is now part of the combined **Gertie's Ice Cream** (see p.150) and **Lindy's Chili** eatery. Start with a bowl for $2.30 and then take some home: pints cost $4.10, quarts $7.90, and gallons $17.95.

Chinese

Wherever you go in Chicago, you're bound to find plenty of inexpensive Chinese restaurants. Dining in Chicago's tight-knit Chinese community is quite different, however, from ordering take-out chop suey from the place on the corner. As Chinatown's main strip is only three blocks long, you might try one very common approach to selecting one of its many eateries for your evening meal—saunter up and down the strip until a particular restaurant intrigues you, or until you find one that meets your dress, ambiance, or pricing criteria. (There's at least one there for everyone.)

A traditional gate on Wentworth (200 W) at Cermak (2200 S) welcomes you to Chinatown. The Chinatown el stop on the Red Line leaves you one block from this point. Although there are some restaurants on Cermak, the bulk of them can be found on Wentworth. **Emperor's Choice** (2238 S. Wentworth, 312/225-8800), **King Wah** (2225 S. Wentworth, 312/842-1404), **Mandar-Inn** (2249 S. Wentworth, 312/842-4014), **Moon Palace** (216 W. Cermak, 312/225-4081), and **Sixty-Five** (2414 S. Wentworth, 312/225-7060) have different atmospheres but all are time-tested favorites with most entrees in the $7-$11 range. For something cheaper, try **Seven Treasures** (2312 S. Wentworth, 312/225-2668). Their colossal menus list hundreds of items priced between $2.50 and $12, most under $7.

Dim sum is the custom (originally Cantonese) of snacking or dining on various types of dumplings and other small portions of delicacies. While many Chinatown restaurants offer daily dim sum from mid-morning to late afternoon, weekends, particularly early Sunday afternoon, may be the best time to go. It seems that the majority of the Chinatown neighborhood is out then, enjoying this social meal that can linger for hours.

Favorites for dim sum (typically $2-$4 per dish) are **Furama** (2828 S. Wentworth, 312/225-6888 in Chinatown and 4936 N. Broadway, 773/271-1161 in Uptown); **Hong Min** (221 W. Cermak, 312/842-5026), known for dreary decor and excellent food; the attractive, new, and exceptionally popular **Phoenix** (2131 S. Archer, 2nd Floor, 312/328-0848); and the pink and cavernous **Three Happiness** (209 W. Cermak, 312/842-1964 and 2130 S. Wentworth, 312/791-1228, both in Chinatown). During busy times, select dim sum from the loaded carts that servers wind through the maze of tables.

Where special needs are met...

Vegetarian Garden (237 W. Cermak, 312/949-1388) employs pork, beef, and poultry substitutes to help create an amazing 100+ dishes (most $7-$9) without meat, eggs, or dairy, including roast duck, vegetable fried eel, orange beef, and chicken with bitter melon! **Mi Tsu Yun** (3010 W. Devon, 773/262-4630), as Chicago's only Kosher Chinese restaurant, employs a rabbi to ensure that meals are prepared accordingly. Pot stickers, egg rolls, sesame chicken, and sweet and sour chicken are house favorites. Closed Fri.-Sat. Apathetic taste buds can be revitalized at **Mei Shung** (5511 N. Broadway, 773/728-5778), a Mandarin restaurant known for its side menu of unique Taiwanese specialties. Closed Mondays.

For lunch bargains on the southwest side:

The complete lack of decor doesn't keep the local business people from packing **Arden Chinese** (6207 S. Kedzie, 773/436-6200) at lunch time. Menu selections ($1.35 to $11) cover the entire range of Chinese and Mandarin cuisine. The chicken dishes are especially tasty. Closed Mondays. **Wing Wah Lau**'s (4340 S. Archer, 773/847-1881) $4.95 all-you-can-eat lunch buffet makes this Brighton Park restaurant a neighborhood favorite. It's a good place for spicy chicken and beef satay.

Coffeehouses and Cafes

If it's teatime, dessert time, snack time, or any time for a break, Chicago has an eclectic and thriving coffee-based culture prepared to help you slow down by pumping you with caffeine, rich desserts, and, often, stimulating entertainment. This suggestion list is hardly exhaustive—Chicago's coffee league needs its own directory—but was devised to introduce a wide range of coffeehouse styles. A snack/dessert and beverage at these places will usually fall between $4 and $6. See also *Chapter 5: Entertainment*, for cafes with live music, improv comedy, and poetry readings.

Anna Held Flower Shop and Fountain Cafe
5557 N. Sheridan, 773/561-1941   **FN**
Like the pink Edgewater Beach Apartments (site of a former luxury hotel) in which it's located, the **Anna Held Flower Shop and Fountain Cafe** can jolt you into a kinder, gentler mindset, or even another era. Let the scent of fresh flowers overwhelm you as you take a seat at the soda fountain for a coffee drink, cake, or ice cream treat.

The Buzz Cup
5750 N. Rogers, 773/205-6196   **FN**
This pub-like corner lot coffeehouse will set you humming upon discovery. Thereafter, you too will be under the spell of its mellow charms. Sink into a couch with a book from their small library. (You'll be able to take it home temporarily to finish.) Pull up to the fireplace with some friends and a

board game. $2-$4 buys some solid nourishment like pastries, square pizza slices, pasta salad, or turkey and swiss on Vienna bread.

Cafe Jumping Bean
1439 W. 18th, 312/455-0019   **W**
A sign of Pilsen's revitalized arts community, **Jumping Bean** rotates the work of local artists that it displays on its walls every six weeks. Cold sandwiches, hot focaccia sandwiches, empanadas, pizza, and desserts provide ample fare to accompany a creative caffeine break.

Earwax Cafe
1564 N. Milwaukee, 773/772-4019   **W**
This popular Wicker Park space holds a second floor store (new and used music and videos) and a first floor cafe. The primarily vegetarian menu includes items like potato pancakes, a portabello sandwich, and a Southwestern wrap. Daily specials run the ethnic gamut and the dessert line-up changes weekly. Banana bread, carrot cake, and white chocolate cheesecake are favored sweets. **Earwax** is a casual and relaxing retreat free of the attitude that plagues similar hip, artsy places elsewhere. If you don't care for coffee, they also have sodas, shakes, smoothies, and juices. Entrees $3.50-$6.50.

Java Express
10701 S. Hale, 773/233-8557   **FSW**
Many routes collide at Java Express—a very friendly, relaxed, neighborhood coffee and sandwich shop. 107th is so narrow here that most of the patrons park with the passenger-side wheels up on the curb. Bike racks outside make it a convenient stop during a bike tour of Beverly. Train schedules are posted inside the shop for the nearby 107th Street station of the Rock Island line. The sound of the train pulling into the station blends in easily with friends, neighbors, kids, and staff members passing the time of day on knock-off oak tables and slatted Breuer-type chairs. Sandwiches range from $3 to $5 (turkey, ham, club, tuna, pb & j, veggie) and are served on thick slices of homemade bread. Two homemade soups and chili are also served each day ($1.50-$3), along with salads and cookies. When you're not having your java express, enjoy one of their twenty-some blends of coffee—perhaps their signature Columbian-bean Beverly Blend—in a thick white mug.

Kopi, A Traveler's Cafe
5317 N. Clark, 773/989-KOPI   **FN**
Kopi (named for the Indonesian word for coffee) is loosely designed for travelers to come and swap road stories and shore up on tips for the next adventure. Slip your shoes off for cross-legged lounging at low tables surrounded by decorative cushions. Perhaps a Thai iced coffee and an order of hummus will tide you over as you plan that real or imagined trip to Nepal. Food choices include scones, muffins, desserts, breakfasts, sandwiches, and international appetizers. Travel books and global treasures are for sale.

Yugoslavian Politics and Chicago Eateries

When the first edition of *A Native's Guide To Chicago* was written in 1994, various *Yugoslavian* establishments in Chicago were closing. By the time the second edition was published in 1996, several specifically *Croatian* or *Serbian* businesses had emerged on the dining scene. As the third edition is released in late 1998, new *Bosnian* places are opening up all the time, particularly in the Lincoln Square neighborhood. In addition to two Bosnian restaurants and a deli, the neighborhood now has at least two Bosnian cafes, both of which take on a nightclub feel after dark: **Cafe Aloha** (2156 W. Montrose, 773/907-9356)—a Hawaiin-themed cafe with poetry nights and a roof-top deck, and **Coffee E** (4807 N. Claremont)—a Euro-style coffee house that often remains open well past midnight.

Columbian

Pueblito Viejo
5429 N. Lincoln, 773/784-9135   **FN**
Step into **Pueblito Viejo** (Old Village) and lose yourself in a recreated Columbian mountain village. The carefully decorated interior, the traditionally clad Columbian waiters, and the live music on the weekends set the stage for the authentic food to follow. The Picada (seasoned and fried chunks of meat, plantain, and yucca), Plato Montañero (mountain platter), and Sancocho de Gallina (parboiled hen) are house specialties. Don't leave without trying the arepas (corn cakes) or empanadas (turnovers). Entrees cost $8-$12. Closed Mondays.

To sample authentic Columbian dishes, it's hard to beat **La Fonda**'s (4758 N. Clark, 773/271-3935) lunch buffet (Tues.-Fri., 11:30am-3pm). The spread changes from day to day but always includes variously prepared meats and poultry, salad, soup, potatoes or cassava, rice, and sweet plantains. Order empanadas ($.95 each) and tropical juices on the side. **Las Tablas** (2965 N. Lincoln, 773/871-2414) is a Columbian steak house that also has a signature paella, seafood, and plenty of traditional sides on the menu. Entrees $8-$12.

Costa Rican

Irazu
1865 N. Milwaukee, 773/252-5687   **N**
Grab one of the few seats at this ramshackle little shop or take your goodies to go. Sandwiches, like steak or black beans and white cheese, run $1.75-$3.25. Try cheap sides like cheese empanadas, plantains or cassava with garlic, and the vegetarian taco ($1-$1.75). Dinners include choices like ceviche-style fish, fried pork chunks with cassava and cabbage salad, and versions of steak, shrimp, and pork chops ($5.50-$6.99). Wash it down with a *licuado*/shake ($1.50): carrot, oatmeal, tamarind, guanabana, mamey, papaya, and lemonade join more familiar flavors. Closed Sundays.

Croatian

Cafe Croatia
5726 N. Western, 773/CRO-ATIA   **FN**
Located across from Rosehill Cemetery, **Cafe Croatia** makes a charming retreat from this somewhat gloomy and lifeless stretch of Western Avenue. A dark and cozy front bar is typically filled with regulars, while the Euro-classy back dining area offers more intimate dining. Traditional combos, dominated by small *tambura* guitars, enliven the restaurant at least one weekend each month with music and dancing. The extensive menu includes roasts, chops, and seafood; *zagrebacki* (veal cutlet stuffed with ham and cheese), *cevapcici* (classic Croatian sausage), and *raznjici* (skewered pork chunks and vegetables) are customer favorites. Start with a regional Zagreb or Dalmation soup and finish with the dessert crepes or walnut torte. Entrees, $8-$16; sides, $3-$9. Outdoor seating in warm weather. Closed Mondays.

Casino Restaurant

9706 S. Commercial, 773/221-5189 **FSE**

This South Chicago restaurant specializes in traditional Croatian dishes, including *muckalica* (dried veal with grilled onions, peppers, and tomatoes) and sausages made from lamb, beef, and pork. Most entrees $8-$9.

Cuban See also: **Caribbean**.

Ambassador Café

3605 N. Ashland, 773/404-8770 **N**

Well-established, luncheonette-style storefront serves Cuban sandwiches and entrees from late morning to late evening. Sandwiches, including the $3 Cuban Sandwich (ham, cheese, steak, and pickles on crusty bread), range from $2.25 to $4.50. Island-style chicken, pork, steak, and seafood entrees come with black bean soup, fried plantains, and rice (all under $10). No rum and cokes or piña coladas here, but the Cuban coffee and tropical fruit shakes are easily potable.

Cafe 28

1800 W. Irving Park, 773/528-2883 **N**

With its exposed brick walls, cheerful paint job, pastry case, and ceiling fans, **Cafe 28** appears to be a fairly typical coffeehouse. When the Cuban and Mexican dinners roll out of the kitchen with a little more adventure than is traditional, you'll know differently. (Incidentally, the current chef is Japanese.) Grilled shrimp quesadillas, duck breast with mole, grilled honey jalapeño pork chops, *ropa vieja* ("old clothes"—a shredded beef classic) with black beans and sweet plantains, *arroz con pollo* (chicken and rice), and tempting vegetarian entrees would set you dancing—even without the background salsa music. Entrees $8.50-$14.50, appetizers $4-$6. Most breakfast and lunch items are $3-$6. Grab a Cuban-style cup of coffee before catching a morning Ravenswood train just a few paces up the block.

Dinner, Other Bargains

Bertucci's

300 W. 24th, 312/225-2848 **S**

Incongruously situated in the heart of Chinatown, this funky, fun Italian restaurant serves delicious food at very reasonable prices. The stuffed artichoke appetizer is great, so are the huge pork chops served with attendant saves spots for patrons, using that time-honored Chicago parking space reserver: plastic milk crates.

Bite
1039 N. Western, 773/395-2483 **W**
Internationally-influenced diner fare comes artfully prepared at this brick and wood artist-slacker-neighborhood spot. Special daily entrees ($7-$11, most under $8) supplement a basic menu of appetizers, soups, salads, pastas, and sandwiches ($1.95-$5.95). Grab a quick bite like a grilled cheese, burrito, or falafel sandwich or a more involved bite like grilled salmon, mushroom risotto, or marinated shark.

Medici
1327 E. 57th Street, 773/667-7394 **S**
Wooden booths and brick walls, adorned with graffiti and student art, chronicle the **Medici**'s decades of existence as a University of Chicago hangout. Though providing something for every taste—from salads and chicken wings to quesadillas and lamb stew—this pub-like coffeehouse is best known for its pizza (the Garbage version includes sausage, ground beef, pepperoni, mushrooms, green peppers, tomatoes, onions and garlic) and its hamburgers (topped, among other things, with barbecue sauce, olives, bacon, chili, and cheese). They say that eggs espresso (still served for breakfast) were invented here in the 60s. Plenty of vegetarian choices. Most menu items range from $4 to $7; the 12" Garbage pizza costs $17.

Mellow Yellow
1508 E. 53rd, 773/667-2000 **S**
Classic, nouvelle, casual, eclectic: the American/lightly French food at this energetic and attractive Hyde Park restaurant includes beloved rotisserie chicken and Taste of Chicago award-winning chili! Vegetarian chili of equal caliber has recently joined the menu. For a delicious meal under $6, choose one of the menu's numerous lighter options (sandwiches, crepes, quiche, burgers, baked potato meals). Sandwiches $4-$7, entrees with soup or salad $4-$13.

Stanley's Kitchen and Tap
1970 N. Lincoln, 312/642-0007 **N**
Upscale home-cooking at great prices and Chicago's largest selection of American whiskeys and bourbons. What a combo. Blackened chicken and catfish, gourmet burgers on black bread, chicken fried steak, veggie lasagna, toasted mac and cheese, meatloaf, pork chops, and pies. Yum.

Mini corn dogs, peanut butter and jelly, black cows. Cool. Entrees $4.95-$9.95, most under $7. Sandwiches are served with mashed potatoes, fries, or tator tots; supper items, with a side dish of choice. Every day has a different dinner special, including the all you can eat homestyle buffet on Mondays and all you can eat catfish on Fridays. Read about their not-to-miss brunch (p. 127).

Do-It-Yourself Stir-Fry

Flat Top Grill
319 W. North, 312/787-7676 (lunch 11:30am-3pm, Fri.-Sun. only) **C**
1000 W. Washington, 312/829-4800 (lunch everyday) **C**
Choose the ingredients for your personal stir-fry from an extensive buffet of meats (chicken, beef, pork, chicken livers, turkey, shrimp, squid), tofu, egg, vegetables, fruits, oils, sauces, vinegars, and flavored waters and deliver it to a chef at the flat top grill for cooking. A wall-sized chalkboard behind the buffet advises on time-tested combinations and proportions. You also select how to enjoy your stir-fry: over noodles (4 kinds), with rice (5 kinds), in a broth, atop lettuce as a salad, and occasionally, folded in pancake-style wrappers, like a burrito. Unlimited trips to the buffet and grill, $9.95. Lunch $6.95.

For a couple bucks extra, **Mongolian Barbecue** (3330 N. Clark, 773/325-2300) offers the same concept, with a larger selection of meat and seafood, plus a soup and salad bar. $11.95.

Doughnuts

Huck Finn Donuts and Snack Shop
4333 S. Kedzie, 773/523-2522 **SW**
3414 S. Archer, 773/247-5515 **SW**
6650 S. Pulaski, 773/581-4285 **SW**
Retirees, workers, families, and couples all come to these popular, diner-like restaurants for their excellent homemade doughnuts ($3.82 a dozen). Try the powdered-sugar-sprinkled doughnut holes ($.13 a piece).

Yum Yum Donuts
3639 N. Clark, 773/549-9109 **N**
In the shadow of Wrigley Field, **Yum Yum Donuts** is known by many Cubs' fans who stop for an affordable Chicago-style hot dog before

entering the ballpark. What commuters and ticket scalpers are more likely to know are the exceptional doughnuts. Try the old-fashioned, cruellers, or honey-glazed chocolate. $4.59/dozen, but if there's a lot left after 3pm (check in after a game), they'll usually cut you a deal.

For the only Kosher doughnuts in Chicago, head to the **Dunkin Donuts** on Devon (3132 W., 773/262-4560).

English

The Red Lion Restaurant and Pub
2446 N. Lincoln, 773/348-2695   **N**
The Red Lion is a classic English pub with good tavern fare (bangers and mash, fish and chips, shepherd's pie, Cornish pasty, seafood chowder, and more), a better beer selection, and just the right atmosphere to make it the perfect place to be stranded during a snowstorm. (That's my winter-weathered Chicago imagination in action.) Dinner $5-$10. Look for the occasional Monday night poetry.

Does **The Red Lion** sound like a place you can go back to again and again? According to Ursula Bielski's *Chicago Haunts: Ghostlore of the Windy City* (Lake Claremont Press), it is one of numerous Chicago eating and drinking establishments that may be haunted by more than enthusiastic patrons. Other nightspots rumored to have supernatural guests include **St. Andrew's Inn** (5938 N. Broadway, 773/784-5540), **Excalibur** (632 N. Dearborn, 312/266-1944), **Hange-Uppe's** (14 W. Elm, 312/337-0561), and **Thurston's** (1248 W. George, 773/472-6900).

Rose & Crown Ltd. London Pub
420 W. Belmont, 773/248-6654   **N**
Stumble into **Rose & Crown** from Belmont or the lakefront path on one of Chicago's many cold, dreary days between October and April and things will cheer up immediately. Inclement weather only helps sets the stage for this authentic English pub. After settling in with a pint of beer from the British Isles, turn to the menu for delicious renditions of England's finest: fish and chips (much extolled), pies, pasties, bangers, burgers. A carved roasted meat (roast beef, turkey, pork, lamb, ham—it's different every week) crowns the traditional spread served on Sundays. Entrees $5-$13.75, most $6-$7. Sunday carvery dinner, $8.50.

Ethiopian   See also: **African**.

Complement your meal with a glass of *tej*, the Ethiopian honey wine.

Addis Abeba
3521 N. Clark, 773/929-9383   **N**
Silverware is prohibited here, as the *injera* (sour, pancake-like bread) is the traditional utensil for scooping up morsels of Ethiopian dishes. Food is served family-style on a *mesob* (woven basket/platter) lined with a large piece of *injera*, so choose widely. For newcomers and those who like a variety, the vegetarian, meat, and fish combos are suggested. Entrees $4.50-$9.75.

Ethiopian Village
3462 N. Clark, 773/929-8300   **N**
Recent redecorating gave a stunning facelift (red walls, black and tan African tablecloths, and glass tabletops) to this Ethiopian standby. Its daily $6.95 all-you-can-eat, mostly vegetarian buffet (late afternoon-10pm) provides the perfect opportunity for extensive sampling and appreciation of the unique Ethiopian spicing (a combination of sweet flavors like cinnamon, nutmeg, cloves, and cardamom, and hot seasonings like cayenne, jalapeño, garlic, and paprika.) Non-buffet entrees $5-$12, most under $7.

Mama Desta's Red Sea Restaurant
3218 N. Clark, 773/935-7561   **N**
Candles, white tablecloths, absent silverware, and shared dishes turn this basic storefront into an intimate dining environment. Spice lovers should look for menu items labeled *wot*, a word designating a typical pungent sauce. *Yemiser wot* is a red lentil favorite; *Doro wot* is a piquant chicken meal. Entrees $6-$8.50.

Far from this unlikely strip of Ethiopian restaurants (all are just down the trendy block from Wrigley Field), **Ethiopian Diamond** (6120 N. Broadway, 773/338-6100) offers these same pungent treats in a neighborhood that's home to many African immigrants.

Ethnic Hybrids

Only in America are you likely to find such a diverse array of unexpected ethnic pairings.

Julie Mai's Le Bistro

5025 N. Clark, 773/784-6000 **FN**

Amidst the remaining decor from an Italian restaurant, Julie Mai serves up a delicious blend of Vietnamese, French, and fusion dishes. Begin with French onion soup, papaya salad with shrimp, or seafood pâté. Follow with an entree like filet mignon, escargot, salmon, lemon chicken, or mushu vegetables. Atmospheric touches include the cozy booths (separated by walls!), dim lighting, and a fish pond in the banquet room. Entrees $7.95-$12.95.

Markelo's Bakery

3520 W. Lawrence, 773/539-9344 **FN**

Sporting Korean, Greek, and various Central American flags in honor of the neighbors, this primarily Greek and Guatemalan bakery loads customers with baked goods, while relieving their pockets of only a few bucks. Sesame-seed bread sticks, loaves of whole wheat, baguettes, cookies, muffins, pastries, spinach and cheese pies, tamales, and cheese or pork-filled *chiles rellenos* all have their place.

Privata Cafe

1957 W. Chicago, 312/850-4720 **W**

The first thing you'll notice upon being seated at **Privata**, besides the funky music, fantasy induced paintings, and an assortment of objects that look like they were taken from the lost and found drawer at a Tijuana dance club, is the addictive black olive salsa with crispy, nearly greaseless chips ready for scooping. They're only the beginning of an odd, yet delicious menu described as "Italian with a touch of Mexico." Most appetizers hover in the $5 dollar range and are considered a bargain by most. The Mexicali Raviolis, Carciopino Quesadillas, and Smoked Jalapeño Hummus are among the favorites. Choose your own pasta for dishes like Paella Sicilliana, Tequilla Crème with Garlic Steak, and Spanish Pesto, which are all under $10 (most are $7). Add homemade sausage, grilled chicken, and steak for $2. The burritos, especially the grilled octopus, are excellent, and of the size that guarantee leftovers. BYOB, but if you forget there's a liquor store conveniently located on the corner. Open for lunch (11am-3pm), and dinner (6pm-10:30pm). Closed on Sundays. The restaurant may be relocating to a site across the street from its present location. (BZ)

How about lunch from **Big Red Rice & Noodle** (3720 W. Milwaukee, 773/588-5129), the take-out joint where neighborhood Poles enjoy hamburgers, hot dogs, fries, and oh, yes... the classic dishes of Thailand. If that menu is too restrictive for your palette, there's always **Steve's Restaurant** (1859 N. Elston, 773/276-1354)—the inexpensive diner where home-cooked Polish entrees, like pierogis and stuffed cabbage, compete with Italian beefs, gyros, tacos, and American fast food standards for the customer's appetite. (Psst. Seniors get a 10% discount.) You probably won't be hungry again until 11pm, but where will you satisfy that craving for stuffed grape leaves, a beef burrito, and an Italian liqueur? The **Beirut Restaurant** (4714 N. Kedzie, 773/509-1800) in Albany Park is one easy solution. If it happens to be the weekend, stay awhile and enjoy the live Mexican or Middle Eastern band. However, if you want something a step up from these ultra-casual places, you can still beat the 2am closing of **The Mecca Restaurant** (6666 N. Northwest Highway, 773/775-1077). A destination for Middle Eastern foodies? Nope—these pilgrims come for Italian, American, and Croatian specialties.

Filipino

Pampanga's Cuisine (6407 N. Caldwell, 773/763-1781), near the city's edge, provides a friendly and tasty introduction to the Spanish-influenced Asian cooking of the Philippines. Suckling charcoal-roasted pig, cured barbecue pork, *longanisa* (spicy sausage), *lumpianitas* (spring rolls), and *pancit* (thick or thin rice noodles) will content the majority of newcomers. Most entrees are under $7. To sample a wider variety of Philippine dishes, head to **Little Quiapo's** (4423 N. Clark, 773/271-5441) weekend buffets. The lunch buffet from 11am to 3pm costs $5.99; the dinner seafood buffet from 5pm to 9pm runs $7.99.

Fish Fry

You've worked hard all week and now you're going to eat as much fried food as your arteries will allow. Put one of the Friday night fish fries at these neighborhood taverns at the top of your feasting list. Ahhh...all you can eat battered and fried fish, french fries, coleslaw, bread, and butter. Beer costs extra.

Lawry's Tavern (1028 W. Diversey, 773/348-9711) offers sole from 6:30pm-10pm for $6.25; **Nantucket Fish House** (2977 N. Elston, 773/583-0456) serves pollack, cod, and ocean perch from 6pm-10pm for $6.95; and **Oinkers** (3471 N. Elston, 773/463-4222) does cod until 10pm for $4.95.

French

In a major metropolis like Chicago, it takes beaucoup francs to experience the *crème de la crème* of the town's French cooking. These bistros and cafes, however, make charming and affordable alternatives.

Cafe Zinc/Bistrot Zinc
3443 N. Southport, 773/281-3443   N
This new Southport hotspot offers the best of French dining with a self-service cafe up front and a restaurant in back. The namesake vintage zinc bar leads from one area to another. Wicker chairs and marble top cafe tables create an authentic Parisian setting for enjoying the informal favorites like crêpes, pâtés, quiche, croques monsieur, salads, soups, and desserts from the deli counter. Everything is under $10 and most items range from $4-$7.50. While bistro meals are costlier ($10-$16), they're still reasonably priced for big city French. Potato salad with salmon and a juniper berry vinaigrette and leek tart with brie are choice appetizers. Dinners range from roast duck with lentils and *poulet grand-mère* (grandmother's chicken) to braised rabbit with spätzle and sautéed skate.

La Crêperie
2845 N. Clark, 773/528-9050   N
This small, dark restaurant is in its 26th year of catering to Chicago's Francophiles via its *Crêpes Bretonnes*—buckwheat crêpes with fillings like *coq au vin*, broccoli & cheese, ratatouille, and seafood in cream sauce. With its candlelit outdoor garden tables (May-Sept.); the occasional live accordion music; dessert crêpes dripping with fresh fruit, chocolate, nutella, crème caramel, and liqueurs; and some of the city's best prices for French wine, **La Crêperie** offers continental romance on a budget. Crêpes, $3.25-$9. Complete $14 dinner comes with soup or salad, one dinner crêpe, and one dessert crepe. All-you-can-eat jambalaya for $6.95 on Tuesdays. Closed Mondays.

Le Loup Cafe
3348 N. Sheffield, 773/248-1830   N
Le Loup (wolf) mysteriously employs a lupine theme to showcase its French Mediterranean fare. Entrees like Duck Madagascar, Shrimp St. Tropez, oysters, and cassoulet are even more enjoyable within the confines of the lovely garden. Entrees $8.95-$12.95. The BYOB policy helps keep this some of Chicago's best, affordable French dining.

Red Rooster Cafe and Wine Bar
2100 N. Halsted, 773/929-7660 (Entrance on Dickens)   N
Rustic and romantic, this cozy, wood-walled restaurant tucked on a Lincoln Park side street woos diners with such dishes as duck à la orange, filet mignon, mustard chicken, and grilled salmon in cabernet sauce. Entrees $7.95-$13.

French Fries

Demon Dogs
944 W. Fullerton, 773/281-2001   N
A buck twenty-five will buy you a glorious bulging brown sack of crispy, salty, greasy fries with the skins still on at this memorable hot dog stand. Owned by Peter Schivarelli, 43rd ward sanitation superintendant and manager of the band *Chicago*, this little shop, tucked under the Fullerton El and sharing the blue demon mascot of nearby DePaul, declares that its food is a "hard habit to break." Can you name that 80s tune? The walls are covered with *Chicago* mementos, including a gold record. Everything on the menu is under $3.

Game

While game is often found at pricier restaurants, these casual tavern settings are known for their unusual meats. **Grizzly's Lodge** (3831 N. Lincoln, 773/281-5112) recreates a North Woods hideaway and boasts buffalo, venison, elk, and wild boar on its menu ($6-$27). The **Lincoln Tavern & Restaurant** (1858 W. Wabansia, 773/342-7778)—also with a lodge-like interior—has a Friday night roast duck special ($9.75). One Saturday every August, they hold an all-you-can-eat-and-drink wild game buffet ($25). Past buffets have included elk ribs, wild turkey, venison, pheasant, and chukar. **El Conejo** (2230 N. Western, 773/486-6558) dishes out typical Mexican fare, plus a slate of rabbit specialties (grilled, fried, or with various sauces). Most are priced near $8.

German

Berghoff Cafe/Berghoff Restaurant
17 W. Adams, 312/427-3170   C
Serving German and American food and their own beers since 1898, this bastion of tradition was the first tavern in Chicago to receive a post-

Prohibition liquor license. Only recently did they begin hiring women for their uniformed waitstaff. Although every penny you spend in the restaurant on sauerbraten, schnitzels, and creamed spinach will be worth it, the more affordable route is the cafe's sandwich line and grill. This is not a modern day concession, but an important element of the **Berghoff** tradition. The dark wood room is adorned with intricate carvings, stained glass, murals, mirrors, and a long, antique bar complete with brass rail where diners stand to eat. Cafe classics include the hot corned beef, roast beef, fried halibut, and bratwurst sandwiches on homemade rye ($3-$5). Enjoy with **Berghoff**'s own beers, bourbons, or root beer on the side.

Chicago Brauhaus
4732 N. Lincoln, 773/784-4444   N
Large, atmospheric restaurant, beer hall, and night club in German Lincoln Square reverberates with live music (German, international, and American) for dancing (slow, fast, polka, ballroom) Wed.-Mon. from 7pm to 2am. Schnitzels (veal or pork tenderloins), Sauerbraten, Roast Goose, Leberkäse (thick fried pork/veal "bologna"), and Königsberger Klopse (meatballs with caper sauce) top the entree list ($8-$15). Sausage plates fall under $6. Popular with groups, older couples, and dancers. Two warnings: Service can be slow (go dance, in the meantime), and the stage isn't visible from most tables in the tiny non-smoking section. Lunch $4.50-$8.95, most under $6. Closed Tuesdays.

Meyer's Delicatessen
4750 N. Lincoln, 773/561-3377   N
Tucked in the last stronghold of German Lincoln Avenue (a couple doors from the **Brauhaus**), **Meyer's** sells a wide array of homemade sausages and breads, along with imported chocolates, mustards, cheeses, German specialty products, beer, and more. Stop in the picturesque **Merz Apothecary** (4716 N. Lincoln, 773/989-0900), which has been down the block for over a century, for homeopathic remedies, fine soaps and bath products, imported shampoos and toothpastes, and Euro-style counter service.

Resi's Bierstube
2034 W. Irving Park, 773/472-1749   N
Beer garden, beer garden, beer garden. Large portions of exceptional homemade food, a friendly all-ages crowd, over 130 imported beers, reasonable prices, and the charming, aforementioned beer garden have brought **Resi's** a high percentage of regulars over the last few decades.

Many groups seem to congregate here, from Germans, Poles, Romanians, Latvians, Greek, Irish, and Mexicans to boaters, skiers, rugby players, cops, contractors, bankers, and pub crawlers. You won't find a lineup of depressing barflies on these barstools: the multi-generational regulars are more likely be discussing politics, history, sports, travel, or sex than drowning their sorrows in good beer. After putting in three years of weekend waitressing here, I feel qualified to recommend the *jagerschnitzel* (pork schnitzel with a brown mushroom gravy), potato pancakes (weekdays only), h*ackepeter* (German steak tartare—weekends only), goulash soup (cold weather months), Kassler ribs (smoked pork chops), f*ricadelle* (well-done hamburger/meatloaf), Russian Eggs (needs too much explanation), *wurst* dinners (pick 2 from 7 kinds of sausage, plus potato salad and kraut), and homemade soups. Try a weiss beer (2 on tap, over 16 in bottles)—**Resi's** was the first tavern in the city to import this German specialty. Dinners ($8.50-$13.50) include a bowl of soup or a house salad and noodles or potatoes. Sandwiches, $4.25-$6.50; sides, $2.25.

Greek

This three-block commercial strip on Halsted is all that remains of Chicago's once, much larger Greektown. However, it has seen some recent cosmetic improvements (note the stately columns) and its many restaurants are as vibrant and crowded as ever. Here are two all-round deals for food, atmosphere, service, and price.

Greek Islands
200 S. Halsted, 312/782-9855   **C**
Greektown classic may draw the biggest crowds on Halsted, with its perpetual bustle, Greek village atmosphere, and great food. Braised lamb in various forms, seafood (sea bass, red snapper, octopus, calamari, cod...), mousaka, pastichio, and most other meals keep customers returning. Entrees, including the 5-7 daily specials, $6-$15, most under $8.

Parthenon
314 S. Halsted, 312/726-2407   **C**
The oldest restaurant in Greektown (1968) claims to have both created flaming saganaki (a melted cheese appetizer delivered with cries of, "Opaa!") and to have introduced gyros to Chicago. Its polished, contemporary dining room is the site of hearty eating, ouzo swilling, spirited gatherings, and intimate meetings. Of the dozens of entrees, narrow your selection to the lamb (roasted, barbecued, braised, chops...)

and seafood (red snapper, codfish, shrimp or scallops flambé...) dishes. Grazing from the appetizer list makes a fine meal, too. Appetizers $3-$8. Entrees $5-$15, most under $10. Ouzo by the 6 oz. carafe $7-$8.

Guatemalan

El Tinajon
2054 W. Roscoe, 773/525-8455   **N**
Decorated with *tinajones*—handleless clay pots—and colorful Guatemalan textiles, **El Tinajon** radiates a warm and friendly atmosphere for enjoying Guatemalan versions of familiar foods like tamales, tacos, and tostadas, along with the restaurant's more distinctive dishes made with chicken, seafood, and black beans. Try *paches de papa* (potato tamales) or *shepes* (corn tamales filled with black beans) for twists on this humble appetizer. *Jocon Cobanero*, a chicken breast simmered in the house green sauce, or *revolcado*, a pork stew embellished with heart, tongue, ear, and liver pieces, are but two typical options for the main course. Entrees $6-$13, most under $8.

Honduran   See also: **Caribbean**.

Salon Garcia
3054 W. Armitage, 773/278-3702   **NW**
This small family restaurant presents the cooking of Honduras, a cuisine which displays elements typical of other Central American countries, as well as the Caribbean. Come on Sundays for the *sopa de caracol*, a snail stew that made them famous. Other daily specials include roasted chicken with beans and fried plantains, roasted pig, and *sopa de mondongo*, (a better way of saying intestines soup). Dinner runs $8-$12. Closed Mondays.

Hot Dogs

For newcomers, visitors, and any residents who need reminding, a Chicago-style hot dog arrives with yellow mustard, relish, raw onions, tomatoes (no ketchup), and celery salt on a poppyseed bun. Grilled onions, a pickle spear, and hot peppers are acceptable additions.

Not just hot dogs, but a dining experience...

Comiskey Park

333 W. 35th, 312/674-1000   **S**

At weekend evening games, the smell of fried onions wafting from the Kosher hot dog carts is enough to make any hot dog lover woozy with desire. The stands are only operable on weekends, however, and are located at various places on the main concourse.

Janson's Drive-in

9900 S. Western, 773/238-3612   **SW**

This low-priced drive-in has been selling hot dog favorites and carrying on the mysterious tradition of taking orders on brown paper bags since 1960. Red hots, spicy dogs, cheese dogs, chili dogs, and chili cheese dogs run under $2. Most of the items on the decently sized menu are under $4. Among their shakes, floats, sundaes, and other ice cream offerings, the fresh strawberry and fresh banana shakes are exceptionally worthy.

Superdawg

6363 N. Milwaukee, 773/763-0660   **FN**

Mr. Hot Dog with his caveman leopard skin, goofy bravado, and red blinking-light eyes poses with a coy Ms. Hot Dog, in her matching dress and bow, atop this landmark (1948) hot dog stand. The pure beef Superdawg ($3.25) comes dressed with all the trimmings (mustard, NO ketchup, piccalilli, a kosher dill, chopped onions, green tomatoes, and the optional hot peppers) on a poppyseed bun, accompanied by the highly touted crinkle cut fries. Burgers, chicken, fish, and Polishes also come Super-style. Call your order over the intercom at your parking spot and a car hop will deliver the goods (and pick up the trash later) for in-car dining. Complete the meal with a malt, shake, or Black Kow ($1.95-$2.25).

Just a hot dog, but an experience in itself:

Weiner Circle

2622 N. Clark, 773/477-7444   **N**

The winner for many is the charbroiled pup ($2.25) at this compact hot dog stand. It's split and darkened on the grill, then dressed appropriately for Windy City palettes. Enhance your meal by visiting after hours with other char-dog diehards. Open until 4am.

Hungarian

Paprikash Hungarian Restaurant
5210 W. Diversey, 773/736-4949   **NW**
Chicago's only Hungarian eatery, this large, friendly bar/restaurant would
shine even if it did have competitors. The Hungarian Farmer's Plate
($5.95) appetizer offers tastes of homeland sausages, salamis, and cheeses;
vegetarians can try the *lecso* (mixed steamed vegetables). Succulent entrees
($7-$13) like chicken paprikash, veal paprikash, beef goulash, and broiled
pork chops will keep you smiling from start to finish. *Somloi* (yellow
sponge cake with mixed fruit, custard, chocolate sauce, and whipped
cream) or *parecsinpa* (crepes with strawberry, apricot, or sweet cheese
filling) for dessert are additional delights. This is a great place to
linger...pick out one of their 30 kinds of Hungarian wine to accompany
your meal and follow everything with some Hungarian schnapps or brandy.

Ice Cream

You can never know about too man ice cream parlors, now, can you?

Betty's Ice Cream
5840 S. Kedzie, no phone   **SW**
Friendly owners and delicious ice cream distinguish this carry-out stand:
"good ice cream for good people," the sign advertises. Place your order
through the window, from the sidewalk. An ice cream cone dipped in
butterscotch is a particular favorite.

Gertie's Ice Cream
5858 S. Kedzie, 773/737-7634   **SW**
3685 S. Archer, 773/927-7807   **SW**
Now part of the **Gertie's Ice Cream** and **Lindy's Chili** chain, this
old-time ice cream parlor is notable not only for the great homemade ice
cream but the over-sized stuffed animals peering through the store-front
windows. Phosphates, sodas, shakes, sundaes, splits, and other creations of
homemade ice cream, yogurt, and whipped cream run $1-$4.

Margie's Candies
1960 N. Western, 773/384-1035   **N**
Everything in this old-fashioned ice cream parlor and candy shop (around
since 1921) throws you back to an earlier era of ice cream eating: the

uniforms, service, dishes, and decor. Ice cream creations start at $2.95 (most individual servings come in under $4) and run up to $35 for a group monstrosity. Also for sale are the hand-dipped candies, balloons, flowers, and stuffed animals.

The Original Rainbow Cone
9233 S. Western 773/238-7075   **SW**
(Closed from December 23rd to February 1st.)
In the summer, the line at this southwest-side institution can stretch out the door and around the corner. Family-owned since 1926, the store's namesake cone is a pile of chocolate, strawberry, Palmer House (New York vanilla with cherries and walnuts), pistachio, and orange sherbet. A small cone costs $1.38; a large one, $2.07. Other delights include sundaes ($2.30 to $3.67) , shakes ($2.30 to $3), and banana splits ($3.67). **Rainbow Cone** also has a stand in Union Station's underground food court and is a popular booth at the yearly **Taste of Chicago** (p.263).

Zephyr Ice Cream Restaurant
1777 W. Wilson, 773/728-6070   **N**
Much of the reputation of this ice cream asylum is due to its Art Deco decor and theme menu. Individual ice cream concoctions run $2.50-$4.50. Try the famous French fried ice cream for $2.50 or share the 10 scoop "War of the Worlds" sundae for $7.50.

Indian/Pakistani

The best spot for Indian dining is Devon Avenue (from about 2200-2700 West), the lifeline of Chicago's Indian/Pakistani community. Top off your lunch or dinner here with a stroll and a browse. (See pp.283-284).

Two time-tested, all-round good deals:

Gandhi Indian
2601 W. Devon, 773/761-8714   **FN**
Various vegetarian, chicken, and lamb dishes round out the tandoori specialties from the clay oven ($4.50-$8.75) and biryani rice specialties ($4.25-$7.45). All-inclusive sampler dinners run $7.45-$9.95.

Udupi Palace
2543 W. Devon, 773/338-2152   **FN**
Though the decor targets the commoners, the completely vegetarian food is

fit for royalty. South Indian favorites include *dosai* (filled with potato and onions) and *udhapam* ("Indian-style pizza" with various toppings). Entrees, $3.75-$15, most under $8; lunch specials, $7.95. Crowded on the weekends.

This strip abounds with lunch and dinner buffets ($4.95-$8.95) of various stripes which make a tasty introduction to Indian and Pakistani cuisine. For starters, try **Indian Garden** (2546 W. Devon, 773/274-4175) and **Sher-a-Punjab** (2510 W. Devon, 773/973-4000).

Want to stick with no-frills and super-cheap? The **Al-Hamra Grill** (6351 N. Western, 773/262-8000) and **Hyderabad House** (2500 W. Devon, 773/764-5880) fit any budget with their $4-$6 entrees. **Hema's Kitchen** (6406 N. Oakley, 773/338-1627) charges $5.50 or less for every dinner. Don't miss Hema's one-person business where the menu educates and everything is fresh, homemade, and made-to-order. Hema recommends the chicken masala—boneless chicken in a rich gravy—for meat-eaters and the spinach & cheese, eggplant & potato, or lentil dishes for vegetarians.

When it's time to go classy (white tablecloths and the like), head to **India House** (2548 W. Devon, 773/338-2929), **Tiffin** (2536 W. Devon, 773/338-2143), or **Viceroy of India** (2516 W. Devon, 773/743-4100), where the prices are higher but still inexpensive.

Besides serving tasty, inexpensive cuisine, the centrally located **Zaiqa** (858 N. Orleans, 312/280-6807) offers other unique features for its customers. Muslims will appreciate their Halal meat and five daily prayer sessions in the basement. Everyone will enjoy the charming outdoor dining, game room (with pool tables and video games), giant parking lot, and enormous TV.

Indonesian

August Moon
225 W. 26th, 312/842-2951   **S**
Located just off Chinatown's main artery is Chicago's sole Indonesian restaurant, ready to wow you with its distinct flavors. *Samba goreng udang* (shrimp with a light, spicy gravy), *redang padang* (hot and spicy marinated beef), and *tumis buncis ayam* (stir-fried crunchy string beans and chicken) come highly recommended. Plenty of vegetarian choices, too. Appetizers, $2-$6; entrees, $8-$15.

On Friday nights beginning at 6pm, the **Logan Beach Cafe** (2537 N. Kedzie, 773/862-4277), a neighborhood coffee house known for its breakfast burritos and other weekend brunch items, serves a 7-course Indonesian extravaganza ($10.75). The changing menu may include turmeric-clove rice, tempeh, fritters (peanut or three-potato), spring rolls, noodles, satay or curry sauce over vegetables, sweet and sour fruit, greens with coconut milk, and *krupuk* chips (seafood or veggie) with *sambal* paste. Vegetarian and non-vegetarian versions available.

Irish

Abbey Pub and Restaurant
3420 W. Grace, 773/478-4408   **NW**
Multi-faceted Irish nightclub caters to many needs. They offer decent Irish and pub fare (entrees $5-$11, most under $9), live music (Irish, folk, rock, other), dancing, Irish sports TV, and neighborhood bar amenities (darts, pool, beer specials).

Kitty O'Shea's
720 S. Michigan, 312/922-4400   **C**
Named for a Dublin pub, this hotel (Chicago Hilton & Towers) bar even imports some of its staff from the old sod. Irish chow and American pub food line the menu. After a meal of shepherd's pie, fish & chips, lamb stew, or corned beef and cabbage, enjoy some bread pudding for dessert, another Guinness or Harp, and the live Irish music. Entrees $7-$10. Live music daily from 9pm to 1am.

Follow up late weekend nights at the bars with a hearty Irish breakfast in the pubs first thing Saturday or Sunday Morning. The classic Irish breakfast is a food spree bound to soak up last night's hangover: eggs, bangers (sausage), black and white puddings (sausage-like), rashers (bacon), potatoes, and soda bread. The **Abbey Pub** (see above) offers this feast 9am-1pm for $5.75, **Bransfields** (4600 N. Lincoln, 773/907-0740) 10am-2pm for $6.25, and the **Hidden Shamrock** (2723 N. Halsted, 773/883-0304) 11am-2pm for $7.50. All places, Saturday and Sunday only.

Israeli

Hashalom Restaurant
2905 W. Devon, 773/465-5675   **FN**
Delectable Israeli and Moroccan eating in a colorful, though sparse, setting. Numerous, estimable appetizers and salads for sampling $1.75-$7.50, most under $4. Entrees $5.75-$10, most under $7. Regulars rave over the eggplant dishes, couscous, beef patties, and a Cornish hen extravaganza bedecked with dried fruits and almonds. Closed Sat.-Sun.

Italian

⇒ **TAYLOR STREET—CHICAGO'S "LITTLE ITALY"**

A pilgrimage to be made at least once each summer...

Mario's Italian Lemonade
1000 W. block of Taylor St.   **C**
This seasonal Taylor Street stand is a Chicago landmark for Italian lemonade. A dozen slushy flavors can be enjoyed in a range of sizes, from a small cup ($.60) to a small bucket ($4.50). The watermelon and traditional lemonade flavors are hits. Open May 1st-October.

To grab some good food fast on Taylor Street, stop in the **Pompeii Bakery** (see p. 181) for original pizza or **Al's Italian Beef** (p.156) for an Italian beef tradition.

The Rosebud
1500 W. Taylor, 312/942-1117   **C**
This Windy City classic—ideal for both romantic outings and lively group dinners—is the proud originator of Chicken Vesuvio. Though this famed invention is still a good bet, take heed of **The Rosebud**'s recent nomination as one of the top 15 pasta restaurants in the country. A single order of one of their signature homemade cavatelli (finger-like dumplings) dishes may be the tastiest pasta bargain in town. The $14.95 entree portion can literally feed 2-4. Add an antipasto salad, a side of Italian sausage, and tiramisu for dessert and you have an affordable feast.

⇒ **SOUTH OAKLEY: CHICAGO'S "HEART OF ITALY"**

Tucked away just east of Western Avenue is a 3-block strip of Italian restaurants dating back to when diminutive alderman Vito Marzullo ruled a large portion of Chicago's southwest side. The restaurants are small and cozy, like eating in the kitchen of someone's Italian grandmother. **Alfo's** (2512 S. Oakley, 773/523-6994) anchors this block and has some coveted private booths. **Bruna's Ristorante** 2424 S. Oakley, 773/254-5500) was opened in 1933, making it the oldest of the lot. Entrees range from $8 to $17, with most under $12. **Villa de Marco** (2358 S. Oakley, 773/847-3168), with a nice, but dated banquet feel, is a little cheaper in price. Don't leave the neighborhood without stopping at **Mila's Restaurant and Bakery** (2401 S. Oakley, 773/579-0800) for homemade pastry delights and cakes. **Mila's** also serves breakfast (eggs, pancakes, French toast), lunch, and dinner (potato pancakes, liver and onions, stuffed peppers, tripe stew, meatloaf, bratwurst). Nearly all entrees are under $5.

Pasta cheap-eats in other neighborhoods:

Pasta Palazzo
1966 N. Halsted, 773/248-1400   **N**
Cross a slick diner with bursts of color (mosaic included) and you have the lively setting for this affordable pasta lollapalooza. Try the Classico (shells with Italian sausage and red bell peppers) or Cavatappi Polo (corkscrews with grilled chicken, mushrooms, sun-dried tomato, and cream sauce) and you're bound to come back for more. Fresh soups, grilled calamari, and polenta appetizers make it harder to finish the main dish. Pasta maxes at $8.95, but most run $5.95-$7.95.

Trattoria Caterina
616 S. Dearborn, 312/939-7606   **C**
Printer's Row trattoria offers 18 fantastic pasta dishes along with a handful of chicken entrees and hot Italian sandwiches. Linguine with Mussels, Ziti Marinera, Angel Hair with Sun Dried Tomatoes, Fettucine Alfredo, or Lasagna Rolls: no entree is more than $9 and most run $5.25-$7. Closed Sundays.

The truly patient who want a neighborhood pasta and pizza powerhouse a step up from the cheap-eats can head to **Mia Francesca** (3311 N. Clark, 773/281-3310). The nightly crowds and hour-long waits (at times, an underestimate) testify to its worthiness.

Old-world baked goods...

D'Amato's Bakery (1124 W. Grand, 312/733-5456) not only bakes some of the greatest Italian breads, but also sells their unique pizza in baker's sheets (party size) for $27-$29. The city's oldest (est. 1908) and largest Italian pastry shop, **Ferrara's Original Bakery** (2210 W. Taylor, 312/666-2200) transports you to a previous era the minute your foot crosses the threshold.

Italian Beefs/Italian Sausages

"Beefs," as we say in these parts, are a Chicago original that have been around since the late 1940s. Thinly sliced beef (with all the fat trimmed) is piled into an Italian or French bread bun, topped with sweet green peppers or hot giardiniera, and given a ritual drenching in the cooking juices.

Al's #1 Italian Beef
1079 W. Taylor, 312/733-8896   C
Featured in Jane and Michael Stern's *Road Food*, in *Gourmet* magazine, on the *Today Show*, and on *Good Morning America*, **Al's** 60-year-old sandwich shop has caught the nation's attention as the apparent inventor and favored vendor of this Chicago culinary icon. Beefs run $3.35. Open until 1am. Closed Sundays.

Mr. Beef
666 N. Orleans, 312/337-8500   C
Another contender for Chicago's best, **Mr. Beef**'s has been serving beefs ($4) with their special giardiniera for 20 years.

Another uniquely Chicago snack, a spicy Italian sausage, parked in a crusty roll and blanketed with soft green peppers, shouldn't be missed by those seeking out regional delicacies.

Benedict's Delicatezzi Italiano
2501 S. Archer, 312/225-1122   SW
An eye-catching little place perched on a corner near Archer and Halsted, **Benedict's** serves an outstanding Italian sausage sandwich smothered in cheese, red sauce, and peppers and an equally yummy Italian sub sandwich loaded with capicola, salami, mortadella and provolone cheeses, and **Benedict's** flavored olive oil. Sandwiches range from $3.25 to $3.75. **Benedict's** also serves homemade cannoli and Eli's Famous Cheesecake.

Go with a friend and get one of each...

Boston Bar-B-Q
2932 W. Chicago, 773/486-9536   **W**
Some of the best and biggest, since 1949. Beefs $3.25, Italian sausages $3.
Closed Sundays.

Freddie's
701 W. 31st, 312/808-0149   **S**
Scrumptious monster sandwiches: beefs $3.50, Italian sausages $3.25 (take
out) and $4.50/$4.25 (dine in, with fries).

Jamaican See also: **Caribbean**.

For home-cooked Jamaican carry-outs and fast food:

The **Caribbean American Baking Company** (1539 Howard, 773/761-
0700) prepares Jamaican baked goods, sweets, and beef patties daily.
Island Delites (1461 E. Hyde Park, 773/324-3100), a no-frills counter-
service restaurant, has ample seating to enjoy its various dinners, combo
plates, and traditional side dishes ($2-$11). **Taste of Jamaica**, part of
Nathan's Deli (1372 E. 53rd, 773/935-4373), makes authentic jerk and
curry dishes, escoveitch fish, and beef patties for admiring carryout
customers (dinners, $5-$12, most under $7).

For sit-down dining, you can probably escape **Back of the Yard** (3474 N.
Clark, 773/281-5224) and **Linette's Jamaican Kitchen** (7366 N. Clark,
773/761-4823) with a full stomach of Jamaican specialties for under $15.
Linette's is homier; **Back of the Yard**, funkier. Both deliver excellent
seafood, beef and vegetable patties, and jerk chicken and pork.

Japanese

Matsuya Restaurant
3469 N. Clark, 773/248-2677   **N**
Beloved and mobbed: This is Chicago's best all-things-considered
Japanese dining, from the grilled squid and soft-shell crab appetizers, to
the Osaka-style sushi and the teriyaki entrees. If you're not already going
with a sushi combination, pick up a piece of salmon, red snapper, or
mackerel on the side. Appetizers $2-$4.20, rice/noodle dishes $5-$6, main

dishes $6-$17, many under $10.

New Tokyo
3139 N. Broadway, 773/248-1193   **N**
Nohana
3136 N. Broadway, 773/528-1902   **N**
These across-the-street neighbors duel for local business with their
comparable $8.50 sushi deluxe dinner deals Mon.-Sat. Both satisfy with
their miso soup, sushi rolls, array of fresh fish (tuna, flounder, salmon, red
snapper, mackerel, octopus...), and tea.

Sai Cafe
2010 N. Sheffield, 773/472-8080   **N**
Paneling on the walls and sports on TV? If you're not hanging out in
someone's basement, you must be waiting in line at the convivial **Sai**'s in
Lincoln Park for some of this town's most enjoyable sushi. You may have
had tuna, shrimp, and yellowtail before (perhaps not this fresh), but what
about a salmon and cream cheese *bagel maki*? Sushi $1.50-$3.50 per piece.

Korean

Recommended lunches:

Bando
2200 W. Lawrence, 773/728-0100   **FN**
Premier Korean restaurant and nightspot with a Vegas feel makes a fun
backdrop for a satisfying noontime repast. $4.95-$5.25 lunch specials
include entree, soup, and rice.

Jim's Grill
1429 W. Irving Park, 773/525-4050   **N**
Korean-American breakfast and lunch shop caters predominantly to
vegetarians. Morning meals include teriyaki and shitaki mushroom
omelettes ($3.95/$3.25). Vegetarian lunch offerings (all $4.50-$4.95)
range from huge bowls of various noodle dishes to items like vegetable
pancakes and vegetable tempura. Meat dishes are priced $4.95-$8.95,
most falling under $6. Closed Sundays.

An unassuming dinner locale with memorable food:

Gin Go Gae
5433 N. Lincoln, 773/334-3895   **FN**
Ignore the unwelcoming exterior and head inside for consistently great
Korean dishes, paying attention to the char-broiled specialties. Waiting for
dinner gives you plenty of time to admire and ponder the table tops—
unexpected collages of old movie posters, vintage comic book pages, and
Cubs memorabilia. Entrees $6.25-$19.95, most under $12. New $4.95
lunch special. Closed Wednesdays.

For grilling Korean barbecue dishes at your own table, head further north
and west. **Jang Mo Lim** (6320 N. Lincoln, 773/509-0211), **Hai Woon Dae**
(6240 N. California, 773/764-8018), **Il Song Jung** (3315 W. Bryn Mawr,
773/463-2121), and **Korean BBQ** (3346 W. Bryn Mawr, 773/588-3112)
are all neighborhood places with table-top grills. Most entrees, $7-$14.

When the newfangled Korean coffeehouses, pool halls, karaoke bars, and
other hangouts close, this 24-hour spot still provides sustenance.

Korean Restaurant
2659 W. Lawrence, 773/878-2095   **N**
Corner storefront prepares tasty marinated and grilled meats, ribs, kim
chee, vegetarian pancakes, noodles galore, and a host of exotic soups that
should soothe any insomniac. Entrees $5-$14.50, most under $9.

Korean, Buddhist, *and* Vegetarian

Guaranteed to be the only such restaurant in the city...

Amitabul
3418 N. Southport, 773/472-4060   **N**
The owners of **Jim's Grill** (p.158) expanded on their customers'
vegetarian favorites and opened this serene and simply-decorated
restaurant—amidst Southport's flurry of trendy eateries and shops—to
promote the pure, healing cuisine of Korean Buddhists. Not only is the
menu 100% vegan (no meat, eggs, or dairy), but the kitchen uses no sugar,
salt, MSG, or chemicals whatsoever in its preparations. The ample menu
includes the expected rice and noodle dishes, plus ten kinds of vegetable
pancakes (in such flavors as soy vegetable, miso, black bean, and kim chee)
and fifteen kinds of vegetarian sushi rolls. The "light" food is compensated

with generous portions. Beverages include sake, plum wine, and herbal teas. Entrees $5.99-$7.99.

Kosher

2700-3000 W. Devon Avenue   **FN**
West of the Indian/Pakistani strip and east of Lincolnwood, Devon Avenue holds the city's largest concentration of Kosher delis, bakeries, grocers, and fish markets. It's an ideal three block stretch for wandering and snacking.

Not too far from this neighborhood, you'll find other businesses offering Kosher specialties. Just west on Devon a couple blocks is the only Kosher **Dunkin Donuts** (3132 W. Devon, 773/262-4560) in the city. **North Shore Baking** (2919 W. Touhy, 773/262-0600) creates dozens of Kosher baked goods, like their beloved seven-grain bread and potato knishes. Salami, bologna, Romanian pastrami, tongue, and liver sausage are among the customer favorites at the **Romanian Kosher Sausage** shop (7200 N. Clark, 773/761-4141). And finally, for an all-American pizza pie, there's **Tel Aviv Kosher Pizza** (6349 N. California, 773/764-3776).

Lakeside Dining

Cafe Brauer
2021 N. Stockton, 312/280-2724   **N**
Lincoln Park's "South Pond Refectory," built in 1908 and beautifully restored in 1989, has indoor tables or outdoor seating on the South Pond. (A quick peak upstairs will explain why many rent this floor out for weddings and other gala events.) Pizza, burgers (including meatless ones), hot dogs, sandwiches, and salads are the main menu items, with animal-shaped fries being the cafe's favorite order. Everything is under $5. Step next door for the **Cafe Brauer Ice Cream Parlor**.

Other dining escapes on Lincoln Park's 1,200 acres are the **Waveland Cafe** (in Lincoln Park at Waveland, 773/868-4132) and **Heartland on the Lake** (Greenleaf & the lake, 773/274-6114). The **Waveland Cafe** is off the **Sydney Marovitz Golf Course** (see p.92) and is a favorite for breakfast after early morning games. Menu items include scones, muffins, bagels, sandwiches, salads, and snacks. Open 6am-8pm daily. Owned by the Rogers Park restaurant (see p.202), **Heartland on the Lake** is a healthy foods concession stand that serves hot dogs, chile, beans and rice, ice cream, smoothies, and more. All items are under $4.

Sesi's Seaside Cafe and Gallery
6219 N. Sheridan, 773/764-0544   **FN**
Hidden in Berger Park, tucked behind the enchanting North Lakeside
Cultural Center, and on the shores of Lake Michigan, lies this peaceful and
refreshing cafe with outdoor seating. Along with the standard coffee drinks
and desserts, the menu offers a range of sandwiches (including hot dogs),
appetizers, and entrees, many reflecting the owner's Middle Eastern
origins. The Mediterranean combo with hummus, dolma, eggplant salad,
and tabouleh and the kabob of seasoned ground beef patties are house
specialties. Entrees $7-$9, other items are under $5. Spending a gray,
winter afternoon at **Sesi's**—lingering over hot drinks and dessert and
looking out on the stormy lake—is as good as an entire weekend away.

Laotian

Nhu Hoa Cafe
1020 W. Argyle, 773/878-0618   **FN**
Pleasant and attractive eatery proffers 40+ Laotian dishes alongside four
times as many Vietnamese ones! Garlic Shrimp, Sweet & Sour Stuffed
Squid, and Tamarind Duck earn a place on the specials list. Menu items
$4.95-$18.95, most under $9. Closed Mondays.

Late-night Wonders

Bar Louie
226 W. Chicago, 312/337-3313   **C**
Dark, wood-laden, and casual neighborhood bar with a sophisticated
finish. The music, posters, mosaics, mural, wine, and martinis set a relaxed
stage for hearty portions of classy sandwiches, salads, pizza, and pasta.
The Luigi steak sandwich, vegetarian muffaletta with goat cheese, calamari
Caesar salad, chicken vesuvio melt, and sausage and provolone pizza come
recommended. Items $3.95-$7.95, most under $6. Open Sun.-Wed. until
1am, Thur. until 2am, and Sat.-Sun. until 3am.

The Hunt Club
1100 N. State, 312/988-7887   **C**
While **The Hunt Club** is of the sports and dance bar variety common to the
Rush and Division Street area, the affordable pizzas, sandwiches, and

salads from its late-night kitchen surpass most in the vicinity. Sandwiches cost $6.95 and include the Kentucky Derby (chicken breast with smoked mozzarella and red pepper mayo) and the Clubhouse Vegetable (grilled veggies on tomato focaccia). The Churchill (chicken with roasted red and yellow peppers) and The Palm Beach (shrimp, chipotle peppers, and roasted garlic) are thin-crust pizza variations ($10-$12) for one or two. The potato salad—on mixed greens, with goat cheese, and bacon—and the spinach salad—wilted by a warm dressing—are favorites among the meal-sized salads ($4.25-$5.25). Food served until 2am Sun.-Fri., until 3am Sat. Dancing Fri.-Sat.

Iggy's

700 N. Milwaukee, 312/829-4449 **C**

Swanky restaurant and bar with a nightclub feel "devoted to the pleasures of late-night dining." Grilled asparagus salad with almonds and Dijon dressing, artichoke heart fritters, crab and ricotta stuffed mushroom caps, jambalaya risotto, and scrambled eggs with cream cheese and scallions epitomize the menu offerings. The coffee (made with espresso and cinnamon) is peerless; the desserts (like Rustica—a richer tiramisu), phenomenal; and the 13 signature martinis ("The Cosmopolitan", "Blue Velvet"), alluring. The food is worth the bucks. Salads and appetizers $4.95-$7.95, egg dishes and entrees $6.95-$14.95 Opens at 7pm (8pm Sun.). Food served until last call: Sun.1:30am, Mon-Fri. 3:30am, Sat. 4:30am.

Los Dos Laredos

3120 W. 26th St., 773/376-3218 **W**

Head to the Mexican Little Village neighborhood for a diverting solution to your insomnia. The late-night **Los Dos Laredos** has been serving their authentic specialties for over thirty years. Fajitas, gorditas, burritos, tacos, and more accompanied by a jumbo 36-ounce margarita are sure to make you full and sleepy. Open 24 hours on the weekends and 8am-4pm Sun.-Thur.

Lucille's Tavern & Tapas

2470 N. Lincoln, 773/929-0660 **N**

A casual, sophisticated bar, specializing in wonderful tapas and fine cocktails, **Lucille's** serves food until 1am nightly. Peanut-crusted catfish with a hoisin and wasabi swirl, pancetta-wrapped shrimp with Chardonnay buerre blanc, and drunken chicken and Monterey jack quesadilla typify their various tapas plates ($3.75-$6.95) which are geared for sharing. Try the daily specials.

The Maxwell Street Depot
411 W. 31st, 312/326-3514   **S**
Known for its pork chop sandwiches and Polish sausage, this Bridgeport
eatery never closes...ever.
For more character, than class...

Stock Yards Truck Stop
4512 S. Halsted, 773/376-1784   **SW**
Truckers' complex with bar, showers, rooms, and store has a 24-hour diner
serving a range of dishes under $5.

White Palace Grill
1159 S. Canal, 312/939-7167   **C**
If it's steak and eggs, liver and onions, chili and the like you're hankering
for, this south of the Loop dive/grill has been serving up the basics for 24
hours a day since 1939. The adjacent bridge offers a marvelous view of
downtown. Most items under $4.

Lithuanian

Chicago boasts the nation's strongest Lithuanian community, most of
which was centered on the south and southwest sides, particularly in the
area bounded by 69th (Lithuania Plaza Court), 71st, Western, and
California. Although most of the original immigrants' descendants have
moved to the suburbs, several Lithuanian restaurants remain in the area.

Healthy Food
3236 S. Halsted, 773/326-2724   **SW**
The owners of this old-world diner claim it's the oldest Lithuanian
restaurant in the world (est. 1938); it's been in their family since 1960.
Their dedication to hearty, wholesome, homemade food is reflected on the
menu and in every delicious bite. Eat *blynai* (Lithuanian pancakes) for
breakfast, lunch, dinner, or dessert, enjoying (in season) fresh (sometimes
even hand-picked) blueberries, strawberries, or gooseberries on top.
Breakfast picks include oat bran and buckwheat pancakes and the vegetable
omelette ($1.50-$7.50, most $3.50-$5). For dinner, the popular 1/2 roast
duck with the trimmings (kraut, applesauce, potatoes, salad...) is the most
expensive thing on the menu at $8.95. Lithuanian sausage, *koldunai* (meat
dumplings), *kugelis* (potato pudding), the meatless garden burger, and fish

also please at supper time.

Seklycia

2711 W. 71st, 773/476-2655 **FSW**

A small, unpretentious neighborhood restaurant, Seklycia was originally opened to earn money for the immigrant human services programs that are held on the second floor. While the clientele is still primarily Lithuanian, you will also find other locals enjoying the homemade food ranging from Lithuanian specialties such as kugelis, blintzes, and dumplings to American standards, such as grilled and broiled fish, chicken, and meatloaf. The soups are outstanding. Entrees in the $6 range.

Lunch

Cafe Penelope

230 S. Ashland, 312/243-3600 **W**

Incongruent pink and quaint cafe in the land of union halls (and just three blocks from the United Center) offers hearty and healthy hot and cold sandwiches, soups, salads, and pizza. Brown bag lunches come with a sandwich (picks like roast beef, Greek feta, and curried eggplant), fresh fruit cup, and homemade cookie. Wonderful hot sandwiches with roasted potatoes include baked meatloaf, Maryland crabcake, and ham barbecue. Dine alfresco under the garden's grape vines. Soups and salads $1.75-$6.50, sandwiches $4.95-$7.95.

Cafe V

1801 S. Indiana, 312/326-9901 **C**

Hopefully, the opening of this small lunch place (with a larger patio for summer dining) signals better things ahead for this neglected neighborhood. Located in the National Vietnam Veteran's Art Museum and just a block from the Prairie Avenue Historic district, **Cafe V** is an appetizing beginning to an afternoon of cultural touring. Sandwiches, like the Triple Turkey Stacker or South Sider (roast beef with onions, peppers, mushrooms, and provolone), come with a side of ever-changing pasta salad and a bag of chips ($6-$7). Salads include a seafood combination and Big Roy's Garbage Salad ($3.25-$7.50). French Toast is the highlight of the weekend brunch. Open weekdays 7am-3pm, weekends 8:30am-2:30pm.

Carmen's Italian Foods

3629 W. 63rd, 773/581-4395 **SW**

This combination deli and grocery store where the staff calls customers "hon" and "dear" sells huge, freshly made sandwiches for take-out (most under $4.) It's also a good place to pick up necessities for a real Italian meal at home: pasta, tomatoes, cheeses, homemade sausages, olive oils, olives stuffed with anchovies, crusty bread, and biscotti. You can even buy empty ricotta cheese storage containers (?!), bar glasses, salt and pepper shakers, pasta bowls, and other cooking supplies.

Deli To Go
4601 N. Elston, 773/202-9700   **NW**
Neighborhood favorite "where you get a mouth full," distinguishes itself with out-of-the-ordinary touches. Choose an "overstuffed" or "understuffed" deli sandwich to suit your appetite or pair a 1/2 sandwich with soup or a side salad. Turkey Teriyaki and Tex-Mex Beef spruce up the specialties list and honey-mustard pasta is a nice coleslaw alternative. Sarsaparilla, birch beer, ginger beer, Kayo, and flavored coffee concoctions accompany routine soda selections. Closed Sundays.

La Cocina Criolla
2418 W. Fullerton, 773/235-7377   **N**
$5-$7 buys authentic Puerto Rican cooking for lunch at this neighborhood bar, grill, and banquet center. Hot sandwiches come with salad and seasoned rice for $5.25. Other specials include the stewed chicken or pork and *jibaros*—green plantains stuffed with steak, tomatoes, and onions ($5.95).

La Milanese
3156 S. May, 773/254-9543   **SW**
Italian/Sicilian sandwich shop on a residential corner of Bridgeport is popular for its enormous sandwiches (Italian beefs and sausages, meat ball, pepper and egg, etc.), including the best breaded steak sandwich in town. Sandwiches cost $2.50-$7, most under $4. Open Mon.-Fri., 10am-4pm.

Leo's Lunchroom
1809 W. Division, 773/276-6509   **W**
The paneling, counter, and post card collection say "old," but the young art crowd and an updated sandwich menu say "new." Extended choice of breads and cheeses, fabulous chunky potato salad. Breakfast $2.75-$6, lunch $2.50-$5.25, most under $4.

Manzo's
3210 W. Irving, 773/478-3070   **NW**
Long a neighborhood favorite for thick pizza, **Manzo's** has expanded into
the lunch trade with a kingly weekday buffet. For $5.95, choose from
cheese and sausage pizza, soup, chicken, BBQ ribs, rice, potatoes, salad,
fruit, garlic bread, and more. Tues.-Fri. 11am-4pm.

Nikki & Pete's Fabulous Deli
1520 N. Halsted, 312/943-6100   **C**
Sleek and spotless little breakfast and lunch deli sits inside an auto shop!
Adorned with models of classic cars, this eatery serves soups, salads,
muffins, and bagels, along with its specialty sandwiches: The '56 T-Bird
is a hot smoked ham and baby swiss ($4.75), the '59 Vette contains roasted
veggies, fresh mozzarella, and special sauce ($5.75), and the Lamborgini is
a marinated chicken breast piled with spinach, fresh basil, and shallots.
Closed Sundays.

Racine Cafe
228 S. Racine, 312/243-9296   **C**
Open since 1961, this sleepy, industry-lauded restaurant is a cafeteria for
the 90s. Postered walls, ample and varied seating, lots of neon, jukebox,
full-service bar, and dim lighting create an unusual hideaway for the
noontime meal. Breakfast $1.95-$5.95. Lunch/dinner $2.50-$5.25. $6.95
dinner buffet Mon.-Fri. (Sept.-Dec. only) may include chicken, pepper
steak, Salisbury steak, fish, pasta, stew, potatoes, salad, soup, garlic bread,
jello, and pudding. Closed Sundays.

Rancho Luna
3312 W. Foster, 773/509-9332   **NW**
Colorful, cool, and clean, the atmosphere at this small storefront soothes,
while the merengue music, wonderful food, and good lunch prices
rejuvenate. Choose from sandwiches like shredded beef, roast pork, and
BBQ chicken ($3.50-$6), fruit shakes ($3), side dishes like yucca, congri,
and tostones ($2-$2.75), and special lunch plates ($4.95—11am-3pm,
weekdays only). Dinner $8-$10.

Sun & Moon
1467 N. Milwaukee, 773/276-6525   **W**
This cheerful Wicker Park deli/cafe offers an ever-changing menu of
innovative and homemade sandwiches, salads, and desserts for dine-in or
carry-out. One of the nine sandwiches ($3.50-$6) available might be goat

cheese with red peppers and onion jam or the turkey burger tarragon. Spicy noodles with a sesame-citrus sauce and succotash with a creamy buttermilk dressing were recent salads. As salads are sold by the pound ($5.75-$8.50/lb.), order a 1/2 pound for an average serving. The array of fresh baked (or frozen) desserts ($1-$3) will beckon before, during, and after the meal. Wash it all down with a coffee drink, smoothie, natural soda, or homemade lemonade.

Urban Market Cafe
2580 N. Lincoln, 773/281-2233   **N**
Former fast food stand gone upscale sandwich and salad shop offers unusual twists on city faves: Chinatown chicken tacos combine stir-fried chicken breast and jalapeños in a flour tortilla ($3.99), the tuna's dressed in lemon pepper and cilantro ($5.29), and the cold turkey breast and havarti cheese sandwich comes brushed with smoky chili pepper mayo ($3.99). Homemade soups, fresh salads, and hot, cold, and sub sandwiches run $2.25-$5.29.

Yellow Wagon
Cottage Grove & 59th   **S**
Fair weather grill on the edge of Washington Park serves cheap charbroiled eats: Rib tips $3.75, steakburgers $3, Polishes $2.50, hot dogs $1.50, tamales $.85, and cans of pop $.60.

Lunch in Bars

There's probably no one that knows more about Chicago watering holes than Tony Gordon and Phil Brandt—the guys who put out Chicago's bi-weekly *Barfly*. Here are some of their recent picks for lunch in little-known neighborhood taverns:

Hiccups (5515 W. Belmont, 773/736-5354) puts a generous chop from the butcher next door between bread from the bakery down the block; tops it with grilled onions, barbecue sauce, and cheese; and serves it with a side of chips, earning Tony and Phil's designation as "the city's best pork chop sandwich." (Sat./Sun. only.) **Candlelite** (7452 N. Western, 773/761-8070), just shy of the city's border with Evanston, serves recommended thin-crust pizza, Italian beefs on garlic bread with mozzarella, and ribs. They also have soups, salads, and other sandwiches. The made-from-scratch cooking makes everything right at **Wrong's Tap** (10014 S. Western, 773/238-5534), where customers must make the painful decision whether to order specially-prepared beefs, Italian sausages, meatball sandwiches, and burgers or the daily special, which may be lasagna, ravioli, pork chops, pepper and egg sandwiches, or another home-cooked treat.

Lunch, Downtown

Over-priced hot spots and links of fast food chains abound in the central business district. Between the two stand many reasonable alternatives. Among the favorites below, you'll find a match for every business, pleasure, and sustenance purpose. Keep in mind that most of these places make their money servicing the weekday business crowd and are not open on the weekends.

332 Deli and Metro Espresso
332 S. Michigan, 312/427-4046   C
Start downstairs at the art-decorated deli for reputable deli sandwiches ($3.49-$4.79) like Kosher pastrami, vegetarian vegetable, white meat chicken salad, and chopped liver. Daily specials ($3.99-$4.99) come with chips or fries and a large soda. After lunch, climb back upstairs for exotic, roasted coffees, homemade desserts, and frozen yogurt. Closed Sundays.

Artist's Viewpoint Cafe
112 S. Michigan, 312/899-5100 (school switchboard)   C
On the top floor of the School of the Art Institute of Chicago, the bi-level campus cafeteria provides a stunning view of Grant Park, Lake Michigan, and the Art Institute's Sculpture Courtyard, as well as a glimpse into the future generation of artists. Sandwiches $2.85, entrees $3-$4. Cheap coffee and vegetarian friendly. If you don't quite fit the image of an art student, explain to the elevator operator where you're headed.

Billy Goat Tavern
430 N. Michigan, 312/222-1525   C
(A staircase will take you to its *below* Michigan Avenue location.)
Tavern with a greasy spoon menu (est. 1934) is legendary because: (a) Back in 1945 when the Wrigleys didn't allow tavern owner Billy Sianas into the World Series with his pet billy goat, he proclaimed that the Cubs were not going to win the pennant—ever (you know the rest of the story), (b) John Belushi memorialized the place with his *Saturday Night Live* "chizborger, chizborger" skits, and (c) It's long been a hangout for Chicago newspaper people, most notably, the late Mike Royko. If you remember that cheeseburgers are primary here and that they serve chips (no fries!), you'll

get along fine when ordering. Closed Sundays.

Boni Vino
111 W. Van Buren, 312/427-0231   **C**
Since 1967, downtown diners have been sitting down at this south Loop Italian restaurant for a relaxing and affordable lunch. Stick with the daily special, pasta, fish, sandwiches, or pizza and your meal will come in under $6. Closed weekends.

Cafe Oaxaca
178 N. Franklin, 312/553-1187   **C**
Fresh and authentic food—resonating with the gustatory pleasures indigenous to Oaxaca, Mexico—is delivered lunch time fast from this sandwich shop setting. The mole dishes are a house specialty. Tacos and tortas ($1.45-$3.75), soups and salads ($1.50-$5.75), complete dinners ($5.75-$7.75), sides ($1-$1.90).

European Sunny Cafe
304 S. Wells, 312/663-6020   **C**
European Sunny Cafe serves up hearty Eastern European lunches that will make you want to crawl to the beach for a nap rather than head back for a productive afternoon at the office. Goulash, stuffed cabbage, pierogi, sausages, and the like join daily Polish specials—some of the only such food in downtown Chicago. It's all yours for about $4 a plate. Outdoor seating in the summer. Closed weekends.

Fast Track
629 W. Lake, 312/993-9300   **C**
Fresh, high-quality fast food: hot dogs, polishes, corned beef, burgers, Italian beefs and sausages, salads, and ice cream shakes and sundaes. Located near the el tracks, **Fast Track** carries a train theme throughout, including a motorized miniature train and elevated track that circles the place. Dine at the outdoor picnic tables during warm weather. Sides $.89-$2.89, salads and sandwiches $1.65-$5.75. Closed Sundays.

HeartWise Express
10 S. LaSalle, 312/419-1329   **C**
The **HeartWise** dietitians do the counting (and reducing) of calories, fat, cholesterol, sodium, and fiber for you (all listed on the menu), so that you can order as freely as you dream about at standard fast food joints. Veggie burgers ($3.75), vegetarian sloppy joes ($3.95), and an Asian Noodle Bowl

with chicken or tofu ($5.25) lead the favorites list. Other interesting and tasty choices include the baked potato topped with black bean chili and low-fat cheddar ($2.89), the Bombay curry wrap ($5.79), and roasted sweet potato wedges ($1.49). Leave room for decadent cinnamon rolls with one gram of fat ($1.69) and low-fat brownies ($1.39). Open weekdays 6:30am-6pm.

King Tut's Oasis
21 N. Wabash, 312/558-1058   **C**
Enter the Wabash Jewelry Mall and pass case after case of gold and gems until you reach this oasis of Egyptian and Middle Eastern food tucked in the back corner. Sandwiches $2.75-$3.50, combination plates $3.60-$6.25. Closed Sundays.

Little Louie's
24 E. Congress, 312/939-3181   **C**
Clean, reliable, and pink sandwich shop offers no frills, just really great prices. Nearly everything—from sausages, beefs, and burgers to Mexican dishes—is priced between $1 and $4.

Mac Kelly's Greens and Things
21 E. Adams, 312/431-1373   **C**
77 E. Madison, 312/346-8072   **C**
180 N. Wells, 312/899-9022   **C**
225 N. Michigan, 312/540-0071   **C**
Build a lunch piece by piece at this do-it-yourself headquarters. Choose from coolers packed with waters, juices, sodas, and fruit; racks lined with bagels, muffins, cookies, and doughnuts; an 80-item salad bar ($4.29/lb.); soup and chili; sandwich and pasta bar; and hot daily specials ($3.99-$4.99). Carry out only. Closed weekends.

Marciello's Down and Under Pizzeria
308 W. Erie, 312/787-6691   **C**
This bright and airy pizzeria and deli (down a staircase and under a nightclub) offers several types of pizza including the award-winning thin crust, Pizza Viva (old-country-style with no cheese and lots of vegetables), and gourmet (decorated with fresh garlic, imported cheeses, pine nuts, artichoke hearts, etc.), along with homemade pastas, salads, and Italian specialty sandwiches. Decent beer and wine-by-the-glass selection. Whole pizzas $10.25-$15.50, 35-item salad bar $3.98/lb., sandwiches $3-$4.55.

Pattie's Heart Healthy
700 N. Michigan, 312/751-7777   C

Heart healthy haven serves low-fat and low-cholesterol entrees, burgers, pizzas, sandwiches, and salads ($4-$6). Try delectable dishes like Grilled Salmon Pattie with lemon-dill sauce, Chicken and Pesto Pasta Salad, Vegetarian Lasagna, and Southwestern Bean Salad. Closed Sundays.

Ronny's Steak House
340 S. Wabash, 312/939-6010   C
16 W. Randolph, 312/346-9488   C

Whether it's fast food or a full meal you need, Ronny's has what you're in the mood for, be it steak, ribs, chicken, pizza, sandwiches, or any of the other dozens of items on the menu!

September's
649 S. Clark, 312/427-7007   C

Dark, unpretentious south-Loop tavern dishes out burgers, charbroiled sandwiches, salads, and authentic Philly cheese steak sandwiches from 11am-Midnight daily. 1/2 slab of ribs is $6; a full slab, $10. Most selections cost less than $6.

Sixty-Five Seafood Restaurant
336 N. Michigan, 312/372-0306   C
225 S. Canal, 312/474-0065   C

These downtown branches of a Chinatown favorite provide seafood, dim sum, and other popular dishes for satisfying lunches under $5.

Soul By the Pound
168 N. State, 312/372-6955   C

It may take several visits to try all the available dishes at this huge buffet, so take a plate and start piling. Pork chops, chitterlings, ribs, catfish, salmon croquettes, greens, succotash, okra, sauerkraut, macaroni & cheese, candied yams, sweet potatoes, banana pudding, peach cobbler, and berry cobbler comprise a fraction of the options! $3.99/pound. Closed Sundays.

Standing Room Only (SRO)
610 S. Dearborn, 312/360-1776   C

Endorsed by Mayor Daley as the "Best Turkey Burger in Chicago" and Governor Edgar as the "Best Turkey Burger in Illinois," **SRO**'s char-grilled, hand packed, 100% turkey burger dominates a menu loaded with plenty of sandwich and salad temptations. They nominate their char-grilled, fresh (never frozen) chicken breast sandwich and falafel in whole wheat pita as "Best in Chicago," but I'd also stand behind their Cajun style chicken and tuna steak sandwiches. Over fifty percent of the menu is heart healthy, including a half dozen vegetarian choices. Sandwiches $4.25-$6.95, most about $5; salads $2.50-$7.75. Despite the name, there's ample seating in this slick Chicago sports-themed sandwich shop.

Taza
39 S. Wabash, 312/425-9988   **C**
As the first U.S. outpost of a popular Saudi Arabian fast food chain, this funky, global-themed chicken restaurant has made a deep impression during its initial test run. Entitled with the Arabic word for "fresh," **Taza** issues not only fresh food, but a fresh perspective on fast food. Amish-raised chicken (brought in fresh daily), marinated in citrus juices and spices and char-grilled to perfection, is the menu's centerpiece. An entire, 20-oz. chicken is served split, on top of store-baked pita bread ($3.99). Other chicken choices (about $5) are sandwiches (grilled chicken, jerk chicken...) and salads (Santa Fe, Tuscan, Greek...). International sides (less than $1.50) include various types of potatoes, rice, and coleslaw. Open daily 7am-9pm.

Venice Cafe
250 S. Wacker, 312/382-0300   **C**
Chalkboard menus, huge portions, red trays, food lines, and cheap prices: sounds like a cafeteria to me. But a cafeteria for made-from-scratch Italian delights? That's **Venice Cafe**, which ironically, looks out on the Chicago River. Fifteen pastas daily, plus pizza, calzones, soups, salads, sandwiches, Italian beefs, Italian sausages, and baked goods challenge one's ability to make quick lunch decisions. Entrees $3.95-$5.75. Closed weekends.

Wellington's
318 W. Randolph, 312/553-0663   **C**
High-quality fast food with incredible selection and terrific prices. Soups like chili, clam chowder, and the seasonal gazpacho run $1.75-$2.25. Salad choices include blackened chicken, beef tostada, and grilled turkey bow tie pasta ($2.95-$5.50). Their own deli and specialty sandwiches vie with the amazing grilled chicken breast concoctions, made blackened, with teriyaki sauce, or as a BLT ($4.95). For further variety, go for a dressed up baked potato or the famous chicken wings ($3.50-$5.25). Closed weekends.

Lunch, Downtown, Quick Gourmet

Corner Bakery
516 N. Clark, 312/644-8100   C
140 S. Dearborn, 312/920-9100   C
900 N. Michigan, 312/573-9900   C
224 S. Michigan, 312/431-7600   C
222 S. Riverside Plaza, 312/441-0821 (Union Station Concourse)   C
676 N. St. Clair, 312/266-2570   C
1121 N. State, 312/787-1969   C
78 E. Washington, 312/201-0805 (Cultural Center)   C
It might be best to make your selection here by reading the menu: the display case hypnotizes with its possibilities. Come to these top-notch bakeries for salads (cashew chicken, curry couscous, red potato and dill), pizza (spinach alfredo with pine nuts, gourmet mushrooms), and sandwiches (roasted vegetable on onion bread, roast beef with horseradish mayo, salami with arugula). Take home an unrivaled loaf of bread (a dozen varieties daily) and colossal baked goods (pecan sticky buns, butterscotch blondies, bear claws, toffee bars...) Lunch items $1.95-$8.95, most $3-$6. Closed Sundays.

Krystyna's
8 E. Jackson, 312/922-9225   C
French-European cafes purvey umpteen fancy dishes, many low-fat and low-cholesterol for discriminating lunchers. 15 croissants (raisin & custard, tart cherry & cream), 21 muffins (lemon crunch, cinnamon coffee cake), omelettes, soups, salads (ratatouille nicoise, seafood Marseilles), pizza (ginger chicken, meatballs teriyaki), lasagnas (chicken cacciatore, champignon à la Russe), and hot and cold sandwiches (baked brie, ham & broccoli, corned beef florentine) all strive for one's attention. Most items $3-$5. Closed Sat.-Sun.

Soprafinna Marketcaffè
10 N. Dearborn, 312/984-0044   C
222 W. Adams, 312/726-4800   C
Classy Italian cafeteria affiliated with the celebrated Trattoria No. 10 dining spot at the original location. Line up for soups, salads, pastas (lasagna toscano, stuffed shells), pizza (Margherita, homemade sausage with three cheeses), and classic Italian sandwiches (chicken Caesar salad, grilled portabello mushrooms, roast beef and avocado). Lunch $2.50-$7.50, most under $6. Closed Sat.-Sun.

Yvette Gourmeteria

311 S. Wacker, 312/408-1242   C

Pricey dining and dancing spot has instituted an affordable gourmet cafeteria to service the lunch time crowd. Fresh soups, salads, sandwiches, pasta, rotisserie chicken, and hot daily specials can be carried out or enjoyed near the indoor fountain, underneath the tall, tropical foliage. Most lunch items run, $3-$5; most breakfast items, $2-$4.

Mexican

With the hundreds, perhaps thousands, of Mexican restaurants in Chicago, most affordably priced and many worth trying, the following are but a few great deals and some of the authors'—and their comrades'—favorites

Arriba Mexico Restaurant

3140 N. Lincoln, 773/281-3939   N

I learned about this hangout years ago from a cousin who had become addicted to their burritos. (They have long since closed and re-opened with great, but not-quite-the-same burritos...hmmm.) When I was a kid and the building housed a McDonald's, I attended birthday parties in its basement. I've run into people in their 3am weekday crowd that I haven't seen in ages. I love this place! Otherwise, it's a fairly typical fast-ish Mexican place with a good following, good prices, and great salsa.

Burrito Station

6446 S. Pulaski, 773/735-3799   SW

Fresh, reasonably priced Mexican fare is served from the open kitchen of this small strip center carry-out. According to two regular patrons, the steak burritos and avocado tostados are awesome.

Doña Torta

3057 N. Ashland, 773/871-8999   N

From the outside—and well, the inside too, **Doña Torta** appears to be just another Mexican fast food place. It's when you first glimpse the menu, take your first bite, or pay your first bill with pocket change that you realize you've found a winner. Let's start with the fourteen Super Tortas (sandwiches) à la Mexico City. None are priced over $3.35 and come in such combinations as grilled steak with bacon & sliced ham and ham & cheese omelette with onions. There are also $3.75 Super Burritos—of the *grande* size we accept as normal in Chicago. The fourteen options for Super Tacos—priced at an easy $1.50—include pork butt and cheese, eggs with chorizo, fried fish with lemon wedge, breaded steak, and beef tongue. There's more. Seven additional burritos are low calorie, four of those are vegetarian. Along with the fresh fruit Super Shakes, **Doña** serves Vitamin Shakes (nutritional powder added), Energy Shakes (carbohydrate powder added), and Protein Shakes (with egg, protein powder, and carbs added).

El Pueblo
2406 S. Western, 773/523-4166   **SW**
If you can get more food for less money in this city, then we'd like to know about it! For at least five years, this banquet hall has served a daily Mexican buffet from 11am-4:30pm for only $3.50. Fill up on nearly a dozen hot dishes (tacos, chile con carne, beef, BBQ ribs, fried chicken, stuffed peppers...), plus tortillas, vegetables, fruits, salads, and chips and salsa.

LaLO's
3515 W. 26th, 773/522-0345   **SW**
4126 W. 26th, 773/762-1505   **SW**
2747 W. 63rd, 773/476-8207   **SW**
Suck down a hefty margarita and dig into the chips & salsa and marinated veggies (carrots, cauliflower, jalapeños, mild whole garlic cloves...), while you peruse the menu at this animated and colorful Mexican neighborhood favorite. Go with a standard (you'll enjoy it) or opt for one of the house or seafood specialties: beef tongue simmered in tomatillo sauce, butterfly-cut skirt steak with guacamole, sopa marina 5 seafood soup, shrimp fajitas. Entrees $4-$14, most under $9.

Nuevo Leon
1515 W. 18th, 312/421-1517 (Pilsen)   **C**
3659 W. 26th, 773/522-1515 (Little Village)   **SW**
Modest family restaurant serves cherished stews, enchiladas, and *mole* dishes. Other specialties include the Steak Nuevo Leon and *Machacado* (scrambled eggs and meat). Entrees $4-$9, many $4-$5.

For vegetarians who want something other than refried beans...

Taco and Burrito Palace #2
2441 N. Halsted, 773/248-0740   **N**
Heavy-traffic, fast-food Mexican place/palace substitutes the typical refried beans in their vegetarian burrito with loads of grilled onions and peppers ($2.75). Huge and messy. Steak, chicken, and other burritos for carnivores

go for $2.25-$3.50.

Garcia's
4749 N. Western, 773/769-5600   N
1758 W. Lawrence, 773/784-1212 (Closed Wednesdays)   N
Busy, family-owned restaurants offer a cheesy, piquant chile relleno nestled
in a soft corn tortilla, making a filling and unusual taco for only $2.

Quesadillas
2165 N. Western, 773/292-0070   N
Large atmospheric restaurant serves a unique, mildly-flavored *nopales*
taco—tender strips of cactus tips and onions—for $1.75.

The consummate collection of Mexican baked goods:

La Baguette Foods, Inc.
3117 W. 26th, 773/254-0006   SW
While various **La Baguette** Mexican bakeries dot the city, none measure
up to this enormous branch where racks and racks of scrumptious (and
cheap) Mexican breads and pastries continually spill forth from the
kitchen. Grab a pair of tongs and start piling goodies onto your round tray.
Across the parking lot is the **Little Village Discount Mall** (p.388), not to
be missed for its great deals and first-hand contact with a little piece of
Mexico.

Middle Eastern See also: **Afghan**, **Israeli**, **Moroccan**, and **Turkish**.

Since the early 1990s, a variety of Middle Eastern restaurants, bakeries,
and grocery stores have opened on 63rd Street between Kedzie and Pulaski.
The first was **Steve's Shishkabab House** (3816 W. 63rd, 773/581-8920).
In addition to the skewered and grilled meats of its name, **Steve's** also
serves other delicious chicken and lamb dishes, garlicky hummus, and
warm homemade pitas. Local rumor has it that the chef at **The Jerusalem**
(3534 W. 63rd, 773/776-6133) once toiled in the kitchen of the Jordanian
royal palace. Try the Arrayes appetizer—finely chopped, seasoned lamb
grilled inside pita bread. **The Nile** (3259 W. 63rd, 773/434-7218) is a good
place for lunch that puts together fresh and tasty sandwiches in a hurry.

A Jordanian revival:

Kan Zaman
5204 N. Clark, 773/506-0191   **FN**

Taking over the former, spartanly decorated **Beirut Restaurant** (see p.143), the Jordanian owners of Kan Zaman have made this space sumptuous and inviting. Two window seating areas are piled with colorful pillows and lined with ornate rugs for more authentic and intimate dining. Choose chicken, lamb, beef, shrimp, scallops, calamari, or a combo to complete a number of traditional dishes ($7.50-$8.95); go for various kababs ($6.95-$10.95) or sandwiches ($2.75-$3.75); or dine vegetarian ($6.95-$7.95). Appetizers ($3.25-$4.95), pastries ($1.75-$2.50), and typical beverages ($1-$1.50) are affordable add-ons. BYOB. (No cork fee if wine is purchased from the liquor store on the northeast corner of Clark and Foster.)

A Persian jewel:

Reza's
5255 N. Clark, 773/561-1898   **FN**
432 W. Ontario, 312/664-4500   **C**

Chicago's favorite Persian restaurant, acknowledged by nearly every critic for food, service, atmosphere, and price, also received another nod for their list. The vested, bow-tied, and charming waiters at the original Clark Street location recently ranked among *Chicago Magazine*'s "25 Sexiest Chicagoans." The voluminous menu holds a specialty for everyone: A separate vegetarian appetizer and entree list ($2.95-$6.95 and $6.95-$12.95), 11 lamb dishes from shanks, to chops, to kabobs ($9.95-$14.95), 10 poultry dishes including turkey, Cornish hen, quail and skinless, low-fat chicken dishes ($8.95-$10.50), seafood delights like salmon kabobs and shrimp and scallop combos ($9.50-$14.95), and more. Lunch entrees $6.95-$9.95.

A Turkish delight:

Cousin's
5203 N. Clark, 773/334-4553   **FN**

Mouth-watering Turkish, Mediterranean, and vegetarian dishes should please nearly every palette at **Cousin's**, where the emphasis is on healthy, fresh, and innovative cooking. Vegetarian mousakka, *imam bayildi* (stuffed baby eggplant), and *manti* (spinach, asparagus, and cheese-filled ravioli topped with fresh pesto, pine nuts, and diced tomatoes) are among the dozen vegetarian entrees that can be vegan with the simple omission of feta cheese. Chicken doner (a chicken "gyro"), lamb chops, saffron shrimp, and more join delectable shish kebabs for meat eaters. Turkish wines, beer, tea, coffee and imported juices compliment the unique dishes and baklava or custard make great finales if you find yourself in the unusual circumstance of still having room after dinner. Sides under $2.25, appetizers and sandwiches $3-$5, kebabs and entrees $8-$13, most under $9.

For a Lebanese slant on Middle Eastern foods, try the small and lively **Andie's Restaurant** (5253 N. Clark, 773/784-8616) where entrees run $4.50-$12.95 (most under $7), and about half the menu is vegetarian; and **Cedars of Lebanon** (1616 E. 53rd, 773/324-6227), a Hyde Park favorite with appetizers priced $1.50-$6.95, vegetarian entrees $3.50-$7.50, and meat entrees $6.75-$10.85.

A take-out treasure:

Middle Eastern Bakery & Grocery
1512 W. Foster, 773/561-2224   **NW**
Head to the deli counter for a tasty carryout bargain for lunch or dinner: 12 falafel balls for $1.95, falafel sandwiches $1.75, stuffed grape leaves $.50, spinach, cheese, meat, or Moroccan eggplant pies $.75-$1.55, and a dozen fresh baked pitas ($1.25). Pick out some olives, cold salads, or imported cheeses for the side and assorted baklava and pastries for dessert.

For more good Middle Eastern fast food, visit the Mediterranean/health food spot **Emerald City** (2852 N. Clark, 773/477-0555). They keep a well-stocked salad bar and carry items like falafel sandwiches, hummus, spinach pies, and fresh fruit and vegetable juices.

Moroccan   See also: **African**, **Israeli**, and **Middle Eastern**.

L'Olive
3915 N. Sheridan, 773/472-2400   **N**
This small, charming restaurant is a gateway to the flavors of the Mediterranean à la North Africa. Moroccan olives, creamy goat cheese hummus, *zaalouk* (roasted eggplant dip), *bastilla* (chicken and almond phyllo pie), couscous variations, *merguez* sausage, baked sea eel, and stuffed sardines can all be tried (or ventured). Small plates and entrees, $1.50-$14.95. Closed Sundays and Mondays.

Perhaps nowhere in Chicago can you get as diverse, delicious, and exotic a lineup of ethnic food as on a quarter-block stretch of North Sheridan, just off the Sheridan el stop. All in a row, from north to south, stand **L'Olive** (3915), **The Tibet Cafe** (3913, see p.200), and **Suya African Bar & Grill** (3911, see below).

A seven-course Moroccan feast ($10.75) is offered Saturday nights at the **Logan Beach Cafe** (2537 N. Kedzie, 773/862-4277). The ever-changing menu may include a potato stew or a chicken pie with walnuts and phyllo dough. Vegetarian option available.

Nigerian See also: **African**.

Suya African Bar & Grill
3911 N. Sheridan, 773/281-7892   **N**
Suya—spicy, grilled beef kabobs—are but the beginning of the many simple, but unusual, dining pleasures at this cheerful Nigerian storefront restaurant. *Fufu* (pounded yam), *semovita* (pounded corn), *kosai* (fried bean cakes), and plantains make good accompaniments for the larger dishes. Hearty stews include okra or the *egusi* (made with meat, spinach, and melon seeds). The seasoned *joloff* rice contains vegetable bits and chunks of goat, chicken, or fish. Can't beat the prices: everything's between $2 and $8. Closed Mondays.

Peruvian

Rinconcito Sudamericano
1954 W. Armitage, 773/489-3126   **N**
Established Peruvian place caters more to the big appetite and the palate than aesthetic inclinations. Peru's lengthy coastline supplies plenty of seafood recipes (stuffed squid, seafood-packed rice, port-style mussels, lobster, shrimp...). Most other entrees are chicken and beef based (like the popular *anticuchos*—grilled beef hearts), but there's lamb, tripe, and rabbit, too. Entrees $8-$13, most under $9.

For further affordable explorations into the pleasures of Peruvian cuisine, try the recently opened **Mi Perú** (4920 W. Irving Park, 773/205-4354) and the long-standing **Machu Picchu** (5427 N. Clark, 773/769-0455).

Pizza

Where do you start listing worthy pizza in the pizza capital of Chicago?

Dishing out perhaps the best-known pizza anywhere, **Pizzeria Uno** (29 E. Ohio, 312/321-1000) birthed the deep-dish pizza that made Chicago famous, back in 1943. Soon afterwards, its sister, **Pizzeria Due** (619 N. Wabash, 312/943-2400), was opened across the street to accommodate the crowds that have persisted to this day. Be forewarned: you must order your pizza at these places before you're even seated.

Other major players on the Chicago-style deep dish and stuffed pizza scene to look for are the many **Bacino's** (heart-healthy stuffed spinach), **Connie's**, **Edwardo's** (all natural), **Gino's**, **Giordano's**, **Ranalli's**, and **Suparossa** restaurants scattered across town. They don't disappoint. Once you've clogged your gills with their cheesy indulgences, check out the unique pizza renditions and environments of the following places:

Chicago Pizza and Oven Grinder Company
2121 N. Clark, 773/248-2570   N
The individual pizza pot-pies are this upscale pizzeria's original claim to fame. Customers love just about everything else on the limited menu as well: the Mediterranean bread (a crispy, seasoned round appetizer that about covers the table), the Salad Dinners (salad concoctions that serve as a meal for 2-4 diners), and the Oven Grinders (overflowing baked sub sandwiches). Pot-pies $7.25, Mediterranean Bread $4.25, Salad Dinners $14.50-$19.50, Oven Grinders $8.75-$9.25. Lincoln Parkers wait 1-2 hours to be seated on the weekends; the host's memory functions as the waiting list. No reservations accepted. Cash only.

The Damen
1958 W. Roscoe, 773/248-9523   N
Blend the look of a jazz club with the feel of a corner bar and the flavors of a first-rate kitchen, and you'll have an instant hit like **The Damen**. With its maze of rooms (the back room was a former speakeasy), sleek open kitchen, brick-oven pizzas, microbrews on tap, atmospheric lighting, piped in jazz, old movies on a big screen, pool, and darts, this can be the right place to bring a date, the kids, or your best buds. Gourmet thin-crust pizzas ($7.50-$9.95) will feed one hungry person or two people who've been munching on the snazzy appetizers. Affordable wine list, cappucino/espresso service, and on Thursday nights at 9pm, live jazz.

Gulliver's

2727 W. Howard, 773/338-2166   **FN**

Perhaps the best-looking pizza parlor in the city, **Gulliver's** has an immense stained glass and antique collection that spruces up its heavy wooden tables and booths, making it both ornate and cozy. The "world famous pizza in the pan" ($6.95/9", $9.95/12", $12.25/14", $14.45/16") is accompanied by a broad menu of Italian (stuffed shells, veal parmesan, fried calamari...), Mexican (red snapper, chimichangas, burritos...), and American (stuffed steakburgers, ribs, grilled tuna, BLT club...) dishes. Sandwiches, $5.45-$7.95; entrees, $6.95-$13.75, most under $9.

Pompei Bakery

1455 W. Taylor, 312/421-5179   **C**

Line up at this long-time bakery (since 1909) at lunch time and select one or more of their incredible pizza slices from behind the glass display case. They've got original square, open faced (look for baked clams with a lemon wedge on Fridays), and stuffed pizza, along with their signature "pizza strude"—a delightful concoction that comes in flavors like "poor boy," roast beef, turkey stuffing, and steak fajita. Hefty slices go for $1.50-$3.25. **Pompei Little Italy** (2955 N. Sheffield, 773/325-1900) duplicates the food but not the character of the original location.

For maximum pizza possibilities, you can't beat Chicago's family-owned chain of **Leona's** restaurants. Choose thin crust or pan; traditional, whole wheat, or garlic parmesan crust; regular or soy cheese; Alfredo, pesto, or tomato sauce; and toppings from a list of two dozen (ricotta cheese, Genoa salami, turkey breast, artichokes, pineapple...). Complimentary cookies arrive with the check.

- 1936 W. Augusta, 773/292-4300   **W**

This is the original location, where the restaurant was built around the family's home.

- 3215 N. Sheffield, 773/327-8861   **N**
- 3877 N. Elston, 773/267-7287   **NW**
- 7443 W. Irving, 773/625-3636   **NW**
- 6935 N. Sheridan, 773/764-5757   **FN**
- 1419 W. Taylor, 312/850-2222   **C**
- 53rd & Woodlawn, 773/363-2600   **S**
- 25th & Western, 773/523-9696   **SW**
- 111th & Western, 773/881-7700   **FSW**

For unusual pizza combinations, head to the bars...

Great Beer Palace
4128 N. Lincoln, 773/525-4906   **N**

Germanesque bar wins kudos for its 24 imported and microbrews on tap, private beer garden tangled with greenery, and unexpectedly good pizza. Two of the thin-crust specialty pizzas ($9-$15) stand out: The German Pizza (potato, mushroom, onion, cheese, herbs, and veal bratwurst) and The Beer Palace Special (thuringer, onion, sauerkraut, apple, cheese, and herbs). Weekends can get rowdy when youthful customers attempt the intemperate Viking Raids. This challenge rewards drinkers with a plastic Viking helmet for finishing six 1/4 liters of different beers.

Simply Ray's
4708 N. Damen, 773/561-1757   **N**

When Chicago's very own Casimir Pulaski Day rolls around in early March, this friendly neighborhood sports bar rolls out Polish Pizza for its Pizza O' the Month. Polish sausage, sauerkraut, and onions join the traditional red sauce and cheese on these thin-crust pies. Not your thing? How about April's Irish Pizza toppings: corned beef, cabbage, and potatoes. What e'er the month, you're bound to be surprised by the kitchen's latest combinations and the happy results for your taste buds. One former monthly special, the *Boofalo*, was such a hit, customers demanded it be added to the regular menu. Grilled chicken soaked in Ray's wing sauce, mozzarella, and blue cheese crumbles top the pizza, which is served with a blue cheese dipping sauce on the side. P.O.M. cost $8.50/9", $10.75/12", and $15.75/16".

Pizza with soul:

Lou Malnati's Pizzeria
3859 W. Ogden, 773/762-0800   **W**

This run-down branch of a big-name Chicago pizza chain was renovated and re-opened in 1995 in conjunction with the Lawndale Community Church in hopes of both revitalizing the area's long gone business district and earning money for the church's community programs. All profits are re-invested in the community, folks needing a second chance are given jobs, and transitional housing is available upstairs for the homeless. In addition to **Malnati's** pizza, pasta, and sandwiches, the restaurant dishes out daily soul food specials: baked chicken, chicken and dumplings, ham hocks, fried catfish, pork chitterlings, corn bread stuffing, red beans, greens, green beans seasoned with salt pork. Having become a popular community hangout and meeting place, insiders refer to the pizzeria as "Malnati's Lighthouse." Closed Sundays.

Lunch time bargains at some favorite pizzerias:

Chesdan's
4465 S. Archer, 773/247-2400   **SW**
$6 soup, salad bar, and pizza buffet. Mon.-Fri., 11:30am-2:30pm.

Edwardo's Natural Pizza
1937 W. Howard, 773/761-7040   **FN**
$4.95 buys a thin-crust 7" pizza with one topping, a salad, and a drink. Mon.-Fri. 11am-2pm.

Giordano's
2124 W. Lawrence, 773/271-9696   **FN**
$3.99 stuffed individual pizza with any three ingredients, plus beer or pop. Mon.-Fri. 11am-3pm. Call ahead so it's ready when you arrive!

Home Run Inn
4254 W. 31st, 773/247-9696   **SW**
75-year-old south side wonder pitches a winning weekday buffet for $5.75. The feast includes seven kinds of pizza, two soups, pasta, salad, and dessert. Mon.-Fri. 11am-2pm, Sat. 11am-4pm.

Pizza Capri
716 W. Diversey, 773/296-6000   **N**
Gourmet "California-style" pizza place serves a mid-day extravaganza for $5.95 that comes with an individual pizza (stuffed spinach, Thai, pepperoni, barbecue...), soup or salad, and unlimited beverage refills. Homemade bread and olive oil while you wait. Substitute a pasta dish (Rotini Tuscani, lime chicken...) or sandwich (smoked turkey, eggplant...) for the pizza.

For the biggest pizza puff in the city...

Damenzo's Pizza and Restaurant
2324 W. Taylor Street, 312/421-1142   **W**
Family owned and operated joint in an old Italian neighborhood offers the largest pizza puff/calzone in the city for $4.75. Other deals include the

gigantic slice of pizza with a soda for $1.99.

Polish

Long having had the world's largest population of Poles outside of Warsaw, Chicago has recently seen a new influx in Polish immigrants (particularly young ones, many professional) to the city. Explore Milwaukee Avenue, primarily between Diversey and Addison, for establishments that can not get more authentic. Along with entrenched Polish delis and restaurants, you'll find newer clubs, coffeehouses, an ice cream parlor, and a video store catering to this younger generation. Two excellent and inexpensive restaurants that have thrived in this area for nearly twenty years are the modest **Home Bakery and Restaurant** (2931 N. Milwaukee, 773/252-3708) and the flashier **Orbit** (2948-54 N. Milwaukee, 773/276-1355), which attracted a visit from George Bush during his presidency.

A budget dining bonanza a couple neighborhoods away:

Andrzej Grill
1022 N. Western, 773/489-3566   **W**
Tiny, bare-bones diner belies the impressive food being freshly prepared in the kitchen. Try pierogis, crepes, tripe stew, or red borscht with meat croquettes for lunch. Dinner entrees like white sausage with onion sauce, stuffed potato pancakes (stuffed with roast pork and topped with gravy), boiled pork shank, and stuffed cabbage come with soup (choose from nine different kinds) and salad (four variations). Vegetarian menu available. Simple pricing: lunch $3.50, soups $1.50, and dinners with soup and salad (thirteen choices + daily specials) $5.50.

To enjoy Poland's star dumpling, the pierogi...

Pierogi Inn
5318 W. Lawrence, 773/736-4815   **FN**
Quaint storefront restaurant owned by former chef to Hugh Hefner. The chalkboard menu lists the day's several choices of pierogi fillings. A plate of dumplings costs $4.50 for 9 and $4.95 for 12. Other entrees run $4.25-$7.95, most under $6.

Caesar's Polish Deli
901 N. Damen, 773/486-6190   **W**
Fans come from near and far for **Caesar's** 12 types of pierogi, including
the late columnist Mike Royko who called them "the Rolls-Royce of
pierogi." Fillings include sauerkraut, cheese, potato, peach, plum, and the
summertime special—organically grown Michigan strawberries. Take
along more goodies from the freezer or deli counter: *nalenski* (rolled crepes
filled with apple, cheese, apricot or prune), *golabki* (stuffed cabbage),
potato dumplings, *kolaczki,* cruellers, Polish rye, homemade soup, chop
suey... Closed Sun.-Mon.

If you're watching your wallet but not your waistline, these popular buffets
offer a filling line-up of Polish favorites:

Ambassador Restaurant
7050 W. Belmont, 773/286-9337   **NW**
Polish smorgasbord from 11am-3pm ($5.25) and 3pm-9pm ($6.25) daily.
Jazz quartet plays Fri.-Sun. 9pm-midnight. No cover.

Czerwone Jubluszko (Red Apple) Restaurants
3121 N. Milwaukee, 773/588-5781   **NW**
6474 N. Milwaukee, 773/763-3407   **FN**
A sizable spread of Polish food, including soup, desserts, ice cream, and
coffee/soda. Served daily 11am-3:30pm for $5.50 and 3:30pm-10pm for
$6.50.

Gilmart Quality Food & Liquor
5050 S. Archer, 773/585-5514   **SW**
Bustling Polish grocery store with a small dining area where you can eat
items purchased at the deli counter or from the $4.99 buffet. A bulletin
board crammed with handwritten notices, mostly in Polish, selling houses
and offering jobs, greets you when you walk in the door.

Staropolska
5249 W. Belmont, 773/736-5230   **NW**
3028 N. Milwaukee, 773/342-0779   **NW**
Jolly Inn
6501 W. Irving Park, 773/736-7606   **NW**
From 10:30am-9pm daily, feast at these plentiful Polish buffets, which
include salad, coffee, and dessert. $5.55 Mon.-Sat. and $6.55 Sun. (Slightly
cheaper at Milwaukee location) Pierogi, sausages, blintzes, dumplings,

potato pancakes, stuffed cabbage, roast chicken, kraut. Soup (all highly recommended, particularly the tripe soup) and soft drinks cost extra.

Tatra Inn
6040 S. Pulaski, 773/582-8313   **SW**
Wear clothes with an elastic waistband when you visit this belly-busting smorgasbord. Fill up on Polish sausage, traditional Polish soups, such as *czarnina* and tripe, schnitzels, stuffed cabbage, turkey, baked ham, broasted chicken, pierogi, mashed potatoes, apple and potato pancakes, and sauerkraut. Eat as much as you can for $6.95. All they ask is that you clean your plate before you go back for more.

Polish Sausage

My first exposure to the definitive polish sausage came when an awe-inspiring friend would habitually arrive at our first period French class—all the way from her south side home to our northwest side girls high school—with a "polish" she picked up off Maxwell Street. I have since learned that many others make similar circuitous journeys to the careworn former neighborhood of the Maxwell Street Market for these peerless onion-heaped sausages.

Two 24-hour stands have been serving "Maxwell Street Polish Sausages" for decades: **Jim's Hot Dog Stand** (1320 S. Halsted, 312/666-0533) and **Original Maxwell** (1316 S. Halsted). $2 apiece.

Pub Grub

Goose Island Brewing Company
1800 N. Clybourn, 312/915-0071   **N**
Considered to be one of the nation's top brewpubs and known to be Chicago's oldest and largest, **Goose Island** has an impressive menu that rivals their vast lineup of award-winning beers. Favorites such as Honkers Ale steamed mussels, the low-fat sausage sampler with hot German potato salad and mango chutney, the Carolina pulled pork BBQ sandwich, and a pepper-crusted burger with stilton on marble rye and served with garlic mashed potatoes are made with their own beers. A free basket of thick, seasoned, homemade potato chips starts all meals ($1 for re-fills) and compliment a pre-meal beer sampling session. Select three or more draft beers to taste and each 5-ounce glass costs only $1. Free tours of the brewpub are given Sundays at 3pm and are followed with brewer-led

tastings. Entrees $10-$17, most under $12, hearty appetizers, pizzas, salads, and sandwiches $3-$9, most $5-$7.

Hog Head McDunna's
1505 W. Fullerton, 773/929-0944   **N**
Hog Head's serves what is arguably Chicago's finest pub food, with specials that can't be beat. Headlining burgers and veggie burgers (macho enough for red meat eaters) with topping options like roasted garlic, havarti with dill, port wine cheddar, and oak smoked gouda lead the broad menu. Beef and Guiness Irish stew served in a sourdough bread bowl, blackened tuna, jambalaya, and char-grilled wings are other choices. This is hearty, homemade, and—relatively-speaking—healthy eating, with better-than-average presentation for a neighborhood saloon. With a drink purchase, customers can relish these dinner time deals: $.10 wings on Mondays, unlimited pasta with salad bar and garlic bread for $1.99 on Tuesdays, $.50 chili on Wednesdays, and 25-ingredient all you can eat taco bar for $1.99 on Thursdays. Order anything on the menu for $2.99 Mon.-Fri. 11am-4pm. Menu items $3.50-$7.75, most under $6.

Schaller's Pump
3714 S. Halsted, 773/376-6332   **S**
A firm Bridgeport address, unshakable White Sox allegiance, past and present politicos from the ward office across the street (including the former Mayor Richard J. Daley) as regulars, St. Patrick's Day revelry, a red meat menu, and the city's oldest liquor license (1881) staunchly establish **Schaller's** South Side credentials. Something "light" from the menu, perhaps corned beef, burgers, or steak sandwiches with the legendary hash browns will run $5-$6. Dinner specials (say, pork chops, stuffed cabbage, chicken, or ribs) with soup and salad are priced in the $8 range. If you miss the traditional weekend accordion music, the jukebox comes well-stocked with 50s-90s classics.

Sedgwick's Bar & Grill
1935 N. Sedgwick, 312/337-7900   **N**
Capacious Lincoln Park gathering place offers homemade victuals that are more than just food to drink by. Appetizing pastas, sandwiches, salads, quesadillas, and appetizers ($3-$8.50, most under $6) are served until 1am nightly. The $6.50 daily specials change weekly and range from pasta salad or a sandwich served with salad and a side dish to beef stroganoff, jerk chicken, and Caribbean-style ribs. A Friday evening happy hour buffet (5:30pm-7pm) and a Saturday pre-closing buffet (midnight-2am) are

absolutely free. Munch on tasty buffalo wings, pizza slices, pasta, egg rolls, raw veggies, and more. Pop in on the weekends for a creative brunch menu combined with pool and big-screen satellite TV (10:30am-3pm).

Puerto Rican   See also: **Caribbean**.

For 500+ years, since Spanish, European, and African culinary traditions first collided with those of the native people, a marvelous and underrecognized cuisine has been brewing on the island of Puerto Rico. To get an inkling of these flavors in Chicago, try one of the following neighborhood standbys. Be careful not to confuse *mondogo* (tripe soup) and *mofongo* (a mashed ball of plantain, fried pork skin, and garlic, sometimes shaped into a bowl to hold chicken broth)—both unique and delicious specialties, but very different things!

In the shadow of Humboldt Park stand these two casual eateries perfect for an affordable introduction to the cuisine of *La Isla*: The proprietors of **Borinquen Restaurant** (1720 N. California, 773/227-6038) recommend their *carne frita con mofongo* (breaded and fried meat with *mofongo*), *bistec con tostones* (steak with fried plantains), and *sopa de mariscos* (seafood soup). Entrees $4.50-$7.50. The **Latin American Restaurant and Lounge** (2743 W. Division, 773/235-7290) lists rice with *grandules* (pigeon peas), pork with rice, *morcilla* (spicy blood sausage), *mofongo*, and *cuchifrito* (fried pig ears) among its menu highlights. Most meals $4.25-$5.50.

Further west, look for the **Sabor Latino Restaurants** (3810 W. North, 773/227-5254 and 3522 W. Armitage, 773/276-3524) for Puerto Rican home cooking in no-frills settings. Snacks and sandwiches $1-$3, non-seafood dinners with rice and beans $4-$8, seafood entrees $5-$10.

Ribs   See also: **Soul Food** and **Southern Eclectic** for more restaurants known for their ribs.

It was for good reason that Hawkeye Pierce ordered ribs all the way from Chicago on the popular television show *M.A.S.H.* We do them right. The following are just a few of the many places for some finger-licking good ribs.

These take-out places draw fans from around the city:

Coleman's #1 Hickory Bar-B-Que (555 N. Cicero, 773/626-9299 and 5754 W. Chicago, 773/287-0363) on Cicero comes recommended by school bus drivers from a nearby depot. **Lem's Bar-B-Q House** (311 E. 75th, 773/994-2428, closed Tuesdays, and 5914 S. State, 773/684-5007, closed Mondays) are family-owned rib stands that have been around for years.

Leon's Bar-B-Q

8251 S. Cottage Grove 773/488-4556 (the original location)	**FSE**
1640 E. 79th, 773/731-1454	**FSE**
1158 W. 59th, 773/778-7828	**SW**
4550 S. Archer, 773/247-4171	**SW**

When you see the big, round pig logo, you know you've found **Leon's**—some of the best ribs around. Slices of white bread come with the order to wipe up the extra sauce. These are dangerous neighborhoods, though, evidenced by the bullet-proof windows at the order counters. Open until 4am, Sun.-Thur. and until 5am, Fri-Sat.

For dine-in ribs, these distinctive barbecue restaurants (one old, one older, and one new) carry easier price tags than many and should not be overlooked:

The large **Glass Dome Hickory Pit** (2801 S. Halsted, 312/842-7600) has straddled the Back of the Yards and the Bridgeport neighborhoods for five decades. Its popularity increases during baseball season, due to the free shuttle service to Comiskey Park. **Twin Anchors** (1655 N. Sedgwick, 312/266-1616) has occupied the same leafy, residential corner in Old Town for nearly 70 years, maintaining its pre-gentrification ambiance and Sinatra on the jukebox. The funky, part-diner, part-club **Smoke Daddy** (1804 W. Division, 773/772-6656) imported a special pit-oven from down south for its authentic, smoky ribs. Other barbecue pleasures include the pork shoulder sandwich, vegetarian sandwich, and chicken breasts. Live blues or jazz nightly, beginning at 10pm.

To grab a slab downtown before or after a symphonic or theatrical event, try these casual Loop favorites: The **Exchequer Restaurant and Pub** (226 S. Wabash, 312/939-5633) serves food nightly until 11pm from a dining room plastered with Chicago memorabilia. The kitchen at **Miller's Pub** (134 S. Wabash, 312/645-5377) stays open until 1am.

Romanian

Little Bucharest
3001 N. Ashland, 773/929-8640 **N**
After more than 25 years, this town's only Romanian restaurant is going stronger than ever. Enjoy generous portions of house specialties like sauerbraten, stuffed cabbage, chicken paprikash, tournedos of veal, spicy *mititei* sausage, and newer vegetarian creations. Dinners $8-$15. Free transportation is available from and to hotels!

Russian

Two elegant places for Russian fare (and food from those lands formerly known as the Soviet Union) are downtown and right across the street from each other...

Russian Tea Time
77 E. Adams, 312/360-0000 **C**
Enjoy Russian, Ukrainian, Georgian, Azerbajiani, and Uzbek cuisine in a refined setting for breakfast ($1.49-$9.95, most under $4) or lunch ($3.95-$7.95), because dinner entrees at $11-$26 break into a different price bracket. In the morning, all choices from the caviar selection on toast, to *blini* (Russian pancakes), *sirniki* (farmer's cheese patties), and buckwheat kasha are real treats. Dough creations like Russian *piroshki*, Ukrainian potato dumplings, and Uzbek *samsa* make great afternoon appetizers. Quail, calf's liver, and chicken croquettes appear on the hot entree list, while vegetarians can delight in an impressive array which includes stuffed eggplant, beet caviar with walnuts and prunes, and Azerbajiani stuffed mushrooms. If you've got the dollars to spend, consider their "elaborate caviar and vodka service." If not, you can appreciate the chandeliers, rich burgundy furnishings, and tuxedo-clad personnel just as well with the fancy tea and coffee service.

Russian Palace
24 E. Adams, 312/629-5353 **C**
With dinners costing $10.50-$13.50 for vegetarian entrees, and $14.90-$32.95 for meat and seafood, lunch time or tea time are the affordable dining hours at the **Russian Palace**. Hot and cold appetizers with frequent appearances of beets, mushrooms, eggplant, and seafood range from $3.75 to $8.70. Dough dishes like blintzes, *piroshki*, *pelmeni*, and *vareniki* run $2.50-$9.90. $4.75-$12.50 entrees include an open-faced assorted smoked

fish sandwich on Russian bread, Chicken Kiev, and Beef Stroganoff.

Less czarist and more peasant-like...

The **Three Sisters Delicatessen & Gift Shop** (2854 W. Devon, 773/973-1919) sells the nuts and bolts needed to prepare a Russian feast at home: bread, pastries, pieorgi, blintzes, caviar, and fish (herring, mackerel, salmon, and more).

Salvadoran

Izalco
1511 W. Lawrence, 773/769-1225   **N**
Basic neighborhood storefront introduces the cuisine of El Salvador. Tamales, empanadas, and pasteles run $1.50-$4. Soups, stews, and entrees cost $4.75-$13.50, most under $7. Menu also includes favorites from Mexico and Puerto Rico. Crowded on the weekends. Closed Mondays and Tuesdays.

Scones

The Breakfast Club
1381 W. Hubbard, 312/666-2372   **C**
Huge toasted raspberry and blueberry scones ($2.50), which are practically a meal in themselves, are served with whipped cream and butter at this pleasant, out-of-the way restaurant that some liken to a Martha's Vineyard cottage. French toast, biscuits and gravy, huevos rancheros, and spinach & feta cheese omelettes are some favorites among their other hearty breakfasts ($5-$7.95).

A Taste of Heaven
1701 W. Foster, 773/989-0151   **FN**
Truly divine scones ($1.65) in chocolate chip, raisin, and various fruit flavors take center stage while sinful bread pudding, eclairs, raspberry crumble bars, lemon bars, brownie bars, rugelah, monster cookies, and such tempt you from the sidelines.

Scottish

The Duke of Perth
2913 N. Clark, 773/477-1741   N
Scottish pub/restaurant serves up shepherd's pie, steak and kidney pie, and fish and chips along with more Americanized offerings. The sizable beer selection accompanies an unsurpassed 75 brands of single-malt Scotch. Recommended beverages include McEwan's beers and the 16-year-old Lagavulin Scotch. Entrees $6.25-$8.25, most under $7.

Seafood (Take Out Joints On the River)

Joe's Fisheries
1438 W. Cortland, 773/278-8990   N
Established adjacent to the Chicago River in 1922, this seafood snack shop sells a wide range of food from lake and ocean. (They "catch their own—but not from the river.") Munch on deep fried specialties (try the smelt or fish chips), smoked fish, shrimp, lobster, oysters, scallops, calamari, and crab. Open until 3am Fri. and Sat.

Lawrence Fisheries
2120 S. Canal, 312/225-2113   C
You wonder what wholesome motive draws someone to a deserted riverside neighborhood in the middle of the night? 24-hour fried shrimp, fish chips, frog legs, scallops, clam strips, catfish, smoked chubs, and seafood gumbo. That's what. Dinners run about $3-$6. Items are also sold by the pound or half-pound.

Seafood (Take Out—Not On the River)

DiCola's
10754 S. Western, 773/238-7071   FSW
Primarily a fish market, **DiCola's** also cooks up some carry-out items. Catfish is the main event, but shrimp, oysters, smelt, and frog legs are also popular. On the weekends and around holidays, the wait can be as long as an hour. Keep yourself entertained by people watching and gazing at the giant fish murals.

Serbian

Skadarlija
4024 N. Kedzie, 773/463-5600   NW
Cozy, windowless Serbian restaurant and nightspot open Wed.-Sun. with
music beginning at 9pm. Salads, appetizers, and desserts run $3.50-$4.50,
entrees $10.95-$15.95. The Gypcy Plate ($31.95) includes traditional
sausages, meat patties, and skewered chunks of pork and feeds 2-4. Closed
Mondays and Tuesdays.

Serbian With a Gimmick

Simplon Orient Express
4520 N. Lincoln, 773/275-5522   N
Intimate and polished Serbian restaurant proffers Serbianized specialties
from every country that the regal Orient Express train passed through on
its historic path from Constantinople to Paris, along with a handful of
Serbian classics. Switzerland, Italy, Bulgaria, Turkey, Greece, and
Romania all have their national dish. There's Veal Goulash from Hungary,
Wiener Schnitzel from Austria, and Veal Cordon Blue from France.
European entrees $7-$14, Serbian entrees $8-$12, sides $2.50-$3.25. A
complete Serbian meal with appetizer, soup, entree, sides, dessert, and
coffee costs $13.95. Open late on weekends.

Smoke-Free Restaurants

Of the restaurants listed in this chapter, the following are known to be
smoke-free: **Chicago Diner** (p.202), **Corner Bakery** (p.173), **Earth Cafe**
(p.202), **El Dinamico Dallas** (p.130), **Lulu's** (p.122), **Pattie's Heart
Healthy** (p.171), and **Soul Vegetarian East** (p.194).

Soul Food

Alma's Place
419 E. 43rd, 773/924-0281   S
Located next to the **New Checkerboard Lounge** (p.212), **Alma's** serves
hometown soul food to a local crowd. Specialties include chittlins, turkey
and gravy, greens and hamhocks, meatloaf, spaghetti, catfish, pinto beans,
and black-eyed peas. Except for the $7 chittlins, all dinners are $5.50.
Alma's other claim to fame is her place's appearance in the movie, *Next of*

Kin, and the appearance of her hamburgers for one of Robert Duvall's scenes in *A Family Thing*. (Alma said that Duvall was so nice, she fixed him some of her special banana pudding, too.)

Gladys' Luncheonette
4527 S. Indiana, 773/548-4566   S

The formica counters and green booths may be what you'd imagine as "luncheonette" decor, but **Gladys'** food surpasses any "luncheonette" expectations. Since 1945, Gladys has been drawing south siders for memorable dishes like smothered chicken, rib tips, oxtails, fried catfish, and ham hocks. Entrees come with your choice of sides (collard greens, black-eyed peas, corn muffins, biscuits....). Though you won't have room, it will be hard to pass on dessert. Sweet potato pie, lemon meringue pie, bread pudding, and peach cobbler are but a few of the favorites. The menu changes daily. Most breakfasts are under $5. Lunch and dinner entrees are $5.50-$12, most under $7. Brunch early Sunday afternoon with a dressed-up after-church crowd.

Lou's and Liz's Restaurant
328 E. 75th, no phone   FSE

Just down the block from the well-known but pricey soul food mecca **Army and Lou's** (422 E. 75th, 773/483-3100) are **Liz and Lou**, still going strong after 30 plus years on the block. Everything's from scratch and dinners range from $4 to $6.50.

For meatless, healthy versions of many of these dishes, head a block or so east to **Soul Vegetarian East** (205 E. 75th, 773/224-0104)—a warm and laid-back restaurant serving breakfast, lunch, dinner, and a Sunday buffet.

Queen of the Sea
212 E. 47th, 773/624-1777   S

The menu at **Queen of the Sea** favors seafood, especially catfish, perch, and bass, but diners can also order chicken, ham hocks, and chitterlings, not to mention an excellent seafood gumbo ($7.50), at this cafeteria-style diner. Dinners $4-$7.

Soul Queen
9031 S. Stony Island, 773/731-3366   FSE

Advertising "Soul Food for all Souls," this south side institution has been around for 50 years, starting in the Bronzeville area and then moving to its current address in Pill Hill. You'll recognize it not only by the huge sign but by owner Helen Maybell's green Excalibur parked out front.

Soup

Soupbox
2943 N. Broadway, 773/935-0769   **N**
Just six weeks before Seinfeld's infamous "Soup Nazi" episode, enterprising (and psychic?) 20-something Jamie Taerbaum converted his summertime Italian Ice shop (**Icebox**) into a literal soup kitchen for the cold months. It's all soup here, so you have only two choices: Which kind? (12 kettles of homemade soup daily, from a rotating selection of 70) and Which size? Tortellini with Chicken, Cream of Asparagus, Tomato Florentine, Minestrone, Chili, Pizza Lover's, Albindigas (Spanish meatballs), Split Pea with Ham, Clam Chowder... $2-$4.

Southern Eclectic   See also: **Cajun/Creole**.

Dixie Kitchen & Bait Shop
5225 S. Harper, 773/363-4943   **S**
Cheerful re-creation of a bayou joint issues first-rate and plentiful Cajun and southern favorites. Start with fried green tomatoes, peach-glazed chicken wings or crayfish and corn fritters ($3.75-$4.95). Sandwiches like the Oyster Po'boy and North Carolina Pulled Pork come with cole slaw and your choice of a side ($5.95-$7.95). Gumbo, jambalaya, and red beans & rice are served with a corn muffin ($5.95-$9.95), and entrees like blackened catfish and country-fried steak come with cole slaw, corn muffin and two sides ($7.95-$10.95). Sides include black-eyed peas, mashed potatoes, greens, and corn. Please save room for dessert: bread pudding with whiskey sauce, peach cobbler, and pecan pie ($3.50).

N.N. Smokehouse
1465 W. Irving Park, 773/868-4700   **N**
Soon after sitting down on one of the wooden benches painted with log-cabin scenes, fresh bread, coleslaw, and large mason jars of water arrive at your table. Specials ($8.25-$8.99) include Filipino *pancit* noodles, Caribbean Tuesdays, Southern Soul Food Wednesdays, and all-you-can-eat BBQ beef ribs Thursdays. Great menu choices ($3.50-$14.95) like BBQ dinners (ribs, smoked chicken, shrimp), BBQ sandwiches (smoked turkey, Texas brisket, Memphis pulled pork), and Seafood Jambalaya make for a tough decision. Enjoy the blues, interesting decor, and eclectic neighborhood crowd while waiting for the food. Lunches run $4.75-$9,

most under $6.

Wishbone

1800 W. Grand, 312/829-3597 (Closed Mondays.)   **W**

1001 W. Washington, 312/850-2663   **C**

Whimsical depictions of barnyard animals and sea life decorate the converted warehouse on Washington where the energetic crowd never lags until the last grit is served at the end of the day. The menu, inviting and lighthearted in its takes on Southern classics, wows with its choices for every meal of the day. (Weekend brunch really packs in the devoted.) The food itself pleases any serious diner, including the health-conscious: baked bone-in-ham with honey mustard sauce, Hoppin' John, cheesy grits, bean cakes with mango salsa, Eggplant Elegant, blue claw crab cakes, stuffed acorn squash. Breakfast, lunch, and dinner entrees, $5-$11.

Spanish

The Spanish, who are late night diners, snack earlier in the evening on tapas, when they stop at a bar for a drink. Tapas are small plates of food that are shared around. Over the last few years, tapas dining has become tremendously popular in Chicago, with several non-Spanish places renaming their appetizers "tapas" or even adopting tapas as their entire menu concept. As Spanish food is generally a more expensive cuisine due to the amount of seafood and types of meat and preparation involved, tapas are a good way to sample some traditional dishes of Spain with your friends without spending a lot of money.

Cafe Iberico

739 N. LaSalle, 312/573-1510   **C**

This bustling, authentic tapas (appetizers) bar has won accolades from all major local newspapers and was elected "The Best Hispanic Restaurant in Illinois" by *Hispanic Magazine*. A large bar area, huge dining room, and a downstairs *bodega* (cellar) can barely contain the enthusiastic crowds. The cold tapas ($2.95-$4.95) list contains all the Spanish standards: olives, artichokes, toasted bread with manchego cheese, tortilla española (potato omelet), cured ham, cold octopus. The hot tapas ($2.95-$4.95) selection does just as well with its special preparations of mussels, scallops, clams, chorizo, squid, and goat cheese. Desserts heavy with caramel and custard ($2.95-$3.50) are also great for sharing. Affordable brandy, amontillado, sherry, vino tinto, and sangria await. Open Sun.-Thur. until 11pm, Fri.-Sat. until 1:30am.

Arco de Cuchilleros (3445 N. Halsted, 773/296-6046) serves tasty renditions of Spanish classics from their smaller quarters on the north side. A pitcher of sangria enjoyed from the pleasant backyard patio will transport you far from Halsted Street. Tapas $2-$6. Closed Mondays.

Submarine Sandwiches

Fontano's Subs
333 S. Franklin, 312/408-0555 (Closed Sat.-Sun.)   **C**
20 E. Jackson, 312/663-3061 (Closed Sun.)   **C**
With piles of everything from Italian meatballs, pepperoni, sausage, and prosciutto to roast beef, corned beef, bologna, and ham at hand, **Fontano's** creates hefty Italian and American sub concoctions topped with giardiniera, peppers, olives, and a hot or mild oregano vinaigrette. 6-inch sandwiches go for $2.25-$4.25 and 10-inchers, $3.75-$6.50.

Grandaddy's Subs
2343 W. Taylor, 312/243-4200   **W**
Most subs with a side salad will cost you under $5. Try one of the Grandaddy Subs for $4.80 or $5.30—they should feed two hungry people. The Great-Grandaddy Subs at $9.60 and $10.60 should feed a family of four. Closed Sunday.

Tim's friend said so...

A gross oversight in this category in past editions was corrected by **Tim's Friend** who politely insisted that the 22-year-old **Potbelly Sandwich Works** (2264 N. Lincoln, 773/528-1405) was guidebook-worthy. From the basic subs, chips, and drinks menu, customers favor the Italian Sub (piled with Italian meats and cheeses) or The Wreck (turkey, roast beef, ham, salami, and Swiss cheese). All sandwiches are $3.83.

Swedish

See the **Andersonville** entry (p.278) in the *Walking* chapter for more information on Chicago's original Swedish neighborhood and two of its long-standing delicatessens.

Ann Sather's Restaurant

5207 N. Clark, 773/271-6677	**FN**
929 W. Belmont, 773/348-2378	**N**
2665 N. Clark, 773/327-9522 (**Ann Sather's Cafe**)	**N**
3416 N. Southport, 773/404-4475 (**Ann Sather Cafe**)	**N**

Extraordinary cinnamon rolls, marvelous homemade food, large portions, cozy atmosphere, and great prices continually put the **Ann Sather's** restaurants at the top of Chicagoans' lists of favorite breakfast spots. [Note: The cafes have limited menus.] Swedish pancakes and meatballs, Swedish waffles with ice cream and strawberries, potato sausage, limpa rye, and lingonberry syrup join more conventional breakfast items on the menu. Special touches accent all meals: try peach, zucchini, or crab in the delectable omelettes. Choose homemade cinnamon rolls, biscuits, or muffins instead of toast, and homemade applesauce or fresh fruit instead of hash browns, as accompaniments to your egg dishes. Enjoy freshly made potato pancakes and ham with the bone left in. Take home cinnamon rolls, loaves of limpa, fruit pies, or monstrous cocoa-laden brownies from the bakery. Breakfast $3.75-$6.75, most under $5.50. Sides $1-$2.95.

Svea Restaurant

5236 N. Clark, 773/275-7738	**FN**

In lieu of **Ann Sathers'** big city bustle, cross the street to **Svea's** sleepy, down-to-earth charm. The Swedish pancakes, Swedish omelette, and Swedish meatballs are as Swedish as they profess. Other authentic favorites, like lox, egg & anchovies, and herring, can be found atop an open-faced sandwich. Menu items range from $2.85 to $7.50, most are under $5.

Swedish Bakery

5348 N. Clark, 773/561-8919	**FN**

A smorgasbord of low-priced and generously portioned baked goods for every occasion: breads (Stockholm limpa, sweet rye), muffins (sour cream poppyseed, cranberry), slices (custard streusel, Italian plum, pumpkin), candies (carrot cake truffles, mini cannoli), coffee cakes (apple walnut, cardamom raisin), cakes (Mocha Log, chocolate raspberry buttercream), cookies (Swedish butter cookies, filbert sandwich), and more. Waits can be long on weekends, giving you plenty of time to scope the three walls of goods and make some choices. Closed Sunday.

Tre Kroner
3258 W. Foster, 773/267-9888   **FN**
Picturesque Swedish and Norwegian cafe serves a limited but sufficient
menu of omelettes, quiches, soups, salads, and sandwiches for breakfast
and lunch ($3.75-$6.50). Try the Oslo Omelette filled with smoked
salmon, dill, and cream cheese or the Stockholm, with caraway and cheese.
Limpa bread and potato sausages make good additions for those with
Viking appetites. With fresh flowers and candle lit tables in the evening,
the dinner ambiance becomes less quaint and more romantic. Lamb,
salmon, and meatballs are house specialties. Complete dinners are under
$10. Closed Mondays.

Thai

Bangkok Spice
1825 W. Irving Park, 773/281-6661   **N**
An artistic paint job that includes a captivating floor-to-ceiling mural
recently spruced up this little storefront whose kitchen offers sensory
pleasures of its own. Pad Thai, Pad See Eiw, and Thai BBQ pork are the
popular menu items, but it's also hard to turn down the $4.95 lunch special
that comes with appetizer, soup, entree, and rice. Most entrees are $5-$7.

Dao Thai Restaurant
230 E. Ohio, 312/337-0000   **C**
Fresh meat, fish, and vegetables are purchased daily, and the herbs and
spices home-grown for the memorable dishes served at this haven for "old
fashioned Thai cuisine." In the summer, savor every spicy morsel from the
lovely outdoor deck. Year round, relish the incredibly low check. Entrees
run $4-$8 and nearly all are under $6.

Noodles in the Pot
2453 N. Halsted, 773/975-6177   **N**
This attractive little storefront stresses their noodle dishes: *Pad Thai* with
chicken, shrimp, or tofu; thick egg noodles topped with broccoli and
roasted duck; *Lard Nar* (fried rice noodles) with chicken or beef. Most
entrees cost $5-$6, lunch bargains are even less.

Siam Cafe
4712 N. Sheridan, 773/769-6602   **N**
Around since before we became a Thai-savvy town, this modest
neighborhood restaurant continues to serve inexpensive meals, including

house specialties like pork satay (BBQ ribs), curries, catfish, cuttlefish, oysters, and greens fried in oyster sauce. Most entrees $4.50-$6.

Star of Siam
11 E. Illinois, 312/670-0100   **C**
Downtown's first Thai restaurant (1984), the **Star of Siam** claims to have helped popularize Thai food in Chicago and the country. Located in a rehabbed warehouse appointed with Thai folk art and some unique seating, this cheap eatery draws a fashionable clientele who gobble the cashew chicken, *Pad Thai*, and chicken satay. Hot fried curry chicken, spicy ginger chicken, and brandy-beef with green curry appear on the specials list. Entrees $5.75-$18, most under $7.

Standing out for their fresh, healthy ingredients; fair prices; options for vegetarians; and all-round quality are **Bamee Noodle Shop** (3120-22 N. Broadway, 773/281-2641) and **Thai Wild Ginger** (2203 N. Clybourn, 773/883-0344). Most entrees at both places fall between $5 and $7. **Thai Wild Ginger** has a $4.95 weekday lunch special (11:30am-4pm) that comes with soup, salad, and choice of entree.

Tibetan

A few years back, Chicago became one of the designated cities in the Tibetan Relocation Project. This national effort helped establish various Tibetan communities in major urban areas as a way for Tibetans to preserve their culture while away from their occupied homeland.

Tibet Cafe
3913 N. Sheridan, 773/281-6666   **N**
Influenced by Chinese and Indian cuisines, the mountains, and the yak, Tibetan food offers unique and pleasing flavors for American taste buds. Appealing to the eye as well as the palette, the **Tibet Cafe** delivers a range of such scrumptious dishes in a lovely setting. This restaurant's light wood interior, accented with bright upholstery on the chairs and butter sculptures on the wall, is mostly the handiwork of its owners—former monks. Be sure to sample any version of *momos*—steamed or fried dumplings filled with meat or vegetables and a staple of Tibetan dining. Among the plentiful vegetarian dishes are curried tofu and spicy potato & cauliflower salad. For meat eaters, try the seasoned beef patty (*Sha-Bhale*) or the curried chicken—both house specialties. Entrees $5-$9. BYOB. Closed Mondays.

Tropical Drinks

Ciral's House of Tiki

1612 E. 53rd, 773/684-1221 **S**
All it takes is a walk in the door of the Hyde Park institution to see why the locals call it "the House of Tacky." The decor is plastic, plastic, and more plastic, from plants to alligators to blowfish suspended from the ceiling. Look past all that to the impressive list of tropical drinks, most of which cost about $3. In addition to the usual Mai Tai, Daiquiri, and Singapore Sling, **Ciral's** serves a Tiki Zombie. Its ingredients are a secret and you're allowed only one per visit. The bar's open Mon. through Fri., noon-4am and Sat., noon-5am. They stay home on Sundays to sleep it off.

Vegetarian

A Natural Harvest

7122 S. Jeffery, 773/363-3939 **FSE**
The Taste of Chicago has exposed thousands (if not millions) over the years to the vegetarian tamales and corn dogs of this South Shore deli and health food store. Make a trip for other veggie substitutes. Ham, salami, chicken, burgers, steaks, tacos, and hot dogs are among the other mock meats/meat dishes prepared to go. The premises include a fresh juice bar that also supplies a range of energy drinks. Items range from $2 to $6.

Blind Faith Cafe

3300 N. Lincoln, 773/871-3820 **N**
While year-round entrees, like corn & potato enchiladas and the black bean burrito made with "chicken" seitan, are healthy and satisfying, ordering a seasonal specialty can be simply divine. The wild mushroom risotto, pumpkin stuffed ravioli with a braised fennel cream sauce, and bourbon squash from last fall's menu are the types of items that are worth **Blind Faith**'s higher price tags. Breakfast $4.95-$7.95, lunch $7-$9, appetizers $5-$7, dinner entrees $9-$12.

Cafe Pergolesi

3404 N. Halsted, 773/472-8602 **N**
True to its 1969 origins, this classic low-key coffeehouse—mentioned in Abbie Hoffman's *Steal This Book*—serves vegetarian dishes, many using their Nuksia meat-substitute invention. Entrees $3.50-$6.50, most under $5. Closed Wed. - Sat.

Chicago Diner
3411 N. Halsted, 773/935-6696   **N**
"Love animals, don't eat them," they say here at Chicago's chief, 20-something vegetarian restaurant, where typical vegetarian ingredients dominate the menu's dishes. Tofu, tempeh, sea vegetables, brown rice, legumes, kale, sprouts, soy cheese, et. al. create standards like burgers, salads, stir-fries, and noodle dishes. Breakfast favorites include biscuits & gravy and the potato hash with tempeh. At dinner, lentil loaf, seitan fajitas, and the future burger are frequent requests. Most entrees $5-$10.

The Earth Cafe
2570 N. Lincoln, 773/327-8459   **N**
Limited-seating ultra-veggie cafe—located in the rear of a New Age gift shop/resource center—is great for cheap lunching or snacking while shopping in the area. Try the vegan soups, burrito, avocado sandwich, or chocolate mousse. The food is 90% organic. Items from the chalkboard menu generally fall between $4 and $7. Closes at 8pm.

Heartland Cafe and Buffalo Bar
7000 N. Glenwood, 773/465-8005   **FN**
This peace/love complex includes a healthy vegetarian (soy, tempeh, tofu, rice, beans) and non-vegetarian (burgers, chicken, turkey) restaurant with a spacious outdoor patio, a bar with an impressive and diverse entertainment lineup, a book store/gift shop, and a newspaper with a message. The nachos, chili with cornbread, outdoor dining, and entertainment come recommended. Breakfasts run under $5; lunch and dinner, $4-$8, with specials up to $10. Visit their new concession stand on the lakefront (see p.160).

Karyn's Fresh Corner
3351 N. Lincoln, 773/296-6990   **N**
"Eat Grass, Don't Walk On It" could be the motto of this astro-turfed raw foods restaurant and shop. This is a "living foods" cafe, as indicated by a menu of almost entirely uncooked foods and sprouting racks of wheat grass and herbs in the open kitchen. Although many of these items are bound to tax even a health-nut's imagination, they will nevertheless impress the adventurous diner. A banana cream pie made from whipped cashews, bananas, and a seed base. Adzuki sprouts pureed to resemble refried beans. Mock turkey created with a skillful blend of seeds and garden vegetables. If such dishes are a stretch for you, there's always the gazpacho. Beverages include teas, tonics, smoothies, and fresh fruit and vegetable juices. Most

dishes, $6-$10, with a $9.95 all-you-care-to-eat vegan buffet. Open daily until 9pm.

Vietnamese

The so-called "New Chinatown" along the 1000 and 1100 blocks of Argyle Street, is actually dominated by Vietnamese shops and restaurants, almost all of which are inexpensive and most of which offer at least 100 dishes. Explore this two block stretch, venturing into a restaurant that interests you, or take one of these recommendations:

Hau Giang Restaurant
1104-06 W. Argyle, 773/275-8691   **FN**
Perhaps Argyle Street's best. Outstanding food and low prices far outweigh the ho-hum decor. Clay-pot specials like shrimp soup with fresh pineapple and catfish soup with sour mustard and taro just nick the surface of the dozens of good finds you'll discover on this 187-item menu. Dishes $4-$13, most under $6. Closed Thursdays.

Lac Vien Restaurant
1129 W. Argyle, 773/275-1112   **FN**
Encyclopedic menu offers 156 fascinating choices (fancy stuffed crabs with house sauce; sizzling platter of abalone, shrimp, crab, fish cakes, and vegetables; sautéed eel in curry and satay sauce...) and Vietnamese classics in a no-frills storefront. Dishes $4-11, most under $6.

And, on the edge of a Korean neighborhood...

Hong Ta
3035 W. Lawrence, 773/267-5408   **N**
With it's low prices and commendable food, you'll want to return again and again to this small, off-the-beaten track Vietnamese restaurant to make your way through its ample menu. Stick with basic items or move on to less familiar terrain: Roasted quail in a sour lime sauce, catfish soup with pineapple and veggies in a tamarind base, green mussel curry with okra, frog legs with chili peppers and lemongrass. Entrees $5.25-$12.95, most under $7. The $4.50 lunch special comes with soup, entree, egg roll, fried rice, and tea.

DINING DISCOUNTS

Look for additional savings at the following restaurants—mentioned in the previous pages—through their participation in one or more discount dining card programs. **IGT** (In Good Taste) takes a 20% discount off the total check, **TransMedia** gives a 25% discount on the entire check, and the **Entertainment Book** offers two entrees for the price of one.

Abbey Pub, Addis Abeba, Ann Sather's, Bacino's Pizzeria, Bamee Noodle Shop, Bangkok Spice, Bertucci's Corner, Blind Faith Cafe, Bransfield's, Cafe Penelope, Chesdan's, Chicago Diner, Clarke's, Connie's Pizza, Cousin's, Dao, Dixie Kitchen & Bait Shop, El Tinajon, Ethiopian Diamond, Ethiopian Village, Gandhi India, Gulliver's, Hickory Pit, The Hunt Club, Hyderabad House, Iggy's, Kan Zaman, Karyn's Fresh Corner, King Tut Oasis, Little Bucharest, L'Olive, Mama Desta's Red Sea Restaurant, Mecca, Nhu Hoa Cafe, N.N. Smokehouse, Orbit, Original Pancake House, Pampanga's Cuisine, The Parthenon, Pattie's Quick & Lite, Russian Palace, Star of Siam, Thai Wild Ginger, Tibet Cafe, Tiffin, Trattoria Caterina, Urban Market Cafe, and **Viceroy of India.**

INTERNET RESOURCES

Chicago Area Restaurant Guide
http://www.dine.com/chicago
Register and receive e-mail reviews, recommendations, and news on Chi-town restaurants. Put up your personal list of reviews and favorite dining spots and read those of others.

Chicago Menus Online
http://menusonline.com/cities/Chicago/locmain.shtml
Menus of dozens of Chicago restaurants. Also, reviews and basic restaurant information.

City-Life Chicago Restaurants
http://www.city-life.com/chicago/restaurants
Comprehensive list of Chicago restaurants, last updated June 1997.

Cuisine Net Chicago
http://www.cuisinenet.com/restaurant/chicago
Search by cuisine, location, price, and amenities. Entry includes one to three paragraphs of description, a price estimate, and a chart of other diners' ratings by service, ambience, and food quality.

Dine Out Chicago
http://dine.package.com/chicago
Reviews, menus, wine list, pictures, directions, description, fact sheet, diners' comments, and online reservations for a limited database of Chicago eateries. Click on the "Spin" button and let it choose a restaurant for you randomly.

Kosher Eating in Chicago
http://condor.depaul.edu/~scohn/NTJC-Fd.html
Master list of Kosher restaurants, take out places, pizza, bakeries, and delis.

Master Vegetarian Restaurant List
http://www.veg.org/veg/Guide/USA/Illinois/Chicago.html
Comprehensive list of restaurants, groceries, delis, coffee houses, etc. that serve vegetarian food. Although last updated February 1996, there's no other list that comes close and most information is still good.

Metromix Restaurant Search
http://www.metromix.com/object/7483.html
Largest online database of Chicago restaurants. Search by region or neighborhood, type of cuisine, and price range. Also restaurant recommendations and feature articles by *Chicago Tribune* staff.

Zagat's Restaurant Guide To Chicago
http://www.pathfinder.com/travel/zagat/Dine/cities/Chicago
Read diners' reviews of some of Chicago's favorite restaurants excerpted from *Zagat's* guide.

OUTLET STORES

Best Kosher Sausage Factory Outlet Store
159 N. Wells, 312/726-6559   **C**

Butternut Bread Thrift Stores
40 E. Garfield, 773/536-7700   **S**
1857 W. 35th, 773/927-5849   **SW**
6655 S. Pulaski, 773/582-5461   **SW**
2925 W. Montrose, 773/478-8875   **N**
3236 N. Damen, 773/528-4004   **N**
Additional 10% discount Tuesdays.

Dolly Madison Cake
2925 W. Montrose, 773/478-8875   **N**
1857 W. 35th, 773/927-5849   **SW**
Additional 10% discount Tuesdays.

Eli's Chicago's Finest Cheesecake
6701 W. Forest Preserve Drive, 773/736-3417   **N**
The yearly taste of Eli's celebration is usually in August or September. Call
for this year's date.

Entenmann's Thrift Stores
4400 S. Pulaski, 773/376-1609   **SW**
3031 N. Pulaski, 773/283-5105   **NW**

Farley Candy Outlet
3025 N. Pulaski, 773/725-1661   **NW**

Heinemann's Bakery Plant Outlet Store
3925 W. 43rd, 773/523-5000   **SW**
Open 24 hours.

Holsum Bakery Thrift Stores
716 E. 87th, 773/488-5109   **FSE**
3230 N. Milwaukee, 773/725-3399   **NW**
4546 N. Magnolia, 773/728-1662   **N**

Hostess Cakes/Wonder Bread Outlet Stores
1301 W. Diversey, 773/281-6700   N
5702 W. 55th, 773/585-7474   SW

Sara Lee Outlet Stores
742 E. 87th, 773/783-6585   FSE
3237 N. Harlem, 773/202-0093   NW
4028 W. 59th, 773/581-9408   SW
6210 N. Western, 773/973-6210   FN
7650 W. Touhy, 773/763-4785   FN

Vienna Beef Outlet
2501 N. Damen, 773/235-6652   N

FARMER'S MARKETS

For four months of the year, from late June to late October, the city of Chicago's **Farmer's Market** (312/744-9187) program offers ample opportunities to purchase fresh and inexpensive produce from regional farmers. Arrive early (7am-8am) for the best selection, but come near closing (2pm-3pm) for the best bargains. Complete schedules are available in season at the information desk in **City Hall** (121 N. LaSalle) or by calling the **Department of Consumer Services** at 312/744-4006, TDD: 312/744-9385.

5 ENTERTAINMENT

Two of Chicago's favorite venues for affordable entertainment: Fireside Bowl (*left*) for all ages punk rock shows and the historic Green Mill (*below*) for jazz and poetry slams. (*Photos by Rames Shrestha.*)

Neighborhood culture: The Old Town School of Folk Music (*above*)
recently moved into the former Hild Regional Library building in Lincoln
Square, making it the largest folk music center in the world.
Pub crawlers commune at The Village Tap (*below*) in Roscoe Village
for its connoisseur's collection of microbrews on tap, popular beer
garden, and assortment of board games. (*Photos by Rames Shrestha.*)

5 ENTERTAINMENT

hen it's time for some rest and relaxation, leaf through this section to find some of the best ways to spend an evening in Chicago. You can amuse yourself and others by volunteer ushering; attending festivals; learning about beer; dancing; or participating in improv comedy, open mic poetry, and open music jams. Or, let them entertain you with live music, movies, theatre, comedy, dance, and poetry. We've got hard-to-beat blues and jazz, improvised Tennessee Williams, free classical music in the afternoon, midnight movies, reggae clubs, spoken word performance forums, Euro-style dance clubs, build-your-own Bloody Mary bars, neighborhood gospel festivals...

LIVE MUSIC

Blues

In the blues capital of the northern U.S. (we like to collect such titles here), big-name blues can be heard seven days a week all over town for very low entrance fees.

Artis
1249 E. 87th, 773/734-0491   **FSE**
An upwardly-mobile, well-dressed crowd gathers nightly at **Artis** to enjoy blues and R&B. Legendary DJ Herb Kent ("the Cool Gent") mans the controls each Tuesday beginning at 8pm. Local bands such as Billy Branch and the Sons of the Blues appear on Sunday and Monday nights at 9pm. Open Sun-Fri. 10 am-2am, Sat. 10am-3am. No cover.

Blue Chicago
536 N. Clark, 312/661-0100 (Closed Mondays)   **C**
736 N. Clark, 312/642-6261 (Closed Sundays)   **C**
Packed with both tourists and residents, these bars remain down-to-earth and friendly in a trendy nightlife area. The clubs open at 8pm, the music begins

at 9pm and goes past midnight. $5-$7 cover allows admission to both clubs.

B.L.U.E.S.
2519 N. Halsted, 773/528-1012   **N**
Small club provides an intimate, quintessential blues bar experience with
some Chicago greats: Big Time Sarah, Magic Slim & The Teardrops, Son
Seals. Music begins nightly around 9:30pm. Most covers $5-$8.

B.L.U.E.S. Etcetera
1124 W. Belmont, 773/525-8989   **N**
Spacious sister club to **B.L.U.E.S.** features the best of local and regional
blues beginning at 9pm Sun.-Thur., and 9:30pm Fri.-Sat. Wednesday is
open blues jam night. Cover $3-$10. Closed Mon.-Tues.

Buddy Guy's Legends
754 S. Wabash, 312/427-0333   **C**
The Grammy winner's club presents local and national acts in a roomy
storefront. Two pool tables and a full kitchen with great BBQ (serving until
midnight) expand your options. On certain nights you might catch the legend
himself roaming through the crowd. Nightly music, cover $3-$10. (BZ)

Delta Fishmarket
228 S. Kedzie, 773/722-0588   **W**
For the most unique blues experience north of the Delta, make a weekend
trip to the **Delta Fishmarket** where organized outdoor blues jams get started
around 2-3pm Friday and Saturday afternoons and continue on into the wee
hours. Grab a seafood dinner from the market, BYOB, BYOC (chair), and
get lost in another world. No charge.

Lee's Unleaded Blues
7401 S. South Chicago, 773/493-3477   **FSE**
The blues begin at 9pm and go until 2am Fri.-Mon. at this cozy, South Side
night spot. No cover, but the drinks do cost at least $.50 more during music
sessions. Order some "unleaded" chili on the side.

New Checkerboard Lounge
423 E. 43rd, 773/624-3240   **S**
Once owned by Buddy Guy and the late Junior Wells, this is the last blues
outpost in a neighborhood rich in blues history. Live music Thur.-Mon.
9:30pm. Covers $5-$7. Don't miss this Chicago favorite, but be wary the
rough neighborhood.

Rosa's Lounge
3420 W. Armitage, 773/342-0452   **NW**
"Chicago's Friendliest Blues Lounge" is owned by a transplanted Italian blues drummer and his mama, Rosa. Visit *www.rosaslounge.com* and join the mailing list to have schedules mailed to you. Music begins 9:30pm Tues.-Thur., 10pm Sat. Cover $5-$7, $10 for the likes of Sugar Blue Melvis.

For South Side neighborhood blues, drop by **Chuck's Derby** (209 E. 51st, 773/373-5100), **Cuddle Inn** (5317 S. Ashland, 773/778-1999), **Jojo Murray Blues House** (7401 S. Halsted, 773/783-3560), or **Red's Lounge** (3479 S. Archer, 773/376-0517) on the weekends. Covers are generally under $5 or even non-existent. North of downtown there's **Lilly's** (2513 N. Lincoln, 773/525-2422), where a mixed bag of Lincoln Parkers and assorted others listen to blues Wed.-Sat. in a bordertown cantina atmosphere. The cover is $3-$5, which sometimes means throwing a few bucks in the tip jar. Music begins around 9:30pm. Just as unexpected is **Smoke Daddy** (1804 W. Division, 773/772-6656), a sleek, diner-like BBQ restaurant with blues/ jazz Sun., Mon., Wed., and Thur. Music starts at 10pm. Never a cover.

Classical

There's no better place to start than **Orchestra Hall** (220 S. Michigan, 312/294-3000) for world-class classical music. The recent creation of **Symphony Center** came with a remodeling of Orchestra Hall that includes improved acoustics, new seating, and renovated public areas. Though generally quite pricey, it's possible to get tickets for as low as $7-$15 here—for the **Chicago Symphony Orchestra** (312/435-6666), as well as for other local ensembles/soloists and visiting musicians. The **Civic Orchestra of Chicago** (the "minor leagues" for the **CSO** comprised of college and graduate musicians, 312/294-3420), the **Chicago Sinfonietta** (a more progressive orchestra, 312/857-1062), and the **Chicago Youth Symphony Orchestra** (high school aged virtuosos, 312/939-2207) routinely play at Orchestra Hall (as well as occasional free concerts elsewhere) and come recommended.

In sharp contrast to the high ticket prices that even lesser-known classical groups command, some of the best classical music in Chicago can be heard for absolutely nothing. The **Chicago Cultural Center** (see p.48), the **Harold Washington Library Center** (see p.48), and **The Chicago Music Mart** (DePaul Center, 333 S. State, 312/362-6700) are often the sites of free performances by noted regional ensembles like the **Newberry Consort**

(312/943-9090), **Chicago Chamber Orchestra** (312/922-5570), and the **Classical Symphony Orchestra** (312/341-1521). Many of these shows take place on the lunch hour, evenings, and Sunday afternoons. Monthly schedules are available. Elegant neighborhood cultural centers, particularly the **North Lakeside Cultural Center** (6219 N. Sheridan, 773/743-4477), the **Three Arts Club** (1300 N. Dearborn, 312/944-6250), and the **South Shore Cultural Center** (7059 S. South Shore Drive, 312/747-2536), likewise offer impressive classical concerts free of charge. Finally, no summer would be complete without enjoying at least one of the many free outdoor concerts performed by the **Grant Park Symphony** (312/742-7638) each season.

Schools, universities, and churches are another solid source of free and inexpensive classical music and opera. **DePaul University** (1 E. Jackson Blvd., 312/362-8000) and the **University of Chicago** (5801 S. Ellis, 773/702-1234), in particular, present both high-quality student performances and well-known guests. The **U of C**'s summer opera theatre wins rave reviews with its outdoor performances on the green and gothic campus. **Roosevelt University** (430 S. Michigan, 312/341-3500) is dependable for free performances, and the reputable **Sherwood Conservatory of Music** (1014 S. Michigan, 312/427-6267) showcases their diamonds-in-the-rough at low cost. Head to Hyde Park where the stunning **Rockefeller Memorial Chapel** (5850 S. Woodlawn, 773/702-2100) sponsors favorites like the *Chapel Choir* and *Carillon* concerts. **St. Luke's Evangelical Lutheran Church** (1500 W. Belmont, 773/472-3383) has a spectacular early music series.

Coffee Houses

Cafe Luna
1908 W. 103rd Street, 773/239-8990   **FSW**
This 1950s child-of-the-beatniks coffeehouse offers folk music every night at 8pm with no cover charge. The atmosphere is artsy and upscale. Coffees run $1.25-$2.75. Sandwiches (with names like Half Moon, Harvest Moon, Tuna Moon, and New Moon) range in price from $2 to $4.95. Luscious homemade desserts include brownies, lemon squares, pies, cakes, and ice cream. There's an open stage Wednesday nights at 8.

Java Jo's Acoustic Coffeehouse and Cafe
3700 N. Halsted, 773/528-3700   **N**
Nightly entertainment may be rock, folk, bluegrass, jazz, Irish, or the sock puppet theater! Cover stays low at $3-$6. Besides the coffee drinks, try other

non-alcoholic beverages like specialty sodas, ice cream shakes, or unique teas. Baked goods and sandwiches are also available for music-time noshing. Open until 8pm Sun., 11pm Mon-Thur., and midnight Fri.-Sat.

Jazz and Java
3428 S. Martin Luther King Drive, 312/791-1300 **S**
Live jazz Fri.-Sat. 8pm-midnight, $5 cover charge. Soups and sandwiches, $2-$4.50. Coffees from $1.25 to $3.

Mountain Moving Coffeehouse for Womyn and Children
1650 W. Foster, 773/973-9934 **N**
Open one Saturday a month from 7:30pm-10pm, the Mountain Moving Coffeehouse is the oldest women-only coffeehouse in the country. No males over the age of 2 are allowed, not even male-to-female transexuals. Music, poetry, literature, and comedy, along with coffee, tea, and baked goods are what you're likely to find at this all-girl coffeehouse which is located inside the Ebenezer Lutheran Church hall. A $15-$20 dollar donation is suggested but not mandatory. Call for details. No alcohol. (BZ)

No Exit Cafe & Gallery
6970 North Glenwood, 773/743-3355 **FN**
The No Exit has been around since the 50s, and for a coffee house it has a decent menu that offers salads, pastas, chili, soups, eggs, desserts, and a special breakfast on Sundays. Scenes for the River Phoenix movie *A Night in the Life of Jimmy Reardon* were shot here. But this Rogers Park perennial is best known for the inexpensive entertainment (mostly jazz and poetry) that graces its tiny stage on a nightly basis ($2-$5 and sometimes free!) Call for details. Open six days a week 4pm-midnight or later, opens 11am on Sunday. (BZ)

Viennese Kaffee-Haus Brandt
3424 N. Southport, 773/528-2220 **N**
Order a coffee drink and a fancy pastry at your marble-topped table and sit back and enjoy the sounds of opera Thursdays at 7:30pm. Owner Larry Cooper, once a professional opera singer in Europe, is one of the regular performers for the *Liederabende* (song nights) at this quaint Austrian-style cafe. Arrive earlier for a dinner of schnitzel or goulash to the sounds of recorded classical music.

Thursdays from 8pm-10pm, a variety of musicians perk up the **Gourmand Coffee Shop** (728 S. Dearborn, 312/427-2610) on Printer's Row. Singer/ songwriters and other acoustic musicians can be heard at the classy **Third**

Coast (1260 N. Dearborn, 312/649-0730) Thur.-Sun. beginning at 9:30pm. On Wednesdays at the beloved **Uncommon Ground** (1214 W. Grace, 773/929-3680) you can enjoy your coffee and baked goods with their songwriters showcase at 8pm. Folk/rock musicians also play on the weekends, when the cover is $1 per set, with 2-3 sets a night.

Country

Carol's Pub
4659 N. 773/334-2402   N
Raucous and spacious neighborhood tavern with live country/western music and dancing beginning at 9pm Thur.-Sat. and an open jam on Sun. Sandwiches and bar food available. Drink specials are simple, $1 bottled beer and 50 cent drafts on Mon., and more 50 cent drafts on Thur.

Lakeview Lounge
5110 N. Broadway, 773/769-0994   FN
Neighborhood bar ("country when country wasn't cool...") hosts country and western bands Thur.-Sat. from 10pm to early morning. Sun. country/ blues open mic 7pm-9pm. No cover.

Eclectic

Déjà Vu
2624 N. Lincoln, 773/871-0205   N
What was not too long ago an ordinary barroom, has been spiffed up by new owners in keeping with these swankier-minded times. Musical offerings include acid jazz, Gypsy King sound-alikes, blues, reggae, and rockabilly. DJs may play 70s/80s tunes or a lounge/swing set. Covers can be free or $3-$5; good drink specials often include top brands. The historic turtle races occur the last Wednesday of every month. Open nightly until 4am, Sat. until 5am.

Elbo Room
2871 N. Lincoln, 773/549-5549   N
A casual, attitude-free club that offers a wide range of rock and jazz stylings. Lounge comfortably with cocktails (or more often, beer) upstairs. Pay the cover charge ($3-$6) only when descending to the basement bar and stage. Wednesday is swing night with the 12-piece Chicago Jump Company. And you can either dance, be a wallflower, or just go limp as a DJ spins import, funk, and acid jazz on Sundays. (BZ)

HotHouse

31 E. Balbo, 312/362-9707   **C**

Subtitled "The Center for International Performance and Exhibition" or "Chicago's home for the Progressive Arts," the **HotHouse** is both home to a host of progressive political and artistic groups and a hip nightclub showcasing an eclectic program of music, dance, poetry, and performance art. One recent month featured mambo, flamenco, samba, fandango, a jazz quartet, big band, a cabaret show, a Zairian dance band, African Soukous, performances by multimedia artists, and a Pablo Neruda birthday party. With hot orange-red walls, warehouse-high ceilings, colorful artwork, interesting sculptures, big-window views of the city, full bar, and a dizzying entertainment schedule, the new **HotHouse** location makes for a sensational new South Loop club. Open daily 11am-2am, Sat. until 3am. Covers range from about $3-$20, most $7-$8.

Ethnic Tunes See also: **Irish**.

Zum Deutschen Eck

2924 N. Southport, 773/525-8122   **N**

Murals, stained glass, pewter vases, steins, wallplates, and other artifacts ornament the walls; Bavarian chandeliers hang from the ceilings; and European chinaware and tablecloths grace the tables at this enormous, Bavarian chalet-style restaurant, banquet hall, and lounge. Since 1956, this has been one of Chicago's favorite places for old world *gemütlichkeit*. Though the food is out of most folks' "budget" category, dessert or a stein of beer is enough to enjoy the live weekend *bierstube* music and infamous sing-a-longs. Fri. 7pm-11:30pm and Sat.-Sun. 6pm-11pm. No Sunday music during July and August. *Schwarzwalder Kirsch Torte* (Black Forest cake), Bavarian Apple Strudel with real whipped cream, or *Zugspitze* (Cherries Jubilee) are specialty desserts. No cover.

For Eastern European music, visit **Skadarlija** (see p.193) Serbian restaurant Wed-Sun. 8pm, 773/463-5600, when the house ensemble performs. **El Nandu** (see p.120) Argentinean restaurant hosts a Latin singer/guitarist Thur.-Sat. at 8pm., 773/278-0900. The seven-member house band at **Al-Khayam** (2326 W. Foster, 773/334-0000) Arabic restaurant plays a variety of Middle Eastern and American music and accompanies the occasional belly dancer Fri.-Sun. 9:30pm-2am.

Folk

Abbey Pub
3240 W. Grace, 773/478-4408   **NW**
Irish bar and nightclub (see below) regularly features folk and bluegrass musicians in addition to traditional Irish and rock bands. $5 contra dancing, with steps taught, Mon., open acoustic stage Tues., folk music Thur. Covers range up to $10 for big name acts, but most hover around $5.

The Old Town School of Folk Music
4544 N. Lincoln, 773/728-6000   **N**
Established in 1957, this venerable folk music school and performance space has become the world's largest center devoted to folk music with its recent move (Sept. 1998) to the renovated Art Deco building of the former Hild Regional Library. Expect a diverse lineup of folk acts, both big and small. Bluegrass, Celtic, Native American, Zydeco, Latin, blues, jazz... Tickets can cost up to $35, but there's plenty of good pickings for $5-$12.

Schuba's
3159 N. Southport, 773/525-2508   **N**
Large tavern and restaurant has a comfortable room for intimate live performances. Although they feature a range of performers, their best and most typical offerings are folkish—acoustic, folk-rock, folk-country, alternative country, bluegrass, etc. Typical covers are $4-$12, with most $5-$8.

Irish

Abbey Pub
3240 W. Grace, 773/478-4408   **NW**
Large Irish nightclub and bar hosts a free Sunday night Irish jam session. The Saturday night Irish bands have a $5-$10 cover. See above for information on the **Abbey**'s folk music schedule and p.153 for a look at their menu offerings.

Augenblick
3907 N. Damen, 773/929-0994   **N**
German name; young, hip crowd; and the popular Tuesday-night Irish folk music: 9pm-midnight or 1am. Arrive early to nab a seat. No cover.

Celtic Crossings
751 N. Clark, 312/337-1005   C
New Irish pub-club enlivened with artwork, two fireplaces, conversation (no TV), and plenty of Guinness offers traditional Irish music Sundays 5pm-10pm and Thursdays 9pm-midnight. No cover.

Kitty O'Shea's
720 S. Michigan, 312/922-4400   C
Named for a Dublin pub, this casual Irish bar and restaurant in the Chicago Hilton and Towers Hotel features Irish music nightly 9pm-1am. No cover. (See p.153.)

Vaughan's Pub
5105 N. Milwaukee, 773/283-8932   FN
Nice neighborhood bar with Irish bands Fri.-Sat 10pm-1am. Always looking for more lasses. No cover.

Jazz

Andy's
11E. Hubbard, 312/642-6805   C
Jazz bar and restaurant, popular with all types, has a free noontime jazz set Mon.-Fri., a $3 after-work set Mon.-Fri. at 5pm, and a later set at 8:30pm for $5. Live music Mon.-Thur. noon-2:30am, Fri. noon-1:30am, and Sat. 8:30pm-2am. Covers $3-$10, with a two-drink minimum on Sat. The kitchen stays open until midnight.

The Clique
2347 S. Michigan, 312/326-0274   S
Not for shy, retiring types, this aggressively social club offers live music, dancing, and comedy. The word is that Mike Tyson put this place on the map. Upstairs, DJs spin dance music; downstairs is for jazz. Dresses are short, pants are tight, and anything to attract the opposite sex, except jeans and baseball caps, is permissible. Cover is usually $10.

The Cotton Club
1710 S. Michigan, 312/341-9787   C
Evoking a similar feel to the mythical Harlem club it's named for, this sleek and classy club (dress code enforced) features nightly jazz up front and a large dance floor in back. Weekends can bring in big names and high price tags. Live music Sun.-Thur. 7pm-midnight, and Fri.-Sat. 10pm-3am. Sundays have a more "alternative" slant to them with female impersonators/

comedy, while Wednesdays are Reggae, and Mondays offer comedians and some excellent fledgling musicians a chance to shine with a night of open-mic. Complimentary buffet after 8pm, Fri. and Sat. nights. Cover varies from $3-$20 depending on the live entertainment, so remember to phone first. (MM and BZ)

Dick's Last Resort
435 E. Illinois, 312/836-7870   C
Gigantic and lively nightclub with a fake-raunchiness files crowds in at long beer-hall type tables, feeds them buckets of fried chicken and fish, plies them with beer, and gives them hours of free entertainment. The regular Dixieland jazz and the Sunday Gospel brunch (10:30am-3pm) are hits. Live music Mon-Thur. 7pm-11pm, Fri.-Sat. 6pm-2am. No cover or drink minimum.

Gold Star Sardine Bar
680 N. Lake Shore Dr., 312/664-4215   C
Tiny 50-seater tucked anonymously inside a high-rise building is too decorous to charge a cover, but will not tolerate jeans, sports shoes, or noise. Nightly live jazz begins at 8pm, 9pm Sat., and includes occasional big name surprises. Drink prices can push the reasonable range, but are justified by the quality of music.

Green Dolphin Street
2200 N. Ashland, 773/395-0066   N
A classy hotspot that recreates a classic jazz ballroom/supper club to showcase an inspiring line-up of jazz styles: acid, experimental, swing, Latin, and more Besides the music and food, enjoy cognac, champagne, cigars, or a shot of single-malt scotch. Live music 9pm-2am. Wed.-Thur. $5, Fri.-Sat. $10. Intimate jazz sets 8pm-12am on Sun.-Mon., no cover. (BZ)

Green Mill
4802 N. Broadway, 773/878-5552   N
Although it's been open since the early 1900s and popular in nearly every successive decade, what remains and what's remembered of The Green Mill are the speakeasy days when Al Capone frequented the place. It was also a favorite of silent movie giants Charlie Chaplin and Gloria Swanson during their days at Essanay Studios on nearby Argyle Street. Regular features include wee-hour jam sessions on the weekends, Sunday night torch singing 11pm-2am, and the 10-year-old, heckling poet's paradise, the Sunday-evening **Uptown Poetry Slam** (see p.252). Live jazz Mon.-Tues. 9pm-1:30am, Wed.-Thur. 5:30pm-1:30am, Fri. 9pm-4am, and Sat. 8pm-5am. The

entrance fee usually $4-$7.

The Note
1565 N. Milwaukee, 773/489-0011   **W**
Located in the Flat Iron Building, **The Note** showcases a range of jazz styles both classic and contemporary. Big band, swing, Latin jazz, acid jazz, free form, instrumentalists, and vocalists are all featured along with the occasional R & B or blues act. Local favorites like Kurt Elling and Fareed Haque appear regularly. Von Freeman leads an outstanding Sunday jam session. Covers are $3-$7, none after midnight. Open 8pm-4am, Sat. until 5am.

Underground Wonder Bar
10 E. Walton, 312/266-7761   **C**
Cozy, low-key, subterranean bar features nightly jazz (classic, Latin, piano, and other styles) until 4am. Cover $4-$6.

Velvet Lounge
2128-1/2 S. Indiana, 312/791-9050   **C**
Chicago jazzman Fred Anderson's bare-bones place, where serious fans and players come for the Sunday night free-form jam after 5:30pm. Cover is $6, $4 on Sundays.

Some no-cover jazz can be heard in outlying neighborhoods: **Big Joe's** (1818 W. Foster, 773/784-8755) features a quartet and jam session Sun. from 8pm to midnight, the **New Apartment Lounge** (504 E. 75th, 773/483-7728) hosts and open jam Tues. at 10pm, and the **Sunnyday Tap** (4953 N. Elston, 773/545-4114) has sets at 9:30pm Wed., Thur., and Sat., and 10pm Fri.

Piano Bars

Slightly higher-priced drinks compensate for the absent cover charge at these establishments.

Coq d'Or Lounge
140 E. Walton, 312/787-2200   **C**
On the scene for 40+ years, Buddy Charles tickles the ivories and honors every possible request at this Drake Hotel Lounge that's been serving since the end of Prohibition. 9pm-1:30am Tues.-Sat.

The Red Head Piano Bar
16 W. Ontario, 312/640-1000   **C**
Classy, dress-up place attracts an older and spiffy crowd. Complimentary appetizers during 5pm-7pm weekday cocktail hours. Dress code enforced. Mon.-Fri. 4pm-4am, Sat. 5pm-5am, Sun. 6pm-4am.

Zebra Lounge
1220 N. State, 312/642-5140   **C**
In business since 1932, this dark, space-constricted lounge with a pervasive zebra motif draws a mixed, upscale crowd for its animated sing-a-longs. Mon.-Sat. 8:30pm-1:30am, until 3am Sat. Magicians perform on Tuesdays.

Punk

Fireside Bowl
2646 W. Fullerton, 773/486-2700   **N**
Chicago's premier venue for punk rock shows just happens to be a bowling alley! Call the punk hotline (773/409-2310) for upcoming performances. Cover is usually $5 for 3 bands. All ages welcome; bar available for those over 21. Be warned that the restrooms may be the most disgusting you've ever experienced.

Keep an eye on these other clubs that also showcase punk bands: **Empty Bottle** (1035 N. Western, 773/276-3600) is the second choice for punk—shows are usually Thur.-Sat. **The Metro** (3730 N. Clark, 773/549-0203) features the big acts, but only on weekends. **Lounge Ax** (2438 N. Lincoln, 773/525-6620) and **Double Door** (1572 N. Milwaukee, 773/489-3160) present shows occasionally as well.

Reggae

Exedus II
3477 N. Clark, 773/348-3998   **N**
With the stage in the window of this small storefront club, you'll have to push your way to the back of the tight room for your allotted inches of dance floor. The live reggae bands begin after 10pm. Cover generally runs $5-$6, but there's no cover on Mondays or before 10pm on Wed. Closed Tuesdays.

Wild Hare
3530 N. Clark, 773/327-HARE   **N**
The live reggae here seven nights a week since 1979 may make **Wild Hare**

the nation's oldest such club and justify their claim as "America's Reggae Capital." Club opens at 8pm, bands start at 9:30pm. No cover charge collected before 9:30pm. Sundays is reggae jam night. Cover $4-$7, more for special shows. Mon.-Tues. no cover, Wed. no cover for the ladies.

Rock/Alternative

For both national and up-and-coming local alternative rock acts, these bar-clubs are a must:

Double Door
1572 N. Milwaukee, 773/489-3160   **W**
Though some find the Double Door a clear indication of Wicker Park's gentrification, most find this spacious club's band bookings in line with the neighborhood's cutting-edge reputation. Live music several nights a week, usually beginning at 9pm. Open until 2am. Cover $5-$12. Closed Mon.-Tues.

Empty Bottle
1035 N. Western, 773/276-3600   **W**
This off-the-beaten-path bar probably presents the most truly on-the-fringe bands of the four, though its offerings range widely to include jazz, punk, local talent, and indie rock. Live music usually Wed.-Sun. and beginning after 9pm. Opens 3-4pm daily, closes at 2am,3am Sat. Cover charges typically run $5-$10, usually at the lower end. Cheap drinks, too. Visit *www.emptybottle.com* for more details. Join their e-mail list to receive the weekly show schedule and a free drink coupon!

Lounge Ax
2438 N. Lincoln, 773/525-6620   **N**
The most entrenched supporter of indie label bands of the four, Lounge Ax features live rock nightly in a small, personal setting that's decked out with Christmas lights and Elvis paraphernalia. Open nightly with music starting around 9pm weekdays/10pm weekends. Cover $2-$10, usually on the cheaper side.

Martyr's
3855 N. Lincoln, 773/404-9494   **N**
This clean, spacious, and relaxed club has catapulted the North Center neighborhood onto the nightlife map with its attention-getting bookings. The hottest local acts, some big names on tour, and a few interesting no-names

are all just as likely to appear on **Martyr's** ample stage in a given week. Although its name refers to deceased greats from the rock world, you're going to find a lot more than classic rock'n'roll here—anything from the local Irish band with the African-American drummer and Asian bass player to new-agey percussionists. Like the others, covers run about $5-$10. Mondays bring free Irish music and half-price pizza.

Fun and inexpensive spots to see local bands include **Beat Kitchen** (2100 W. Belmont, 773/281-4444) with its interesting musical offerings and creative menu. The **Morseland** (1218 W. Morse, 773/764-6401) incorporates the first two floors of a house, with the second floor still divided into separate rooms. Shoot pool in one bedroom, listen to the jukebox from a couch in another, or play the organ in the third. **Phyllis' Musical Inn** (1800 W. Division, 773/486-9862) remains from the 50s when this section of Division was filled with polka clubs and referred to as "Polish Broadway." **Phyllis'** now hands the stage over to rock groups, jazz ensembles, and bands of every stripe in between looking to break into better local-act venues. Most cover charges at these places are $3-$7.

These distinctive and to different degrees, historical, mid-sized concert halls should be visited at least once. Wait for your favorite national acts to come to town. The **Aragon Ballroom** (1106 W. Lawrence, 773/561-9500) with its dated "exotic" Mediterranean decor, still stands after an earlier heyday as a 1940s big band dance hall. An old-time theater, the **Metro** (3730 N. Clark, 773/549-0203) now hosts rock, alternative, and punk bands. The **Park West** (322 W. Armitage, 773/929-5959) went from a strip club to an eclectic entertainment center with a kind of 70s panache. Also serving many entertainment functions since it was built in 1918, the **Riviera** (4746 N. Racine, 773/275-6800) now presents a range of concerts, including major rock, alternative, rap, and jazz acts.

For quick online updates of Chicago's music scene:

Blues
http://nitescape.com/chicago/blues
Clubs, schedules, and blues links.
Jazz
http://209.25.44.164/main/jazz.htm
Venues, upcoming concerts, and musicians' pages.
Rock and Pop
http://209.25.44.164/main/rock.htm

Favorite Local Bands' Schedules
http://www.mcs.net/~cheeks/chifav/
Classical
http://tezcat.com/~andyhat/music/concerts.html
An impressive search feature for local classical concerts.
Folk, Acoustic, and Celtic
http://www.mcs.net/~candre/chicago.html
New Music
http://www.cs.nwu.edu/~tisue/chicagonow
Free jazz, avant-classical . . . anything experimental.
Punk and Ska
http://chicagomusic.com/shows
Christian Rock/Alternative
http://www.ccm.net/~slloyd/
New City's Music Hub
http://www.newcitychicago.com/listings/music.html
Search New City's shows listing by day of week, type of music, club/venue, and band/act. Includes a list of recommended shows. Updates are made daily.

CLUBS

Big Band

Twice a month, several hundred senior citizens meet at either **St. Elizabeth's Church** (4058 S. Michigan, 773/268-1518—every third Sunday, 4pm-9pm) or the **Montford Point Marine Hall** (7011 S. Vincennes, 773/873-6600—every first Sunday) to twirl around the floor to big band music performed by the *Roland Brown Merchants Band Co.* At **St. Elizabeth's**, the $15 per person admittance fee includes dinner and dancing. A cash bar serves everything from soda to mixed drinks ($1-$4). Dancers can bring their own beverages, but will need to purchase set-ups.

Dance Clubs

Small-to-medium-sized neighborhood dance clubs are typically free of the attitude of the nightclub scene, are generally more affordable, and can even be more interesting as well.

The veteran **Club 950** (950 W. Wrightwood, 773/929-8955) focuses on its large central dance floor, the site for doing your own thing to 80s pop and alternative, electronic, punk, gothic, and new wave. Open Wed.-Sun. 7pm-2am. Covers $3-$5, usually none before 10pm. **Exit** (1315 W. North, 773/395-2700) is Chicago's punk headquarters, where dancers can listen to plenty of music from the good old days, plus current metal, ska, and anything hardcore. Open 8pm-4am nightly, Sat. until 5am. Call for nightly themes. Cover free-$5. Still another alternative old-timer, **Neo** (2350 N. Clark, 773/528-2622) has featured the Tues. "Morphea" gothic night for over ten years. Other evenings find techno, industrial, punk, and other dark and alternative dance music at the DJ table. Open Thur.-Tues. from 10pm to 4am, Sat. to 5am. Covers range from free to $5. Located underneath The Metro, the **Smart Bar** (3730 N. Clark, 773/549-4140) plays some jazz, but mostly house and other urban dance styles, nightly until 4am, Sat. until 5am. Covers run from $1-$7, with higher prices after midnight and on weekends. At **El Jardin Fiesta Cantina** (3407 N. Clark, 773/327-4646), margaritas are king, and a post-college sports bar crowd rules the sizable two-floor club on weekends for dancing to rock, disco, retro, and Latin music. Open Wed.-Sun. 6pm-2am. $5 cover on Fri. (men only) and Sat. Much further north, **Hollywood East** (5650 N. Broadway, 773/271-4711) appeals to a variety of neighborhood tastes with offerings of Latin, Caribbean, disco, reggae, techno, house, and stepping. Open Thur.-Sun. 6pm-2am, cover can vary from free to $7. Defying categorization, Wicker Park's **Mad Bar** (1640 N. Damen, 773/227-2277) delivers top DJs for funk, house, techno, and other bass-heavy grooves; poetry nights; live Latin music (salsa, samba, Flamenco); good coffee with their good booze; and more. Plus, they're biker-friendly. Covers can be free or $3-$6.

With weekend cover charges starting at $10 and moving towards $15 at the city's biggest and best nightclubs, the bargain bet would be to test drive them first at a lower price during the week.

The **Convent's** (1529 W. Armitage, enter on Elston, 773/395-8660) theme is evidenced everywhere from the servers clad in Catholic schoolgirl uniforms to the VIP rooms dubbed "Heaven" and "Hell." Music here means house, Latin, and dance music in Spanish and English. The dress code is "casual but neat." Go Sun.-Thur. for a cover in the $5 range; Monday is gay night. Outrageous, enormous, extreme, and body-pounding loud, **Crobar's** (1543 N. Kingsbury, 312/413-7000) gothic industrial landscape attracts wild crowds, including frequent visitor, Bulls rebounder Dennis Rodman. Techno, disco, and anything with a low and definite beat rule the expansive floor of dance-crazed patrons. When it's busy, if you don't have "the look," you may be waiting outside all night. Wednesday is "Ladies Night" with an alternative twist, cover $4, $8 after midnight. Sunday is gay and lesbian night, cover is $8. New on the scene, the Asian-themed **Dragon Room** (809 W. Evergreen, 312/751-2900) draws a moneyed, urbane crowd for sushi and all-night dancing. Go Thur. for drink specials and a $3 cover. Inside Magnum's Steak and Lobster is **Faces** (223 W. Ontario, 312/440-3223)—a contemporary, cosmopolitan club for disco and dance hits. Wed. and Thur. cover is $5, women pay nothing on Thur. Open 8pm-4am. **Karma** (318 W. Grand, 312/321-1331) delivers three floors of sophisticated clubbing amidst a Hindu/Indian theme. Drenched in velvet and lit with candles and strobe lights, you'll want to return again and again for partying or lounging. Go Thur. 10pm-4am for $5. On the lighter side is **Polly Esther's** (213 W. Institute, 312/664-0077), one of a chain of large retro clubs. Follow your nostalgia to the ground level dance floor which is all 70s or downstairs to the all-80s "Culture Club." No cover Wed. or Thur. Open 8pm-3am.

Some of the bigger clubs with more affordable weekend fees are **Club 151** (151 W. Ohio, 312/832-1110), **Drink** (702 W. Fulton, 312/733-7800), and the **Excalibur Entertainment Complex** (632 N. Dearborn, 312/266-1944). **Club 151** offers patrons (whose ages span four decades) fun and free dancing without the club scene attitude. Dance tunes emphasize the popular from all recent eras and include pop, rock, alternative, and swing classics. Open Sun.-Thur. until 2am, Fri.-Sat. until 3am. **Drink** is the coolest of this trio, a capacious, psychedelic nightspot with dancing first and drinking a close second. (Specialty bars are devoted to tequilas, cognac, beer, vodka, and fruity drinks.) Open Thur.-Sat., $5 cover after 9pm. Women and those with a college ID and driver's license are free on Thursdays. Gussy up a bit, no gym shoes allowed. The **Excalibur Entertainment Complex** joins a lounge area, dance club, singles bar, restaurant, arcade, pool hall, and more in 60,000 ft.^{2} under the roof of one castle-like fortress. Listening and dance music may be "Top 40," house, retro, R & B, disco, Latin, industrial, alternative, lounge, or jazz at any given moment or in any particular corner. Open 5pm-4am nightly, until 5am Sat. There is typically no cover to enter, but charges for certain rooms may hover in the area of $5.

Depending on what you want or what you can tolerate, the Division Street singles bars clustered between Dearborn and State make for inexpensive evening of dancing, drinking, and mingling.

Far from the moneyed or edgy crowds of the city's top nightclubs, these pubs o' fun draw just-barely-post-collegiate types, frat drinkers, out-of-towners, suburban kids, sports buffs, neighborhood party people having a big evening downtown, or any combination thereof. The young and the reckless certainly appreciate the absence of cover charges and the ridiculously cheap drink and shot specials—particularly for the womenfolk. The following bars have the most active dance floors of the of the pack: **The Alumni Club** (15 W. Division, 312/337-4349), **Bootleggers** (13 W. Division, 312/266-0944), **Mother's** (26 W. Division, 312/642-7251), and **P.O.E.T.'s** (5 W. Division, 312/943-7638). Located a block or so off the strip, **Hangge-Uppe's** (14 W. Elm, 312/337-0561) has probably the best dancing crowd and facilities of them all, with first floor and lower level DJs spinning different types of music for each dance floor. Open until 4am Fri./5am Sat.

Folk

Folk dancers should access the **Folk Dance Council of Chicago** Web page at *http://members.aol.com/fdccpub/index.html*. With a few clicks, you'll be in touch with all the clubs, dances, and lessons you can hope for. Bulgarian singing and basic Balkan Dance lessons, Irish set dancing, Scottish country dancing, international folk dancing for seniors, Norwegian folk dancing performances, ethnic dance parties, and Cajun/Zydeco lessons are just a few of the many options that are happening nearly every week in Chicagoland.

Gay and Lesbian

Berlin
954 W. Belmont, 773/348-4975   **N**
This big, dance video club, with frequently-changing theme nights, attracts mostly gay men during the week and a mix of gays, straights, and "I'm too drunk to cares" on the weekends. Male dancers, drag contests, disco balls, feather boas, dancing platforms, and lots of camp. Every Wednesday is Women's Obsession Night for lesbians, and the last Wednesday of the month is Disco Wednesday. Open 5pm-4am nightly, 5am Saturdays. Cover charge $2-$5. (BZ)

Fusion
3631 N. Halsted, 773/975-0660   **N**
During the week this address is the Brazilian restaurant Rhumba, featuring a drag show with Carmen Miranda, aging USO singers, etc. But on the weekend, the tables are removed and it becomes Chicago's largest gay dance club, wowing 'em with its myriad rooms and levels, laser lighting, video technology, special events, music, and diverse (though generally, young) crowd. Open 10pm-4am Fri., 10pm-5am Sat. Cover $5-$10. (BZ)

GirlBar

2625 N. Halsted, 773/871-4210   **N**

GirlBar is one of the last all-girl bars in the city, but on Wednesdays it becomes "boybar" and on the first Friday of every month it's salsa night. Large facility includes a game room and an outdoor deck. By the way, this is the bar that Jay Leno (or at least a Leno dummy) was ejected from during his visit to Chicago. $5 cover on Friday and Saturday. Open 6pm-2am Sun.-Fri., 6pm-3am on Sat. (BZ)

The "Boystown" neighborhood (see p.279) offers an abundance of nightlife opportunities for gay men. Check out **Manhole** (3458 N. Halsted, 773/975-9244), a "tame," mainstream leather bar which requires leatherwear or shirts-off on weekends before access to the backroom dance floor is permitted. **Sidetrack's** (3631 N. Halsted, 773/477-9189) is an all-ages gay video bar with TVs at every turn to watch videos with varying nightly themes, such as show tunes; comedy; 60s, 70s, and 80s music. **Roscoe's** (3354 N. Halsted, 773/281-3355) combines a cafe, neighborhood bar (TV watching, pool tables, couches), dance floor, and gimmickry (70s and 80s nights, "post office," palm readers). Wed. night entertainment includes comedy acts and game show send-ups like $25 Pyramid and Family Feud. **Spin** (800 W. Belmont, at Halsted, 773/327-7711) is open nightly for dancing and various theme events until 2am, Sat. until 3pm. Cover charges range from free to $3. For country/western dancing, including frequent lessons, head to **Charlie's** (3726 N. Broadway, 773/871-8887), where there are regular drink specials and free admission.

In other neighborhoods, there's **Big Chick's** (5024 N. Sheridan, 773/728-5511), a predominantly-gay, used-to-be-lesbian neighborhood bar with great drink prices, weeknight euchre (see p.90), weekend dancing, and free Sunday buffets at 4pm. Guys also gather at **Scot's** (1829 W. Montrose, 773/528-3253) bar in Ravenswood, particularly for Tues. night martinis and old movies. **Charmer's** (1502 W. Jarvis, 773/465-2811) art deco establishment has been standing since 1929 and now lures mostly gay men, some women, and some neighbors for its friendly bar atmosphere, darts, and trivia nights. Despite its River North location, **The Generator** (306 N. Halsted, 312/243-8889) dance club keeps its cover charges between $3 and $5. The crowd is primarily gay African-American males, but is mixed enough for anyone else to feel comfortable joining in the fun.

Other entertainment alternatives include the mostly-gay **Gentry** (440 N. State, 312/836-0933) cabaret/piano bar, where there's never a cover charge; **Lolita's Cafe** (4400 N. Clark, 773/561-3356), a Mexican restaurant that dishes up drag shows Fri. and Sat. at midnight; and **The Legacy** (3042 W. Irving Park, 773/772-3084), a gay club that features live gay and lesbian rock bands four nights a week.

German

Chicago Brauhaus
4732 N. Lincoln, 773/784-4444   N
The authentically-clad house band at this large restaurant/beer hall plays German, American, international, polka, ball room, and popular music for dancing from 7pm-midnight Mon. & Wed., 7pm-1am Fri., 1pm-5pm and 7pm-2am Sat., and 1pm-5pm and 7pm-midnight Sun. Closed Tuesdays. No cover. (See p.146.)

Latin Dance

Leave the jeans and gym shoes at home...

Tania's
2659 N. Milwaukee, 773/235-7120   NW
This large and beautiful Cuban restaurant and club hosts live music four days a week for salsa, merengue, and cumbia dancing. DJs play other nights. The music goes until 2am during the week, 3am or later on the weekends. DJs begin around 8:30pm, live music after 9:30pm. No cover charge for women, $10 for men on the weekend.

Tropicana D' Cache
2047 N. Milwaukee 773/489-9600   N
Chicago's premier Latin nightclub presents a changing lineup of entertainment events. Look for live tropical and Caribbean music Thur.-Sat., salsa and merengue lessons, large orchestras, and amateur boxing (Tues. after midnight). The international Spanish-speaking majority along with interested gringos make up a sharp, classy, and high-energy crowd. Cover can be free-$12. Ladies get in free before midnight Thur. and before 10pm Sat. Open 8pm-4am Thur., until 5am Fri.-Sat.

Polish

On the northwest side, a string of small-to-medium-sized dance clubs featuring both DJs and live bands, cater predominantly to Polish and Polish-American crowds with other Europeans and neighbors mixed in.

Most of these places have no cover charge or a minimal one, tend to be dressy, and play a range of international pop/dance music.

Jedynka

5610 W. Diversey, 773/889-7171 **NW**

With 10,000 ft.^{2}, 3 rooms, and four bars, **Jedynka** is probably the largest nightclub on Chicago's Northwest Side. It takes that responsibility seriously and delivers big for its patrons. Their facilities include a vodka bar, a cappuccino bar, pool tables (tournament pool on Wed.), "champion" DJs playing Europe's newest dance music, and elaborate hi-tech light shows. Brimming with a variety of contests and special events, the club has a five-year tradition of packing the last Friday of every month with gifts and surprises for those whose birthday occurs in that month. They've also been known to give away free bottles of champagne of guests' birthdays or name days. Open Tues.-Sun. 7pm-2am, until 3am Sat. No cover before 10pm. Sundays is 70s & 80s Euro-retro night.

Dance until the early morning hours on weekends at the **Cardinal Club** (5159 W. Belmont, 773/736-4662). **Club 4-5-6** (7429 W. Addison, 773/889-7365) stays open until 4am Wed.-Sat. Along with its Polish clientele, **Maryla Polonaise** (3192 N. Milwaukee, 773/545-4152) also has a large Hispanic following. Their DJs add house, techno, and even some Latin tunes to the international dance music lineup. Open nightly from 9pm-2am.

Polka

Baby Doll Polka Club

6102 S. Central, 773/582-9706 **SW**

Named for a 1948 hit by accordionist and late owner Eddie Korosa, this tavern across the street from Midway Airport has been Polka Central since 1955. A live polka band plays every Saturday at 9:30pm and Sunday at 5:30pm. Drinks are cheap and there's never a cover charge. The **Baby Doll Polka Club** is open until 2am, seven days a week.

Major Hall

5600 W. Grand, 773/237-8089 **NW**

Don't fight it, polka is back! And every Tuesday morning the Major Hall holds polka parties, showing that at least for some people, it never went away. The "Pensionaires" play their brand of polka to an almost all-seniors crowd though anyone with "happy feet" is welcome. Lunch is $2 and coffee costs a quarter. If anything, this is the only wholesome place in the city where you can get a mixed drink at 9 in the morning. (BZ)

Polonia Banquet Hall
4604 S. Archer, 773/523-7980   **SW**
The site of many a Southwest-side wedding reception, **Polonia** holds frequent polka nights. One of the most popular celebrates *Paczki* Day (pronounced "poonch-key"), the Polish version of Mardi Gras, centering around the consumption of *paczki*, jelly-filled pastries sprinkled with powdered sugar. Cover charge is $6-$7. Call for upcoming events.

Local polka dance groups meet at varying locations—sort of a floating polka party. For a current list, contact the **International Polka Association** (4145 S. Kedzie, 773/254-7771).

Stepping

If you have to ask what this is, don't show up at one of the clubs until you've learned a few steps. But we'll give you this hint: it's a uniquely Chicago African-American dance phenomenon, often compared to gliding across the dance floor. You can practice in the privacy of your own living room with the help of *Steppin' on Club Seven*, which appears each Saturday night at 1am on Channel 7. When you're ready to join the couples on the dance floor, try one of these places:

East of the Ryan 914 E. 79th, 773/874-1500	**FSE**
Infinity 9156 S. Stony Island, 773/375-1800	**FSE**
Mr. G's 1547 W. 87th, 773/445-2020	**FSE**
Mr. Ricky's Note 118 E. Cermak, 312/842-0400	**C**
Original 50 Yard Line 69 E. 75th, 773/846-0005	**FSE**
The Other Place 377 E. 75th, 773/874-5476	**FSE**
Strictly Business 1355 S. Michigan, 312/663-4463	**C**
Taste Entertainment Center 6331 S. Lowe, 773/873-6700	**S**
What's Poppin' 7710 S. Halsted, 773/846-4200	**FSE**

Swing

The Jub Jub Club
2447 N. Halsted, 773/665-7557   **N**
The hip, young, and fashionably tattooed (but fun for us regular folk as well) congregate here for good-old-fashioned-wacky-nutty fun. They have music, they have food, and on Wednesdays for a $2 cover they have swing! So put

down your martini and grab a partner. Open 5pm-2am Sun.-Fri., 5pm-3am Sat. (BZ)

Olive

1115 N. North Branch, 312/280-7997   **C**

Every night is swing night at **Olive**, and as their name might imply, they have martinis. Live music nightly. Open 7pm-2am Wed.-Fri., 7pm-4am Sat., closed Mon.-Sun. (BZ)

Want the lounge scene without a swing band distracting you from your cocktail culture? Try **The Leg Room** (7 W. Division, 312/337-2583) downtown, the **Holiday Club** (1471 N. Milwaukee, 773/486-0686) in Wicker Park, and **Plush** (2500 N. Southport, 773/472-1502) in Lincoln Park.

Boogie Sites:

Dance Clubs
http://www.centerstage.net/chicago/dance/clubs
Phone/address directory for 68 Chicago dance clubs. Search by dancing style and location. Not up-to-the-minute, but still current and useful.

Dancing in Chicago
http://www.ee.princeton.edu/~aria/chicago_dance.html
A guide to places where one can dance (ballroom, Latin, swing, country & western) in the Chicago area, with information on locations, prices, schedules, directions, and general descriptions of the establishments. Not absolutely current, but still an excellent resource.

Chicago Clubs
http://207.24.161.48/chiclubs/dbfull1.asp?which=IL
Incomplete but useful guide to Chicago clubs has a place for visitors to add comments about local nightspots.

Gothic Chicago
http://www.yourplanb.com/gothchgo
Information on Chicago's gothic scene.

Chi-Town Squares
http://www.mcs.net/~jdpope/ctshomep.html
Gay and lesbian square dance club.

DRINK

Bars for Beer Education

The Map Room
1949 N. Hoyne, 773/252-7636   **N**
With 26 beers on tap, a first-rate imported beer and microbrew selection,
daily drink specials, and occasional beer classes (about $10 to sample), **The
Map Room** is the perfect classroom for learning more about beer *and*
geography! Maps line the tables and walls, globes are scattered about, and a
travel club convenes here. Drink specials, imported coffees, wine tastings,
and international theme nights add to the enticing brew at this comfortable
bar. Look for the free buffet of ethnic foods Tues. at 7:30pm. A lineup of
live music so diverse it's rivaled only by their beer selection can be heard for
free Fri. at 9:30pm and Sat. at 10pm.

Sheffield's
3258 N. Sheffield, 773/281-4989   **N**
Serene and atmospheric in the winter, thanks in part to dim lighting, wooden
features, and a fireplace, this well-loved bar gets crowded and crazy when
the beer garden opens in the summer. Join the Joseph Sheffield Memorial
Beer Society by trying every beer on the menu (free T-shirt and two
Sheffield's pint glasses upon completion). A booklet explains each of the
over five dozen kinds to help you learn the differences between ales, porters,
pilsners, bocks, ciders, rye beers, wheat beers, oatmeal stouts, cream stouts,
lambics, pale ales, lagers, and any stray cousins. The bar also sponsors
quarterly beer tastings and special events to further their support of the
current beer renaissance. Open 2pm-2am Mon.-Fri., 12pm-3am Sat., and
12pm-2am Sun.

Bars for Beer Selection

Hop Leaf
5148 N. Clark, 773/334-9851   **FN**
Posters on the walls; wooden tables, chairs, and stools; big booths; candles;
and interesting magazines and jukebox make for a spiffy neighborhood
tavern. You'll want to return repeatedly to try the 18 different beers on tap,
a rotating selection of over 110 bottled beers (1/4 are Belgian), and the
Swedish Glögg. Ask for recommendations. Free pretzels and chips. Open
daily 3pm-2am, until 3am Sat.

Quenchers

2401 N. Western, 773/276-9730 **N**

Beer lovers can always have their thirst, for just about anything, quenched at this large corner bar, established in 1979 before the current beer boom. With 225 different kinds of bottled beer (many unusual and most imported) and 17 more on tap (try the rogue or Belgian ales), this is most likely the largest assortment of beer assembled in Chicago. The owner's famous chili and the standard bar popcorn will intensify your need for something thirst quenching. Have another—these prices are easily some of the best in town for this type of selection. Open Mon.-Fri. 11am-2am, Sat. 11am-3am, and Sun. noon-2am.

Village Tap

2055 W. Roscoe 773/883-0817 **N**

The over 30 draft beers on hand at the **Village Tap** is not only an impressive quantity, but one of the most craftily maintained collections of microbrews around. They like to push Midwestern labels, including Bell's from Michigan and Chicago's Goose Island. The backyard beer garden is a big draw; indoor accessories include board games, a pinball machine, and an encyclopedia set. Open 5pm-2am Mon.-Fri., noon-2am Sat.-Sun.

Bars for Bloody Marys

Build your own hangover cure on Sundays at these well-stocked Bloody Mary Bars.

From 10am-3pm, **The Fireside** (5739 N. Ravenswood, 773/564-7433) restaurant and bar sets out 110 ingredients to add to your vodka and tomato juice, including a wide variety of pungent spices and fiery hot sauces. **Hoghead McDunna's** (1505 W. Fullerton, 773/929-0944) and **Jack Sullivan's** (2142 N. Clybourn, 773/549-9009) provide over 50 ingredients so that patrons can concoct their own Bloody Marys from 10am-3pm both Sat. and Sun.

If you prefer, rely on the house's special recipe served at these bars seven days a week:

Twisted Spoke's (501 N. Ogden, 312/666-1500) $5, 16 oz. *Road Rash Mary* blends juices, vodka, olives, peppers, onions, salami, cheese, and spices and throws in a beer on the side. The changing recipe of **Sheffield's** (3258 N. Sheffield, 773/281-4989) Bloody Mary may include accouterments like okra, hot peppers, artichoke hearts, and a squirt of dark beer.

Bars for Games

The Blue Frog Bar and Grill
676 N. LaSalle, 312/943-8900   **C**
Folks head to the Blue Frog to play one of their 100+ board games, including the ever-popular Trivial Pursuit, Operation, Mousetrap, and Don't Break the Ice. A well-stocked bar and a full-service kitchen keep gamesters satisfied, whether they're waiting to "get out of jail free" or watching others "roll again." Open Mon.-Fri. 11:30am-2am, Sat. 6pm-3am. Closed Sundays.

Guthrie's
1300 W. Addison, 773/477-2900   **N**
Large windows, high wooden stools, checkered tablecloths, old maps, and pictures of boats and harbors make this quiet and quaint neighborhood tavern (when not packed on weekends or after Cubs' games) perfect for spending an evening with friends and one of the board games from the backroom cabinet. Bar prices are on the higher side of average. Open 4pm-2am Mon.-Fri., 2pm-3am on Sat., noon-2am on Sun.

Lakeview Links
3206 N. Wilton, 773/975-0505   **N**
Cavernous, two-story bar has something different and engaging around every corner: pool, ping pong, foosball, pinball, shuffleboard, jukeboxes, and a decent beer selection. Local bands perform on the weekends for low cover charges. (Look for Lightening and Thunder—a Neil Diamond tribute act which includes some Blondie, ABBA, and *Grease* hits.) Couches and stuffed chairs are available for the comfortable viewing of sports events on jumbo-screen TVs. Open 4pm-2am daily.

Bars with Unique Features

Danny's
1951 W. Dickens, 773/489-6457   **N**
This house-turned-bar has been spruced up with plush couches, crazy artwork, candles, low and colored lighting, unique furniture, and plenty of turns and alcoves. Grab a niche for lounging or romancing. Open Sun.-Fri. 7pm-2am, Sat. 7pm-3am.

Old Town Ale House
219 W. North, 312/944-7020   **C**
Journalists, writers, actors, and late-night employees are among those who
join the more down-and-out at this shoddy, shabby, and uniquely-adorned
neighborhood fixture. Its bookshelf is filled with classics, its jukebox is
filled with everything (classical, jazz, opera, rock, soul, oldies...), and its bar
stools are filled with characters. Located in one of Chicago's ritziest 'hoods,
this decidedly downscale place seems to make it on everyone's list of
favorite Chicago bars. Open noon-4am daily.

Saga Launder Bar
1344 W. Newport, 773/929-9274   **N**
A pool table, darts, pinball, TV, jukebox, cafe food, and a great beer
selection are just steps a way from your spinning clothes. After throwing
your dirty laundry into the machines up front, head to the bar in back to
relax. An illuminated sign lets you know when your washers have stopped.
Laundry day just hasn't been the same in this neighborhood... Open seven
days a week 7am-11pm for laundry and 11am-2am for food and beer.

Bars for a Wide Selection of Fine and Unusual Spirits in a Funky Setting

Artful Dodger
1734 W. Wabansia, 773/227-6859   **N**
The funky 14-year-old Bucktown/Wicker Park neighborhood bar that once
promoted its glow-in-the-dark signature drink, "The Aqua Velva," is now
cashing in on the fine booze, beer, and cocktail craze and pushing their
remarkable stock of aged tequilas, wines, sherries, ports, cognacs, single
malt scotches, rums, bourbons, microbrews, and imported beers. Open 5pm
daily, Sat. at 8pm. DJ spins alternative music five nights a week in its back,
black-lit dance room. $2 cover Fri.-Sat., free all other times.

Delilah's
2771 N. Lincoln, 773/472-2771   **N**
A host of odd and splendid bottles to call you from behind the bar—
particularly the impressive assemblages of bourbon, scotch, beer, and wine.
To accompany the liquid experimenting, you couldn't ask for more eclectic
background entertainment. Punk rock, ska, gothic, old metal, and more have
their theme-nights at the DJ table. Similarly, the music spinners pay a
musical tribute to folks like Johnny Cash, Tammy Wynette, and Johnny
Thunder on their birthdays. Expect the occasional fashion show, look alike

contest, or a 16-mm screening from The Psychotronic Film Society. Wed. is insurgent country night. Open Sun.-Fri. 4pm-2am, Sat. 4pm-3am. Never a cover charge.

Southwest Side Bar Recommendations

Bohica
5518 S. Archer, 773/581-0397   **SW**
Bohica welcomes diversity. Word has gotten around that everyone who enters this Southwest-side bar is made to feel at home, which means the crowd ranges from nerdy to funky. The outdoor beer garden is popular in warm weather.

Groucho's
8355 S. Pulaski, 773/767-4888   **SW**
This friendly bar has been around for a long time, catering to all age groups. It's not fancy, but the bar is huge so there's always room. **Groucho's** has an admirable beer selection for this part of town, with two dozen bottled brews and four on tap. Prices, at $1.75-$.250, are easy to swallow too. The usual bar games are available, including pool, darts, and Trivial Pursuit. Live rock or blues on Sat. nights. Open nightly until 4am, Sat. until 5am.

Schaller's Pump
3714 S. Halsted, 773/847-9378   **SW**
Located across the street from the 10th Ward Democratic headquarters, this Bridgeport tavern has been a popular meeting place for machine politicians for a century. The rest of the clientele are long-suffering White Sox fans. No trip to the neighborhood is complete without stopping for a brew (and a shot, if you're so inclined) at **Schaller's** long bar. See p.187 for food details.

Internet access to local bar news:

Barfly
http://www.barflynews.com
Independent news and reviews of Chicago's drinking establishments.
Chicago Bars Online
http://www.barsonline.com
Database of downtown and Northside Chicago bars (mostly Near North and North Central). Search bars by neighborhood and type. Information on daily drink specials included. Punch in some preferences and they'll return a customized route for your next pub crawl free!

Center Stage's Chicago Bar Search and Directory
http://www.centerstage.net/chicago/bars
Master phone/address directory of nearly 600 Chicago bars. Search based on the closest El stop, neighborhood, crowd type, and venue type.

Chicago Gay and Lesbian Bars List
http://www.mcs.net/~hcarter/bars.html
Search by area (includes suburbs) and bar type. Includes information on daily specials.

Coffee at Night

Cafe Lura
3184 N. Milwaukee, 773/736-3033   **NW**
Sharing a name with a pub in Lodz, Poland, **Cafe Lura** is quite a discovery for anyone whose beaten path doesn't include the Northwest-side Polish stronghold where it's located. The dark and heavy wood and brick gothic decor is unlike any American coffeehouses in these parts. Beyond espresso, cappuccino, and other caffeinated beverages, cocktails, ice cream, dessert, and a small food menu are available to support your nighttime lounging. A cover charge of $5-$10 may apply for evenings of live jazz, blues, or Polish music.

Don's Coffee Club
1439 W. Jarvis, 773/274-1228   **FN**
On the outside Don's looks like any other college-town coffeehouse, but once inside you get the feeling that you've just walked into the living room of that eccentric aunt that no one invites to Thanksgiving. The atmosphere is warm and inviting, with ceiling fans, couches, a piano, stacks of records and books, old pictures, pink flamingos, ceramic-parrot lamps, soft lighting, and Don's music of choice (usually from the 40s and 50s) crackling beautifully in the background. The menu changes regularly (peanut butter and jelly sandwiches, bratwurst, pie, etc.), but the selection of coffee is always the same: regular or decaf. Don serves your coffee personally, presents an annual prom in September, and hosts Sunday Night Swing sessions during the summer. The only advice I offer is, "look before you sit," because Don's cats are a permanent fixture of the club that like to sleep on or under the furniture. Open 7pm-1am Sun.-Wed. and 7pm-1am Fri.-Sat. Closed Thursdays. (BZ)

THEATER

This section will hopefully bring theater-going into your realm of daily activity options. Relieve the theater of its special occasion status, dragging it down to the routine level of movie-watching, and your life will change. In fact, most inexpensive theater and comedy choices listed here will cost you less than the price of a first-run movie. Volunteer ushering is even cheaper than the rent-a-movie-and-stay-in standby. The Friday and Sunday editions of the *Chicago Sun-Times* and the *Chicago Tribune* and the weekly editions of the *Reader* (free) and *New City* (free) are the best places to find comprehensive listings of what's playing where, when, and for how much.

Inexpensive Theater Options

Chicago's inexpensive theater scene holds something for everyone: drama; comedy; experimental works; political works; classics; student, amateur and professional performances; works-in-progress... Nearly every production staged at the 61 theaters below costs under $12 Scan the newspaper listings carefully—some of these theaters have "pay what you can" nights.

CODE:
$ $6 & under
$$ $6.01-$12

A Red Orchid Theatre ($$)
1531 N. Wells, 312/943-8722   N

About Face Theatre ($/$$) and **Famous Door Theatre ($/$$)**
Jane Addams Center
3212 N. Broadway, 773/409-4863   N

American Theater Company ($$)
1909 W. Byron, 773/929-1031   N

Angel Island Theatre ($$)
731 W. Sheridan, 773/871-0442   N

Annoyance Theatre ($/$$)
3747 N. Clark, 773/929-6200   N
Look for the late night shows Fri. and Sat. after midnight.

Athenaeum Theatre ($$)
2936 N. Southport, 773/935-6860 **N**

Bailiwick Repertory ($$)
Bailiwick Arts Center, 1229 W. Belmont, 773/883-1090 **N**

Baird Hall Theatre ($$)
615 W. Wellington, 773/248-0577 **N**

Beverly Arts Center (FREE/$/$$)
2153 W. 111th, 773/445-3838 **FSW**
For more information on the **Beverly Arts Center**, see p. 31.

Black Ensemble Theatre ($$)
Uptown Center Hull House, 4520 N. Beacon, 773/769-4451 **FN**

Blue Rider Theatre ($$)
1822 S. Halsted, 312/733-4668 **C**

Boulevard Art Center (Free/$/$$)
6011 S. Justine, 773/476-4900 **SW**

Chicago Dramatists Workshop ($/$$)
1105 W. Chicago, 312/633-0630 **C**
Watch plays-in-progress by Chicago dramatists Sat. at 2pm for $3.

Chicago Kids Company ($)
Richard J. Daley College
7500 S. Pulaski, 773/539-0455 **FSW**
Wright College
4300 N. Narragansett, 773/539-0455 **NW**

Chicago State University Breakey Theatre ($$)
9501 S. Martin Luther King Jr. Drive, 773/995-2952 **FSE**

Chicago Theatre Company ($$)
500 E. 67th, 773/493-0901 **S**
This is one of Chicago's three theaters specifically devoted to works by and
about African-Americans.

Chocolate Chips Theatre Company ($/$$)
Kennedy-King College, Katherine Dunham Theatre
6800 S. Wentworth, 773/994-7400   **FSE**

Chopin Theatre ($$)
1543 W. Division, 773/296-6850   **C**

Columbia College Theater/Music Center ($$)
72 E. 11th, 312/663-0581   **C**

Cook County Theatre Department ($$)
2255 S. Michigan, 312/842-8234   **S**

Eclipse Theatre Co. ($/$$)
2074 N. Leavitt, 773/862-7415   **N**

ETA Creative Arts Foundation (FREE/$/$$)
7558 S. South Chicago, 773/752-3955   **S**
An African-American cultural center, **ETA Creative Arts Foundation**
offers an ambitious schedule of original works by African and African-
American playwrights. See p.31 for a more detailed look at its
comprehensive arts programming.

Head up 75th Street about a mile for noteworthy soul food at **Lou's and
Liz's** (p.194) or **Soul Vegetarian East** (p.193). If you can spend a little
more, visit **Army and Lou's** (422 E. 75th, 773/483-3100) for the best in
town.

Factory Theater ($$)
1257 W. Loyola, 773/274-1345   **FN**

Footsteps Theatre ($$)
5230 N. Clark, 773/878-4840   **FN**

Fourth Wall Productions at Wright College ($$)
4300 N. Narragansett, 773/481-8535   **NW**

Greenview Arts Center ($$)
6418 N. Greenview, 773/508-0085   **FN**

Griffin Theatre Company, Calo Theatre ($$)
5405 N. Clark, 773/769-2228   **FN**

Heartland Studio ($$)
7000 N. Glenwood, 312/409-4207 **FN**
This performance space is part of a healthy foods restaurant/bar/store complex. (See p. 202.)

Irish Heritage Community Theatre ($/$$)
4626 N. Knox, 773/282-7035 **NW**

Ivanhoe Theatre ($$)
750 W. Wellington, 773/975-7171 **N**

Latino Chicago Theater Company ($$)
The Firehouse, 1625 N. Damen, 773/486-5120 **N**

Latino Experimental Theatre Company ($$)
1822 S. Paulina, 312/243-4149 **W**

Lifeline Theatre ($/$$)
6912 N. Glenwood, 773/761-4477 **FN**

Live Bait Theater ($$)
3914 N. Clark, 773/871-1212 **N**

Loyola University of Chicago Centennial Forum ($$)
6525 N. Sheridan, 773/508-3847 **FN**

Lunar Cabaret ($/$$/"Pay what you can")
2827 N. Lincoln, 773/327-6666 **N**
Cabaret space features performance art, unusual theatrical offerings, and folksy and fringe musical acts. Coffee, tea, and light coffeehouse fare are available. BYOB.

Merle Reskin Theatre ($/$$)
60 E. Balbo, 312/362-8455 **C**
Expect a diverse theater schedule, including works by The DePaul Theatre School, plays for children, and performances by The Chicago Opera Theater.

National Pastime Theater ($/$$)
4139 N. Broadway, 773/327-7077 **N**

Neo-Futurarium ($/$$)
5153 N. Ashland, 773/275-5255   **FN**
Located above a funeral parlor, the Neo-Futurarium has been performing *Too Much Light Makes The Baby Go Blind*, their popular 30 plays in 60 minutes requiring audience participation, for quite a while. Fri.-Sat. 11:30pm, Sun. 7pm. Pay $4 plus the roll of a die ($5-$10). Doors open at 10:30pm. No reservations are accepted, so get there early because the theater fills up quickly. Crowds are lighter on Sundays.

Northeastern Illinois University ($$)
Stage Center, 5500 N. Saint Louis, 773/794-6652   **FN**

Paul Robeson Theater ($$)
South Shore Cultural Center
7059 S. South Shore, 312/747-2580   **FSE**

Performance Loft ($/$$)
Second Unitarian Church of God
656 W. Barry, 773/529-8337   **N**

Profiles Theater ($$)
4147 N. Broadway, 773/525-9565   **N**

Puppet Parlor ($/$$)
1922 W. Montrose, 773/774-2919   **N**

Raven Theatre ($/$$)
6931 N. Clark, 773/338-2177   **FN**

Stage Left Theatre ($$)
3408 N. Sheffield, 773/883-8830   **N**

Steppenwolf Studio Theatre ($$)
1650 N. Halsted, 312/335-1650   **N**

Strawdog Theatre Co. ($$)
3829 N. Broadway, 773/528-9696   **N**

Sweet Corn Playhouse ($/$$)
5113 N. Clark, 773/409-2876   **FN**

Theatre Building ($$)
1225 W. Belmont, 773/327-5252   N

Theatre on the Lake ($$)
Fullerton & the lake, 773/348-7075   N
The Chicago Park District sponsors a full summer lineup of popular musicals and plays staged by drama troupes from the city's parks.

Tin Fish Theatre ($$)
4223 N. Lincoln, 773/769-2056   N

Torso Theatre ($$)
2827 N. Broadway, 773/549-3330   N
Buy drinks downstairs at **Renaldi's Pizza Pub** (773/248-8903) for the theater's BYOB shows.

Trap Door Theatre ($$)
1655 W. Cortland, 73/384-0494   N

TurnAround Theatre ($/$$)
3209 N. Halsted, 773/296-1100   N

University of Chicago University Theater ($)
Reynolds Club, 5706 S. University, 773/702-3414   S

University of Illinois at Chicago Theatre ($$)
1040 W. Harrison, 312/996-2939   C

Viaduct Theatre ($/$$)
3111 N. Western, 773/612-1884   N

Victory Gardens Studio ($/$$)
2257 N. Lincoln, 773/871-3000   N

Voltaire ($/$$)
3231 N. Clark, 312/409-9793   N

Theaters That Use Ushers

Volunteer ushering is an ideal way to keep current with what's playing on the moderate to high-priced theater front. It involves little more than dressing in black and white, collecting tickets, passing out programs, directing payees to their seats, making sure no intermission refreshments leave the lobby, and picking up left-behind programs at the end. Show up an hour early for a briefing on the theater and its seating policies, perform your simple duties, and take an empty seat once the show begins.

There are three basic ways to connect with ushering opportunities: 1) Almost all of the theaters below depend solely on volunteer ushers. Find the dates and times of their current productions in a newspaper and call with the specific day and time you would like to work. If it's open, they'll pencil you in. If not, you can talk about other available shows. 2) Theaters that still need ushers for upcoming shows often put a notice in the *Reader* classifieds (section 4) under the *Theater/Performing Arts* or *Wanted* headings. 3) Some theaters have a volunteer list/organization from which they draw their ushers. Contact the theaters you're interested in and sign up.

Athenaeum Theatre
2936 N. Southport, 773/935-6860   N

Bailiwick Repertory
1229 W. Belmont, 773/883-1090   N

Briar Street Theatre
3133 N. Halsted, 773/348-4000   N

Center Theater
1346 W. Devon, 773/508-5422   FN

Chopin Theatre
1543 W. Division, 773/529-5510   C

Court Theatre
5535 S. Ellis, 773/753-4472   S

European Repertory Company
Baird Hall, 615 W. Wellington, 773/472-6233   N

The Firehouse
2257 N. Lincoln, 773/549-5788   N

Goodman Theatre
200 S. Columbus, 312/443-3800   C

Lifeline Theatre
6912 N. Glenwood, 773/761-4477   **FN**

Mercury Theater
3745 N. Southport, 773/325-1700   **N**

Organic Touchstone Theatre
2851 N. Halsted, 773/327-5588   **N**

Pegasus Players
O'Rourke Performing Arts Center at Truman College
1145 W. Wilson, 773/271-2638   **N**

Royal George Theatre Center
1641 N. Halsted, 312/988-9000   **N**

Steppenwolf Theatre Company
1650 N. Halsted, 312/335-1650   **N**

Theatre Building
1225 W. Belmont, 773/327-5252   **N**

Theatre on the Lake
Fullerton and the Lake, 773/348-7075   **N**

If you enjoy volunteer ushering, you might want to join **The Saints**, a volunteer group that supports the performing arts. In addition to ushering, **Saints** members are offered other ways to volunteer for theater groups in exchange for show tickets. Some of the city's best theaters like the Shubert or Chicago Theater only use **Saints** members for their volunteer ushers. Monthly meetings have guest speakers from Chicago's theater community and allow ushers to sign up to usher several shows at once. Annual fee: $30, $10 for students ages 16-22.

Discount Theater Tickets

Finally, if you want to see the big-time stuff and don't want to pass out programs in exchange, you have the wonderful **Hot Tix** alternative.

Hot Tix Booths, 1-900-225-2225 or 1-888-225-8844
($1 per minute for information on available tickets)

108 N. State	C
Michigan & Pearson (Water Tower Visitors Center)	C
214 S. Wabash (Tower Records—cash only)	C
2301 N. Clark (Tower Records—cash only)	N

Buy your theater tickets the day of the performance, in person at one of the **Hot Tix** booths, and get them for 1/2 price—subject, of course, to availability. Mon.-Sat. 10am-6pm and Sun. noon-5pm.

Check your **Entertainment Book** (see p.204) for 1/2 price coupons for 2-4 tickets at local theaters. The **Bailiwick Arts Center, Center Theater, Footsteps Theatre Company, Greenview Arts Center, Lifeline Theatre, Raven Theatre, Shattered Globe Theatre, Stage Left Theatre**, and **UIC Theater** are regular participants in this program.

Chicago theater information on the Net:

Phone/Address Directory for 139 Chicago Theatres
http://centerstage.net/chicago/theatre/theatres/directory
Chicago Theatre Homepage
http://chicagotheatre.miningco.com
News of Chicago's theater scene: openings, events, recommendations, and reviews.

COMEDY AND IMPROV

Most comedy clubs have the last laugh as they tack on the two (over-priced) drink minimum rule to your already too-high cover charge. I've omitted those types and employed the same code used for theaters to lead you to a performance that's kinder on your pocketbook. Again, a weekly *New City* or *Reader* can give you details of current shows.

CODE:
FREE Indicates no charge, but please, if at a cafe or bar, have at least one
　　　 drink to support the establishment.
$　　 $6 and under
$$　 $6.01-$12

Annoyance Theatre ($/$$)
3747 N. Clark, 773/929-6200   **N**
Finish up an evening of weekend drinking in Wrigleyville at one of the
Annoyance's late Fri. and Sat. 12:30am $5 shows, which permit drinking
and smoking to the annoyance of some and the delight of others. The
theater's schedule is loaded with comedic productions, including a once-a-
month interactive bingo show (see pp.80-81) and the long-running *Co-ed
Prison Sluts*.

Factory Theater ($/$$)
1257 N. Loyola, 773/274-1345   **FN**
This theater's evening and round-midnight weekend comic productions are
on the order of their popular *White Trash Wedding and a Funeral*.

Gallery Cabaret (FREE)
2020 N. Oakley, 773/489-5471   **N**
Free "Improv Orgy" at 10:30pm Wed. at this Bucktown bar and paneled-
wall gallery.

The Hungry Brain (FREE)
2319 W. Belmont, 773/929-6288   **N**
Sundays from 8:30pm-11pm, the Second City Players Workshop hosts "The
Sunday Night Improv Thing," an open mic for improvised comedy.

ImprovOlympic Theatre ($/$$)
3541 N. Clark, 773/880-0199   **N**
Long-form improv shows and some sketch comedy can be seen Wed., Thur.,
and Sun. at 8pm, and Fri.-Sat. at 8pm and 10:30pm for $8. Fridays at
midnight is the $5 "Cage Match," which pits two local improv ensembles
against each other. The audience chooses the better to return the following
week and face a new challenger. "Improv Jams" Sat. at midnight are free for
participants.

Ivanhoe Theater ($$)
750 W. Wellington, 773/975-7171   **N**
Check out performances by The Free Associates, who use a particular genre
as their foundation for an improvised show. Recent styles include Tennessee
Williams, Shakespeare, gothic romances, Bible epics, hospital dramas, and
detective stories.

Jimmy's Woodlawn Tap (FREE)
1172 E. 55th, 773/643-5516   S
U of C neighborhood bar hosts the audience-interactive improv troupe,
Sheila, Wed. at 9pm.

No-Exit Cafe ($)
6970 N. Glenwood, 773/743-3355   FN
Rogers Park coffeehouse presents the improvised "Bang Bang" show Wed.
at 10:45pm for $2.

O'Bar & Cafe ($$)
3343 N. Clark, 773/508-6969   N
Improv comedy Wed. at 8pm, $5.

Off-Off-Campus ($)
Blue Gargoyle, 5655 S. University, 2nd Floor, 773/702-3414   S
The University of Chicago student improv group performs Fri. at 8pm for
$4.

Philosofur's ($/$$)
2833 N. Sheffield, 773/477-3661   N
Restaurant, bar, and pool hall features a stand-up comedy group Wed. at
8:30pm and Improv Theater Sports Thur. at 8pm. $3-$10 cover required for
comedy shows only.

The Playground ($)
Cafe Ashie, 5419 N. Clark, 773/561-7363   FN
Jako's, 4300 N. Lincoln, 773/883-5389   N
The Playground is a consortium of some of the city's best new improv
ensembles. Its member groups perform on a rotating basis at these North
Side restaurants. Shows at **Cafe Ashie** are at 8pm, Fri. and Sat.; shows at
Jako's begin at 9pm Fri. and at 9pm and 10:30pm Sat. $5.

Second City (FREE/$/$$)
1616 N. Wells, 312/337-3992   N
The famed, original Chicago comedy company has a $5 show Sun. at 3pm,
a $5.50 show Mon. at 8:30pm, and special free improv shows after regular
performances, Mon.-Thur. at 10:30pm, late Sat. at 1am, and Sun. at 10pm.
No drink minimums.

Second City's Donny's Skybox Studio ($$)
1608 N. Wells, 4th Floor, 312/337-3992   N
More comic stage productions from the funny Second City people.

Second City E.T.C. (FREE/$/$$)
1608 N. Wells, 312/642-8189   N
Second City's second stage performs free improv shows after the night's
regular acts, Wed. & Thur. 10:30pm, late Sat. at 1am, and Sun. at 10pm. No
drink minimums.

Sidelines Grill ($)
2843 N. Halsted, 773.528-7569   N
Wrigleyville sports bar features comic sketches and improv for $5, Thur. at
9pm.

Turnaround Theatre ($$)
3209 N. Halsted, 773/296-1100   N
Turnaround's "Comedy Sportz" involves two teams competing in short
improv games. Fri. 8pm, Sat. 8pm and 10:30pm, $12. The theater presents
other improv shows and comedic stage productions as well.

POETRY AND PERFORMANCE ART

Though still the greatest strugglers in the starving artists' club, poets do have
a variety of changing and established forums in Chicago where they can
publicly express themselves. For audiences who lean toward the creative and
the literary, this means a whole new world of inexpensive entertainment.
Most poetry readings will cost you no more than the amount of coffee or
alcohol you want to drink. To keep abreast of new developments in the
poetry circuit, look to the monthly literary publication, *Strong Coffee*, and
the weekly arts newspaper, *New City* ("Words" listing). Both of these
periodicals are free and can be found in abundance at coffee shops and
various alternative venues.

Cafe Aloha
2156 W. Montrose, 773/907-9356   N
The Tuesday night open mic at this Bosnian Hawaiian-themed bar/coffee
place draws poets, performance artists, and musicians. 7:30pm, FREE.

Cafe Descartes
2458 N. Lincoln, 773/935-0324   **N**
The Friday night "Half-n-Half" begins with an hour of spoken word open mic at 8pm and is followed with "expressionist parlor games" at 9pm. FREE.

Club 950
950 W. Wrightwood, 312/365-2679   **N**
"Deadly Variety" show at small dance club features poetry, theater, music, film, video, and more. First Sunday of every month at 9pm, $3.

Gallery Cabaret
2020 N. Oakley, 773/489-5471   **N**
Bar hosts a performance open mic, Thur. at 9pm. FREE.

Green Mill's Uptown Poetry Slam
4753 N. Broadway, 773/878-5552   **FN**
Staged at the legendary **Green Mill** jazz club, this internationally known poetry open mic/variety show includes a role for the opinionated audience. Sun. 7pm-10pm $5. (See p.209.)

Joy Blue
3998 N. Southport, 773/477-3330   **N**
Neighborhood bar opens its mic for poetry and spoken word performance, Wed. at 8:30pm. FREE.

Mad Bar
1640 N. Damen, 773/227-2277   **N**
Monday is "Mental Graffiti" open mic poetry night at this popular Wicker Park bar. 7:30pm, FREE.

Myopic Bookstore
1726 W. Division, 773/862-4882   **W**
Alternative bookstore hosts "Salon de Thax," a spoken word performance show with guest artists. Sun. at 8pm, FREE.

No Exit
6970 N. Glenwood, 773/743-3355   **FN**
Coffeehouse/performance space sponsors the on-going "In One Ear" open mic for poetry, spoken word, and comedy. Wed. at 8:30pm, $2.

Red Lion Pub
2446 N. Lincoln, 773/348-2695   N
English pub features "Twilight Tales," a spoken word series with a different
program each week. Mon. 8pm-10pm in upstairs dining area, $2.

Sheffield's
3258 W. Sheffield, 773/281-4989   N
Bar hosts open mic for poets and other performers Mon. 9:30pm. $3, $2 for
performers.

6511
6511 S. Kedzie, 773/737-6703   SW
Southwest-side Irish bar features Irish poetry readings the third Sat. of every
month from Sept.-May at 9pm. FREE.

34th St. Cafe
3364 S. Halsted, 773/927-1501   SW
This Bridgeport cafe sponsors "Word Night" the 1st, 2nd, and last Tuesday
of each month, welcoming poets, musicians, and ranters to the mic.

Weeds
1555 N. Dayton, 312/943-7815   C
Bar's "Uncensored Poetry Night" is a fixture on the spoken word circuit and
can get raunchy and raucous. Could be the all the tequila. Mon. 9:30pm,
FREE. The Saturday open mic draws musicians, comics, and variety show
acts, 8pm.

DANCE

Following are the most likely places you can see dance performances in
Chicago for under $12. To keep up with the dance set, pick up a **Chicago
Dance Coalition** monthly calendar at the coalition's office (200 N.
Michigan, 312/419-8384) or at the tourist information booth in the **Chicago
Cultural Center** (78 E. Washington). The **Dance Hotline** (312/419-8383)
can also update you on current events.

Chicago Cultural Center
78 E. Washington, 312/744-6630   C

Dance Center of Columbia College
4730 N. Sheridan, 773/989-3310   **FN**

Harold Washington Library Center
400 S. State, 312/747-4800   **C**

Links Hall
3435 N. Sheffield, 773/281-0824   **N**

Northeastern Illinois University
5500 N. St. Louis, 773/794-6138   **FN**
Keep an eye out for the Ensemble Español Spanish Dance Theater and their vibrant flamenco performances.

MOVIES

With the following list in hand, you will never have to pay $7.50-$8 for a movie in Chicago again. In fact, $8 can allow a savvy moviegoer to see a movie nearly every day of the week! Paying less won't interfere with seeing first-run or big name movies. Nor does seeing such movies "second-run" make them a second-rate experience. Use moviegoing to expand your knowledge of the cityscape. With the wide range of inexpensive movie choices in Chicago, it's easy to combine the familiar escape to the silver screen with an adventure to a new neighborhood.

Matinees

The newly merged **Loews/Cineplex Cinemas** essentially monopolize first-run moviegoing in Chicago—with **General Cinema**'s 14-plex in the Ford City Shopping Center being one exception—demanding $7.50-$8 per show. Matinees are your ticket around those prices. Each of the following theaters offers discounted prices before 5pm or 6pm during the week and for the first show on weekends and holidays. Bargain prices are $4.50-$4.75. Seniors and children under 12 always pay the reduced rate.

62nd & Western 2258 W. 62nd, 773/476-4959		**SW**
600 N. Michigan 600 N. Michigan, 312/255-9340		**C**
900 N. Michigan 900 N. Michigan, 312/787-1988		**C**
Biograph 2433 N. Lincoln, 773/348-4123		**N**
Bricktown Square 6420 W. Fullerton, 312/739-6083		**NW**

Broadway Cinema 3175 N. Broadway, 773/327-4114	N
Burnham Plaza 826 S. Wabash, 312/922-1090	C
Chatham 14 210 W. 87th, 773/487-1625	FSE
Esquire 58 E. Oak, 312/280-0101	C
Fine Arts 418 S. Michigan, 312/939-3700	C
Ford City 14 7601 S. Cicero, 773/582-1838	FSW
Hyde Park 5238 S. Harper, 773/288-4900	S
Lawndale 3330 W. Roosevelt, 773/265-1010	W
Lincoln Village 1-6 6341 N. McCormick, 773/604-4747	FN
Lincoln Village 7-9 6101 N. Lincoln, 773/604-4747	FN
McClurg Court 300 E. Ohio, 312/642-0723	C
Pipers Alley 210 W. North, 312/642-7500	N
Plaza 3343 W. Devon, 773/539-3100	FN
Water Tower 845 N. Michigan, 312/422-4463	C
Webster Place 1471 W. Webster, 773/327-3100	N

The Cheap Movie Theaters

Chicago is not the second city when it comes to cheap moviegoing. Most people don't realize that "the dollar shows" we know, love, and rely on in Chicago are virtually non-existent in New York City. (We have seven.) Hey—the popcorn costs more than the movie at many of these places.

Brew & View at The Vic
3145 N. Sheffield, 312/618-8439   N
The historic Vic Theatre has added cheap movie house to its list of incarnations (both a former theater and nightclub, it still doubles as a concert hall). Admission is always $4 for 2-3 movies. The first one starts around 8pm, the second at 10/10:30pm, and the 3rd movie (weekends only) at midnight. There's a full bar (with $1-$2 drink specials nightly), full concession stand, Bacino's Pizza, a grand staircase to the 2nd floor balcony, and a gutted first floor with benches and tables for more convivial viewing. Thursdays, buy the mandatory $2 Brew & View cup at the door and fill it up with beer or soda for 25 cents all night. This is a rowdy time—like renting videos with your closest two hundred friends. Must be 18 to enter, and 21 with ID to drink.

Finish an evening at **Brew & View** with a trip to the local **Dunkin' Donuts** (Belmont & Clark), so long a notorious hangout for rebel teens that it is sometimes referred to as the *Punkin' Donuts*.

Davis Theatre
4614 N. Lincoln, 773/784-0893   **N**
Movies at the **Davis** cost $1.50 Mon. and Tues. and for the first shows on
other days. Otherwise, seats are $2.50. **The Davis Art** movie of the week is
an art movie, independent flic, foreign film, or mega-blockbuster that
commands a higher ticket price and helps keeps the other movies cheap: $4
before 6pm, $6 afterwards.

Before a weekend matinee, browse through the German delis and gift shops
in Lincoln Square (4700-4800 N. Lincoln). After an evening show, head to
the same area for some sudsy *gemütlichkeit* at the **Chicago Brauhaus**
(p.146 & p.230), **The Huettenbar** (4721 N. Lincoln, 773/561-2507), or
The Hansa Clipper (4659 N. Lincoln, 773/271-0657).

Logan Theatre
2646 N. Milwaukee, 773/252-0627   **NW**
The Logan is the only neighborhood theatre that has matinees daily. They
show 4-6 movies weekly, with some double features. Pay $2 at all times.

The Patio Theatre
6008 W. Irving Park, 773/545-2006   **NW**
This once elegant, if now a bit shabby, historic theatre, takes you back to the
days of the movie palace to enjoy your $2 show. As **The Patio** remains
whole—undivided into the narrow screening corridors of other theaters, it
only shows one movie at a time. (It also makes it hard to heat, so be prepared
to wear your coat on those sub-zero winter nights.)

The Portage Theatre
4050 N. Milwaukee, 773/202-8000   **NW**
Choose from 2 movies weekly. Cost is $1 on Mondays and $1.50 otherwise.

Inspired to try, prove, or develop power and prowess after seeing Arnold,
Seagal, or Van Damme on the big screen? The **Saracan Archery Range**
upstairs (p.76) will provide a nearby arena for your exploits.

Three Penny Cinema
2424 N. Lincoln, 773/935-5744   **N**
The features here tend to be critically acclaimed, art, independent, or foreign
flics. Unfortunately, **The Three Penny** recently ended their cheap Monday
night movie, but fans of their discriminating selection of movies can still
benefit from their six-movie discount pass at $24. The normal price tag is
$6.50, $3.50 for seniors, and $4.50 for students with IDs. The concession

stand offers herbal iced tea, sparkling water, fancy juice combos, and popcorn refills.

The Village Theatre
1548 N. Clark, 312/642-2403   **C**
4-6 different movies ($2.75, $5.00 for "Art" shows) are shown weekly, often including a double feature. All movies are $2 on Tuesdays. The Village has popularized midnight shows in Chicago as an alternative to the weekend bar scene. Cult favorites, revivals of recent hits, and offbeat classics are selected for their four Fri. and Sat. night midnight shows ($5.50). **Mitchell's** (p.124) on the corner is great for late-night snacks (open 24 hours on the weekends) and chow that will carry you through a double feature.

A sister theater of **The Village** is **The Village Theatre North** (6746 N. Sheridan, 312/764-9100) which is the "community theater" for the Loyola/ Rogers Park area. Formerly the 400 Theatre, **The Village North** shows 4-6 movie selections a week. Prices are $4.50 daily before 5:30pm and $7.50 after 5:30pm. Seniors, college students with IDs, and children under 12 pay $4.50. Increased prices are justified by the coming attractions, which include valet parking, wall-to-wall curved screens, and stadium seating. They also feature four choices Fri. and Sat. at midnight and keep alive the 400's tradition of regular screenings of *The Rocky Horror Picture Show*.

> For over a dozen years, the Oscars have been made by Chicago trophy makers R. S. Owens & Co. at 5535 N. Lynch in Chicago's Northwest-side Jefferson Park neighborhood.

Alternative Movie Houses

Chicago Filmmakers
1543 W. Division, 773/384-5533   **C**
Chicago Filmmakers is a 22-year-old independent film house and forum/ resource center for filmmakers. They usually screen a couple of movies, mostly experimental stuff, weekly. Films are $6, but members pay a reduced admission. Memberships begin at $25, or $15 for filmmakers, students, and seniors. A $50 Co-op Membership gives filmmakers access to equipment and classes. Consider volunteering and seeing movies for free.

Facets Multimedia

1517 W. Fullerton, 773/281-4114   **N**

The **Facets** complex includes three theaters (for film, video, and live performance), classroom/conference space, and an enormous one-of-a-kind video rental library. A broad range of independent, unusual, classic, and rare movies are shown (at least one each day) for $7 apiece. A $50 Cinematheque Membership gets you ten free movie passes and numerous other perks, including a discounted admission and video rental fees. Call for a film schedule or pick up a bimonthly calendar at various locations. Facets also publishes *Facets Non-Violent, Non-Sexist Children's Video Guide.*

Film Center at the School of the Art Institute

Columbus Drive and Jackson, 312/443-3737   **C**

The **Film Center** is a research center and archive as well as a non-profit theater that offers one of the nation's best programs of independent, international, and classic films. Pick up the center's monthly *Gazette* or call the number above for information on upcoming films. Over 500 are shown annually; most cost $5. For film buffs, you can't beat gold card membership: $50/year for 1 or $75/year for 2 (the members can live at different addresses). Besides entitling you to some free passes, a subscription to the *Gazette*, free weekly lectures, and a discounted admission price of $3, gold card membership allows you to see over 50 sneak previews of major new releases (i.e., many Hollywood films) a year for free. For membership details call 312/443-3733.

Music Box Theatre

3733 N. Southport, 773/871-6604   **N**

Although with tickets priced at $7.75 the **Music Box** is no longer an inexpensive movie option, this classic theatre, renovated a few years back, is a must-see and do for its architecture and offerings. Some consider its lineup of foreign films, art movies, documentaries, animation fests, weekend midnight shows, and classics to be the country's best. Save by buying a $27 pass for 5 movies. Check out Sat. and Sun. matinee classics at 11:30am for $5.75, when a live organist regularly plays in the main theater. Quarterly schedules are available outside the theatre and periodically in the *Reader.*

Other Free or Inexpensive Film Options

Finally, for when you're really broke or really bored, some great moviegoing opportunities you may have never thought of...

Celluloid Movie Bar
Liquid Kitty, 1805-1807 W. Division, 312/707-8888 **W**
Celluloid is the "movie bar" component of Liquid Kitty, a totally hip, see-and-be-seen retro bar draped in red velvet and accented with orange, yellow, fish tanks, and candles. Three movies are shown nightly at approx. 7:30pm, 10pm, and midnight—everything from the latest hits to cult classics. Seating is at bar tables, in seven rows of theater-style seats, or unavailable. Sun.-Thur. is free, Fri. and Sat. command a $7 cover charge. Dress as fashionably as you can muster.

Chicago Cultural Center Film Series
78 E. Washington, 312/744-6630 **C**
Recent films reflecting a monthly theme are shown every Tues. at 5pm in the Cultural Center's theater at no charge. Call for or pick up a monthly schedule.

Harold Washington Library Center Films
400 S. State, 312/747-4100 **C**
The HWLC shows a variety of free films every month in their auditorium or video theatre on the lower level. Call for a schedule or pick one up at any library or the Chicago Cultural Center.

LaSalle Classic Film Series
4901 W. Irving Park, 773/777-7200 **NW**
See old movie classics on the big screen at this bank's clean and roomy theater (also used for financial seminars and community events) Sat. at 8pm for $3, seniors $2. Popcorn $.75-$1, buttered $1-$1.25. Enter through the parking lot. Pick up or call for a seasonal schedule.

Sulzer Regional Library
4455 N. Lincoln, 312/744-7616 **N**
Feature film series shows a variety of recent and classic movies every Wednesday at 1pm for free in the Louis Lerner Auditorium. One Saturday every month, a captioned film for the deaf and hearing impaired is shown. The monthly schedule you can pick up at the library will also have information on other films, classes, concerts, workshops, meetings, and children's activities.

University of Chicago Doc Films
Max Palevsky Cinema at Ida Noyes Hall
1212 E. 59th, 773/702-8575 **S**
University of Chicago film group shows recent, classic, and documentary

movies daily during the academic year, both for the campus community and all Chicagoans. Recently named "Best Student Film Society" in the country by *Entertainment Weekly*, this is the country's longest continuously running student film society (since 1932). The Max Palevsky Cinema is even outfitted with the latest Dolby SR surround sound technology. Movie times are approximate: Mon.-Wed. at 7pm, Thur. at 7pm and 9:15pm, Fri. & Sat. at 6pm, 8:45pm, and 11pm, and Sun. at 2pm and 7:30pm. Admission is $3, $4 on weekends. Call for recorded message of weekly and upcoming offerings.

University of Chicago International House Films
1414 E. 59th, 773/753-2274   **S**
The film society of the International House at the University of Chicago shows international, classic, and recent movies for $3 on Thur. and $4 Fri./Sat. most Thursday (7:30), Friday (8 & 10), and Sunay (8) evenings. Pop and popcorn are only 50 cents each. Call for or pick up a quarterly schedule.

Two bars, **Delilah's** (2771 N. Lincoln, 773/472-2771) and **Iggy's** (700 N. Milwaukee, 312/829-4449), show movies regularly on Sunday nights. **Delilah's** screens student films, and **Iggy's** shows recent classics and popular flics.

Arnie Bernstein celebrates the vital role of Chicago and Chicagoans in moviemaking history in his new book *Hollywood on Lake Michigan: 100 Years of Chicago and the Movies.* The history/guide book includes exclusive interviews, celebrity anecdotes, trivia, an in-depth look at the silent era in Chi-Town, sightseeing suggestions, 80 photos, and more.

Online updates for on-screen entertainment:

Chicago Movie Phone Online
http://www.movielink.com/?TP:Regional+FP:MainMenu+Mld:CH
Find movies playing near your or the location of a movie you wish to see. Also, show times and show prices.
Chicago Film Office
http://www.ci.chi.il.us/WorksMart/SpecialEvents/FilmOffice
Learn about movies currently being filmed in Chicago, extras casting, procedures for filming, etc.

Chicago Reader Movie Reviews, Past and Present
http://www.chireader.com/movies
Searchable database of 6,000 brief reviews.
Dinner and a Movie
http://www.dinnerandamovie.com
Choose a restaurant by cuisine, price range, rating, or location and a movie
by title, time of day, theater, or rating, and the database will spit out some
compatible options for you.

DOWNTOWN AND FREE

Four grand central city institutions offer continuous and diverse
complimentary programming for the public.

Chicago Cultural Center
78 E. Washington, 312/744-6630   C
A monthly schedule, WBEZ (91.5 FM), and the FINE-ART hotline can all
provide you with specific information regarding the procession of free
entertainment offered at Chicago's public cultural headquarters. Especially
popular are the classical *Dame Myra Hess Memorial Concerts* held
Wednesdays at 12:15pm in the exquisite Preston Bradley Hall.

Harold Washington Library Center
400 S. State, 312/747-4800   C
The auditorium in the lower level of the main branch of Chicago's library
system is frequently open for free public music, dance, and drama
performances. Pick up a monthly schedule of shows in the library's lobby or
at the Chicago Cultural Center. You can also call 312/747-4800 for dance,
312/747-4700 for drama, and 312/747-4850 for music information.

James R. Thompson Center
100 W. Randolph, 312/346-0777   C
Regular noon-time entertainment is offered in the atrium mall of this state
government building. Pick up the monthly *Center Stage* brochure at 100 W.
Randolph or call for details.

Under the Picasso
Daley Civic Center at Washington and Dearborn, 312/346-3278   C
Every weekday of the year from noon-1pm, near the Picasso in the Daley
Civic Center, the City of Chicago's Department of Cultural Affairs sponsors
a range of cultural events: choral and instrumental music concerts, drama,

dance, lectures, ethnic celebrations, fashion shows, exhibits, farmer's markets, and much more. For the monthly schedule, stop by City Hall. For the week's activities, dial FINE-ART.

PUBLIC CELEBRATIONS

Summer in Chicago is our reward for surviving the harsh, grueling winters. May through September, a constant stream of music fests, food feasts, art fairs, block parties, parades, fireworks, street fairs, historical house and garden walks, neighborhood fests, church carnivals, ethnic festivals, and picnics offers us abundant opportunities for eating, drinking, music listening, dancing, hanging out, spectating, browsing, marching, playing, gambling, lounging, strolling, meeting our fellow Chicagoans, and out-and-out carousing.

Consult weekend newspapers, tourist information centers, or the events hotlines for exact times and dates. (See *Chapter 9: Keeping Informed* for more details on these resources.) To use as a rough guideline, the last line of each festival entry gives the typical time of year for the event.

The Big Grant Park/Lakefront Summer Events

Ahh... There's nothing quite like partying with hundreds of thousands of your neighbors in Chicago's grassy front yard of Grant Park or on the sandy shores of Lake Michigan: World-class music and summertime food favorites abound, the music and people watching are free and sensational, there are surprisingly few problems considering the number of people hoarded together, and the amount spent on eating and drinking is up to you...

Chicago Blues Festival, 312/744-3315   C
Grant Park (Jackson & Columbus)
Food and art have joined this music extravaganza as the Chicago favorite and world's largest free blues fest continues to grow.
Memorial Day weekend or first weekend in June.

Chicago Gospel Festival, 312/744-3315   C
Grant Park (Jackson & Columbus)
Nation's largest free gospel fest draws local and national acts performing traditional and contemporary gospel styles.
2nd weekend in June

Grant Park Music Festival, 312/819-0614   C
Grant Park (Jackson & Columbus)
The Grant Park Concerts Society has been presenting free, evening summer concerts for 60+ years. Send a SASE to the society at 520 S. Michigan, Suite 343, Chicago, IL 60605 for a schedule of the almost 40 concerts presented each season. Bring dinner, beverages, and a blanket; stretch out; and enjoy a relaxing evening under the stars!
Concerts run mid-June through late August

Annual Chicago Country Music Festival, 312/744-3315   C
Grant Park (Jackson & Columbus)
Listening and dancing to local and national country acts.
Last weekend in June

Taste of Chicago, 312/744-3315   C
Streets extending from Jackson & Columbus intersection
Lavish food-sampling fest of 65+ area restaurants accompanied by both loads of street musicians/performers and a packed schedule of "official" musicians and performers. Pay for the food; the music, as always, is free. Chicagoans' number one public extravaganza.
Usually the 10 days up to and including the July 4th weekend

Fourth of July Concert and Fireworks, 312/742-7638   C
Lakefront/Grant Park/Navy Pier for viewing, fireworks and music begin after dark.
Hard-to-beat fireworks fête and accompanying classical music concert lures millions to the lakefront for an Independence Day celebration.
July 3, yearly

Venetian Night, 312/744-3315   C
Viewing area along lakefront between Navy Pier and the Adler Planetarium, begins after dark.
A parade of illuminated and decorated boats coasts along Lake Michigan, with fireworks and the Grant Park Symphony in the background.
A Saturday between late July and mid-August

Air and Water Show, 312/744-3315   C
Best lakefront viewing spot is North Ave. Beach
Two million people pack the lakefront to view stunt pilots and power boat racers in the country's oldest such event and one of the nation's largest free spectator events.
Late August, though date tends to vary

Chicago Jazz Festival, 312/744-3315   C
Grant Park (Jackson & Columbus)
World's largest (...surprise!) free outdoor jazz fest showcases the many
faces of jazz with local, national, and international acts.
Labor Day weekend

Viva! Chicago Latin Music Festival, 312/744-3315   C
Grant Park (Jackson & Columbus)
Local, national, and international performers provide a weekend of Latin
jazz, merengue, and salsa along with newer forms.
Usually weekend before Memorial Day or weekend after Labor Day

Chicago Celtic Music Festival, 312/744-3315   C
Grant Park (Jackson & Columbus)
New music fest celebrates the music, dance, and Celtic traditions from
Brittany, Galacia, Ireland, Canada, the United States, and the United
Kingdom.
Weekend in mid-September

Music Festivals

43rd Street Blues Fest, 773/924-1330   S
4314 S. Cottage Grove
This free, one-day celebration of "gut-wrenching blues" is sponsored by the
Mid-South Planning and Development Commission not only to provide
entertainment for the community, but to educate people about the rich local
talent. Past performers have included the late Junior Wells, Vance Kelly,
and Otis Rush. One or two food vendors usually set up booths, but for some
real hometown cooking, try **Alma's Place** (see p.193) next door to the
famed **Checkerboard Lounge** (see p.212).
Wednesday before the annual city Blues Festival the first weekend in June

Concerts in the Park, 312/747-0816   Citywide
Chicago Park District sponsors over 80 summer concerts in over 60 Chicago
parks. Call for a schedule.
Various dates/times throughout July and August

North Pullman Jazz, Blues, & Gospel Festival , 773/928-6300   FSE
Gately Park at 101st & Cottage Grove
*The Farmer's Almanac is consulted for a good weekend (usually late July
or early August).*

South Shore Cultural Center Jazzfest, 773/734-2000   **FSE**
South Shore Cultural Center at 71st & South Shore Drive
1st weekend in August

Jazz in the Alley, 773/624-4620   **S**
Dunbar Park at 2900 S. Indiana
Last Sunday in August

Art Fairs

57th Street Art Fair, 773/493-3247   **S**
57th St. at Kimbark
Established in 1948, this is the oldest juried art fair in the Midwest. It attracts serious artists from throughout North America. Approximately 300 artists exhibit their paintings, photography, sculpture, woodworking, etc. Wide variety of food and refreshments are available at the Ray School. Free.
1st weekend in June

Community Art Fair, 773/363-8282   **S**
Bixler Park, 57th & Kenwood
An off-shoot of the 57th Street Art Fair, this juried fine arts and fine crafts fair is sponsored by the Harper Court Arts Council. Free.
First full weekend in June

Old Town Art Fair, 312/337-1938   **N**
1800 N. Lincoln Park West & 1800 N. Orleans
Chicago's oldest outdoor (49 years & counting) art fair. $3 donation.
2nd weekend in June

Wells Street Art Festival, 773/868-3010   **C**
Wells Street from Scott St. to North
20+ year old Chicago staple. $3 donation.
2nd weekend in June

Art Experiences, 312/751-2500   **C**
Various downtown locations
The *American Society of Artists* sponsors 5-6 art fairs every summer on Michigan Avenue, at the Water Tower, at Navy Pier's Gateway Park, at the Thompson Center (100 W. Randolph), and at the Plaza of the Americas (420 N. Michigan). Call for the year's list of art fairs.

Festival of Ethnic Arts, 773/445-3838   **FSW**
Beverly Art Center, 2153 W. 111th
Family-oriented festival centers around ethnic music, dance, food, and
children's events.
3rd weekend in June

DuSable Arts & Crafts Festival, 773/947-0600   **S**
DuSable Museum at 740 E. 56th Place
Arts & crafts fair and family festival of the DuSable Museum of African-
American of history and culture.
Mid-July

Gold Coast Art Fair, 312/787-2677   **C**
River North neighborhood, bounded by Ontario, Wells, Superior, and State
1st or 2nd weekend in August

New East Side Artworks Festival, 312/551-9290   **C**
Michigan Avenue and Lake Street
Mid-August

Broadway Art Fair, 773/348-8608   **N**
Belmont and Broadway
A 27-year city tradition.
3rd weekend in August

Bucktown Arts Fest, 773/227-4629   **N**
2200 N. Oakley
Last weekend in August

Around the Coyote Art Exhibition, 773/342-6777   **W**
Milwaukee, North, and Damen
Visit the studios and galleries of Wicker Park's cutting edge visual and
performing artists.
2nd weekend in September after Labor Day

Neighborhood Fests

St. Casimir's Day Festival, 773/778-7500   **SW**
Lithuanian Youth Center, 5620 S. Claremont
A free celebration of the feast day of the patron saint of Lithuania and of the
Lithuanian Boys and Girls Scouts of Chicago who sponsor this arts and
crafts festival. Visitors can also enjoy Lithuanian food, entertainment, and

games.
First Sunday in March

Printers Row Book Fair, 312/987-9896   **C**
Dearborn from Congress to Polk
Former printing district turned fashionable restaurant, club, and shopping strip hosts this jumbo book fair.
Last weekend in May

Central Lakeview Street Festival, 773/868-3010   **N**
Belmont between Clark and Sheffield
Food, entertainment, and miscellaneous vendors lure the neighborhood's youthful majority.
1st weekend in June

Park West Antiques Fair, 773/477-5100   **N**
Main gate at 600 W. Fullerton
Summer streetfest focusing on buying, selling, and admiring antiques.
1st weekend in June

Taste of the Heart of Italy Street Fest, 773/254-6168   **SW**
2400-2500 S. Oakley
Close-knit Heart of Italy neighborhood's food and entertainment fest.
1st or 2nd weekend in June

NAES Annual Pow Wow, 773/761-5000   **FN**
Mather Park, California & Peterson
An annual celebration of Native American cultures, ponsored by Native American Educational Services (NAES), includes food, crafts, entertainment, and ceremony. Donation required for entrance.
Early June

Fiestas Puertorriquenas, 773/292-1414   **W**
Humboldt Park at 1400 N. Sacramento
Large Puerto Rican summerfest and independence day celebration includes carnival rides, games, live music, and Puerto Rican and other ethnic foods.
6 days up to the second Sunday in June

St. Symphorosa Festival, 773/767-1523
St. Symphorosa Church, 6200 S. Austin
This block party that has grown into a festival features food booths hosted by area restaurants, bingo, beer tent, raffle, adult and kiddie games, and live

entertainment.
Usually the first weekend after the Fourth of July

Taste of River North, 312/645-1047   **C**
State between Kinzie & Grand
A showcase of food from local restaurants, arts & crafts, and entertainment, with live musicians/performers on the House of Blues stage.
2nd weekend in June.

Black Kings & Queens Family Fest, 773/445-5445   **FSE**
Fernwood Park, 10436 S. Wallace
A relatively new summer festival based on the Juneteenth celebration marking the emancipation of the last African-American slaves on June 19, 1865 in Galveston, Texas. The date changes each year, so contact the South Side Help Center at for more information.
Mid-June

Andersonville Midsommerfest, 773/728-2995   **FN**
Clark from Foster to Balmoral
Swedish mid-summer fest with food, drink, arts and crafts vendors, and local bands.
3rd weekend in June

Lincoln Avenue Street Fair, 773/348-6784   **N**
Lincoln from Belden to Webster
Lincoln Park neighborhood fest packs in the crowds for food, entertainment, and shopping.
Mid-late June

Calumet/Giles/Prairie Historical House Walk, 312/225-2257   **S**
3100 S. Calumet
Tours of historic homes and attendant festivities.
Last Saturday in June

Gay and Lesbian Pride Festival, 773/348-8243   **N**
Lincoln Park at North Lake Shore Drive West & Wellington
Parade begins at 2pm at Halsted & Belmont and ends with music fest/rally in Lincoln Park.
Last Sunday in June

Kwanzaa Summer Festival, 773/264-1298   **FSE**
Abbott Park at 49 E. 95th
African-American celebration with food, entertainment, and children's activities.
1st Saturday in July

Rock Around the Block, 773/472-7171   **N**
Lincoln between Belmont and School
For a $3 donation, enjoy 30 local bands on 3 stages, food, arts and crafts vendors.
2nd weekend in July

Annual Brighton Park Lithuanian Fest, 773/847-0664   **SW**
4300-4700 S. Western
Lots of food and music (including Polish, Lithuanian, country, and rock).
Weekend in mid-July

Taste of the East Side, 773/721-7948   **FSE**
106th & Ewing
Food and music extravaganza on Chicago's far Southeast Side.
Weekend in mid-July

Sheffield Garden Walk and Festival, 773/929-9255   **N**
Webster & Sheffield
Tour private gardens, browse through rummage sales, and enjoy local food and entertainment. Kid's corner includes a petting zoo. $4 admission.
Weekend in mid-July

Dearborn Garden Walk & Heritage Festival, 773/472-6561   **C**
1200-1600 N. Dearborn
Tour 60+ award-winning private gardens at the oldest garden walk in the country in the tony Gold Coast area. Fest includes plant sales, music, food, children's activities, and more. $5 donation.
3rd Sunday in July

Chinatown Summer Fair, 312/225-6198   **S**
2200-2400 S. Wentworth
Fireworks, sidewalk sale, traditional arts and crafts, food, children's carnival, folk dancing, and martial arts.
Last/2nd to last Sunday in July

Newberry Library Book Fair & Bughouse Square Debates   **C**
312/255-3510
60 W. Walton
Noted humanities library combines big book fair with debate fest for well-known orators and those on a soapbox.
Last weekend in July

Taste of Lincoln Avenue, 773/534-5460   **N**
Lincoln Ave. between Fullerton and Wrightwood
Food, 40+ bands, 60+ arts and crafts vendors, and a kids' carnival.
Last weekend in July

Fiesta del Sol (Festival of the Sun), 312/666-2663   **C**
Blue Island from 18th to Cermak
Mexican street festival draws 500,000+ for food, entertainment, music, dancing, arts and crafts, carnival rides, etc.
Last week in July/first week in August

Wicker Park Greening Fest, 773/868-3010   **W**
Wicker Park at 1500 N. Damen
Historic house walk, food, music, and resale and art vendors.
Weekend in August

Oz Park Festival, 773/929-8686   **N**
Lincoln Park on Cannon Drive, east of the zoo
The Medieval family fair and neighborhood fest with live music/theater, food, crafts, etc. has outgrown Oz Park and now has a new Lincoln Park location. $4 admission
1st weekend in August

Hegewisch Fest, 773/646-6880   **FSE**
Baltimore from 132nd to 134th
Neighborhood fest of an old Polish community on the city's southernmost edge.
1st weekend in August

Original Old Timers of Lilydale Festival, 773/928-1251   **FSE**
Abbott Park at 49 E. 95th
Jazz and gospel music set the stage for dancing, food, and art exhibits.
1st Saturday in August

Taste of Midway Festival, 773/767-8183   **SW**
5500 S. Lorel
St. Camillus' parish food fest with beer garden, music, games, rides, and children's activities.
1st or 2nd week in August

"Northalsted" Market Days, 773/868-3010   **N**
Halsted between Belmont & Addison
Large food, art, and entertainment streetfest, heavily organized and attended by Chicago's gay community.
2nd weekend in August

Midwest Buddhist Temple's Ginza Festival, 312/943-7801   **N**
435 W. Menomonee
Japanese food, dancing, drumming, crafts, and martial arts.
2nd or 3rd weekend in August

Taste of Austin, 773/921-2121   **W**
Columbus Park at Jackson & Central
Elaborate neighborhood food festival at a beautiful, historic, and spacious city park.
Weekend in late August/early September

Argyle Fest, 773/784-2900   **FN**
Argyle from Sheridan to Kenmore
Asian and American music, dancing, arts and crafts, food from local restaurants, clowns, and children's activities.
Last Sunday in August

Taste of Polonia Festival, 773/777-8898   **FN**
Copernicus Plaza at 5216 W. Lawrence
Polish and American music, dancing, folk dance performances, bingo, and 20+ Polish and American food vendors. Small entrance fee.
Labor Day weekend September

Ukrainian Fest, 312/357-1750   **W**
Smith Park at 2526 W. Grand
Folk dancing, traditional and contemporary musical acts, folk art, and food booths. Suggested donation of $5 entitles you to a raffle ticket for major door prizes.
Weekend after Labor Day

German-American Fest, 773/561-5535   N
Lincoln & Leland
Folk dance, musical performances, and carnival games, serve as the background for lots of German food and even more beer.
Weekend closest to Sept. 17th (Von Steuben Day)

North Lakeside Festival, 773/743-4477   FN
North Lakeside Cultural Center/Berger Park at 6100 N. Sheridan, Somewhat new arts, entertainment, and food renaissance festival for a beautiful park district cultural center in a scenic lakefront location.
Last weekend in September, though future dates may vary

PARADES

For more parade news, contact the mayor's parade department at 312/744-0477.

Chinatown New Year Parade & Lion Dance, 312/225-6198   S
24th Place & Wentworth to Cermak & Princeton. Call for time.
Sunday after the Chinese New Year's Day. Generally, February.

Chinese New Year Parade on Argyle, 773/728-1030   FN
Argyle from Broadway to Sheridan. Call for time.
Usually after the Chinatown Parade in mid-late Feb. Call for date.

South Side Irish St. Patrick's Day Parade, 773/238-1969   FSW
Western between 103rd and 114th. Call for time.
Supposedly the largest Irish neighborhood parade outside of Ireland—a raucous event that can last up to three hours.
Sunday before March 17th

St. Patrick's Day Parade, 312/942-9188   C
Dearborn between Wacker and Van Buren, 11am
Vegetable dye turns the green Chicago River bright green for the day!
March 14th

St. Jude Police Memorial Parade, 312/746-8458   C
Chicago Avenue between Michigan and State, 8:40am
1st Sunday in May

Polish Constitution Day Parade, 773/889-7129   C
Dearborn between Wacker and Van Buren, 11:45am
Saturday in early May

Greek-American Parade, 312/822-9888   C
Dearborn between Wacker and Van Buren, noon
Second Saturday in May

African Liberation Day Parade and Picnic, 773/268-7500   W
Austin & Jackson. Call for time.
Saturday in late May

Philippine Independence Day Parade, 312/744-0833   C
Dearborn between Wacker and Van Buren, noon
Saturday in early-mid June

Puerto Rican Day Parade, 773/292-1414   C
Dearborn between Wacker and Dearborn, noon
1st or 2nd Saturday in June

Gay and Lesbian Pride Parade, 773/348-8243   N
Halsted from Belmont to Broadway, south to Diversey, east to Sheridan,
2pm
Last Sunday in June

India's United Independence Day Parade, 312/744-3315   C
Dearborn between Wacker and Van Buren, noon
First Saturday in August

Bud Billiken Parade and Picnic, 312/225-2400   S
39th & King Dr. to 55th & Washington Park, 10am
This historic, back-to-school parade of the South Side's African-American
community is the country's third largest, after the Rose Bowl Parade in
Pasadena and Macy's Thanksgiving Day Parade in Manhattan.
Second Saturday in August

Mexican Independence Day Parade - Downtown, 312/744-3315   C
Dearborn between Wacker and Van Buren, 12:30pm
Saturday in mid-September

Mexican Independence Day Parade - Little Village, 312/744-0477 **SW**
26th between Troy and Kostner, noon
Sunday after the downtown parade

Chicago's Labor Day Parade, 312/744-3315   C
Dearborn between Wacker and Dearborn, noon
Labor Day

Central American Independence Parade, 312/556-8239   C
Dearborn between Wacker and Dearborn, noon
Saturday after Labor Day

Von Steuben German Day Parade, 773/561-8670   C
Dearborn between Wacker and Dearborn, 10:30am
Saturday closest to September 17th

Double-Ten Parade, 312/225-6198   S
Wentworth from 24th Pl. to Cermak. Call for time.
Chinatown parade commemorates the 1911 overthrow of the Manchu
dynasty by Sun Yat-Sen and his Nationalistic Party.
1st Sunday in October

Columbus Day Parade, 312/828-0010   C
Dearborn between Wacker and Van Buren, noon
Columbus Day

Veteran's Day Parade, 312/744-7582   C
Dearborn between Wacker and Van Buren, noon
Veteran's Day

63rd Street Christmas Parade, 773/436-1000   **SW**
63rd & Tripp to 63rd & Western
This is the city's largest holiday parade averaging 75 entrants with some 20
floats, 12 performing groups, the requisite politicians, and of course, Santa
Claus. Neighborhood residents line up along 63rd Street early in the day to
stake out their spots with lawn chairs and to visit with each other.
Saturday before Thanksgiving

6 WALKING

Gardens and outdoor sculptures are but a few of Chicago's multitude of treasures best discovered on foot. (*left*) The Illinois Centennial Monument in Logan Square at Kedzie and Logan Boulevards and (*below*) the Art Institute's scultpure garden flanked by prairie grasses and traditional shrubbery. (*Photos by Rames Shrestha.*)

6 WALKING

alking earned its own chapter in this book because it is the ideal way to know any place intimately. Much of the information in this book, in fact, comes from the thousands of miles I have hiked over a lifetime on Chicago sidewalks.

Walking exposes us as closely as possible to our surroundings. It allows us to pick up more environmental information than any other mode of transport. Walking is an active endeavor that requires attention and decision making. This close contact with the streets helps us to develop ever more intricate mental maps of Chicago, which then provide us with increasingly reliable information about the city. And, as the budget-conscious know, walking is free entertainment.

The three sections of this chapter: **Neighborhoods, Historic Districts, and Ethnic Enclaves for Roaming and Exploring**; **Good Parks for Walking**; and **Downtown Walking Tours** should provide a good start for your efforts to better know and appreciate the sights and sounds of the Chicago streets.

NEIGHBORHOODS, HISTORIC DISTRICTS, & ETHNIC ENCLAVES FOR ROAMING & EXPLORING

Here's a hefty introduction to "the city of neighborhoods." The approximate boundaries and brief descriptions of 41 distinct areas of the city given here, matched with your spirit of adventure and lots of free time, should be all you need to begin your exploring.

Andersonville

(Clark about 1500 W) from Foster (5200 N) to Bryn Mawr (5600 N) **FN**
Valkommen! Clark from Foster to Bryn Mawr is the business strip of Andersonville—Chicago's Scandinavian headquarters. The **Swedish American Museum Center** (see p.59), Swedish restaurants (see p.196), bakeries, bars, and gift shops can be found here as well as a host of newer Middle Eastern restaurants and grocers (see p.176). **Erikson's Delicatessen** (5250 N. Clark, 773/561-5634) and **Wikstrom Gourmet Foods** (5247 N. Clark, 773/878-0601), some of the country's only Swedish delis outside of Minnesota, have thrived here since the early 1920s. Drop in to stock up on imported cheese, chocolate, cookies, brown beans, fresh and frozen lingonberries, potato sausage, and herring of all persuasions. Don't miss **The Swedish Bakery** (see p.198) for an eye-popping smorgasboard of baked goods and **The Landmark** (5301 N. Clark, 773/728-5301), a three-story mall of arts, crafts, Scandinavian goods, and more. Traditional festivities for **St. Morten's Gos Day** (Sat. in early Nov.) and **St. Lucia Day** (Sat. in early Dec.) make Andersonville a great destination for atmospheric holiday shopping. The onset of winter is also the beginning of glögging season. Make the rounds to Andersonville's restaurants, bars, and shops to sample variations of glögg—the spiced and fruity wine of the season. Cozy up to the fireplace with a glass at **Simon's** (5210 N. Clark, 773/878-0894), the oldest Swedish tavern in Chicago. Their 93-year-old recipe is considered the best in the area.

Argyle Street

Argyle (5000 N) between Broadway (1200 W) & Kenmore (1040 W) and Broadway between Lawrence (4800 N) & Foster (5200 N) **FN**
A "New Chinatown" emerged in Uptown over the last fifteen years, becoming home to many Vietnamese, Thai, Cambodian, and Laotian immigrants. Asian restaurants, bakeries, grocers, gift shops, and services prosper along Argyle and Broadway. Look for the pagoda on the Argyle el stop (Howard-Dan Ryan/Red Line).

Beverly Hills/Morgan Park Ridge Historic District

Bounded by the curving Prospect (about 1500 W), 115th (1500S), Hoyne (2100), and 89th (8900) **FSW**
Here in the middle of the Illinois flatlands are hills created some 12,000 years ago by the waters of the long-gone Lake Chicago and a continental glacier. Longwood Drive, which runs north and south through the neighborhood, rides the crest of the Blue Island Ridge. After Lake Chicago

receded, marsh lands and prairie grasses flourished. These eventually produced a lush, rolling terrain. Today, beyond the wide expanses of lawn and towering trees are 3,000 homes and other structures that are on the National Historic Register. **Longwood Drive** [91st to 115th Streets] and **Walter Burley Griffin Place** [104th Street between Wood (1800 W) and Prospect (1600 W) and named for the architect-student of Frank Lloyd Wright] are also Chicago landmark districts. Within these streets are approximately fifty Prairie-Style houses as well as examples of fourteen other architectural styles including Queen Anne, Victorian, Gothic Revival, Tudor, Italianate and English Country.

The fate of Beverly Hills/Morgan Park was of great concern in the early 1970s when African-American families began moving into the area and rumors about white homeowners fleeing to the suburbs circulated. The **Beverly Area Planning Association (BAPA)** worked to allay these fears and to bring about a rejuvenation of the area. Today Beverly Hills/Morgan Park is reasonably well-integrated and home to many professional couples and their families. House values into the high six-figures give the name Beverly Hills a double meaning.

The 1922 English Manor-style **Driscoll House** (10616 S. Longwood Drive) is now the headquarters for the **Ridge Historical Society** with a museum and a research library. It is generally open on Sunday and Thursday from 2 to 5 pm, but the archivist is on duty from 9am to 2pm Monday, Wednesday, Thursday and Friday, and from 9am to 5pm on Thursdays and is very accommodating about opening the museum for visitors. Admission is free. The Society, which also sponsors various historical exhibits and holds bi-monthly general meetings with speakers on historical topics, can be reached at 773/881-1675. At the **BAPA** office (10233 S. Wood, 773/233-3100), you can pick up maps for walking and biking tours (MM)

Boystown

Broadway (600 W) from Grace (3800 N) to Diversey (2800 N) and Halsted (800 W) from Grace to Belmont (3200 N) **N**
These sections of Broadway and Halsted in Lakeview are the main drags of gay Chicago. There's eclectic shopping during the day and restaurants, bars, and clubs galore at night. For three days in August a large section of Halsted is blocked off for the annual street party known as "Market Days," which attracts thousands of people to the area (see p.271). The party is a celebration of gay pride crossed with a neighborhood fest complete with music, food and drink booths, transvestite square dancers, the ROTC (Righteously Outrageous Twirling Corps), vendors, and a good dose of bare

skin and outrageous outfits. The city of Chicago plans to recognize the area as gay and lesbian friendly with special rainbow gateways, street improvements, landscaping, and new street lights. It would be the first officially designated gay district in the United States. (SW and BZ)

Bridgeport

Bound by Wentworth (200W), Pershing (3900S), Ashland (1600), the diagonal Archer, and the Stevenson Expressway   **S/SW**

One of Chicago's oldest and most famous neighborhoods, Bridgeport gets its name from the port created when a too-low bridge at Ashland Avenue and the Chicago River necessitated the unloading and re-loading of barges in order to pass. Its fame stems from its being the center of Chicago's Democratic Party machine and as the site of **Comiskey Park** (333 W. 35th), home of the Chicago White Sox. Although first populated by European immigrants, people of Mexican, Chinese, and Italian descent now comprise 50% of its population. But, thanks to politics, it is the Irish who are most associated with Bridgeport. This working class neighborhood has produced several Chicago mayors, including the Daleys, and more than its fair share of police officers and firefighters. Much of the political power emanates from the **Hamburg Athletic Association** (3523 S. Emerald) whose members include the first Mayor Daley, federal judge Abraham Lincoln Marovitz, and the current Mayor Daley.

The original 1910 **Comiskey Park** (called White Sox Park by the locals) was razed in 1991 and replaced across the street by a modern stadium complete with skyboxes. A plaque commemorating the original park stands in the north parking lot. Bridgeport's architecture is quintessential Chicago with blocks of brick bungalows and two-flats. In recent years, however, a number of upscale townhomes and condominiums have been constructed. Another neighborhood renovation project is underway at **Bubbly Creek**, part of the South Branch of the Chicago River and long a place of legend in the neighborhood.

The **Friends of the Chicago River** (312/939-0490) offers walking tours and canoe trips of the area, and in the summer sponsors the ***World's Least Glamorous Cruise***, a quirky historical trip down the Chicago River to Bubbly Creek. (MM)

Bronzeville

Bounded by 31st Pershing Road (39th St.), the Dan Ryan Expressway, and Cottage Grove.   **S**
In the early 1900s, thousands of African-Americans migrated from the Southern states to Chicago in search of jobs. Racially and politically motivated housing restrictions caused many of them to settle in this southside neighborhood near the lakefront. By the 1930s, Bronzeville, as this area came to be known, was a mecca of African-American culture. Stately greystones, many of which are still standing today, occupied the residential streets. Black-owned businesses flourished, including Supreme Life, the nation's first black-owned and operated insurance company, the Binga Bank, one of the first black-owned banks, and the *Chicago Defender* newspaper (2400 S. Michigan). Duke Ellington, Louis Armstrong, Scott Joplin, and Nat "King" Cole all lived here for a time in the early days of jazz and ragtime. At the **Wabash Avenue YMCA** (38th and Wabash), Carter G. Woodson established Negro History Week in 1926, the precursor to Black History Month.

After the Second World War, housing opportunities opened up and most of Bronzeville's more well-to-do residents moved elsewhere. The Chicago Stockyards closed, putting much of Bronzeville's working class out of work. Buildings fell into decay. In the late 1990s, a group of local business people began to revitalize Bronzeville. Eight buildings are under consideration for historic landmark status by the Chicago City Council. The wide boulevards have been cleaned up, homes are being restored and several townhouse developments are planned. Other projects include converting the **Supreme Life Insurance Building** (3501 S. Martin Luther King Drive) into an African-American tourism and visitors center, creating a military museum in the former **Eighth Regiment Armory** (3533 S. Giles, 312/939-0490) to honor the African-American soldiers of the World War I Eighth Army Regiment, and establishing a retail and entertainment complex in the **Alco Drugs Building** (35th and King Drive). Contact the **Mid-South Planning Commission** (773/924-1330) for information on the progress of these projects.

A bronze map, designed by Gregg LeFevre, sits in the median strip at 35th and King Drive identifying over 120 historic sites between 21st and 52nd and Wentworth Avenue and the lakefront. At 3624 S. King Drive, for example, you will find the former home of social reformer Ida B. Wells and Ferdinand Lee Barnett, founder of the *Conservator*, Chicago's first black-owned newspaper. The house was designated a National Historic Landmark in 1974.

The campus of the **Illinois Institute of Technology (IIT)** occupies the eastern edge of Bronzeville. **The Commons Building** (3200 S. Wabash) was designed by Mies van der Rohe, who headed the school's College of Architecture from 1938 to 1958. In the late 1990s, IIT received grants from Chicago philanthropists Jay and Robert Pritzker, Robert Galvin, and the Robert R. McCormick Tribune Foundation. The school plans to use this money to build its first new structure in 25 years, a campus center designed by Dutch architect Rem Koolhaas that is supposed to span beneath the Green Line elevated tracks. (MM)

Monument to the Great Northern Migration
26th Place and King Drive
What looks at first like feathers attached to the suit of this 15-foot-tall bronze man are actually the soles of shoes representing the thousands of African-Americans who migrated to Chicago at the turn of the 19th century. It was created by artist Alison Saar.

Statue of the Black Doughboy
35th Street and King Drive
Erected in 1927, the statue's base memorializes the black soldiers who died in the First World War. The statue itself, designed by Leonard Crunelle and added in 1936, immortalizes George Giles, a highly decorated WWI vet.
(MM)

Burnham Park/"Printers Row"

Bounded by Clark (100 W), Congress (500 S), the lakefront, and Roosevelt (1200 S), pushing further south and west all the time. **C**
Burnham Park is a trendy neighborhood on the rise (even the mayor—a lifelong Bridgeport resident—moved here a few years back), prized for its convenient just-south-of-the-Loop, just-west-of-the-lakefront location. Major housing developments (quite suburban-like); art galleries; and jazz, blues, and comedy clubs join the long-standing Lake Shore Drive museum trio (**Aquarium, Planetarium,** and **Natural History**) and **Grant Park.** Dearborn Street between Congress and Polk is "**Printers Row,**" the former printers' strip (until the early 70s) which now contains restaurants, bars, a coffeehouse, a hotel, and a bookstore.

Chinatown

Cermak (2200 S) between Princeton (300 W) & Wentworth (200 W) and Wentworth from Cermak to 24th Place (2450 S) **S**

The original "Old Chinatown" in Chicago overlapped with the Levee vice district near Clark and Harrison in the south Loop. In 1905, however, various civic organizations and the state's attorney pushed the vice lords south to 22nd and Wabash. The Chinese, who could not afford the rents of their new, unwelcoming landlords, followed the crime bosses south, where they established themselves along Wentworth. Chinatown remains—to this day—one of the most tightly preserved ethnic communities in Chicago. Chinese gift shops, grocers, and restaurants line these two blocks of Wentworth and a block of Cermak Road.

Clybourn Corridor

Bounded by the Chicago River, Fullerton (2400 N), Halsted (800 W), and North (1600 N) **N**

The diagonal Clybourn Avenue, running parallel to the Chicago River, cuts through a rapidly disappearing industrial zone that's been pretty well taken over by popular shops, restaurants, and night clubs. Unless you drive down Kingsbury Street, you would probably never notice what little industry does remain. Everything new here has taken on gigantic proportions: **Sam's Wine and Liquors** (See p.351), **Whole Foods** (1000 W. North, 312/587-0648) natural foods supermarket, **Goose Island Brewery** (See p.186), **Best Buy** (1700 N. Marcey, 312/988-4067) electronics store, **Super Crown** (1714 N. Sheffield, 312/787-4370) book store, **Crate & Barrel** (850 W. North, 312/573-9800) housewares, **Erehwon** (1800 N. Clybourn, 312/337-6400) outdoor gear, **Smith & Hawken**'s (1780 N. Marcey, 312/266-1988) upscale garden shop, **Liquid** (1997 N. Clybourn, 312/528-3400) swanky swing dance joint, **Bub City** (901 W. Weed, 312/266-1200) country nightclub complex, and **Webster Place** (see p.255) multi-plex theater. Following Clybourn four blocks southeast to Division (1200 N) brings you to Cabrini Green, the infamous Chicago housing project that now has a questionable future. It sits on prime real estate that has had developers salivating for years. (SW and BZ)

Devon Avenue

Devon (6400) from Leavitt (2200 W) to Kedzie (3200 W) **FN**

English immigrants renamed Church Street "Devon" in the 1850s after their home county. Soon afterwards the neighborhood began its steady growth towards the "International Market Place" to which it currently likens itself. Devon at Leavitt begins a full strip of Indian and Pakistani restaurants, services, sari shops, jewelers, video rental stores, and general merchandisers, followed by a stretch of Jewish and Russian shops, kosher restaurants, delis, bakeries, grocers, and fish markets that start at Washtenaw (2700 W). There are also the occasional Chinese or Greek eatery and emerging Arabic and Assyrian businesses. The **Croatian Cultural Center** is at 2845 W. Devon.

Downtown/The Loop

Bounded by Wacker (350 N), Lake Michigan, Van Buren (400 S), and Jefferson (600 W)   C

Chicago's downtown core gets its name **"The Loop"** from the late 1800s' streetcar tracks that encircled the central business district. Today's el tracks trace that same route. The six detailed walking tours in this chapter are designed to familiarize you with downtown streets and sights, particularly its impressive array of public art and architecture.

Downtown at Night

For nighttime downtown strolling, try Michigan from Oak (100 N) to Balbo (700 S).   C

The areas east of this Michigan Avenue strip contain elegant hotels and homes along with office buildings, night life, and green space. Follow, too, the Chicago River for spectacular and romantic views.

Edgewater/Bryn Mawr Avenue

Bounded by Foster (5200 N) Lake Michigan, Devon (6400 N) and Ravenswood (1800 W)   FN

Known in the past both as the celery-growing capital of the Midwest and for its swanky heyday in the 1920s, Edgewater continues to be a neighborhood of interesting contrasts. Despite its lakefront barricade of high-rises (each with its own private beach), lovely old homes, jazz age history, cultural diversity, and pockets of urban desperation, its good and bad go unnoticed by many Chicagoans. A recent listing for a four block stretch of Bryn Mawr (5600 N)—from Broadway to the lake—on The National Register of Historic Places will perhaps change that. Several buildings on this strip (dating from the 1900s to the 1920s) have been recognized, particularly the hotel apartments which were popular in the 20s, and many are being restored. Look for the **Edgewater Presbyterian Church Community House** (1020 W. Bryn Mawr), **Manor House Courtyard Apartments** (1025 W. Bryn Mawr), the **Bryn Mawr Apartment Hotel** (1043 W. Bryn Mawr), the **Belle Shore Apartment Hotel** (1062 W. Bryn Mawr) and the **Illinois Aikido Club** (1103 W. Bryn Mawr). Stop in the **Anna Held Flower** and **Ice Cream Shop** (see p.133) on the ground floor of the **Edgewater Beach Apartments** (5555 N. Sheridan, see p.20) for an afternoon escape.

Gold Coast

Bounded by La Salle (150 W), North (1600 N), Lake Shore Drive and Michigan on the east (about 100 E), and Chicago (800 N) **C**
The **Gold Coast** began as the big money, big power place it is today when Bertha and Potter Palmer (of Palmer House fame) boldly packed up from their posh Prairie Avenue neighborhood in 1882 and moved north of downtown. The historic parts on Dearborn (*36 W*), State (*0 E/W*), and Astor (*50 E*), between North and Division (*1200 N*) contain the grandest structures, including the **McCormick Mansion** (1500 N. Astor) and the **Residence of the Roman Catholic Archbishop** of Chicago (1555 N. State Parkway).

Greek Town

Halsted (800 W) from Madison (0 N/S) to Van Buren (400 S) **C**
The building of the University of Illinois and the Eisenhower Expressway in the 1960s disrupted—and, ultimately, destroyed—large portions of Greek Town. Yet, its concentration of restaurants on Halsted Street has continued as a popular destination for both out-of-towners and city dwellers in search of affordable food, fun, and drink. Along with several commendable Greek restaurants, the strip holds Greek bakeries, grocers, gifts shops, and bars.

Hegewisch

Bounded by the Calumet River, Brainerd, 100th Boulevard, and the state of Indiana **FSE**
One of Chicago's least-known neighborhoods, Hegewisch is tucked away in the far southeast corner of Cook County, a stone's throw from Indiana. It was founded in 1883 by Adolph Hegewisch, the president of U.S. Rolling Stock Company. Like his fellow railroad car manufacturing magnate George Pullman, Hegewisch wanted to create a company town. His attempt failed miserably and, in 1889, Hegewisch became part of the city of Chicago. Local rumor has it that Adolph Hegewisch took off for Mexico to escape his creditors.

A predominately white blue-collar community of modest bungalows, Hegewisch feels more like a small town than a neighborhood in a large metropolis. Most families have lived here for generations and many of the houses are known by the family name. Hegewisch has produced its share of colorful citizens including White Sox player and automobile dealer Tony

Piet, lightweight boxing champion Battling Nelson, writer Eugene Izzi, and former alderman turn radio-talk show host Ed Vrdolyak, who earned the nickname Darth Vadar during the infamous Council Wars waged after the election of Chicago's first African-American mayor, Harold Washington.

Hegewisch boasts the only state park within city limits (**Wolf Lake/William Powers Conservation Area**, see p.61), the only goose and duck hunting within city limits, a PGA golf course (**Harborside**), and 40-plus taverns serving its 8,000 residents. A feisty group of those residents has successfully fended off attempts to raze the neighborhood and build an airport, and is currently working to revitalize the area, particularly **Wolf Lake**. Check out **Aniol's True Value Hardware** (13416 Baltimore, 773/646-0730). It's been family-owned and operated for three generations and the current proprietor is the unofficial historian of Hegewisch. Make time to visit one or two of the local eating and drinking establishments such as **Doreen's Pizzeria** (13201 Baltimore, 773/646-0063) or **Club 81 Too** (13157 Avenue M, 773/646-4292)—a friendly tavern that serves lobster tails at its Friday night fish fry. (MM)

These days **Bubbly Creek** in Bridgeport and **Wolf Lake** in Hegewisch are being groomed as recreation havens, but what secrets are lurking under those waters? After all, Bubbly Creek did not get its name because it's a well-spring of champagne. Upton Sinclair called it "a great open sewer," exposing the practice of meatpackers from the Stockyards who dumped leftover blood and carcasses into the Chicago River's south fork. Gases from decomposing flesh...*that's* where those bubbles came from. Rumors also persist that after the city's 1919 race riots, several African-American packinghouse workers were drowned in the creek. As for Wolf Lake, those infamous child killers Leopold and Loeb dumped their victim Bobby Franks there in 1924. Seventy-three years later, the body of the son of El Rukn leader Jeff Fort, Antonio Fort, was pulled from its waters. Denizens of both Bridgeport and Hegewisch can be prompted to tell stories of someone they know, or someone their neighbor's brother-in-law knows who fell into the depths, never to be seen again. (MM)

Hyde Park

Bounded by Cottage Grove (800 E), Hyde Park (5100 S), Lake Michigan, and 61st (6100 S)   **S**

Developed by attorney Paul Cornell in the mid-1880s as a strictly residential suburb, Hyde Park's name was chosen to evoke the gracious living associated with London's park of the same name. Thanks to Cornell's active involvement to create a park system south of Chicago, Hyde Park is bounded by Jackson Park to the south and Washington Park to the west. In spite of vehement opposition from Cornell and other residents, Hyde Park was annexed to Chicago with several other large townships in 1889 to increase the city's odds for hosting the 1893 Columbian Exposition. Cornell's dream of luring a major academic institution to Hyde Park was realized in 1890 when John D. Rockefeller and the Baptist Church founded the **University of Chicago**. The university, whose faculty collects Nobel Prizes (64!) like some people collect parking tickets, is the focal point of the community. Free one-hour tours of the campus are given Monday through Saturday at 10am beginning at **Ida Noyes Hall** (1212 E. 59th Street).

Hyde Park has retained a somewhat independent status, a sort of idyllic island surrounded by blighted neighborhoods. It is alternately seen as progressive, snobbish, integrated, segregated, elitist, and populist, depending on the speaker's point of view. In any event, it is a thriving, bustling community with architectural jewels, eclectic and affordable restaurants, and the wide variety of the kind of funky stores that usually inhabit a college town. (MM)

Kenwood Mansions

Bounded by Cottage Grove (800 E), 47th (4700 S), Lake Michigan, and Hyde Park (5100 S)   **S**

This square of Kenwood has the city's largest concentration of mansions and was designated a Chicago landmark in 1979. Known for being a pillar of black/white racial harmony in an infamously segregated city, Kenwood is bounded by the University of Chicago to its south and some of Chicago's most hurting neighborhoods to the north and west. It was founded by Chicago dentist John A. Kennicott in 1856, who named it after his mother's ancestral Scotland estate. Other wealthy families soon built palatial homes in the area. Kennicott's house once stood at 43rd Street and the Central Railroad line. Among those still standing are the **C.S. Bouton House** (4812 S. Woodlawn), an example of the Italianate style; the **Elijah Muhammed House** (4835 S. Woodlawn), now the home of Nation of Islam leader Louis Farrakhan; the **Julius Rosenwald House** (4901 S. Ellis), built for the Sears executive and major Chicago philanthropist; and two Frank Lloyd Wright-designed houses (4852 and 4858 S. Kenwood). Also keep an eye out for the **K.A.M. Isaiah Israel Temple** (1100 E. Hyde Park), home of Chicago's oldest Jewish congregation; and Jesse Jackson's **Operation PUSH headquarters** (930 E. 50th). (MM and SW)

The Lakefront   FSE/S/C/N/FN

Chicago has about thirty miles of Lake Michigan shoreline as its eastern boundary with 29 beaches dotting that strip from **Rogers Park** (about *7700 N*) to **Calumet Beach** (about *10000 S*). Walking, running, biking, in-line skating, wading, swimming, sunning, picnicking, romantic strolling: the lakefront offers endless possibilities for relaxation and rejuvenation. (And, it's hard to get too much of this lakefront bonanza!) Here's an introductory checklist of lakefront opportunities:

⇒ Any lakefront activity in spring, summer, fall, and winter.

⇒ Any lakefront activity in the rain and the snow (with ice on the water).

⇒ Any lakefront activity at sunrise and dusk.

⇒ Any lakefront activity after dark [note: beaches technically close at 11pm. At night, the grassy, hilly stretch of land that juts into the lake and leads to the Adler Planetarium is a popular spot for lovers to lounge and stargaze. Lesser known, is that you can creep up behind the nearby Shedd Aquarium and watch the dolphins at play in its Oceanarium.

⇒ Chicago skyline view from the north, as from the North Avenue Chess Pavilion.

⇒ Chicago skyline view from the south, as from Promontory Point at 55th and the lake.

⇒ Lakefront people watching the first warm days of spring and the first hot days of summer.

⇒ Being packed at the shore with hundreds of thousands of others out for an event like the **Air and Water Show** or **Venetian Night** (see the **Public Celebrations** (pp.52-64) section of *Chapter 5: Entertainment*, for more details).

⇒ The Fourth of July fireworks display.

Lincoln Park

Bounded by North (1600 N), Diversey (2800 N), the Chicago River, and Lake Michigan.   **N**

While technically **Lincoln Park** covers a much wider region (most of which is good for meandering and admiring costly homes), its accepted hub is Fullerton/Halsted/Lincoln—the "De Paul Area." Packed with chic shops, used book and music stores, caffeine outposts, restaurants, bars, and clubs, Lincoln Park surges with activity from dawn to well past midnight. The nightlife is concentrated along Lincoln from Armitage (2000N) to Diversey (2800 N), with Halsted being home to some prominent blues clubs (see p.211).

Lincoln Square

Lincoln from Leland (4700 N) to Lawrence (4800 N)   **FN**

After a brief stint in the 1960s as the "New Greek Town," **Lincoln Square** began fortifying the last vestiges of Lincoln Avenue's German roots and molding a unique one-block commercial strip for itself to preserve this heritage. As a result, German delis, bars, a restaurant, gift shop, and apothecary now do an energetic business in the area. Recent Eastern European additions—including two coffeehouses, a bakery, and a Bosnian deli—and popular Greek and Mexican restaurants, add a multi-ethnic flavor. The newer toy shop, book dealer, music store, and upscale pastry cafe— precipitated by an ongoing influx of singles and professional families— mingle with steadfast retailers of European clothing, linens, and crystal. All of this is tucked in an outdoor mall setting complete with a shady bench-lined courtyard, gazebo, active events lineup, and music over the speakers. Not surprisingly, Lincoln Square is now a frequent destination for foreign visitors, school groups, and tour busses—perhaps the most visited ethnic district outside the city's center.

Little Italy/Taylor Street

Taylor (1000 S) from Morgan (1000 W) to Ashland (1600 W)   **C**

Like the old Greek neighborhood, this old Italian neighborhood was greatly diminished by the 1960s construction of the Eisenhower Expressway and the University of Illinois. Taylor Street remains its lifeline with a host of well-established Italian restaurants, bars, bakeries, and grocers. Recent development of the area's housing options (in part because of U of I) has brought newer Chinese, Thai, barbecue, pizza, and other establishments to the strip, where its banners declare that the neighborhood is still, "Working Together-Growing Together." Side streets are clean, lined with trees, and full of refurbished houses and apartments. This little enclave is disrupted, though briefly, by 2-3 blocks of dilapidated housing projects. (See p.154 for food recommendations in the area.)

Little Village/"La Villita"

Bounded by Ogden, Western (2400 W), the Chicago Sanitary and Ship Canal, and the city limits at the train tracks (about 4600W) **SW**
On either side of the giant arch that straddles 26th Street, La Villita's main artery, you can buy just about anything, from clothing and piñatas to live chickens. It's a good bet for authentic Mexican food and night life too. The **Little Village Discount Mall** (about 3050 W. 26th) is an indoor bazaar that has the look and feel of an urban Mexican marketplace.

Logan Square/Boulevards Historic District

Logan (2600N) from Western to Kedzie, Kedzie (3200 W) between Palmer & Logan, Humboldt (3000 W) between Milwaukee & North ending in Humboldt Park, Palmer Square at Palmer (2200 N) & Kedzie, and Logan Square at Milwaukee (about 3100 W) & Logan **N**
While many feared a homogenized gentrification for **Logan Square** when its solid, reasonably-priced bungalows, two-flats, and graystones were discovered, more restrained development over the last twenty years still leaves the neighborhood socially diverse. The mansion-like graystones that line **Logan Boulevard** (2600 W to 3000 W) are the heritage of its first turn of the century residents who earned the street the early "Boulevard of Millionaires" nickname. These and other homes along Logan Square's massive boulevards, with their expansive green stretches, make up the **Boulevards Historic District** which contains the northwestern portion of Chicago's boulevard system as outlined by Daniel Burnham's visionary 1909 "Chicago Plan." Working class families inhabited the surrounding streets at the community's origin and have continued to predominate until the present. Although the commercial areas reflect the largely Hispanic population, newer businesses are catering to a growing number of young professionals and artist-types. **Logan Beach Cafe** (see p.153) coffeehouse agreeably co-exists with a slate of taco places and the new **Boulevard Cafe** (3137 W. Logan, 773/384-8600) supper club joins **Tania's** (see p.230) long-standing Cuban supper club in its appeal to an upscale clientele.

Magnificent Mile   C

Michigan (100 E) from Oak (1000 N) to the Chicago River (about 400 N)
Chicago's Rodeo Drive—a 3/4 mile stretch of magnificently expensive shopping...

Old Edgebrook   FN
Bounded by Devon (6400 N), the diagonal Caldwell (about 5600 W), the diagonal Lehigh following the railroad tracks (about 5400 W), Central   at about 5350 W, and the North Branch of the Chicago River.
Tucked in the forest preserves of northwest Chicago stands this charming mini-neighborhood developed in 1894 as a suburb for railroad executives.

Old Town
Bounded by Armitage (2000 N), Lincoln Park (just west of the lake), North (1600 N) and Halsted (800 W)   **N**
Perhaps the original gentrified neighborhood, **Old Town** abounds with boutiques and restaurants—especially along Wells (200W), Halsted (800W), and Armitage (2000 N)—that cater to people who not only have a taste for the finer things in life, but also the money to pay for them. Well-kept, well-gardened old houses and tree-lined streets (some with cobblestone and old-fashioned street lamps) make aimless meandering a worthy Old Town diversion. The entertainment this neighborhood is known for, however, stems from the fabled **Second City** (see p.250) and **Steppenwolf** (1650 N. Halsted) theaters. The birthplace of improvised comedy, **Second City** is where members of the original and subsequent casts of *Saturday Night Live* got their starts. Original ensemble members John Malkovich, Laurie Metcalf, and Gary Sinise, are among the many TV and film stars who have performed on the **Steppenwolf** stage. (SW and BZ)

Pill Hill
Bounded by 91st (9100 S), Euclid (1934 E), 93rd (9300 S), and East End (1700E)   **FSE**
A four-block square of suburban-like residences that were built by white doctors in the 1960s, thus earning the neighborhood its name. Today the area is inhabited primarily by black professionals. The houses are enormous, often dwarfing the city lots on which they sit. Note that most of the 60s-style landscaping has been retained

Pilsen
Bounded by 16th (1600 S), Halsted (800 W), the Chicago River (about 2700 S), and Damen (2000 W)   **W**
Pilsen was originally settled by Czechoslovakian immigrants who named their new home after the Czech town where the pilsner brewing process was invented. It was the power base from which Anton Cermak rose to the mayor's office only to be killed in Miami in 1933 in an assassination attempt on President Franklin Delano Roosevelt. Pilsen began its transformation into

its current status as Chicago's Mexican arts community in the 1950s. Many of Pilsen's structures are adorned with murals, mosaics, and other outdoor artwork. The vibrantly decorated **Casa Aztlan** (1831 S. Racine) serves as a center for dance, art, and theater instruction. The **Mexican Arts Center Museum** is at 1852 W. 19th. The **Pilsen East Artists Colony** (19th and Halsted) houses several hundred sculptors, painters, ceramists, writers, actors, and photographers who hold an arts fair each October. Like every good artsy neighborhood, Pilsen has its requisite coffeehouse in the form of **Cafe Jumping Bean** (1439 W. 18th, 312/455-0019).

Two annual festivals bring crowds of people to Pilsen. One is the **Fiesta del Sol**, a warm weather feast of food, music, and culture traditionally held the last week of July and/or the first week of August. The other, more solemn, celebration is the **Via Cruces**, or Way of the Cross, which reenacts the Christian story of the Last Supper and Jesus' journey to his crucifixion each Good Friday. The procession begins at **Providence of God Church** (built in the 1920s), 18th and Union. (MM and SW)

Pullman Historic District FSE
Bounded by 111th (11000 S), Langley (700 E), 115th (11500 S), and a slanting Cottage Grove running parallel to the train tracks at about 500 E
George M. Pullman built this community in the 1880s to house the employees of his Pullman Palace Car Company, which manufactured railroad sleeping cars. Designed by architect Solon S. Beman and landscape architect Nathan Barrett, the town was self-sufficient with houses, a school, a church, a shopping arcade, a theater, stables, a hotel and a market. Note the varying sizes and styles of the houses; they correspond to the level of the workers who once lived within. You will also notice that most of the structures are red brick with green and red trim, echoing the colors of the original Pullman cars. The 1894 strike by Pullman employees, led by union organizer Eugene Debs, resulted in more control for the workers and changed the face of U.S. management-labor relations. Two years later, Pullman received the "World's Most Perfect Town" award.

Pullman was annexed by the city of Chicago in 1889. In 1960, developers threatened to raze the neighborhood in order to build an industrial park. The Pullman Civic Organization was formed to preserve the area. It became a state landmark in 1969, a national landmark district in 1971, and a city of Chicago landmark in 1972. Today, Pullman's residents are typically teachers, retirees, police officers, and students. In addition to the civic organization, the community has several other active community groups including the Historic Pullman Foundation, the Gay and Lesbian

Association, the Arcade Park Garden Club, and the Pullman Seniors Club.

The shopping arcade was demolished in 1926. In its place stands a utilitarian building housing the **Historic Pullman Visitors Center** (11141 S. Cottage Grove). It is open on Saturdays 11am-2pm and Sundays noon-3pm. Guided walking tours are given at 12:30pm and 1:30pm on the first Sunday of the month from May to October.

At the restored **Hotel Florence** (11111 S. Forrestville), Saturday Continental breakfast, Sunday brunch, and First Friday night theme dinners are served. On the second floor, you can view the room where George Pullman stayed when he was in town. (His home was in the historic Prairie Avenue district further north. The family had it torn down to prevent anyone else from purchasing it.)

Be sure to see the **Greenstone Church** at 112th and St. Lawrence. Also noteworthy is the **Retreat Restaurant** (605 W. 111th), the former home of Henry H. Sessions, Pullman's first general superintendent and once the finest residence in Pullman. (MM)

River North

Bounded by the Chicago River (on the southern and western edges), Oak (1000 N), and Wabash (50E)   **C**
Marked with non-stop growth and re-creation since its successful 80s gentrification, this former industrial zone now encompasses the largest concentration of galleries (about 90!) outside of Manhattan. Factories and warehouses of yesteryear have been either razed or remodeled for lofts, condos, auction houses, fine antique dealers, pricey furniture retailers, elite health clubs, day spas, sleek hair salons, restaurants galore, and trendy clubs (cigars and martinis abound). There is also a growing collection of oversized, theme park style dining experiences: **Ed Debevic's** interactive 50s diner (640 N. Wells, 312/664-1707), **Hard Rock Cafe** (63 W. Ontario, 312/943-2252), **Michael Jordan's Restaurant** (500 N. LaSalle, 312/644-3865), **Rainforest Cafe** (605 N. Clark, 312/787-1501), **Planet Hollywood** (633 N. Wells, 312/266-7827), and the **Rock'n'Roll McDonald's** (600 N. Clark, 312/664-7940). As the neighborhood's ad people say, there's something for everyone from the "most wide-eyed visitor to the most jaded urbanite." Guess who goes where?

Rogers Park

Bounded by Lake Michigan, Devon (6400 N), Ridge (running diagonally from about 1850 W to 2100 W), Howard (7600 W), Hermitage (1732 W) and Juneway (7736 N) **FN**
This most northeastern of Chicago neighborhoods is unique in that has always served both as a settling place (with its spacious single-family homes) and a transition neighborhood—especially for newly arrived immigrants (almost 80% of residents rent rather than own). Settled first by Native Americans, followed by Luxembourgers, Germans, English, and Irish, then later by Russian Jews and African Americans, and most recently by Hispanics, Asians, Caribbean Islanders, and Middle Easterners, Rogers Park's eclectic population includes large numbers of Loyola and Northwestern University students, young families, and retirees. Basically, the neighborhood has been home to members of every ethnic and religious group just short of Yoda's, with each group leaving their mark on the neighborhood in the form of shops, restaurants, churches, graffiti, etc. A sampling of Rogers Park congregations turns up African-American Baptists, Nigerian Christians, Mennonites, orthodox and reform Jews, Buddhists, Hindus, Muslims, Sikhs, and Hare Krishnas. Not surprisingly, a recent study of fifty cities across the U.S. ranked Rogers Park first in economic, racial, and religious diversity. Visitors enjoy its beaches, bars, coffeehouses, bookstores, and theaters. Residents benefit as well from an active neighborhood known for its schools, grass roots activism, and strong community organizations. (SW and BZ)

Roscoe Village

Bounded by Western (2400 W) Belmont (3200N) Cornelia (3500 N) and Ravenswood **N**
Roscoe Village—one of those picturesque names coined by real estate agents and developers to draw new life to an old neighborhood—refers in most minds to an eclectic, low-key business district along Roscoe between Western (2400 W) and Ravenswood (1800 W). This one time underdog has been growing steadily for the past few years adding new shops, restaurants, and of course, condos to service the rise in yuppie families and 20-something residents. Daytime strollers can browse **Sterns Psychology Book Store** (2004 W. Roscoe, 773/883-5100), **Shangri-la's** (see p.269) for a great selection of vintage clothing, pulp fiction, and LPs, or the gigantic **Village Discount** (see p.385) resale store for super bargains. Stop in **Big Hair** (2012 W. Roscoe, 773/348-0440) for a cheap haircut or to witness the latest in alternative hair styles and dye jobs. Note that 2 blocks south on Belmont is **Antique Row** (see p.19). Hip, neighborly nightlife can be found

at the singular **The Damen** (see p.180) and the **Village Tap** (see p.235). (SW and BZ)

South Chicago
Bounded by the Calumet River (about 9500 S), the slanting South Chicago Avenue, Lake Michigan, and 79th (7900 S) **FSE**
The burgeoning steel industry brought European immigrants seeking jobs at the Wisconsin Steel Company and USX Corporation South Works plants from the late 1800s to the First World War. They were then joined by Mexican workers and their families. The area thrived until a dark day in March of 1980 when the Wisconsin Steel Company closed. Although the closing of the South Works steel plant in 1992 has only added to the neighborhood's depressed state, the community somehow manages to hold together in the face of continued unemployment. On the plus side, the Southeast Chicago Development Commission is working hard to get city, state and federal funds to rejuvenate South Chicago.

Our Lady of Guadalupe Church (3200 E. 91st) was founded in 1926, making it the city's oldest Mexican immigrant church. Ironically for South Chicago, the church also houses the **National Shrine of St. Jude** (3200 E. 91st) , the patron saint of lost causes. (MM)

Southport
Southport (1400 W), bounded by Belmont (3200 N) and Irving Park (4000 N) **N**
Just a hop, skip, and a drunken stumble from Wrigley Field—Southport is booming! Once home only to a few pizza joints, several neighborhood taverns, and a multitude of closed shops, the auspicious arrival of Starbucks in the early 1990s would change this nondescript stretch for good. Just a few years later, this is a hip strip of yuppie commerce with unique ethnic eateries (**Tango Sur**—p.120 and **Amitabul**—p.159), upscale French and Italian dining, a Viennese coffee house (see p.215), vintage clothiers, antique dealers, and pricey home furnishings and gift boutiques. Among the latter are *Fourth World Artisans* (3453 N. Southport, 773/404-5200), *Fly Paper* (3402 N. Southport, 773/296-4359), *Bibelot* (3349 N. Southport, 773/348-6365), and *Whimsy* (3234 N. Southport, 773/665-1760). Entertainment options include the classic **Music Box Theater** (see p.258) for an artsy foreign flic, **Southport Lanes** (see p.84) for hand-set pin bowling, or the **Saga Launder Bar** (see p.237) for combining laundry day with a trip to the corner bar. (SW and BZ)

South Shore
Bounded by the lakefront, 79th (7900 S), South Chicago (running diagonally from 400 E-1600 E), the IC tracks (about 200 E), and 67th (6700 S)   **FSE**
Long the home of an upwardly mobile middle-class—first WASPs, then Irish Catholics and Jews, now African-Americans. The community's crowning jewel is the **South Shore Cultural Center** (7059 South Shore Drive), overlooking Lake Michigan. The approach to the center's front door is framed by a columned promenade. Its 65 attendant acres include a beach (known for its romantic ambiance and spectacular view of downtown Chicago), a public golf course, tennis courts, stables, and a stage. Built in 1906 as the preeminent South Shore Country Club (White Christians only, please. Blacks and Jews need not apply), the building and grounds were purchased by the Chicago Park District in 1974. In its infinite wisdom, the park district announced plans to demolish the building. Luckily the community banded together to save it. After you've visited the Cultural Center's art gallery and peered into its ballrooms, dining rooms, and solarium, hike up 71st Street to the **Jeffery-Cyril Historic District** [the 700 S. blocks of Cyril (1934 E) and Jeffery (2000 E)] to view a patch of 1920s apartment buildings, many of which have been rehabbed. On the other side of 71st, running to 67th, Constance (1836 E), Bennett (1900 E), Euclid (1934 E) is **Jackson Park Highlands**, a ridge-top neighborhood developed between 1905 and 1940 and home to a trendy, integrated middle-class. Your visit should also include Chicago's oldest cemetery, **Oak Woods** (1035 E. 67th); Chicago's premier African-American theater, the ornate, muraled, Middle Eastern-inspired **New Regal Theater** (79th and Stony Island), built in 1927 as the Avalon movie theater; and the Afrocentric **ETA Creative Arts Foundation/Cultural Center** (7558 S. South Chicago). (MM and SW)

Streeterville
Bounded by Michigan (100 E), Oak (1000 N), Lake Shore Dr. (cutting diagonally from about 240 E to 500 E), and Water (about 420 N)   **C**
Named for an 1889 squatter, George Wellington Streeter, who set up house on a sandbar that is now the **John Hancock Building**, this neighborhood east of Michigan Avenue is now one of the city's most moneyed areas. It's home to numerous luxury hotels and apartments, restaurants, bars, and the multi-use recreational complexes of **North Pier** and **Navy Pier**.

Tri-Taylor Historic District

Bounded by Oakley (2300 W), Polk (800 S), and Ogden (cutting diagonally from about 2300 W to 1932 W)   **W**

Triangular near south district has been on the National Register of Historic Places since 1983 for its well-preserved two and three story row houses from the late 1800s.

Villa Historic District

Bounded by the diagonal Avondale which runs parallel to the Kennedy Expressway at about 3750 N, Hamlin (3800 W), Addison (3600 N), and Pulaski (4000 W)   **NW**

Procured in 1907 by developers Albert Haentze and Charles M. Wheeler for the purpose of single-family bungalow building, this historic area is comprised mostly of Chicago and California bungalows, with some Frank Lloyd Wright and Louis Sullivan touches thrown in for good measure.

Wicker Park/Bucktown

Bounded by Western (2400 W), Fullerton (2400 N), the Kennedy Expressway (cutting diagonally from about 2200 W to 1300 W), and Division (1200N)   **N/W**

Once the stomping grounds of writer Nelson Algren, the bustling commercial intersection of Damen, Milwaukee and North Avenue (sometimes referred to as "the crotch") joins Wicker Park (to the south) and Bucktown (to the north). These two once neglected neighborhoods were rediscovered by artists and have long since skyrocketed to heights of hipness and gentrification. After Manhattan and San Francisco, Wicker Park/ Bucktown holds the United States' highest concentration of working artists. It has also been the breeding ground for various indy label musicians who have achieved national and international fame in the 1990s. The area's galleries, artists' work spaces, coffee shops, slick eateries, poetry open mics, performance spaces, and four o'clock bars testify to this convergence of creativity and trendiness. While Bucktown is yuppier, Wicker Park is an urban catwalk for the younger (tattoos, piercing, 'zines, anarchists, and connoisseurs of all things hip). Both include streets filling up with incredible rehab projects. Check out Wicker Park's **Beer Baron Row** on Hoyne (2100 W) between Pierce (1532 N) and Schiller (1400 N). While German brewery chiefs like Schlitz were living it up in these 1880s mansions, humbler German immigrants were tending to their backyard goat farms further north in Bucktown.

Wrigleyville

Bounded by Byron (3900 N), Sheffield (1000 W), Newport (3434 W), Southport (1400W)   **N**

This section of residential Lakeview overflows with nightlife for the youngish, thanks in part to the beer and bar culture surrounding **Wrigley Field** (Clark and Addison). The area is active all year round but really kicks into gear in spring, when baseball returns to the northside, bringing with it cars, street vendors, and crowds of people spilling out of the bars, shouting: *Cubs win! Cubs win!* (on a good day). Despite the neighborhood's frat party image, you'll find great Mexican and Asian food, three of Chicago's four Ethiopian restaurants (see p.141), the city's two most popular reggae clubs (see p.222), a handful of small theater companies, a great used book store, vintage clothing, antique dealers, and the **Metro** (see p.65)—a common venue for highly-alternative music—in the immediate vicinity of the ballpark. Clark Street, Wrigleyville's main artery, has remained a well-traveled path since its origins as Green Bay Road—a busy Indian trail that stretched all the way to Green Bay, Wisconsin. (SW and BZ)

Where are the largest concentrations of Chicago's least represented ethnic groups? The *Local Community Fact Book--Chicago Metropolitan Area 1990*, published by the University of Illinois Board of Trustees in 1995, supplies these data: Belgians, Dutch, Finnish, French Canadians, Scottish, Swiss, and Welsh reside in Lakeview; Hmong, Laotians, and Nicaraguans in Albany Park; Gaumanians, Hawaiians, and Hungarians in West Ridge, Eskimos, Dominicans, and Ukrainians in West Town; Ecuadorians, Hondurans, and Panamanians in Logan Square; Portuguese, Salvadorans, and Subsaharan Africans in Rogers Park; Colombians and Thais in Lincoln Square; Norwegians and Peruvians in Edgewater; Aleuts in Chicago Lawn; Samoans in Uptown; Danish in Norwood Park; Slovaks in Gage Park, and Czechs in Garfield Ridge.

GOOD PARKS FOR WALKING

Of Chicago's 560+ parks, these eight stand out for their size, greenery, beauty, popularity, and recreational opportunities. All provide a refreshing, scenic escape from the city din, but be careful; not all are located in the safest of neighborhoods.

Columbus Park

Bounded by Austin (6000 W), Adams (200 S), Central (5600 W), and the Eisenhower Exp. (about 750 S)   **W**

Designed by Prairie School architect and landscaper Jens Jensen in 1920, much of **Columbus Park** was restored to its original state by the Park District in 1992. Its 134 acres contain lagoons, pools, a small waterfall, plenty of wildflowers, beautiful park buildings, and a golf course.

Grant and Burnham Parks

Bounded by Randolph (150 N), the lakefront, 56th (5600 S), and on the west, Michigan (100 E) from Randolph to 11th (1100S) and the train tracks from 11th to 56th   **C/S**

Thanks to the foresight of early Chicagoans, the land that comprises **Grant Park** was set aside by early settlers (*1836*) to be public land forever free of buildings. Commonly referred to as Chicago's "front yard", Grant Park is the site of endless public activities, most notably, free summer concerts and festivals (see p.262). Stretching several miles along Lake Michigan to the beginning of Jackson Park, this area abounds with gardens, beaches, recreational facilities, and the trio of big museums near Roosevelt (*1200 S*).

Jackson Park

Bounded by 56th (5600 S), the lakefront, 67th (6700 S), and Stony Island (1600 E)   **S**

Located on the lake and behind the **Museum of Science and Industry** (see p.55), much of this park's 562 acres were developed for the 1893 Columbian Exposition. Don't miss the Japanese garden on the Wooded Island which has existed in various forms since that era. It's now called the **Osaka Garden** (see p.61) for Chicago's Japanese sister city which donated a traditional cedar entrance gate and money for restoration and landscaping in 1995. Other park highlights include the still, reflective **Columbian Basin** (behind the museum) that leads to the lagoon system and **Promontory Point** with its lighthouse-looking field house and great view of the cityscape.

Lincoln Park

Bounded by Ardmore (5800 N), Lake Michigan, Grand (530 N), and on the west, roughly, Lake Shore Drive (about 1000 W-250 E)   **FN/N/C**

Lincoln Park is the city's largest (1,212 acres) and perhaps best maintained and most used park. In addition to its great amenities for lakefront recreation, Lincoln Park also contains a zoo, rookery, conservatory, lagoons, ponds, cafes, a new wildlife preserve, the **Chicago Academy of Sciences** (now closed for restoration), the **Chicago Historical Society** (see p.52), **Theatre on the Lake** (see p.244), and numerous monuments and sports facilities.

Marquette Park
Bounded by Central Park (3600 W), Marquette (6700 S), California (2800 W), and 71st (7100 S) **FSW**
This large neighborhood park is enlivened by lagoons, a golf course, and a rose garden.

River Park
On both sides of the Chicago River between about 2850-2950 W. Lawrence (4800 N) and about 3200-3300 W. Devon (6400 N) **FN**
River Park's quiet, lengthy strip of land surrounding the Chicago River contains a meandering sidewalk perfect for cycling, skating, jogging, or an evening stroll.

Washington Park
Bounded by Martin Luther King Dr. (400 E), 51st (5100 S), Cottage Grove (800 E), and 60th (6000 S) **S**
Planned and landscaped in the 1870s, this 366 acre park just west of the **University of Chicago** has a large lagoon, plenty of shade, and a new aquatic center (see p.287). The **Lessing Monument** in its rose garden (57th and Cottage Grove) commemorates an 18th century German writer whose plays spoke for religious tolerance, particularly towards Jews. Be on the lookout for the ghost of Studs Lonigan, title character from James T. Farrell's famed trilogy. Both author and character hung out here as boys in the 1920s.

DOWNTOWN WALKING TOURS

Following are six walking tours of the city's center, designed to expose you to Chicago's great wealth of architecture and public art, while familiarizing you with the downtown area in general. Three concentrate on buildings: **Downtown Buildings (Classic)**, **Downtown Buildings (Modern)**, and **Luxury Hotel Lobbies**. The other three are art-centered: **Public Art (Classic)**, **Public Art (Modern)**, and **Indoor Public Art**. To complete a tour takes anywhere from 1-1/2 to 4 hours, depending on the tour, one's pace, the amount of time spent at each stop, the weather, etc. As some of them can get quite long, it is easy enough to stop anywhere in the tour and pick it up at another time or on another day. Maps for each tour can be found after the site descriptions.

Downtown Buildings (Classic)

This walking tour will show you twenty-five of Chicago's famous downtown buildings, all of which were built prior to 1930. It's designed to introduce you to many of the well-known "big" landmark buildings and cultural institutions as well as a few lesser-known jewels.

1. East Lake Shore Drive Historic District,
East Lake Shore Drive between Michigan and North Lake Shore Drive
Marshall & Fox, Fugard & Knapp, Benjamin H. Marshall (1912-1929)
This historic block of Lake Shore Drive is a cohesive stretch of regal stone structures, the most recent having been built in 1929.

2. Fourth Presbyterian *Church*, 866 N. Michigan
Ralph Adams Cram, Howard Van Doren Shaw (1914-1925)
Include the courtyard in your appreciation of this beautiful Gothic church that was designed for one of the city's toniest congregations.

3. Water Tower and Pumping Station, 806 and 811 N. Michigan
William W. Boyington (1866-1869)
These Gothic structures are most widely recognized for being the only downtown buildings to survive the Great Chicago Fire of 1871. The **Water Tower** is on the west side of the avenue and the **Pumping Station** is on the east side of it.

4. Quigley Seminary and Chapel of St. James, 831 N. Rush
Zachary T. Davis (1919)
With the seminary modeled after the Palais du Justisce in Rouen, France and the chapel modeled after Paris' Sainte-Chappelle, it's not surprising that this may be Chicago's best example of French Gothic architecture. Recently added to the National Registry of Historic Places, the crowning jewels of this property are the fourteen enormous stained glass windows in the St. James Chapel. Made of antique glass, the seventy-year-old windows are the focus of an emergency preservation campaign (*www.windows.org*) that is receiving technical assistance from the chief stained glass expert of France's Ministry of Culture. Docent tours of the chapel are given Tues., Thur., Fri., and Sat. from noon-2pm. Look for special events on the grounds, including traditional choral, classical, and folk music concerts, as well as things like

E Lake Shore Dr.

W. Oak St.
W. Oak St.
W. Delaware Pl.
W. Locust St.
W. Chestnut St.
W. Chicago Ave.
W. Superior St.
W. Huron St.
W. Erie St.
W. Ontario St.
W. Ohio St.
W. Grand Ave.
W. Illinois ST.
W. Hubbard St.
W. Kinzie St.

Wacker Dr.
W. Lake St.
W. Randolph St.
W. Washington St.
W. Madison St.
W. Monroe St.
W. Adams St.
W. Jackson Blvd.
W. Van Buren St.
E. Congress Pkwy.

N. cleveland Ave.
N. Hudson Ave.
N. Sedgwick St.
N. Franklin St.
N. Wells St.
N. Kingsbury Ave.
N. Orleans St.
N. Milwaukee
N. Dearborn St.
N. State St.
N. Rush St.
N. Reed St.
N. Wabash St.
N. Michigan Ave.
N. Fairbanks Ct.
N. Lake Shore Dr.
DeWitt Pl.
E Lake Shore Dr.

N. Desplaines St.
N. Jefferson St.
N. Clinton St.
N. Canal St.
N. Wacker Dr.
N. Franklin St.
N. Wells St.
N. Lasalle St.
N. Clark St.
N. Dearborn St.
N. State St.
N. Wabash Ave.
N. Michigan Ave.
N. Columbus Dr.
N. Lake Shore Dr.

1
2 3
4
3
5
6
25
24
7
15
13 14
16 23
8
17
9 10
18
12 19 22
11
21
20

N

W — E

S

Walking Tour Map - Downtown Buildings - Classic

the more imaginative herb festival.

5. Episcopal Cathedral of St. James, Wabash and Huron
Edward J. Burling (1857), Rebuilt by Burling & Adler (1875), Restored by Holabird & Root (1985)
If you can get inside the building, its Victorian features are worth seeing.

6. Medinah Temple, 600 N. Wabash
Huehl & Schmid (1913)
Shriner convention center/circus arena distinguishes itself with Arabic architectural flourishes.

7. Merchandise Mart, North of the River between Franklin and Wells
Graham, Anderson, Probst & White (1930), Renovated by Beyer Blinder Belle, Jack Train Associates (1992)
The world's most spacious commercial building, the **Merchandise Mart** was recently sold by the Kennedy Family, who had owned it since purchasing it from Marshall Field in 1945.

8. Civic Opera Building, 20 N. Wacker
Graham, Anderson, Probst & White (1929)
A hunk of rock chiseled into an Art Deco opera hall, theater, and office building.

9. St. Patrick's Roman Catholic Church, 140 S. Desplaines
Carter & Bauer (1852, 1856)
Chicago's oldest church, a.k.a. "Old St. Patrick's," shines from an incredible restoration which highlights intricate Celtic-inspired artwork from the early 20th century.

10. Union Station, 210 S. Canal
Graham, Anderson, Probst & White (1913-1925), Lucien Lagrange Associates (1992)
Featured in the movie *The Untouchables*, the main waiting area will return you to a previous era.

11. Board of Trade Building, 141 W. Jackson
Holabird & Root (1930), Addition by Murphy/Jahn, Shaw & Associates, Swanke, Hayden, Connell (1980)
A remarkable building that unites a 1930 Art Deco beauty with a 1980 Postmodern annex. A dramatic illustration of this union can be seen from the 12th floor's twelve-story lobby.

12. The Rookery, 209 S. LaSalle
Burnham & Root (1885-1888), Renovated by Frank Lloyd Wright (1907), Renovated by William Drummond (1931), Restored by McClier Corp. (1992)
An awe-inspiring local favorite since its 1992 restoration! The thick, ruddy exterior conceals an airy interior of spectacular lighting and lacy ironwork. Try the elevators, balcony, and spiral staircase for new sightseeing and perspectives.

13. City Hall, 121 N. LaSalle
County Building, 118 N. Clark
Holabird & Roche (1911)
A square block holds the square building whose western half is City Hall and whose eastern half is the County Building. The more staid exterior hides an elaborate ground floor. Wander this public-friendly building, checking out all the local governmental offices.

14. Chicago Temple, 77 W. Washington
Holabird & Roche (1923)
Housing the First United Methodist Church of Chicago, this is the world's tallest church (568 ft.). The sanctuary is open from 7am to 9pm and daily tours of its Sky Chapel (located in the spire) are given at 2pm. The chapel, the world's highest place of worship, was created in 1952 with a donation in honor of Charles Walgreen, founder of the local drugstore chain. Stained glass windows on its eastern exterior wall (facing the Miro court) detail the church's history.

15. Chicago Theater, 175 N. State
Rapp & Rapp (1921), Restored by Daniel P. Coffey & Assoc. (1986)
Plush former movie palace turned concert hall and theater.

16. Marshall Field & Company, 111 N. State
D.H. Burnham, Graham Burnham & Co. (1892-1914), Renovated by HTI/ Space Design International (1992)
Chicago's original, and still thriving, luxury department store.

17. Carson Pirie Scott & Company, 1 S. State
Louis Sullivan (1899), Addition by D.H. Burnham & Co. (1906), Addition by Holabird & Root (1961)
Another choice downtown department store for generations, **Carson**'s architectural highlight is its exterior ironwork done by architect Louis Sullivan.

18. Marquette Building, 140 S. Dearborn
Holabird & Roche (1893-1895), Renovation and restoration by Holabird & Root (1980)
A heavy marble staircase, bronze portrayals of Native American chiefs and European explorers, and mosaics that include glass and mother-of-pearl tiles created by Tiffany's make up some of the over $4 million in artwork that graces the **Marquette Building**'s lobby. The mosaics and bronze panels over the outside doors recount some of the adventures of French Jesuit explorer Jacques Marquette.

19. Monadnock Building, 53 W. Jackson
Burnham & Root (1889-1891), Addition by Holabird & Root (1893)
The tallest building with weight-bearing walls in the world—this is about as tall as one can build a stone building with windows (16 stories), without making the walls unreasonably wide. Take the elevators to the top floor and walk down the intricate staircase to best appreciate the recent restoration.

20. Auditorium Building/Roosevelt University, 430 S. Michigan
Adler & Sullivan (1887-1889), Auditorium Theatre restored by Harry Weese & Assoc. (1967)
You won't be able to see the theater without a ticket for a performance, but if the box office is open, you should be able to sneak a peek at the lobby. Go around the corner to Michigan, and enter Roosevelt University which is in the same building. Formerly a hotel's public space, the first and second floors of the school, connected by a grand staircase, still retain much of their original splendor.

21. Fine Arts Building, 410 S. Michigan
Solon S. Beman (1885), Renovated by Andrew N. Rebori (1917)
Originally opened as a showroom for Studebaker vehicles, Charles Curtiss turned this lovely old building into the United States' first artists' colony about ten years later. Current tenants include voice and instrument instructors, instrument repair, violin makers, a sheet music store, rare book dealers, art studios, architects, dance groups, an interior design school, and non-profit organizations. The 10th floor walls are covered with murals from some of the colony's early occupants and its studios have skylights. There are many delightful surprises as you wander through the building. Each floor's lobby has its own unique details. Plaques on doors commemorate famous former tenants—like Frank Lloyd Wright and Laredo Taft—and their years of occupancy. The Daughters of the American Revolution (DAR) in Room #828 has been the longest inhabitant—from 1898 to the present! Occupants open their offices and spaces to the public during monthly open

houses.

22. Chicago Symphony Center/Orchestra Hall, 220 S. Michigan
D.H. Burnham & Co. (1905), Addition by Howard Van Doren Shaw (1908), Remodeled by Harry Weese & Assoc. (1967), Rehabbed by Skidmore, Owings & Merrill (1981), Renovation by SOM (1997).
The just-finished renovation has created the **Chicago Symphony Center** around **Orchestra Hall**. The updates to the building's traditional grandeur include a restaurant and expanded educational and administrative spaces.

23. Chicago Cultural Center, 78 E. Washington
Shepley, Rutan & Coolidge (1897), Renovated by Holabird & Root (1977, 1993)
See p.48 for a complete description.

24. Wrigley Building, 400 and 410 N. Michigan
Graham, Anderson, Probst & White (1919-1924), Plaza by L.R. Solomon, J.D.
The gum family owns this charming, riverside landmark, recognized by its white color and intricate clock tower.

25. Tribune Tower, 435 N. Michigan
Howells & Hood (1923-1925), Addition by John Mead Howells, Hood & Foulihoux, Leo J. Wessenborn (1934)
This Gothic beauty is the result of an international architecture contest calling for "the world's most beautiful office building," conducted to honor the *Tribune*'s 75th anniversary in 1922. Pieces of famous structures from all over the world (all clearly identified) are built into the lower portion of the exterior walls. Touch remnants of the Alamo, the Arc de Triomphe, the Great Pyramid, the Great Wall of China, the Taj Mahal, Westminster Abbey, and dozens more.

Downtown Buildings (Modern)

Beginning with the Bloomingdale's Building and ending with the new Harold Washington Library Center, this 20-building tour shows off our new stuff. The buildings you will see and explore along the way were built between 1959 and 1991.

1. 900 N. Michigan, 900 N. Michigan
Kohn Pedersen Fox, Perkins & Will (1989)
New Art Deco Bloomingdale's building is layer upon layer of condos,

offices, and luxury shopping—with piped in classical music.

2. John Hancock Center, 875 N. Michigan
Skidmore, Owings & Merrill (1969)
Modern skyline staple had world-record height at the time of construction. Its new sunken plaza has a patio for outdoor dining, enlivened with a waterfall and pool.

3. Chicago Place, 700 N. Michigan
Skidmore, Owings & Merrill, Solomon Cordwell Buenz & Assoc. (1990)
Postmodern tribute to Chicago with shopping on floors one through eight and condos on top. Ride the glass elevators to the 8th-floor food court to see fountains, tropical greenery, a tacky skyline sculpture, and a view of the city. Take the escalators down to marvel at the interior design and customer-sparse shops.

4. North Pier, 435 E. Illinois
Christian A. Eckstrom (1905-1920), Renovated by Booth/Hansen & Assoc., Austin Co. (1990)
Really a "classic" building (it was a former exhibition hall), but its new use as a shopping, eating, clubbing, and high-tech gaming center has bumped it into the modern era.

5. Lake Point Towers, 505 N. Lake Shore Drive
Schipporeit-Heinrich, Graham, Anderson, Probst & White (1968)
Tripartite, glass-walled towers are based on an early-twentieth century design by Mies van der Rohe that was executed much later by a couple of his students.

The shopping, entertainment, and living complexes of North Michigan end here and we move to more corporate and government edifices.

6. NBC Tower, 454 N. Columbus
Skidmore, Owings & Merrill (1989)
Postmodern broadcasting/office skyscraper with a polished, marble lobby.

7. Amoco Building, 200 E. Randolph
Edward Durell Stone, Perkins & Will (1973)
Amoco recently spiffed up the plain rectangular prism that is the former Standard Oil Building with a multi-level plaza, bedecked with fountains, flora, flags, and sculpture. When it was discovered in the early 1990s that the six-ton layer of Italian marble that coated the building was too flimsy for

W. Oak St.

W. Oak St.

E Lake Shore Dr.

W. Delaware Pl.

W. Locust St.

W. Chestnut St.

N. Rush St.

DeWitt Pl.

1+2

W. Chicago Ave.

Mies Van Wy

N. cleveland Ave.

N. Hudson Ave.

N. Sedgwick St.

W. Superior St.

W. Huron St.

3

W. Erie St.

N. State St.

N. Rush St.

W. Ontario St.

N. Dearborn St.

N. Wabash St.

N. Michigan Ave.

N. Fairbanks Ct.

N. Lake Shore Dr.

N. Franklin St.

N. Wells St.

W. Ohio St.

W. Grand Ave.

N. Kingsbury Ave.

W. Illinois ST.

4+5

N. Orleans St.

W. Hubbard St.

6

W. Kinzie St.

8

N. Milwaukee

Wacker Dr.

N. Dearborn St.

9

W. Lake St.

W. Randolph St.

N. Franklin St.

N. Wells St.

N. Lasalle St.

15

N. Clark St.

N. State St.

N. Wabash Ave.

N. Michigan Ave.

7

N. Columbus Dr.

N. Lake Shore Dr.

W. Washington St.

16

10

W. Madison St.

N. Desplaines St.

N. Jefferson St.

N. Clinton St.

N. Canal St.

N. Wacker Dr.

14

17

W. Monroe St.

13

W. Adams St.

11

18

W. Jackson Blvd.

12

19

W. Van Buren St.

20

E. Congress Pkwy.

N

W ✦ E

S

E. Harrison St.

Walking Tour Map - Downtown Buildings - Modern

Midwestern winters, it was all removed and replaced with brawny granite. Now marble from this project (that emptied the quarry that once supplied Michelangelo) can be bought in the gift shop in the form of trinkets and expensive decor. For the record, this building has out-scraped the John Hancock as Chicago's second tallest structure.

8. Marina City Towers, 300 N. State
Bertrand Goldberg Assoc. (1959-1967)
Beehive? Corn cob? Once considered an innovative housing and social solution for urban singles, **Marina City** was the first mixed-use apartment building in the United States.

9. 333 W. Wacker, 333 W. Wacker
Kohn Pedersen Fox, Perkins & Will (1979-1983)
Much lauded for its design elegance, this green glass building purposely curves with Wacker Drive and the Chicago River and reflects the city around it.

10. Northwestern Atrium Center, 500 W. Madison
Murphy/Jahn (1987)
Blue glass waterfall/ "cash register" train station is an Art Deco tribute.

11. Sears Tower, 233 S. Wacker
Skidmore, Owings & Merrill (1968-1974)
At 110 Stories and 1,454 feet, it's no wonder this world record holder has its own zip code. Sears is no longer headquartered here.

12. 311 S. Wacker, 311 S. Wacker
Kohn Pedersen Fox, Harwood K. Smith & Partners (1990)
The immediate neighbor south of the Sears has its own Guinness standing— it's the world's tallest concrete-framed building. The exterior blandness is somewhat offset by its inner wintergarden—a pretty lobby filled with tropical plants and a sizable fountain. At night its illuminated top resembles a castle—or, as some have said, Bart Simpson's hair.

13. 190 S. La Salle, 190 S. LaSalle
John Burgee Architects with Philip Johnson, Shaw Assoc. (1987)
A Postmodern building with an appealing lobby containing lots of marble, a gold-leafed ceiling, and interesting artworks.

14. Chemical Plaza, 10 S. LaSalle
Moriyama & Teshima, Holabird & Root (1989)
Chemical Plaza retains the 1912 Otis Building base and tops it with a tower of blue and green painted aluminum and glass. Ignore the ordinary inside.

15. Thompson Center, 100 W. Randolph
Murphy/Jahn, Lester B. Knight & Assoc. (1979-1985)
Squat salmon and periwinkle glass state government building is easily Chicago's most strongly disliked. Some think its construction signaled the beginning of the end of Chicago's reign as architectural capital extraordinaire. I personally like how it matter-of-factly sits across from the classic, stone fortress of City Hall and kitty-cornered from the ultra-minimalist box of Daley Center: three government buildings from different universes just hanging out on the same corner. Its internal structure is original, dizzying, and according to anecdote, suicide-inspiring.

16. Richard J. Daley Center, Dearborn and Washington
C.F. Murphy Assoc., Loebl, Schlossman & Bennett, Skidmore, Owings & Merrill (1965)
The Daley Center appears an unremarkable, tall and narrow block of glass and steel to those unschooled in the joys of Spartanism. The plaza, which contains it, however, is redeemed by "the Picasso," the fountain, and the eternal flame which reside there, as well as the multitude of outdoor cultural events and activities that take place there.

17. First National Bank, Dearborn and Monroe
Perkins & Will, C.F. Murphy Assoc. (1969)
Another Modernist skyscraper, the bank building is enhanced by its sloping design and popular plaza, which contains an enormous fountain and a Marc Chagall mosaic.

18. Chicago Federal Center, Dearborn between Adams and Jackson
Ludwig Mies van der Rohe, Schmidt, Garden & Erikson, C.F. Murphy Assoc., A. Epstein & Sons. (1959-1974)
At the center of this trio of steel-and-glass block government buildings stands Alexander Calder's bright orange steel sculpture, **Flamingo**, offering some color, curves, and originality.

19. Metropolitan Correctional Center, 71 W. Van Buren
Harry Weese & Assoc. (1975)
Triangular prison and administrative center is the incarceration facility that offers every prisoner a view.

20. Harold Washington Library Center, 400 S. State
Hammond, Beeby & Babka, A. Epstein & Sons International (1991)
After the Thompson Center, this Postmodern hodgepodge of Chicago design symbolism is the city's next most despised building by those in the architectural know. I, on the other hand, think it's magnificent and am tickled that it belongs to the public. See p.49 for a full description.

Luxury Hotel Lobbies

14 downtown hotels most worthy of gaping and gawking...

[**Note:** See them now, because they are not listed in the *Lodging* chapter of *this* book.]

TIPS ON DOING A LUXURY HOTEL LOBBY

Casual dress and the admiration of art, architecture, and affluence is generally acceptable, but be prepared for the occasional question or questioning looks. The size and location of a hotel, the time of day, and your demeanor and behavior all determine how easy it is to remain anonymous and free from contact with hotel personnel. "Just looking" usually suffices if someone offers to "help you with something." It's easier to wander in and out unnoticed during the day, but the view and ambiance are more spectacular at night.

Once inside the lobby, explore! Climb staircases, follow hallways, and when possible, definitely peek into the ballrooms... Stay away from the floors with the guests' rooms and you should be okay. And remember, thank the doorstaff when they hold the door for you.

1. The Knickerbocker Hotel, 163 E. Walton
Building dates back to 1927, hotel to 1979.

2. Drake Hotel, 140 E. Walton
Luxury hotel since 1920. A pianist entertains in the lounge Tues.-Sat. 9pm-1:30am.

3. Four Seasons Hotel, 120 E. Delaware, 7th Floor
Part of the Bloomingdale's building since the late 1980s.

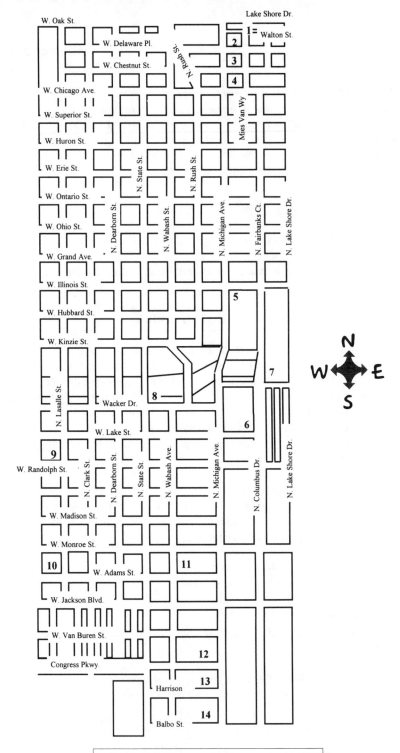

Walking Tour Map - Luxury Hotel Lobbies

4. Ritz-Carlton Hotel, 160 E. Pearson, 12th Floor
Luxury lodging has been part of Water Tower Place since 1975.

5. Hotel Inter-Continental, 505 N. Michigan
Built in 1929 as the Medinah Athletic Club.

6. Fairmont Hotel, 200 N. Columbus
Pink granite elegance since 1987.

7. Hyatt Regency, 151 E. Wacker
Constructed in 1974 as part of the Illinois Center complex. Atrium lobby added in 1980.

8. Stouffer Riviere Hotel, 1 W. Wacker
Plush lodging since 1991.

9. Bismark Hotel, 171 W. Randolph
125 year old hotel at its present location since 1926. Also investigate the adjacent **Bismark Palace** from the ground (if the doors are open) or from the inside via the hallway to the left of the reception desk (if it's locked).

10. Midland Hotel, 172 W. Adams
A den of luxury since 1926.

11. Palmer House, 17 E. Monroe
This is the longest continuously operating hotel in the United States, the first entirely fireproof hotel in America, the first hotel with elevators, and the first hotel with electric lights and telephones in the rooms. It first opened in 1871 and the current building dates to 1927. However, the **Palmer House** is no about statistics but rather fabulousness. Even guests' pets receive the red carpet treatment here.

12. Congress Hotel, 520 S. Michigan
Built as an annex (1893) to the Auditorium Hotel (now Roosevelt University) of the Auditorium Theatre across the street.

13. Blackstone Hotel, 636 S. Michigan
Hotel dates back to 1908, its companion theater to 1910.

14. Chicago Hilton & Towers, 720 S. Michigan
Once the largest luxury hotel in the world. Building began in 1922 on its 25 floors and 3,000 (now 1,600) rooms.

Downtown Public Art (Classic)

From Financial Plaza to Solidarity Drive (the roadway to the Adler Planetarium), this walking tour will introduce you to 24 public art works, most from the late nineteenth and early twentieth centuries. You'll encounter a facade, a bridge, a string of busts, statuary and fountains galore, and a great view of the lake.

1. San Marco II, Financial Place (156 W) near Congress
Ludovico de Luigi
Sculpted horse on a pedestal.

2. Ceres, Board of Trade at 141 W. Jackson
John Storrs (1930)
Over 300 feet above the ground, atop the Board of Trade (home of heavy grain trading) stands a statue of Ceres, Roman goddess of agriculture, carved without facial features because the artist didn't figure on anyone getting close enough to notice.

3. Merchandise Mart Hall of Fame, North of the Chicago River between Franklin and Wells
Minna Harkavy, Milton Horn, Lewis Iselin, Henry Rox, and Charles Umlauf (1953)
The busts of eight great American business honchos, many Chicagoans, perch on marble pillars facing the Mart's main entrance.

4. Heald Square—in the middle of East Wacker Drive at Wabash:

⇒ **The George Washington-Robert Morris-Hyam Salomon Memorial**
Lorado Taft and Leonard Crunelle (1941)
George Washington rendered in stone with two obscure men who helped fund the American Revolution. Purportedly, the memorial is the only example in statuary history when this founding father is not standing alone.

⇒ **Father Time** *(1926)*
Father Time on an old-time clock at 35 E. Wacker.

Just east of Heald Square is another concrete island:

⇒ **The Children's Fountain**, East Wacker at Wabash *(1982)*
Classic-style fountain fancifully decorated with kids, birds, and beasts.

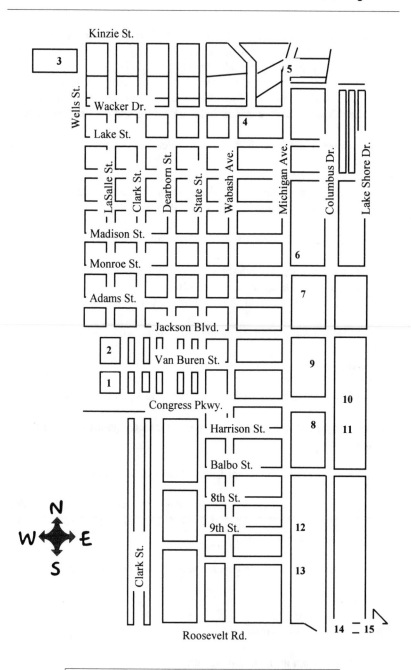

Walking Tour Map - Downtown Public Art - Classic

5. Defense, Regeneration, The Pioneers, and The Discoverers,
Michigan Avenue and the Chicago River
James Earle Fraser and Henry Herling (1928)
A sculpted relief at each corner of the Michigan Avenue Bridge recognizes
the early inhabitants and history of Chicago. Note the metal boundary lines
set in the sidewalk near the bridge that mark off the site of Fort Dearborn.

6. Alexander Hamilton, East side of Michigan between Madison and
Monroe
Bela Lyon Pratt (1918)
Early American statesman, *The Federalist Papers* author, and unsuccessful
duelist is commemorated in his own Grant Park alcove.

7. In the square block that contains the Art Institute:

⇒ **The Chicago Stock Exchange Arch**, Columbus and Monroe
Louis Sullivan and Dankmar Adler (1893)
Saved from the 1972 wrecking ball that hit the Chicago Stock Exchange.

Over the bridge and around the corner onto Michigan:

⇒ **Lions**
Edward Kemeys (1894)
Chicago's bronze mascots flank one of the world's great art museums.

In the courtyard to the right of the main entrance, against the wall of the
southern wing:

⇒ **The Fountain of the Great Lakes**, Michigan near Jackson
Lorado Taft (1913)
Inspired by a myth sentencing husband-slaying sisters to eternally hauling
water in sieves, this work represents the Great Lakes of Huron, Ontario,
Erie, Superior, and Michigan.

8. On Congress, east of Michigan, at the gateway to Grant Park:

⇒ **Eagles**
Frederick Hibbard (1931)
Bronze eagles set in fountains.

⇒ **The Bowman and The Spearman**
Ivan Mestrovic (1928)

Native Americans on horseback are posed—one on each side of the parkway—as if to shoot an arrow (no bow) and as if to throw a spear (no spear).

9. Abraham Lincoln, North of Congress in Grant Park
Augustus Saint Gaudens (1926)
"The Seated Lincoln" by the renowned sculptor.

10. Where Congress Parkway ends, east of Columbus Drive:

⇒ **(Clarence) Buckingham Fountain**
End of Congress, east of Columbus
Bennett, Parsons, and Frost in Chicago and Marcel Francois Loyau and Jaques Lambert in Paris (1927)
See p.43 for a complete description.

⇒ **Crane Girl, Dove Girl, Fisher Boy, and Turtle Boy**
End of Congress, east of Columbus
Leonard Crunelle (1905)
Four figures in four small fountains can be found on the grounds surrounding **Buckingham Fountain**.

11. Theodore Thomas Memorial/The Spirit of Music, East side of Columbus near Congress
Albin Polasek (1923)
A bronze goddess of music memorializes Theodore Thomas, founder of the Chicago Symphony Orchestra.

12. General John Logan Memorial, Michigan at 9th
Augustus Saint Gaudens (1897)
Horse-top Illinois congressman and civil war hero raises the enemy flag he captured during wartime.

13. Rosenberg Fountain, Michigan at 11th
Franz Machtl (1893)
Greek goddess Hebe, cup-bearer to the Mount Olympus crowd, beautifies the top of this drinking fountain—thanks to the patronage of Joseph Rosenberg, whose successful relatives founded Michael Reese Hospital and co-founded K.A.M., Chicago's original Jewish congregation.

14. Christopher Columbus, Columbus and Roosevelt
Carl Brioschi (1933)
Bronze figure of the 1492 explorer stands on a marble base.

15. Big Beaver, Roosevelt at Lake Shore Drive
Norman Tait, of the Nishga Band of the Isimshian Tribe (1982)
Traditional carving depicts the legend of how one family came to adopt the beaver as its totem animal.

16. On Solidarity Drive—the roadway leading to the Adler Planetarium:

⇒ **Thaddeus Kosciuzsko Memorial**
Kasimir Chodsinski (1904)
A monument remembering the Revolutionary War general and military engineer of Polish descent.

⇒ **Karel Havlicek**
Joseph Strachovsky (1911)
Statue honors the Bohemian writer, statesman, and martyr.

⇒ **Nicolaus Copernicus**
Bertel Thorvaldsen (1973)
A tribute to the Polish scientist who boldly suggested that the earth revolves around the sun.

Downtown Public Art (Modern)

Besides exposing you to 19 modern outdoor works of art (from 1960s to the present), this tour will wind you through some of Chicago's trademark plaza spaces.

1. Celebration of the 200th Anniversary of the Founding of the Republic,
Behind the Art Institute on Columbus Drive between Monroe and Jackson
Isamu Noguchi (1976)
This modern fountain was commissioned for the American Bicentennial.

2. Over the bridge and around the corner, enter the Art Institute's northern courtyard on Michigan, near Monroe:

• **Large Interior Form**
Henry Moore (1982)

This sculpture is cast from the inner portion of Henry Moore's **Large Upright Internal/External Form** which stands in the **Three First National Plaza** lobby (#4 in the **Indoor Public Art** walking tour).

⇒ **Cubi VII**
David Smith (1963)
Chunks of welded stainless steel.

⇒ **Flying Dragon**
Alexander Calder (1975)
From the same zoo as Calder's famous **Flamingo** (#14 in this tour).

3. Communication X9, 150 N. Michigan
Yaacov Agam (1983)
Vertical, silver-and-rainbow painted aluminum outgrowth.

4. The **Amoco Building**'s (200 E. Randolph) landscaped plaza contains various pieces of contemporary sculpture. Although some of the artwork goes unlabeled here, the Amoco Plaza has markers identifying its trees and plants.

⇒ **Untitled**
Harry Bertoia (1975)
Sculpture of upright copper rods are set in a reflecting pool. They vibrate when the wind blows, creating music.
⇒ **Deer**   *John Kearney (1986)*
Mama, Papa, and Baby deer sculpted from car bumpers.

5. Chicago Totem, 400 E. Randolph
Abbott Pattison (1963-1964)
To the degree the sculpture is perplexing, the view down Lake Shore Drive to the Field Museum is magnificent.

6. Children of the Sun, 211 N. Stetson, roof
Osamu Shingu (1990)
Four 17-ft. mobile structures animated by the wind.

7. Splash, 205 N. Michigan
Jerry Peart (1986)
Colorful bouquet of aluminum.

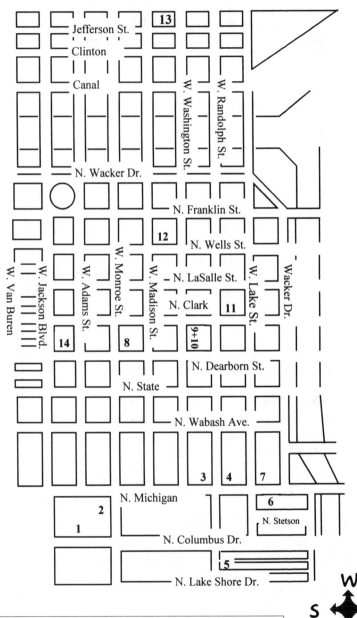

Walking Tour Map - Downtown Public Art - Modern

8. Four Seasons, First National Plaza at Dearborn and Monroe
Marc Chagall (1974)
This stone and glass mosaic that interprets Chicago's changing seasons underwent a recent cleaning and restoration. A new glass roof will now protect it from the elements.

9. Miro's Chicago, Washington between Dearborn and Clark
Joan Miro (1981)
An enigmatic figure of stone, wire, steel, bronze, and ceramic tiles created by the preeminent Spanish artist.

10. Untitled, Daley Plaza at Washington and Dearborn
Pablo Picasso (1967)
The original and most prominent work of modern public art in Chicago—the unidentifiable Picasso. Daley Civic Center Plaza also contains an eternally burning flame dedicated to the U.S. armed services personnel who served in Korea and Vietnam.

11. Monument with Standing Beast, 100 W. Randolph
Jean Dubuffet (1984)
Monstrous fiberglass mystery greets visitors at the entrance of the State of Illinois' Chicago office building.

12. Dawn Shadows, 200 W. Madison
Louis Nevelson (1983)
Abstract shadows configured in painted black steel.
13. Batcolumn, 600 W. Madison
Claus Oldenburg (1977)
You've heard of wiffle balls? This is a 100-ft., steel wiffle baseball bat.

14. In the Federal Plaza at Dearborn and Adams:

⇒ **Flamingo**
Alexander Calder (1974)
Except for the American flag, this abstract red steel flamingo is the only spark of color in the Federal Plaza.

⇒ **Ruins III**, Jackson and Clark
Nita K. Sunderland (1978)
Granite pillar people stand amid stone ruins and shavings.

15. Pritzker Park, State and Van Buren
Ronald Jones (1992)
Symbolically designed park is a combination of greenery and sculpture, including a granite wall evoking René Magritte's *The Banquet*. Adjacent to the Harold Washington Library Center, the park is dedicated to Cindy Pritzker, of the Chicago philanthropic family, for her contributions to the library's development.

Indoor Public Art

This walking tour of 17 pieces of indoor public art in downtown Chicago takes you from office buildings to the fifth floor of the Board of Trade to the base of the Sears Tower. All artwork is located in the building lobbies unless otherwise noted.

1. Stone Arbor, 20 N. Michigan
Carolann Haggard (1985)
Abstract marble and granite fountain.

2. 35 W. Wacker:

⇒ **Rite of Spring**
Bryan Hunt (1985)
Abstract fountain.

⇒ **Doorful of Syrup**
John Chamberlain
Abstract of enameled steel or mishmash of bumpers and fenders?

3. 77 W. Wacker:

⇒ **Twisted Columns**
Ricardo Bofil (1992)
Tall, twisted marble columns wade in a fountain.

⇒ **Les Grandes Paupiers**
Antoni Tapies
Droopy painting of "the big eyelids."

⇒ **Three Lawyers and a Judge**
Xavier Corbero
Large, formless stone figures.

Wacker Dr.

Lake

3 **2**

Franklin

Wells St.

Lasalle St.

Clark St.

Dearborn St.

State St.

Wabash Ave.

Michigan Ave.

1

Madison St.

4

Monroe St.

5+6

10

Adams St.

11

W. Jackson Blvd.

7

Wacker Dr.

12

8

W. Van Buren St.   **9**

Walking Tour Map - Downtown - Indoor Public Art

N
W   E
S

4. Large Upright Internal/External Form, 70 W. Madison
Henry Moore (1983)
Bronze humanoid figure ("Internal Form") nestles in larger humanoid figure
("External Form").

5. Untitled, a.k.a. Radiant I, 30 W. Monroe
Richard Lippold (1958)
Spiny metal and steel wire abstract fountain.

6. Untitled, 33 W. Monroe
Chryssa (1980)
Immense white acrylic light sculpture.

7. The Town-Ho's Story, 77 W. Jackson
Frank Stella
This is not a spray-painted pile of metal trash from the city dump. It is "poetic aluminum" reflecting the artist's familiarity with ***Moby Dick***, the architecture of the federal building, and the belligerent nature of city living!?

8. Original Entryway Gates to the 1930 Trading Floor,
Board of Trade, 141 W. Jackson, 5th Floor Visitors' Center
Decorative bronze and nickel gates faithfully served at the entrance of the North Trading Room for over fifty years.

9. In the **Chicago Board Options Exchange** (141 W. Van Buren):

⇒ **Clouds Over Lake Michigan**
Ruth Duckworth (1976)
A stoneware mural.

⇒ **Stone Fabric**
Robert Winslow (1987)
Black marble abstract.

10. 190 S. LaSalle:

⇒ **The 1909 Plan of Chicago**
Helena Hernmarck (1987)
Wool and linen yarn tapestry depicts a portion of Daniel Burnham's ambitious 1909 plan for Chicago's lakefront, boulevards, and parks.

⇒ **Chicago Fugue**
Anthony Caro (1987)
Welded bronze sculpture.

11. Universe, Sears Tower, 233 S. Wacker
Alexander Calder (1974)
Crude forms ("spine," "sun," "flowers," "pendulum," and "helix") in constant motion represent the cosmos.

12. Gem of the Lakes, 311 S. Wacker
Raymond Kaskey (1990)
A classical Neptune figure supervises this large, gushing fountain. Check
out the enormous palm trees and other tropical foliage in the lobby.

INTERNET RESOURCES

Neighborhood Search
http://chicago.digitalcity.com/community/neighborhoods/neighbor.htm
Profiles of Chicago's 77 distinct communities, including neighborhood
demographics and information on schools, churches, libraries, parks, and
health facilties.
Neighborhood Rent Statistics
http://chicago.digitalcity.com/community/housing/rent.htm
Outdated, but still useful: the 1990 median monthly rent for Chicago's 77
different neighborhoods.
Neighborhood Violent Crime Statistics
http://chicago.digitalcity.com/community/crime/overall.htm
Detailed information on violent crime in Chicago's neighborhoods.
Buyer's and Renter's Guide for 375+ Chicago Area Communities
http://www.greaterchicago.com
Facts and figures for city and suburban neighborhoods (e.g. average home
value, school report cards, property taxes, appreciation rates), plus details of
interest and links to related sites.
Chicago Neighborhood Tours
http://www.ci.chi.il.us/Tourism/NeighborhoodTours/Welcome.html
Learn about the Department of Cultural Affairs' new half-day bus tours of
different Chicago neighborhoods that leave every Saturday morning from
the Cultural Center. Visit South Shore/Greater Grand Crossing, the West
Side, Uptown, South Side/Bronzeville, Near South Side/Prairie Avenue
Historic District, Andersonville/Lincoln Square, Chinatown/Pilsen, Wicker
Park/Humboldt Park, and Devon Avenue.

⇒ Consult the following Web sites for more information on these specific
communities:

Beverly Hills/Morgan Park
http://www.bapa.org
Bridgeport
http://www.uic.edu.orgs/LockZero

Chinatown
http://www.tezcat.com/web/chinatown-FAQ
Douglas/Grand Boulevard (Bronzeville)
http://aman.interman.net/bronzeville/bville.htm
Near West Side/East Garfield Park
http://www.chicagohs.org/Neighborhoods/NWEGIntro.html
Pilsen/Little Village
http://www.chicagohs.org/Neighborhoods/PLVIntro.html
Rogers Park/West Ridge
http://www.chicagohs.org/Neighborhoods/RPWRIntro.html
http://www.wecaretoo.com/Organizations/IL/rpwrhs.html

7 LODGING

Scenes from the Lincoln Avenue motel strip.
The Lincoln Motel (*above*) and the Rio Motel (*below*)
(*Photos by William Arroyo.*)

7 LODGING

Big-name hotel chains, local bargain hotels, quaint boutique hotels, bed and breakfasts, youth hostels, university dorms, retreat centers, and outlying motels provide a wide range of lodging choices for Chicago visitors who inevitably have a wide range of preferences for where they lay their head and hat... as well as varying interpretations of "budget" accommodations.

DOWNTOWN HOTELS

Not a deal in Little Rock or Kalamazoo, but a bargain in New York, Paris, or Tokyo: the hotels listed here, mostly chain operations, offer their share of Chicago's more than 25,000 downtown hotel rooms under $100 a night (while most others begin at $150). Rates may vary with availability, convention schedules, day of the week, and season, but most can be cut with the help of various discount travel services. Ask for weekend rates, as many hotels empty out when business travelers and conventioneers go home.

Best Western
162 E. Ohio, 312/787-3100   **C**
Rooms range from $99 to $189. Located 1/2 block off of Michigan Avenue.

Best Western
125 W. Ohio, 312/467-0800   **C**
Rooms range from $89 to $144. Located in the River North restaurant, nightclub, and art gallery district.

Best Western Grant Park Hotel
1100 S. Michigan, 312/922-2900   **C**
Rooms begin at $89. Located south of the Loop near Grant Park and the big museums.

Cass Hotel
640 N. Wabash, 312/787-4030   **C**
$64/single, $69/double. Located in the River North restaurant, nightclub, and art gallery district.

Days Inn Michigan Avenue
520 S. Michigan, 312/786-0000   **C**
Rooms begin at $69. Located on the south side of the Loop and across from Grant Park.

Harrison Hotel
65 E. Harrison, 312/427-8000   **C**
$60/single, $70/double. Located just south of the Loop, near Grant Park and Printers Row.

HoJo Inn by Howard Johnson
720 N. LaSalle, 312/664-8100   **C**
$83/single, $93/double, $100/2 double beds, suites $110-$135. Located in the River North restaurant, nightclub, and art gallery district.

Motel 6
162 E. Ontario, 312/787-3580   **C**
$59/single, $69/double. When conventions are in town, $79/single, $89/double. Located 1/2 block off of Michigan Avenue.

Ohio House Motel
600 N. LaSalle, 312/943-6000   **C**
$83/double for 1-2 people, $90/king or triple, $100/2 double beds, $105/suite. Located in the River North restaurant, nightclub, and art gallery district.

Quality Inn
1 S. Halsted, 312/829-5000   **C**
Pre-discounted rooms begin at $99. Located just west of the Loop, in Greektown.

HOTELS IN OTHER AREAS

These strategically located hotels provide lower-priced, quality rooms in popular areas.

Best Western Hawthorne
3434 N. Broadway, 773/244-3434   N
$40/single or double. Weekly rates available.

Comfort Inn
601 W. Diversey, 773/348-2810   N
$73-$104/single, $85-$120/double. Located 3-4 blocks from Lincoln Park
and Lake Michigan on the city's north side.

Days Inn Gold Coast
1816 N. Clark, 312/664-3040   N
Weekdays $65-$85/single, $69/double. Weekends $70-$95/single,
$91/double. Located across the street from Lincoln Park, Lincoln Park Zoo,
and Lake Michigan, on the city's near north side.

Days Inn Midway Airport
5400 S. Cicero, 773/581-0500   SW
$79/single, $85/double. Continental breakfast and shuttle to and from the
airport included in price. Located near Midway airport, on the city's
southwest side.

Days Inn Near North
644 W. Diversey, 773/525-7010   N
$74/single, $94-$99/double. Located 3-4 blocks from Lincoln Park and
Lake Michigan, on the city's north side.

Holiday Inn-Midway Airport
7353 S. Cicero, 773/581-5300   FSW
$89/single, $90/double. Located near Midway Airport, on the city's
southwest side.

Hyatt at University Village
625 S. Ashland, 312/243-7200   C
Weekdays $82.50-$159/single or double with AAA or other discount card.
Weekends $99-$204/single or double. Located near the University of
Illinois, UIC Medical Center, and Rush-Presbyterian St. Luke's Medical
Center, on Chicago's near west side.

Ramada Inn Lake Shore
4900 S. Lake Shore Drive, 773/288-5800   S
$79/single, $85/double Sun.-Thur., $89/single, $95/double Fri.-Sat. Located
across from Lake Michigan, near Hyde Park and the University of Chicago,

on the city's south side.

NEIGHBORHOOD INNS OF CHICAGO

Neighborhood Inns of Chicago has been renovating old transient residences, turning them into charming, one-of-a-kind, Eurostyle boutique hotels. Located in the lively east Lakeview neighborhood, each hotel is just a short walk from numerous restaurants, clubs, theaters, unique shopping, the lakefront, and Wrigley Field.

City Suites Hotel
933 W. Belmont, 773/404-3400   N
$95/single, $109/suite. 45 rooms and a Chicago Prohibition-era theme.

Park Brompton Inn
528 W. Brompton, 773/404-3499   N
$85/single, $119/suite with 2 double beds and adjoining sitting room with sleeper. Third and fourth guests in a suite each cost $10 extra. 52 rooms and a British ambiance.

Surf Hotel
555 W. Surf, 773/528-8400   N
$85/small single, $99/large single, $119/with two double beds. $10 extra per person. 55 rooms done in a French country style.

ROOM LINK-UP SERVICES

For bed and breakfast rooms and apartments in Chicago's better neighborhoods, and discounted rooms at better hotels, make use of one of the link-up services below. Be sure to also consult discount travel services connected with AAA, banks, credit cards, entertainment cards, frequent flyer clubs, and professional organizations.

Bed & Breakfast Chicago
312/951-0085
One of the original B & B reservation services in the country, **Bed & Breakfast Chicago** links travelers with unique lodging in Chicago's North Shore, Lincoln Park, Gold Coast, Downtown, and Hyde Park neighborhoods. Rooms with breakfast run from $75 to $105 per night.

Self-contained apartments cost $105-$185 a night. Although you won't be staying in the typical country inn bed and breakfast, the 60-70 active units in the system are all charming urban alternatives, ranging from cozy coach houses to elegant town homes to stunning high-rise apartments.

The Heritage Bed & Breakfast Registry
75 E. Wacker, Suite 3600, Chicago, IL 60601
800/431-5546, 312/857-0800
Another option for reserving private rooms and apartments in Chicago is the new **Heritage Bed & Breakfast Registry**. Visit *www.heritageregistry.com* for details and pictures of all locations. The site also provides some historical background and local color, including this splendid piece of trivia: Chicago, Rio, and Havana are the only three North American cities which enjoy a downtown that is located next to the beach. Rooms downtown run $115-$150/night. Those in Lincoln Park go for $75 to $125. Two night minimum, except for some last-minute reservations.

Hot Rooms
773/468-7666/1-800-HOTEL-00
Free reservation service links you with discounted (up to 50%) rooms at 15 downtown hotels, up to three months in advance. Be warned: even after big price cuts, nightly rates generally range from $75-$225.

Hotel Reservations Network
1- 800-964-6835
Free hotel booking service reserves blocks of rooms at major economy, first class, and deluxe hotels, and passes the savings (up to 65%) on to you. "A chocolate on your pillow doesn't have to cost you a mint."

HOSTELS

Not just for youths, hostels are the ideal choice for anyone who doesn't need big hotel amenities (like a private bathroom), for people who like to meet other travelers, or for those who would prefer spreading their money around the city rather than concentrating it in the hands of major hotel chains. Reservations are strongly recommended, especially in the summer when space/rooms go fast. Prices quoted are per night.

Arlington House International Hostel
616 W. Arlington Place, 773/929-5380   **N**
$15 for those with a hostel membership, $18 for non-members, $32 for a

private single (no bath), $38 for private double (no bath), $51 for a private double (with bath). 24-hour check-in.

Chicago International Hostel
6318 N. Winthrop, 773/262-1011   **FN**
$13 for basic accommodations, $35 for private room with 3 beds (no bath), $40 for private double (with bath). Family rooms available. Reservations advisable. Check-in 7am-10am and 4pm-12am. Weekday midnight curfew, weekends 2am.

Chicago International House
1414 E. 59th, 773/753-2270   **S**
$21 with hostel card, $36 without membership. All private rooms. Reservations mandatory. Located on campus of the University of Chicago.

Chicago Summer Hostel
731 S. Plymouth, 773/327-5350   **C**
Newly remodeled dormitory accommodations (they belong to Columbia College during the school year) are maintained by Hosteling International to provide a much-needed downtown hostel and help handle the overflow of summer visitors. Open early June to early September. 2-3 people per room. 24-hour access. Reservations recommended. $19 members, $21 non-members.

For general hostel/membership information, contact:

American Youth Hostels Inc. - Metropolitan Chicago Council
2232 W. Roscoe, 773/327-8114   **N**

DORMS AND DORM-LIKE

Illinois Institute of Technology
3200 S. Wabash, 312/567-5075   **S**
Three miles directly south of downtown—just a bus ride away—the **IIT** dorm rooms have an attractive price for summer travelers of all ages. Private rooms for one person are $26/night and rooms shared with another are $21 per person. Community bathrooms are located on each floor. Laundry and cafeteria available. One-time linen set-up included. Reservations accepted one week in advance with credit card guarantee.

Three Arts Club
1300 N. Dearborn, 312/944-6250   **C**
The landmark **Three Arts Club** has been a supportive residence for emerging women artists since 1912. Its beautiful building—complete with outdoor courtyard, wooden floor ballroom, and exhibition space—in Chicago's ritzy Gold Coast neighborhood is quite a find for budget travelers. Laundry, multi-purpose art studio, pianos, and TV lounges are open to guests. Private rooms are $40/night, $225/week, and $750/month, and include breakfast and dinner. Upon request, slightly lower double occupancy rates are available. The one catch is that during the school year (early September-late May) only women travelers are allowed to rent rooms; it goes co-ed for the summer. Reservations are accepted with a one-third, non-refundable deposit.

NO-FRILLS NEIGHBORHOOD MOTELS

Chicago is not a Club Med sort of destination where one's lodging is an integral part of the experience. Stay inside and you might as well have stayed home. The hardier, more adventurous, more tolerant, more financially constrained traveler may prefer saving their dollars for seeing the town and check into one of these no-frills neighborhood motels.

All are easily accessible by public transportation and cost somewhere between $35 and $60 a night—at least half the price of a downtown hotel. Granted, some of these establishments make more money as outposts for amorous trysts and spicy cable TV programming than on visits from thrifty tourists, and yes, more than one has served as a clandestine site for partying teens. However, even at these locations, the linen is clean and the rooms are safe.

For the budget-conscious and for the not so particular who will be out exploring Chicago all day anyway, the neighborhood motels present a viable alternative to pricier accommodations. Borrowing a Motel 6 motto, "These are rooms to stay in, not to live in."

Far North

Chicago Lodge
920 W. Foster, 773/334-5600
$56/one bed, $60/2 beds. Located 2-3 blocks from Lake Michigan, Foster

Beach, and the northern end of Lincoln Park.

Edens Motel
6020 N. Cicero, 773/725-4500
$38.50/two double beds, $46.50/king bed.

Edgebrook Motel
6401 W. Touhy, 773/774-4200
$35/single, $45/double.

Esquire Motel
6145 N. Elston, 773/774-2700
$37/all rooms.

Heart of Chicago Motel
5990 N. Ridge, 773/271-9181
$50/single, $57/double, king or two double beds. AAA rated. Continental breakfast included.

Lakeside Motel
5440 N. Sheridan, 773/275-2700
$38/single, $55/double. Located near Lake Michigan and the northern end of Lincoln Park.

Sheridan Chase Motor Hotel
7300 N. Sheridan, 773/973-7440
$50/single, $60/double. Located near Loyola University's Lake Shore Campus.

North Lincoln Avenue Strip

This 13-motel strip on Lincoln Avenue always strikes me as misplaced, both in the quantity of motels and in their style. It could be a retirement community for motels who put in their 50 years at the Wisconsin Dells. What are they all doing here? Built in the 1950s, these motels experienced a ten-year heyday, as they were on Highway 41 (Lincoln Avenue), which joined the Edens Expressway at Peterson at the end of the strip. Alas, the 60s brought the Kennedy Expressway, which bypassed this city detour, making it faster than ever to go from southeastern Wisconsin to northeastern Indiana.

Acres Motel
5600 N. Lincoln, 773/561-7777
$40/weekdays, $45/weekends. Call first—this motel's acreage is slated for something more reputable...a library.

Apache Motel
5535 N. Lincoln, 773/728-9400
$40/weekdays, $46/weekends.

Diplomat Motel
5230 N. Lincoln, 773/271-5400
$42/single, $47/double.

Guest House Motel
2600 W. Bryn Mawr, 773/561-6811
$43/all rooms.

Lincoln Inn
5952 N. Lincoln, 773/784-1118
$35/weekdays, $45/weekends.

Lincoln Motel
5900 N. Lincoln, 773/561-3170
$35-$45/1 bed.

O-Mi Motel
5611 N. Lincoln, 773/561-6488
$35/weekdays, $45/weekends.

Patio Motel
6250 N. Lincoln, 773/588-8400
$45/weekdays, $55/weekends.

Riverside Motel
5954 N. Virginia, 773/561-7460
$39/weekdays, $44/weekends.

Spa Motel
5414 N. Lincoln, 773/561-0313
$46/all rooms.

Stars Motel
6100 N. Lincoln, 773/478-6900
$35/weekdays, $40/weekends.

Summit Motel
5308 N. Lincoln, 773/561-3762
$40/all rooms.

Tip Top Motel
6060 N. Lincoln, 773/539-4800
$35-$45/weekdays, $44-$55/weekends.

South

Michigan Inn Motel
3536 S. Michigan, 312/326-3042
$43/all rooms.

Michigan Plaza Motel
2600 S. State, 312/791-1110
$44/all rooms.

Climax Motel
6625 S. Martin Luther King Drive, 773/363-7000
$47/weekdays, $51/weekends, $57/deluxe rooms.

Royal Michigan Motel
3756 S. Michigan, 773/536-4100
$41/all rooms.

Southwest

Rainbow Motel and Pink Palace
7050 W. Archer, 773/229-0707
Budget-minded travelers check in at the **Rainbow Motel** for $55/single, $65/double and romantically inclined couples stay at the **Pink Palace's** fantasy-themed suites for $139 Sun.-Thur. and $169 on weekends. If the *Wine and Roses* heart-shaped bed or the "Hawaiian" room's artificial flowers don't do it for you, maybe the large cards on the *Vegas* room wall or the space-capsule bed of *Space Walk* will!

These four are all within 1/2 mile of Midway Airport:

Rollin' Wheels Motor Hotel
5335 S. Pulaski, 773/582-9600
$44/single, $48/double.

Skylark Motel
5435 S. Archer, 773/582-2100
$50/single, $55/double, $110/rooms with hot tubs. 24-hour restaurant on premises.

Sportsman's Inn Motel
4501 S. Cicero, 773/582-3700
$60/all rooms.

Tangiers Motel
4944 S. Archer, 773/582-0900
$55-$63/1 bed, $65.50/2 beds.

Far Southeast

Barbara Ann's Motel 2
7621 S. Cottage Grove, 773/487-5800
$41/weekdays, $60/weekends.

Camelot Motel
9118 S. Cottage Grove, 773/488-3100
$38/all rooms.

Dunes Motel
9401 S. Stony Island, 773/731-2400
$50/single, $60/double.

New Riviera Motel
9132 S. Stony Island, 773/221-6600
$46/all rooms.

Seville Motel
9101 S. Stony Island, 773/731-6600
$46/all rooms.

Zanzibar Motel
8161 S. Stony Island, 773/768-1430
$50/all rooms.

Far Southwest

Aloha Motel
8515 S. Cicero, 773/767-3100
$35/weekdays, $48/weekends.

Grand Motel
10022 S. Halsted, 773/881-3500
$47/all rooms.

New Halsted Motel
8220 S. Halsted, 773/651-0333
$44/all rooms.

Hogan's Motel
8903 S. Ashland, 773/881-4200
$45/all rooms.

Regency Castle Lodge II
1140 W. 95th, 773/238-8500
$55/all rooms.

Saratoga Motor Inn
7701 S. Cicero, 773/582-8400
$60-$65/double, $50/60 king. Water beds and hot tubs cost extra!

SHOPPING

Definitely not your suburban shopping centers: the historic Maxwell Street Market (*top*) and the Logan Square Megamall (*bottom*) offer unique atmospheres for bargain hunting and snacking. (*Photos by Rames Shrestha.*)

8 SHOPPING

Not only will this chapter assist you in "owning more, spending less," it will also direct you to unique stores and flea markets that are as fun for browsing—and even people watching—as they are for buying.

OUTLET STORES

Outlet stores sell new, generally brand-name merchandise at reduced prices. The items they carry may be last year's model, have slight imperfections, or merely be overstock that a manufacturer is trying to push. Included among the outlet stores in this list are some off-price shops and major discount centers, also well loved for their great bargains.

Accessories and Jewelry

Sun King
44 E. Chicago, 312/649-9110   **C**
826 W. Armitage, 773/975-SUNS   **N**
Discounted designer and brand-name sunglasses—regular and prescription. If you (unlike me) don't get your shades from the drugstore, there are great deals to be had here. Ray Ban, Matsuda, Calvin Klein, Armani, Revo, Persol, and others can run from $30 to $500. Certified opticians and optometrists on staff.

Wabash Jewelry Mall
21 N. Wabash, 312/263-1757   **C**
Twenty merchants sell gold, silver, diamonds, gems, and watches below retail, from their various stations, in this large store front on "Jewelers Row." Some, specializing in loose diamonds, can help you design a unique piece for yourself. **King Tut's Oasis** in the back corner is no mirage—this Middle Eastern fast food stand is an affordable jewel you can indulge in again and again.

Audio Equipment

Saturday Audio Exchange
2865 N. Clark, 773/935-8744   **N**
Open only on Thursday evenings (5pm-9pm) and Saturdays (10:30am-5:30pm), the **Saturday Audio Exchange** sells, buys, and exchanges home audio and home-theater audio equipment. Although the stock is made up of samples, demos, seconds, and used items, everything comes well guaranteed. All merchandise comes with a 90-day full exchange option. From 90 days to a year after purchase, products may be returned for a store credit of 2/3 the price paid. Many items also come with full manufacturer's warranties.

Baby Goods

Rubens Baby Factory Store
2340 N. Racine, 773/348-6200   **N**
No tedious browsing through rack after rack at this minimalist outlet: discounted goods are displayed in a small section of the factory's office. Crib and bassinet sheets, bibs, cotton diapers, pajamas, and the ever-favorite $1.99 assortment of undershirts comprise the majority of available products. Open Mon.-Fri.

Cameras, Film, and Film Processing

Central Camera Company
230 S. Wabash, 312/427-5580   **C**
In business since 1899, **Central Camera** still offers old-fashioned style counter service and the area's largest selection of discounted new and used photo equipment (includes binoculars, books, camera bags, and dark room supplies) from its cramped quarters reminiscent of a bygone era. With its convenient downtown location, their color film developing service is a blessing for tourists. Bring film in by 10am and pick it up the next day with a free second set of prints. Opens 8:30am Mon.-Sat.

Clothing

Burlington Coat Factory
4520 S. Damen, 773/254-0054   **SW**
7340 W. Foster, 773/763-6006   **FN**
While off-price coats—for every season and occasion, from all possible

materials—are the emphasis here, some women's sportswear and designer clothing, men's suits and ties, and children's togs are also sold. Everything is 10-70% below department store prices.

Dan Howard's Maternity Factory Outlet

4242 N. Knox, 773/777-2700, x 119   **NW**
Dan Howard's casual, business, formal, and sleepwear for expectant mothers runs at least 25-50% off the retail price at this outlet location. Most items run $10-$20, but dresses hover in the area of $40.

Fitigues Outlet
1535 N. Dayton, 312/255-0095   **C**
Fitigues' outlet carries remainders from last year's stock of cotton separates at about a 30% discount for in-season clothing and a 50% reduction for off-season items.

Fox's
2336 N. Clark, 773/281-0700   **N**
Women's off-price designer clothing store features sportswear, suits, dresses, and coats at 50-70% off retail prices.

The Gap Factory Outlet
2778 N. Milwaukee, 773/252-0594   **NW**
Irregular and discontinued Gap clothing for men, women, children, and babies. Heavy on the jeans, trousers, and cotton shirts.

Gingiss Formalwear Outlet
542 W. Roosevelt, 312/347-9911   **C**
Know one of those nice guys that will end up going to half a dozen proms? Send them here to buy used (previously rented) tuxes, formalwear, and accessories. Buying one of these tuxes is cheaper than renting one twice—coat, pants, shirt, cummerbund, and bow tie "packages" start at just over $100.

I.B. Diffusion
5020 W. Roosevelt, 773/473-8048   **W**
A true "warehouse outlet," this local clothing manufacturer sells directly to the public from their factory location. Find their sportswear, cruisewear, knit coordinates, linens, sweaters, T-shirts, and jackets at discounts of 30-70%.

Irv's Men's Clothing
431 N. Orleans, 312/832-9900   C
2841 N. Laramie, 773/286-7293   N
Long a staple for Chicago's men's wear, **Irv's** delivers designer and brand name accessories and clothing—from suits to sportswear, including big sizes—at 35-50% below retail. Labels include the likes of Perry Ellis, Chaps, LeBaron, Bill Blass, and San Remo.

A small stretch of Roosevelt Road, just south of downtown and not far from the old Maxwell Street Market, has long been noted for its reputable haberdashers. In fact, the notorious zoot suit was invented along this strip by Harold Fox of **Fox Brothers Tailors** (556 W. Roosevelt, 312/922-5865) back in the early 1940s. Today this area is still a men's wear center, particularly for high-quality, off-price clothing. 555 W. Roosevelt Road is home to three such clothiers: **Eisenstein Clothing** (312/738-0028) carries brand name irregulars, returns, and close-outs (mostly suits) for 50-75% off. Any flaws are pointed out to the customer. **Meyerson Associated Clothing** (312/421-5580) specializes in large sizes at a 20-30% discount. The only place in the United States to buy certain current-season European designer clothes at a discount is in the chockfull, 2nd floor store of **Morris & Sons** (312/243-5635). Expect 30-50% markdowns—more in the clearance section. On the same street, you can buy a tux for a bargain at **Gingiss Formalwear Outlet** (p.345) or stock up on low-cost necessities at **Chicago Hosiery and Underwear Company** (601 W. Roosevelt, 312/226-0055). Walk a couple blocks to **Joseph Cinofsky Discount Men's Wear** (560 W. Harrison, 312/922-5560) for even bigger savings (50-90%) on irregular and second-quality clothing for men.

Land's End Outlet
2121 N. Clybourn, 773/281-0900   N
Men's and women's Land's End sportswear and outdoor clothing. Scan the racks carefully and you might find your own initials among the items mis-monogrammed for others. Sheets, towels, and bags are also sold.

Mark Shale Outlet
2593 N. Elston, 773/772-9600   **N**
Spiffy work and play clothes for the urban professional from local clothier Mark Shale and others at deep discounts. Translation: you can find a $375 suit for a low $149.

Maternity Works
51 E. Randolph, 312/332-0022   **C**
1730 W. Fullerton, 773/529-0564   **N**
Remainders from some of the town's finest maternity shops end up on the racks of **Maternity Works**, where they're sold for at least 50% off the original price. Both locations have a variety of casual, business, and formal pieces, but the downtown store has the better selection of career clothes.

Computers and Supplies

Computer Discount Warehouse
315 W. Grand, 312/527-2700   **C**
When it comes to the 30,000 products (major computer brands, peripherals, and accessories) they sell, not only does **CDW** pass on the "right price" to its customers, but they pride themselves on passing on the "right advice" as well. Readers of *Computer Shopper* agree: they recently awarded them six first-place titles—best place to buy notebook PCs, printers, scanners, monitors, and software and best vendor Web site (*http://www.cdw.com*).

Cosmetics

The Cosmetic Center
2817 N. Broadway, 773/935-2600   **N**
8119 S. Cicero, 773/284-5502 (No nail service.)   **FSW**
After the exhausting chore of sifting through the enormous selection of department store and brand name cosmetics sold at moderate discounts, visit the in-house salon for a hair cut, makeover, or manicure.

Devon Discount Distributors
2454-59 W. Devon, 773/743-1058   **FN**
Largest independent fragrance distributor in Chicago sells name-brand and designer (Armani, Versace, Gaultier, and pals) fragrances and related products at discounts up to 85%. Drastic discounts also apply to their cosmetics, health and beauty supplies, film, and batteries.

Crafts

Gone to Pot
1432 W. Irving Park, 773/472-2274   **N**
For one-of-a-kind items for gift giving or home use, make a trip to this "seconds" outlet to find irregular and discontinued handmade crafts from artisans around the country. Pottery, blown glass, sculpture, wood, jewelry, frames, clocks, lanterns, switchplates, quilts, and more carry price tags 30-60% less than retail.

Fabric

Fabric Outlet
4518 N. Kedzie, 773/539-8011   **NW**
The **Fabric Outlet** sells the designer and first-quality fabric remnants from the owner's main business to the public. Perhaps 1,000 different pieces of fabric, left over from custom drapery, bedspread, and upholstery projects, are available at any time. All sell for $8.95/yard, down from the original $50-$60/yard.

Textile Discount Outlet
2121 W. 21st Place, 773/847-0572   **W**
Four rooms on each of three floors take up thousands of square feet to display thousands of fabrics, trimmings, and sewing doodads. Whether it's for outfitting the bride, re-upholstering a chair, or any project in between, you will—if you spend enough time—find what you're looking for. If you don't, it's because you discovered something better and at a better price.

Furniture

The typical finds at these furniture outlets and liquidators are listed below:

Furniture Factory Outlet
2700 N. Elston, 773/276-3000   **N**
Bedroom, dining room, and living room sets. Layaway and delivery available.

Furniture Liquidation Center
4515 S. Western, 773/523-4191   **SW**
Bedroom and living room sets, dinettes, couches, sofa sleepers, carpets, and appliances.

Furniture Liquidators of America
4425 S. Western, 773/579-0200   **SW**
Living and dining room pieces, carpeting, headboards, mattresses, bunk
beds, stereos, TVs, and VCRs.

Landmark Furniture Liquidators
5853 S. Halsted, 773/783-3100   **S**
New, used, and antique furniture. Come for a lamp, foot stool, curio cabinet,
Queen Anne chair, or bunkbeds and leave with a record player, old radio,
musical instrument, or fish tank besides.

M Furniture Outlet
5323 S. Western, 773/434-1666   **SW**
Kitchen, bedroom, and living room sets, plus stand alone pieces. Layaway
and financing available.

Golf & Tennis Equipment

Chicago Tennis & Golf Company
1880 W. Fullerton, 773/489-2999   **N**
For $55/year, serious golfers and tennis players stand to save a bundle by
joining the **Chicago Tennis & Golf Company's** buyer's club. Membership
entitles buyers to a price much lower than the discounts already found at this
independent, family-owned store. For example, a golf bag marked down to
$160 for regular customers recently went for $119 for club participants. Top
equipment and apparel brands include Callaway, Titleist, Cobra, Prince,
Foot-Joy, Wilson, Head, Nike, and more. Indoor golf and tennis demo lanes
available to test the products.

Crown Golf Outlet
4727 W. Montrose, 773/777-7110   **NW**
Save 20-30% on Crown golf clubs by purchasing them from a small
showroom attached to the **Crown Golf** warehouse. Used and demo sets of
clubs are sold at a 50% discount. Carts, bags, balls, and gloves are also
available.

Nevada Bob's Discount Golf
60 E. Lake, 312/726-4653   **C**
Especially proud of their deals on premium golf club brands, **Nevada Bob's**
guarantees the lowest prices on clubs, clothing, shoes, and tee-time
accessories.

Greeting Cards and Party Supplies

Card & Party Warehouse
1880 W. Fullerton, 773/342-1500   **N**
1265 N. Milwaukee, 773/227-9900   **W**
4216 W. Belmont, 773/736-4900   **NW**
6253 N. McCormick, 773/478-6200   **FN**
Mix and match from the stuffed aisles and you'll have the semblance of a
party before you know it: invitations, catering supplies, coordinated paper
products and plastic cutlery, streamers, table favors, mylar balloons, boxed
greeting cards, gift wrap, ribbon, and disposable cameras. Party goods
discounted 50-70%.

Factory Card Outlet
2585 N. Elston, 773/486-0948   **N**
5125 S. Pulaski, 773/585-7733   **SW**
6520 W. Fullerton, 773/637-4874   **NW**
8045 S. Cicero, 773/582-7787   **FSW**
One of the oldest and largest discount superstores for party supplies,
greeting cards, and special occasion merchandise, **Factory Card Outlet**
offers 20-60% off coordinated party supplies and sells $.39 greeting cards
(over 4,000 top quality available) every day. Also, party favors and
novelties, serving ware, costumes, seasonal decorations, gift wrap, piñatas,
banners, and more.

House and Garden

1730 Outlet Company
1730 W. Wrightwood, 773/871-4331   **N**
1730 delivers big savings on miscellaneous high-quality housewares for
indoors (cloth napkins, placemats, dish towels, candles, candleholders, area
rugs...) and out (lanterns, cintronella and other garden torches, wooden
window boxes, flower baskets...).

American Kitchen & Bath Outlet
2211 N. Elston, 773/395-3500   **N**
If, before you can accessorize your home at the housewares outlets, you
need some major home improvements, this is the place to begin your
savings. Just about everything necessary to renovate a kitchen or bathroom
is here at a 30-90% markdown: cabinets, sinks, faucets, bathtubs, toilets,
appliances, fixtures, and tile.

Northwestern Cutlery and Supply
810 W. Lake, 312/421-3666   **C**
Most come here for deals of up to 35% off on kitchen knives, particularly
the Henckel and Wusthof brands. Bargains on cutlery sets and Swiss army
knives are another draw.

Smith & Hawken Outlet
1780 N. Marcey, 312/266-1988   **N**
Leftovers from the upscale **Smith & Hawken** catalog—which sells
everything remotely related to gardening—can be found here at healthy
discounts. Some standard buys are plants, tools, bulk seeds, statuary,
fencing, topiaries and topiary supplies, and metal and rattan outdoor
furniture. Recent favorites include handmade pots and French rain shoes.

Stacy's Choice
2716 N. Paulina, 773/868-0152   **N**
Stacy's loyal following keeps abreast of their latest bargains via a phone
message that reports new arrivals and special markdowns. They return again
and again for incredible deals on holiday stuff—particularly year-round
Christmas decorations and accessories, special occasion and party items,
home and garden decorations, and craft and cake decorating supplies. It's
enough to fill even the most reluctant of homemakers with glee.

Liquor

Cardinal Liquors
3501 N. Central, 773/725-0900   **NW**
4905 N. Lincoln, 773/561-0270   **FN**
With their great selection, low prices, and even better sales, it's no wonder
that these full-service neighborhood liquor stores have been in business for
56 years. Some of their can't-find-anywhere-else stock includes specialty
Polish, Hungarian, and Russian products.

Sam's Liquors
1720 N. Marcey, 312/664-4394   **N**
This huge, 50-year old warehouse business recently moved a half block to
become the slick "34,000 square foot wine, spirits, food and cigar playpen"
described in its 160-page catalog. It's still one of the finest full service wine
and spirits dealers in the Midwest, offering perhaps the best prices around,
great sales, and an incredible selection.

Wine Discount Center
1826 1/2 N. Elston, 773/489-3454   **N**
An impressive wine selection, which ranges from low-end, unusual, and obscure brands to fine labels—all at hard-to-beat prices—is what allows the **Wine Discount Center** to operate successfully just a stone's throw from the mega stores.

Zimmerman's Discount Liquor Store
213 W. Grand, 312/332-0012   **C**
Having been in business for 65 years, **Zimmerman's** is the original beverage superstore of the Chicago area. Not only that, but because they attempt to carry every brand of spirits on the market and sell it to the public at a good price, they may also deserve their billing as the "world's largest discount liquor store." **Zimmerman's** does their alcohol sales the old-fashioned way—no slick interior, no lush gourmet food section, no upscale bar gadgets. In their partially underground showroom (the warehouse is on the second level), you'll find the largest selection of red Bordeaux wines and imported liqueurs in the area and one of the largest collections of single malt scotches.

Luggage

Irv's Luggage Warehouse
820 W. North, 312/787-4787   **N**
Pay a visit to **Irv's** before your next trip for the best name brands in luggage at factory direct prices. Whether you need a garment bag, duffel bag, passport pouch, or full set of luggage, you'll appreciate the 20-70% cut in prices—not to mention additional savings from the regular coupon offers in local papers. Find current styles, discontinued models, closeouts, and irregulars from makers like Andiamo, Atlantic, Briggs & Riley, Dakota, Eagle Creek, Hartmann, Samsonite, Skyway, and TravelPro. Also save money with their luggage repair service.

Mattresses

Two long-time family businesses provide Chicagoans with remarkable options for discounted bedding:

The Mattress Factory
2850 W. Irving Park, 773/478-1239   **N**
Founded on Roosevelt Road over 100 years ago, **The Mattress Factory**

keeps up with the new (futons and more futons) and accommodates the old (mattresses for odd-sized and antique beds) with merchandise marked down 20-60% from the list price.

The Mattress Factory Outlet Store
2828 W. 48th, 773/376-9522   **SW**
The 60-year-old Heller Brothers bedding manufacturer sells a range of sizes, plus made-to-order mattresses at their wholesale warehouse for about 50% less than what you'd pay elsewhere.

Two newer dealers also offer good discounts: **Mattress King** (1444 W. Belmont, 773/472-5120) sells all of their mattresses, including a selection of therapeutic ones, at wholesale prices. **Marjen of Chicago Discount Furniture & Bedding** (1536 W. Devon, 773/338-6636) handles all variations of mattresses, futons, box springs, and bed frames at affordable prices.

Office Supplies

Arvey Paper
175 W. Jackson, 312/986-1820   **C**
3555 N. Kimball, 773/463-0822   **NW**
Warehouses stock more paper and envelope styles than you can imagine, plus all the other office supplies your home, business, or graphic design project could need. Although the everyday low prices, monthly sales, and volume discounts are outstanding, even more remarkable is the friendly, helpful staff, most of whom seem to be high school and college-aged students.

Restaurant Supplies For the Home

Edward Don Co. Outlet
2525 N. Elston, 773/489-7739   **N**
While you can find an astounding range of glassware, dinnerware, flatware, commercial cookware, utensils, and cleaning supplies at **Edward Don**, the epicenter here is kitchen gadgetry. 500 kitchen gadgets—most specialized and many imported from Switzerland, Hungary, and Poland—draw those who want just the right flour sifter or cheese grater.

Krasny & Company

2829 N. Clybourn, 773/477-5504   **N**

From the mundane ketchup and syrup dispensers, bread baskets, and ashtrays used at corner diners to the over 600 kinds of specialty glassware found behind hotel bars: **Krasny** has the kind of items you've long admired at eating and drinking establishments of every caliber and have always wanted to take home. Other perks of shopping at this accessible wholesaler include the industrial cookware and bulk herbs and spices.

Shoes

Adams Factory Shoe Outlet

3655 W. Irving Park, 773/539-4120   **NW**

If sturdiness means more to you than fashion, then read on. This 52-year old family shoe store deals in irregulars, closeouts, and overstocks of American made shoes and is known for their wide range of sizes—women's 1-14, men's 5-18, also wide-widths. Their "full-service" includes a cup of good coffee!

Chernin's Shoe Outlet

1001 S. Clinton, 312/341-5131	**C**
3035 N. Pulaski, 773/282-2626	**NW**
5139 S. Pulaski, 773/284-7272	**SW**
6560 W. Fullerton, 773/804-0494	**NW**

Browse the ample collections of discontinued, irregular, and closeout Chernin shoes for women (sizes 5-13), men (sizes 6-17), and children, at these outlet stores. Besides the regular discounts of up to 50% off, take off an additional 50% on a second pair of shoes.

Chicago Shoe Outlet

3212 N. Lincoln, 773/528-4433   **N**

Good discounts on men's casual and sports shoes from names like Nike, Reebok, and Fila. Some women's shoes.

Nine West Outlet

2739 N. Clark, 773/281-9132   **N**

Nine West's women's shoes end up at their outlet stores with friendlier price tags a year later. While their selection contains evening, casual, and canvas shoes, they mostly handle leather dress shoes. On the back racks, older shoes can be found at deeper discounts.

Wolinsky & Levy
3259 N. Ashland, 773/880-5648 **N**
W & L discounts their designer and brand name shoes (casual, dress, and some athletic) for men and women 25-75% easily. If that's not enough, check out the *discount* racks! Also, socks, purses, and Ray Ban sunglasses.

UNIQUE BROWSING

Things you would find only in a big city. Things that are great to look at, but you don't need, don't want, or can't afford. Things that make distinctive, memorable gifts. Things that make you go hmm...

Alternative Stuff

Alternative Shopping Complex
Clark and Belmont, 773/348-5000 **N**
Five stores under one roof sell "alternative" products for the urban hip: **The Alley** (773/883-1800) deals in motorcycle gear, leather jackets, boots, clothing, jewelry, and alternative lifestyle paraphernalia. At the **Architectural Revolution** (773/752-7837), find columns, statues, gargoyles, and other decorative plaster items to spruce up the house and garden. **Blue Havana** (773/242-8262) is a premium cigar shop, with a decent selection of ashtrays and humidors. Sterling silver necklaces, rings, charms, bracelets, watches, and earrings are the **Silver District**'s (773/871-3900) specialty. And, for those of age, **Taboo-Tabou** (773/723-3739) carries lingerie, condoms, and—ahem—adult toys.

99th Floor
3406 N. Halsted, 773/348-7781 **N**
Welcome to a world of leather, latex, hardware, hair dye, and Zippo lighters. The **99th Floor** traffics in "eclectic and extreme" shoes, boots, clothing, jewelry, and accessories for an underground and alternative clientele.

Architecture and Design Stuff

Chicago Architecture Foundation Gift Shop
224 S. Michigan, 312/922-3432 **C**
875 N. Michigan, 312/751-1380 **C**
Architecture books, Tiffany-style lamps, decorative gargoyles, jewelry, and assorted home accessories—many with Frank Lloyd Wright motifs—are

among the carefully chosen items for sale. Unique and educational children's toys like Archiblocks, Geomobiles, and origami and rubber stamp kits are also architecturally inspired.

The Good Design Store
6 N. Michigan, 312/251-0175   **C**
Gift shop of the Chicago Athenaeum Museum of Architecture and Design honors the well-designed: from furniture and housewares to lighting and fixtures to tools and electronics. Clipboards from old computer boards, whimsical tea kettles, the perfect blue wine goblet, improved-upon garden tools, and the ideal leather backpack are items you might find in an international collection that hails from the United States, Japan, Germany, Israel, Portugal, Italy, and other nations.

Art by Locals

Gallery 37 Store
State and Lake, 312/251-0371   **C**
Gallery 37 is an eight-year-old project of the Chicago Department of Cultural Affairs. It pairs talented Chicago students—over 7,000 to date—earning an hourly work program wage, with local and international artists/instructors. This boutique, in the Renaissance Hotel building, sells much of the exceptional artwork created during these year-round internships: jewelry, stationery, hand-painted scarves and ties, T-shirts, ceramics, wall hangings, furniture, mosaic works, pillows, flower pots, wooden boxes, and more. All store proceeds go back into the program.

Illinois Artisans Shop
100 W. Randolph, 312/814-5321   **C**
Located in the James R. Thompson Center, the **Illinois Artisans Shop** markets arts and crafts from Illinois artisans. Woodworkers, feltmakers, quilters, beaders, photographers, painters, potters, and sixty different jewelry artisans are among the dozens of artists displaying their handiwork here. From fine art to county fair crafts, from the practical to the purely decorative, **the Illinois Artisans Shop** is impressive in its range of merchandise and its reasonable price tags.

Boulevard Artisans
6011 S. Ashland, 773/434-1617   **SW**
Community arts center sells a variety of ethnic arts and gifts created by its students and teachers, including jewelry, ceramics, dolls, clothing, greeting cards, and photography. Closed Mon. and Tues.

Building Parts

Salvage One
1524 S. Sangamon, 312/733-0098   **C**
Five-floor, 100,000 ft.^{2} warehouse sells salvaged parts—nearly everything—of American and European buildings from the 18th, 19th, and 20th centuries. The largest salvage company in the nation, **Salvage One** obtains many of its vintage architectural furnishings from buildings slated for demolition or renovation and then re-sells them to individuals restoring, renovating, or constructing other buildings. Think piles of doors, bins of doorknobs, and racks of switchplates and you're just warming up. While items like handrails, gates, chandeliers, mirrors, benches, bars, urns, statuary, and mantels can be re-used for their original purposes, things like ironwork, woodwork, paneling, stained and leaded glass, hardware, finials, columns, marble, and terra cotta require more imagination.

Cookie Jars

Jazz'e Junque
3831 N. Lincoln, 773/472-1500   **N**
What exactly constitutes *jazzy junk*? How about what's probably the world's largest cookie jar collection, along with unusual salt and pepper shakers, funky 50s tablecloths, vintage cookbooks, and other kitschy kitchen objects? Cookie jar guises include Elvis, Miss Piggie, sports cars, and even a replica of the **Jazz'e Junque** shop! 10% off on Wednesdays.

Costumes

Fantasy Headquarters
4065 N. Milwaukee, 773/777-0222   **NW**
A block-long mega store equipped for every disguise and party need: 5,000 masks, 10,000 costumes for sale or rent, makeup and accessories (stage blood, fake noses, glow-in-the-dark facial decorations), 1,000 wigs on display (30,000 in stock), adult novelties and gag gifts, and party goods (luau decorations, streamers, helium tanks). Medieval garb, gangster attire, and Blues Brothers costumes are perennial favorites, while characters from the movie *Scream* are recent rental hits.

Hats

Hats Plus
4706 W. Irving Park, 773/286-5577   **NW**
Revamp your image again and again from the 10,000 hats and 10,000 caps
in over 500 styles at **Hats Plus**. The management lists the Panama and straw
hats; fedoras; 30s and 40s style hats; golf, fishing, and baseball caps; and
Greek fisherman's caps as their most popular styles. But if you prefer, you
can always walk away topped with a propeller beanie, ear-flap hat, lambskin
beret, Stetson, or furry Siberian number.

"Six Corners," in previous decades, was one of the northside's major
shopping districts. For being past its prime, this Irving Park/Milwaukee/
Cicero intersection remains strangely vibrant despite its five-and-dime
appearance and makes a wonderful destination for an afternoon of
specialty browsing. Graze at **City News Stand**'s (below) buffet of
publications, don beanie after beanie at **Hats Plus** (above), plan next
year's Halloween get-up at **Fantasy Headquarters** (p.357), and grab a
used game cartridge from **Windy City Games** (p.377). Also near by are
Saracan Archery Range (p.76), the **Portage Theater** (p.256), and
LaSalle Movie Classics on Saturday nights (p.259).

Kites

The Kite Harbor
North Pier, 435 E. Illinois, 312/321-5483   **C**
It's always springtime and playtime amidst the colorful assortment of kites,
windsocks, windchimes, whirligigs, and other unusual flying toys (airplanes,
boomerangs Frisbees, single line and dual line stunt kites) at **The Kite
Harbor**. For land-based pleasures, they have yo-yos, juggling equipment,
and remote control boats and cars.

Magazines and Newspapers

City News Stand
4018 N. Cicero, 773/545-7377   **NW**
This small and friendly neighborhood store has a periodical lineup that can't
be beat in Chicago—or maybe anywhere else for that matter. You'll find

Sunday papers from Maui and Prague, old monster magazines, *Shotgun News*, obscure literary journals, and at least 6,000 other newspapers, magazines, and publications, including their own monthly newsletter, *The Mag Bag*. Open daily 8am-11pm.

Quimby's
1854 W. North, 773/342-0910   **W**
Alternative bookstore carries the city's largest collection of 'zines, underground comics, and other independent and imported publications. *The Baffler, Lumpen, Rocktober, Libido, Schizo*, and *Acme Novelty* are some local productions they recommend.

Magic

Izzy Rizzy's House of Tricks
6034 S. Pulaski , 773/735-7370   **SW**
For over a quarter of a century, southsiders have picked up their tricks, gags, costumes, and adult party favors and games at **Izzy Rizzy's**. More recently they've been able to find how-to videos, tarot cards, voodoo kits, and virtual reality pets. Izzy is opening a second store at 64th and Cicero in late 1998.

Models

Stanton Hobby Shop
4718 N. Milwaukee, 773/283-6446   **NW**
Plastic model cars and Japanese sci-fi robots top what models hobbyists are currently buying at **Stanton**. But never fear, model kits, tools, guides, and accessories for everything else that moves—trains, planes, boats, tanks, cars, rockets, and more—are strongly represented, along with vinyl model figures of the ever-lovable Jason and Freddy Krueger.

Movie, Radio, and TV Memorabilia

Metro Golden Memories
5425 W. Addison, 773/736-4133   **NW**
If Seinfeld and Howard Stern don't figure in your Golden Age of broadcasting, **Metro Golden Memories** has another era's memorabilia for you. Jack Benny, Fibber Magee & Molly, Bergen & McCarthy, Bette Davis, Joan Crawford, Tyrone Power, Clark Gable, and James Cagney are the stars here. Find related new and used books, posters, scripts, statues, collector's plates, stills, and more. Popular and hard-to-find movies and tapes of radio

programs are for sale or rent.

Paper

The Paper Source
232 W. Chicago, 312/337-0798   **C**
Admirers of **The Paper Source**'s extravagant array of homemade papers, miscellaneous paper and wood gifts, classy stationery items, and an extensive rubber stamp and ink pad collection include Chicago artist and regular customer Ed Paschke. Regular classes on topics such as envelope making, paper lampshades, book binding, rubber stamping, calligraphy, and collage will give those with a creative inkling even more reasons to patronize this shop.

Posters

Poster Plus
200 S. Michigan, 312/461-9277 (Across from the Art Institute)   **C**
3366 N. Clark, 773/929-2850   **N**
Idle away a couple of hours lingering over the thousands of vintage and contemporary posters on display. Once inspired, you may want some of their fine art for everyday life: O'Keefe mousepads, Degas serving trays, Kadinsky mugs, Magritte puzzles, etc.

Spy Stuff

Spy Shop Inc.
1156 N. Dearborn, 312/664-0976   **C**
Want to spy on your baby-sitter or employees? Hidden cameras are one of the top sellers among the scary surveillance and home protection gadgets the **Spy Shop** proffers its voyeuristic, stalked, stalking, paranoiac, 007 wannabe, and average American customers. Topics typically familiar only to private investigators and covert agencies are available in its mind-boggling assortment of books. Conceal your identity, track down a long-lost someone, start a revolution...

Surplus Stuff

American Science and Surplus
5316 N. Milwaukee, 773/763-0313   **FN**
Countless aisles and bins overflow with an extraordinary array of other

companies' unrelated leftovers, mistakes, etc. Find what you need for that science, art, or home improvement project super cheap: tubes, cords, magnets, wires, motors, lenses, compasses, doll heads, plastic body parts, rubber animals, light blue masking tape, and thousands of additional items.

Creative Reuse Warehouse
721 W. O'Brien, 312/421-3640   **C**
Reduce, reuse, recycle is the idea behind this non-profit distributor of business scraps and surplus. From its 10,000 ft.^{2} warehouse near Halsted and Roosevelt Road, **Creative Reuse Warehouse** makes items otherwise headed for a landfill available at low cost to teachers, artists, non-profit groups, and the public. Select items have price tags, but the general fee is $3/bag. Most of these goodies are "raw" (fabrics, leather, yarns, plastics, wood pieces, metals, and plenty of whatchimacallits) and require imaginative re-use.

Voodoo/Hoodoo Stuff

Augustine's Spiritual Goods
3114 S. Halsted, 312/326-5467   **SW**
The owners of this Bridgeport shop, native Chicagoans themselves, take their voodoo and spirituality seriously. Jokesters and unattended children will be asked, politely but firmly, to leave. The shop's wide-ranging inventory includes potions, amulets, talismans, house blessings, tarot cards, candles, books on wicca and witchcraft, and Christian religious statues. **Augustine's** also provides astrological services such as natal and relationship reports.

Other one-and-onlys...

Yodel over to **Austrian Station** (3504 N. Elston, 773/583-8288) for Austrian items like crystal, beer steins, traditional clothing, and of course, Beanie Babies. Their phone message provides a quick Beanie Baby update! **Hip House** (6560 W. Fullerton, 312/745-2300) outfits professional and amateur DJs with accessories and equipment from turntables, mixers, and record bags to new, old, and imported records, tapes, and CDs. **Magic & Vanity** (447 N. Wells, 312/595-9660) sets a comfortable stage for female cancer patients and cancer survivors to purchase customized scarves, wigs, special makeup, hats, prostheses, and clothes. **Stoner Enterprises** (4427 N. Milwaukee, 773/202-0090) deals in goods specifically for the police officers and firefighters on your gift list. Yep, keychains, coffee mugs, condom caddies, jewelry, leather goods—including radio holders and wallets—and gold pendants designed solely for these civil servants.

Free Shopping in Chicago?

Sure, on "Trashing Day." According to Northsider Nina Sandlin, Chicago's most popular moving days, May 1st and Oct 1st, are the best days for "trashing." That is, visiting the alleys and dumpsters in better neighborhoods—especially those with a high concentration of renters—to recover some of the goods those with plenty of *disposable* income discard when they move. Some of her regular finds include housewares, furniture, plants, expensive clothing, plastics, office supplies, and gift wrap!

RESALE SHOPPING

Extensive coverage of Chicago's resale options is provided below for various reasons. First and foremost, this is where you'll spend the least amount of money for the most stuff. Secondly, as most of these places are operated by individuals or non-profit organizations, they are "unique" to Chicago. K-Mart, Sears, and Marshall Field's, can be patronized in any old city. These stores and markets can lure you into new neighborhoods to explore. Then, as any experienced resale shopper can tell you, it's not just about acquiring things—it's a hobby, an adventure. You'll often have to search for what you want, but you'll just as often be surprised by the unexpected finds. What about the societal gains? This is recycling far beyond the realm of bottles and cans. Local charitable organizations benefit when you buy from them. Finally, second-hand merchandise is the perfect affordable option for those who don't want to wear or own the same things as everyone else. Instead, you can wear and own the same things that people did 2, 5, 10, and 20 years ago.

Specialty Resale Stores

You won't be rummaging through a haystack of junk to find the needle you want at these places. This listing contains specialized resale shops, most dealing with high-quality merchandise. They sell the sort of things you may not mind buying used: appliances, books, building parts, children's clothing and goods, furniture for home and office (including hotel/motel furniture), leather and Levi's, men's suits, music, sporting goods, vintage clothing, and women's designer and consignment clothing.

⇒ APPLIANCES

Before shelling out for big-ticket appliances like stoves, refrigerators, washers, and dryers, you may want to check out the second hand items available at **McCoy New & Used Furniture & Appliance** (7257 S. Halsted, 773/994-9000) or **Southwest Furniture & Appliance** (825 W. 47th, 773/247-4300 and 2934 N. Milwaukee, 773/227-4224). For these appliances plus temperature control appliances (heating units, water heaters, air conditioners, etc.), there's **A-1 Appliance** (2094 N. Milwaukee, 773/489-6732) and **Vargus Used Appliances** (3248 W. 25th, 773/762-2340).

⇒ BOOKS

After-words
23 E. Illinois, 312/464-1110   C
New downtown independent bookstore sells both new and used books with a notable literature and poetry section. Does out-of-print book searches and offers internet access to its customers ($8.99/hour, $2.50 for 15 minutes, or $20 for 5 hours/month).

The Armadillo's Pillow
6753 N. Sheridan, 773/761-2558   FN
Small, general used book store draws Loyola University students and the neighbors. The jewelry, gifts, and incense make it a bona fide Rogers Park establishment.

Aspidistra Bookshop
2630 N. Clark, 773/549-3129   N
Enormous collection includes significant literature, fiction, drama, history, science, art eastern religion, and philosophy sections.

Bookends
4740 N. Lincoln, 773/561-0110   N
Collection of used and remaindered books includes a nice children's selection. Plus, book accessories, Chicago titles, children's play area, and

special events

The Bookies Paperbacks & More
2419 W. 103rd, 773/239-1110   **FSW**
Trade-in past reads for merchandise credit. Collection includes horror,
mystery, romance, general fiction, and new releases. Rock, jazz, and
classical, records, CDs, and tapes are also available.

Bookleggers Used Books
2935 N. Broadway, 773/404-8780   **N**
Varied collection includes art, photography, architecture, fiction, literature,
philosophy, religion, and a sizable selection of audiobooks.

Bookseller's Row
408 S. Michigan, 312/427-4242   **C**
Large downtown store resells all subjects with major art, photography,
literature, mysteries, and Chicago sections.

The Bookworks
3444 N. Clark, 773/871-5318   **N**
Rare and general used book collection includes photography, history, and
literature. Some used CDs and records are also available.

Ex Libris Theological Books
1340 E. 55th, 773/955-3456   **S**
Used scholarly theology and religion bookstore attracts University of
Chicago academics.

Fagin N Books
459 N. Milwaukee, 312/829-5252   **C**
Specialty store deals in used anthropology, archeology, botany, zoology,
and natural history books.

The Gallery Bookstore
3827 N. Broadway, 773/975-8200   **N**
General used book and magazine store is open daily. The Florence Hanley
Memorial Wing—their special collection of mystery, sci-fi, and horror—is
open weekends only.

Login Medical Book Store
1910 W. Harrison, 312/733-4544   **W**
Used and new medical books aimed at students, doctors, dentists, nurses,

and other medical professionals.

Myopic Books
1726 W. Division, 773/862-4882   **W**
Coffee and food are available for sustenance while you peruse **Myopic Books'** large collection of fiction. Open 11am-1pm.

National Law Resources
328 S. Jefferson, 312/382-8282   **C**
Largest law book dealer in the United States stocks plenty of used books aside their new ones.

Officer Bob's Paperbacks
4340 N. Milwaukee, 773/736-9522   **NW**
General used bookstore sells mostly paperbacks. Open Tues.-Sat.

O'Gara & Wilson Ltd.
1448 E. 57th, 773/363-0993   **S**
A suitable neighbor for the University of Chicago, **O'Gara & Wilson** carries used, rare, antiquarian, and scholarly titles in the humanities—especially history, art, religion, and philosophy.

Powell's Book Stores
2850 N. Lincoln, 773/248-1444   **N**
1501 E. 57th, 773/955-7780   **S**
828 S. Wabash, 312/341-0748   **C**
Large, general used bookstores stock scholarly titles in all fields and have notable history, philosophy, art, photography, and fiction collections.

Prairie Avenue Bookshop
418 S. Wabash, 312/922-8311   **C**
Called the "best architectural bookshop in the world," by the *London Financial Times*, the United States' largest architectural bookstore sells new and used books on architecture, interior design, and urban planning.

Selected Works
3510 N. Broadway, 773/975-0002   **N**
Broad collection includes many scholarly subjects: classical studies, philosophy, theology, history, poetry, and literature. Also, sci-fi, mysteries, books on the Occult, and second-hand sheet music.

Shake Rattle & Read Book Box
4812 N. Broadway, 773/334-5311   **FN**
Special book sections include pop culture, Hollywood, military, cookbooks, and mysteries. Also sells used CDs, cassettes, and records (mostly rock and jazz), comics, and magazines (check out the vintage rock 'n' roll magazines).

The Stars Our Destination
1021 W. Belmont, 773/871-2722   **N**
Named for Alfred Bester's 1957 classic *The Stars My Destination*, this 10-year-old used science fiction, fantasy, and horror bookstore is one of the largest such stores in the country. Frequent author events and signings are posted in the store as well as the house newsletter.

Turtle Island Books
7001 N. Glenwood, 773/465-7212   **FN**
New Age, metaphysical, and occult specialties, plus a general collection that is primarily fiction. Tarot decks, essential oils, and other New Age gifts round out their stock. Tarot readings on the premises. Closed Wednesdays. Open until 9pm Thurs.-Sat.

The UIC Medical Bookstore
828 S. Wolcott, 312/413-5550   **W**
Large selection of new and used medical books and multimedia.

⇒ **CHILDREN'S ITEMS**

Perfect places for those reluctant to spend big on the material accouterments of fleeting childhood stages...

Clothes (infant-size 14), furniture (cribs, beds, bassinets, dressers, hi-chairs), bedding and receiving blankets, toys (bikes, outdoor equipment, plush stuffed animals), strollers, nursery decorations, and more make **First Seconds Resale** (4266 N. Milwaukee, 773/777-2200) a great resource for parents. Most items are sold on consignment, but cash is paid for toys and furniture. **Once Upon A Child** (5316 N. Milwaukee, 773/594-1705) and **Sweet Little One's** (3519 N. Lincoln, 773/525-8963) have similar items, as do **The Second Child** (954 W. Armitage, 773/883-0880) and **Children's Wearhouse** (2640 W. Pratt, 773/761-3572), which also carry maternity clothes.

⇒ CLOTHING (BRIDAL)

Cynthia's Consignments
2218 N. Clybourn, 773/248-7714   N
With over 200 high-fashion wedding gowns—none more than two years old—**Cynthia's** has the largest and most impressive designer bridal consignment in the city. In fact some of her stock is so current, the same dresses are still selling at full-price on the racks of the area's elite bridal shops. Though many of the dresses have been worn once, others are samples and exclusive end-of-the season buyouts from those designer boutiques. Dresses for the mothers of the bride and groom, veils, and bridal accessories are also available. Everything is over 70% off retail.

I Do Designer Bridal Consignment
6742 W. Belmont, 773/205-1234   NW
It's easy to say "I do" to the wide range of prices, sizes, and styles available at this all-bridal consignment shop: the "once-worn" wedding gowns (cleaned and bagged), veils, lingerie, accessories, and mother of the bride dresses from the 1930s to the present can be bought for at least half of the original price. Alterations on the premises.

Check out **Flashy Trash**, **Silver Moon**, **Wacky Cats**, and **Wild Thing** in the **Vintage Clothing** section (pp.368-370) for vintage wedding gear.

⇒ CLOTHING (LEATHER AND LEVI'S)

LeGarage
1649 N. Damen, 773/278-2234   N
Over 5,000 vintage Levi's, black jeans, overalls, flannels, police jackets, leather jackets, other leather clothing, and boots

JR's Blue Revolution
3125 N. Broadway, 773/525-1431   N
Over 2,000 pairs of Levi's and other trustworthy denim brands, leather jackets/clothing, and other vintage items.

⇒ CLOTHING (MEN'S)

Duomo
2906 N. Broadway, 773/325-2325   N
In the spirit of Chicago's many designer resale and consignment shops for

women, comes this one for men who want to dress fashionably without spending a fortune. Very particular in its selection, the store's stock includes end-of-season merchandise from the area's most exclusive boutiques along with cleaned and pressed consignment clothing no more than two seasons old. Expect Calvin Klein, Claude Montana, Hugo Boss, Armani, Versace, and peers on the labels.

Monitor Formal Wear
1422 W. Wilson, 773/561-0573   **N**
While they promote their wares to entertainers, caterers, and waiters, **Monitor** probably has a piece of used or vintage formalwear just for you, too. Suits, tuxedos, dinner jackets, sports coats, vests, cummerbunds, shirts, shoes, scarves, canes, and jewelry are all available for an affordable special occasion transformation.

Suitsmart
115 N. Wabash, 2nd Floor, 312/553-0200   **C**
Known for their service as well as their selection, **Suitsmart** was the first in the area to handle gently used men's clothing. (Their inventory also includes closeouts and overstocks.) Used and new items are all department store and designer brands, up-to-date in style, free of major flaws, and well-labeled with size information. Find an array of suits and dress clothing from a $25 sport coat to a pair of $199 wool-lined slacks. Tailoring available.

⇒ **CLOTHING (VINTAGE)**

Beatnix
3400 N. Halsted, 773/281-6933   **N**
Everything necessary for a 60s/70s look can be found here. Bell bottoms? Platform Shoes? Wigs? Something plaid, polyester, or otherwise wacky in texture, color, or cut? They've got it. Just maybe, you want a retro tux for say...catering or table waiting as they suggest? Plenty of leather and buckskin jackets, jewelry, purses, bags, belts, and ties await.

Dandelion
2117 N. Damen, 773/862-9333   **N**
Dandelion's vintage items take up about half the store. Their apparel hails from the 1940s to the1980s, with most from the 60s and 70s. Shoes and accessories available.

Flashy Trash
3524 N. Halsted, 773/327-6900   N
Flashy Trash brings on the glamorous and not so glamorous of the 20th century in its loaded 3,000 ft.[2] store, containing a jumbled mix of new and vintage items for men and women. Some of their stuff is "dead stock," meaning it previously sat in warehouses for 20 or so years collecting dust. A brief register of their noteworthy items must include vintage jeans, beaded dresses, lingerie, swim suits, evening gowns, and bridalwear; classic tuxedos (many with tails) dating from the 1920s; sequined sweaters; Victorian jewelry; old and new hats; polyester shirts; bowling shirts; Hawaiian shirts; denim and corduroy clothing; overalls; Zippo lighters; and last, but not least, pinup girl decals.

Hubba-Hubba
3338 N. Clark, 773/477-1414   N
If vintage spells romance for you, hurry over to **Hubba-Hubba** for items from the 1950s and earlier, as well as newer vintage-inspired articles. Start a search for that special occasion dress or tuxedo here or pick up a beaded sweater or gabardine jacket for everyday use. Dripping in lace, pearls, crystal, and rhinestones and perfumed with a floral scent, the second floor's jewelry, accessories, frames, housewares, and linens offer girly girl shopping at its best.

Lost Eras
1511 W. Howard, 773/764-7400   FN
Largest collection of vintage clothing—10,000+ items!—and antiques in the midwest draws theater people and vintage lovers alike with its ample representation of eras past.

Kismet Vintage Clothing
2923 N. Southport, 773/528-4497   N
One of the first vintage dealers in the area (opened in 1980), **Kismet** specializes in items from the 1920s to the1950s. Casual and formal clothing include suits, furs, formalwear, wedding dresses, shoes, hats, and purses. Some vintage drapes and Art Deco furniture round out their selection.

Shangrila
1952 W. Roscoe, 773/348-5090   N
Self-described as the "smallest and least expensive" of the local vintage dealers due to their "high turnover," **Shangrila** mixes some contemporary used clothing into their selection of goods from the 1930s to the 1970s. Along with their casual and fancy attire, you'll find shoes, handbags, and

jewelry. Grab something from their collection of pulp novels and LPs to help authenticate a new look.

Silver Moon
3337 N. Halsted, 773/883-0222   **N**
They "don't do junk here" is what I'm told. Instead, they pack two rooms with inviting vintage from the 1890s to the1960s. One room is devoted to clothing, with a notable selection of hats and men's suits, tails, and tuxes. The other displays a collection of wedding gowns, jewelry, accessories, shoes, and antiques and oddities from the 40s and earlier.

Strange Cargo
3448 N. Clark, 773/327-8090   **N**
Modern vintage of the 50s-70s comprises the strange cargo pedaled here. Police jackets, Levi's 501s, overalls, bowling shirts, and old models of athletic footwear—unused Converse, Nike, Keds and more—top the big sellers list. Also, women's casual and formal apparel, jewelry, and hats.

Wacky Cats
3109 N. Lincoln, 773/929-6701   **N**
Women's causal and formalwear, wedding gowns, men's shirts and suits, hats, shoes, and accessories dating from the 1940s to the 1970s make up the **Wacky Cats** inventory.

Wild Thing
2933 N. Clark, 773/549-7787   **C**
Although they deal in clothing from the1940s to the 1970s, **Wild Thing**'s specialty is "retro elegance." That means less of the 70s casual clothing and more suits, ties, beaded tops, and cocktail dresses from the 40s and 50s. Also, lingerie, wedding gowns, Hawaiian shirts, and large-size dresses.

Wisteria
3715 N. Southport, 773/880-5868   **N**
"Vintage emporium" emphasizes its "hep" swing wear for men and women. Other vintage items from the 1930s to the 1960s include women's suits, nightwear, bowling shirts, hats, and purses.

⇒ CLOTHING (WOMEN'S)

Even with resale and consignment being one of the fastest growing areas of the American retail industry, an insider's estimate that the Chicago area has over 100 such shops for women's clothing is still extraordinary. What's no surprise is why savvy shoppers love them: their turn-over system keeps stock fresh and seasonal—prices are typically marked down systematically over a period of weeks to keep things moving. The better places take only clothes less than two years old, that have been dry-cleaned (or at least washed), pressed, and supplied on a hanger. What's not sold in a reasonable amount of time is either returned to the consignor or donated to charity.

Absolutely Fabulous
2821 N. Halsted, 773/244-2330   **N**
Everything from jeans to businesswear for those sized 2-16. Jewelry, purses, and other accessories add a fabulous finish to your new wardrobe. Those placing their clothes on consignment are given store credit rather than cash. Closed Mondays.

Bella Moda Consignment House
947 N. State, 312/642-0330   **C**
The **Bella Moda** mode is designer and couture. They carry top of the line business, casual, and evening attire, with handbags, jewelry, and scarves of the same ilk.

Buy Choice Resale
3860 N. Lincoln, 773/296-4525   **N**
Free of the downtown attitude, **Buy Choice** may actually deserve the owners' self-election of their store as "Chicago's Friendliest Consignment Shop." Their selection includes everything from casual to formal department store and designer clothing (petite to plus sizes), plus shoes (to size 11), hats, jewelry, and sunglasses. Closed Mondays.

Buy Popular Demand
2629 N. Halsted, 773/868-0404   **N**
Another friendly consignment shop, **Buy Popular Demand**'s only irksome quality is the overstuffed racks that make it hard to browse quickly. Get on their mailing list to be notified about their great seasonal sales.

Cynthia's Consignments
2218 N. Clybourn, 773/248-7714   **N**
Cynthia's specializes in high quality, top designer (Calvin Klein, Moschino, Prada, and cohorts) consignment clothing: cleaned, pressed, no more than two seasons old, and probably from a socialite more fashionable than thou—or me, at least. Other garments aren't even "gently used," rather stock overruns and year-end leftovers from exclusive city and North Shore boutiques. Evening gown rentals also available. See **Clothing (Bridal)** on

p.367 for information on **Cynthia's** designer bridalwear bargains.

Owner Cynthia Hodgkins is also a singer, actress, model, and former Miss Chicago, Miss Illinois, and 1987 Miss America talent winner.

The Daisy Shop
67 E. Oak, 6th Floor, 312/943-8880   C

Called "a jewel of a resale shop" by local fashion editors, **The Daisy Shop** is the place to spend your money after simply browsing through the exclusive Oak Street boutiques. Armani, Chanel, Lagerfeld, and Mizrahi are but a few of the 75 couturiers the shop discriminatingly accepts—its 2000-item inventory gleaned from the best dressed women in Chicago, Boston, New York, and Palm Beach. Lest you have nothing to complement your haute purchases, the shop also carries fine jewelry, appraised signed costume jewelry, and authenticated accessories on consignment for completing any ensemble.

Designer Resale East
658 N. Dearborn, 312/587-3312   C

Don't be surprised to find certain price tags here inching perilously up into the hundreds of dollars. The designer and couture clothing, shoes, and accessories at **Designer Resale East** are likely closeouts or consigned by that sliver of society that can afford to buy things they never wear—you'll find the original tags still on some of this stuff. Yet, there are big bargains for what it is, as well as bargains for the rest of us, especially when pieces are marked down to move.

Elliott Consignment
2465 N. Lincoln, 773/404-6080   N

Free parking, given its Lincoln Park location, is quite a selling point for this two-story clothing and furniture consignment shop. Their racks contain current casual and formal—designer and better brands—apparel and acessories (mostly women's, some men's). Housewares include collectibles, antiques, china, pillows, couches, and tables. Layaway available.

Encore II Resale
9513 S. Western, 773/779-6288   FSW

Consignment store's designer and quality-label stock ranges from casual to corporate to formal attire for women of all sizes. Jewelry, handbags, scarves, and more available for accessorizing.

Entre-Nous Resale Shop
21 E. Delaware, 312/337-2919   **C**
Boutique-style consignment shop handles only the crème de la crème of designer clothing. Expect high quality and prices to match.

Exquisite: A Women's Resale & Consignment Shop
4262 W. Irving Park, 773/736-2422   **NW**
Clothing (sizes 2-26) and accessories aimed at the business woman on a budget. **Exquisite** carries only seasonal clothes less than five years old, but no vintage clothing, jeans, or T-shirts.

Gem's Consignment
3304 N. Central, 773/282-4511   **NW**
Dresses make up a large portion of **Gem's** consignment clothing. Shoes, accessories, and jewelry are available to complete an outfit.

McShane's Exchange
815 W. Armitage, 773/525-0282   **N**
1141 W. Webster, 773/525-0211   **N**
Great prices and selection make designer clothing accessible to women of all budgets at these extremely popular consignment shops. As they like to say: We're "14 blocks above Bendel's [Henri Bendel's at 900 N. Michigan Avenue] and about 80% below."

My Sister's Closet
5413 W. Devon, 773/774-5050   **FN**
This 16-year-old business deals in resale clothing and "samples" for women and children. Accessories available include shoes, purses, scarves, fine and costume jewelry. Perfume, home decor, and antiques are also sold.

New To You
10037 S. Western, 773/779-6969   **FSW**
Moderate to upscale clothing, jewelry, shoes, and accessories consignment store includes a large selection for the full-figured woman. Small sections for men and children. Closed Sundays.

Obsessions Resale Boutique
7424 N. Western, 773/761-5279   **FN**
This resale and consignment shop sells casual and business attire, shoes, purses, and jewelry. They're trying to expand their already large selection of 14+ sizes.

Selections
2152 N. Clybourn, 773/296-4014 **N**

Armani, Escada, DKNY, Ralph Lauren, Dana Buchman...these are the types of labels (and relative price tags) to expect from **Selections'** selection of better consignment clothing and accessories. Small men's section. Closed Mondays.

Style and Substance
2249 W. 111th, 773/881-8007 **FSW**

Designer clothing (DKNY, Ellen Tracy, Liz Claiborne, and Armani) is chosen, at this consignment shop on the city's periphery, to appeal to a wide range of customer styles and sizes. Also, shoes, purses, and scarves.

⇒ CLOTHING (WOMEN'S AND MEN'S)

Disgraceland
3330 N. Clark, 773/281-5875 **N**

Disgraceland specializes in high-quality casual wear (mostly current, some vintage) from labels like the Limited, Gap, and Betsy Johnson—lot of jeans, shoes, and boots. Also, jewelry, hats, scarves, and accessories.

Ragstock
812 W. Belmont, 2nd floor, 773/868-9263 **N**

60s & 70s retrowear, flannels, military surplus, kimonos, and inexpensive new clothing for those inclined towards mix-and-match creative dressing.

Threads, Etc.
1400 N. Milwaukee, 773/276-6411 **W**

Better casual and formal threads for men and women: Brooks Brothers, Armani, Polo, Mark Shale, Ann Taylor, Ann Klein, Liz Claiborne, Gap, Levi's, Express, and Banana Republic typify the labels available here. Collection includes jeans, leather, formalwear, shoes, accessories, purses, belts, jewelry, and some vintage items.

⇒ COMPUTERS

Chicago Computer Exchange
5255 S. Harper, 773/667-5221 **S**

In this basement level store in the Harper Court shopping district area, computer terminals, consoles, and innards are stacked from floor to ceiling. There's even a bathtub next to the staircase filled with computers. The operation is exactly what it's name says: you can bring in new or used computers and sell or exchange them for other computers. The Exchange also offers delivery, set-up, and networking services.

Chicago Cyber Exchange
237 W. North, 312/337-4882   **C**
Though used computer games and software are the big-sellers here, they're just some of the ways that one can save on the high costs of being a technophile. Used hardware is also available, including complete computer systems. Staff members build, fix, restore, and maintain systems. All software is checked for viruses and to ensure it's in proper working order. Trade old computers for new software; receive in-store credit for most software and cash for current titles.

⇒ FURNITURE (HOME)

Betty's Resale Shop
3439 N. Lincoln, 773/929-6143   **N**
If there's one place northsiders think of when they think used furniture, it's **Betty's** ...everyone seems to know about it. I suppose you can't miss it, with furniture stacked floor to ceiling, only foot-wide aisles allowing passage, spilling over into an adjacent lot, and sprawling out onto the front sidewalk. Open seven days a week, 9am-8pm, this neighborhood fixture took off as property values rose and young professionals started moving in. Now, you'll see Betty and "Betty, Jr." outside all day long unloading truck after truck of used furniture—paying and collecting with fistfuls of cash. Some say "over-priced junk," others say "great finds" (if you can tolerate the cats). It's probably somewhere in between and definitely an experience.

Other northside places include **Broadway Used Furniture** (6241 N. Broadway, 773/761-9945), **Chicago Recycle Shop** (5308 N. Clark, 773/878-8525), **Interiors on Consignment** (2150 N. Clybourn, 773/868-0797), and **Lake Shoppe New & Used Furniture** (4009 N. Broadway, 773/525-2518). They all carry a range of living room, dining room, bedroom, and kitchen furniture, but **Chicago Recycle** also carries antiques, collectibles, and some elaborate carpeting, and **Lake Shoppe** has box springs and mattresses. **Interiors on Consignment** is quite posh and has a decent selection of lamps, lighting, fixtures, and sofa beds.

Heading west, there's **Justine Furniture Inc.** (5303 W. Chicago, 773/261-7065) for bedroom and dining room sets, dressers, chairs, and couches. **Nancy's** (3642 W. Belmont, 773/478-5059) on the northwest side deals in furniture for every room of the house, plus oil paintings, dishes, and linens.

Southward, **Curtis Furniture Exchange** (5925 S. Halsted, 773/487-3450), **McCoy Real New & Used Furniture & Appliance** (7257 S. Halsted, 773/994-9000), and **Mose's New & Used Furniture** (504 E. 71st, 773/994-4900) carry the typical assortment of couches, lamps, tables, dressers, dinettes, and bedroom sets. **Curtis** and **McCoy** also handle stoves, refrigerators, and freezers.

⇒ FURNITURE (HOTEL/MOTEL)

Cooper Furniture Inc.
1929-33 S. Halsted, 312/226-2299   **C**
Don't stay at the Four Seasons, Ambassador East, Hyatt, Hilton, or Marriott as often as you would like? Maybe you need a trip to this 7-floor jungle to pick up some used pieces from these hoteliers for your own home. **Cooper Furniture** has been in the business for over 60 years, redistributing hotel items like bedding, carpeting, lobby furniture, chandeliers, mirrors, paintings and prints, telephones, electronics, and tablecloths to the public. Open seven days a week.

Less monstrous are **Fort Pitt Associates** (3500 S. Morgan, 773/247-3523) and **Windy City Furniture** (2221 S. Michigan, 312/225-9777), which also deal in used hotel/motel furniture. Armoires, dressers, beds, sofas, chairs, tables, lamps, mirrors, and carpets: they resell nearly everything but the "Do Not Disturb" signs.

⇒ FURNITURE (OFFICE)

While these stores don't offer garage sale prices, their office furniture is still available well below the list price. On the near north side, choose between **Chicago Office Furniture** (1030 W. North, 312/649-7100) and **Gently Used Office Furniture** (1300 W. North, 773/276-6200). Further north, are the **Direct Office Furniture Warehouses** (5041 N. Western, 773/271-3000 and 7232 N. Western, 773/465-3300). All carry a wide variety of chairs, desks, file cabinets, and workstations/modular units. Sometimes there's even wall paper, carpeting, hanging files, manila folders, floppy disks, and the like to be found.

⇒ GAMES

Windy City Game Exchange
3900 N. Cicero, 773/202-1077   **NW**
Buy, sell, and trade used video game cartridges and systems, from older
models to the most hi-tech. Chicago's best collection: Atari Jaguar, Super
Nintendo, Nintendo 64, Gameboy, Sega, Sony Playstation, Turbo Grafix 16,
3DO, computer games, and more.

⇒ MOVIES

Audio Visual
2449 N. Lincoln, 773/871-1928   **N**
From Jim Mahercy, owner of the **Second Hand Tunes** chain of used music
stores, comes the opportunity to buy, rent, and sell cult, classic, foreign,
independent, rare, and out-of-print movies. Don't know what you want to
watch? Let the hilarious categories guide you to something of interest:
Medical Melodramas, Friendly Animals, Classic TV Commercials, Worthy
Sequels,1950s Sex Hygiene Scare Films, Gangsta Flicks, Technology Run
Amok, Bad Sci-Fi. Before taking home *Santa Claus Conquers the Martians*,
stay and browse the used music, audio books, and video game selection.
Also, posters, postcards, and magazines.

⇒ MUSIC (RECORDS, CASSETTES, AND CDS)

Beverly Records
11626 S. Western, 773/779-0066   **FSW**
Current and dusty 45s, 78s, LPs, tapes, and CDs. Big band, country/western,
jazz, karaoke, and soundtracks. Collectibles and rare finds.

Chris & Heather's Record Roundup
2034 W. Montrose, 773/271-5330   **N**
It's a sure bet that you've never been in a record *or* resale store quite like the
one recently opened by local cartoonist Heather McAdams and her musician
husband Chris. While they carry all styles of music on vinyl, about 1/2 of the
collection is old country music or "weird spoken word stuff." Heather's
artwork, found art, old toys, knickknacks, and 16mm films are also sold.
Some of those films may be shown during one of their regular public
viewings. Hurry in, partner—the candy banjos and clocks made out of
records are going fast.

Disc Go Round
2412 N. Lincoln, 773/519-1133   N
3182 N. Clark, 773/404-4955   N
Buy, sell, trade, and exchange CDs, primarily rock, jazz, and R & B. Also sells posters, patches, bumper stickers, and other accouterments of fandom.

Disconnect Records
3131 N. Broadway, 773/248-5195   N
New and used CDs include imports, box sets, and local bands. Plus, videos, movies, posters, T-shirts, and collectibles.

Dr. Wax
5210 S. Harper, 773/493-8696   S
2523 N. Clark, 773/549-3377   N
1203 N. State, 312/255-0123   C
Records, tapes, and CDs. Alternative, jazz, reggae, rock, soul, and imports.

Evil Clown Compact Disc
3418 N. Halsted, 773/472-4761   N
Buy, sell, or exchange used CDs, cassettes, and records. Alternative, Britpop, dance, Gothic, imports, indie rock, industrial, jungle, Krautrock, new wave, old jazz, punk, and technopop.

Frank's Record Store
4309 W. 63rd, 773/582-2559   SW
Classical, country, jazz, pop, rock, and soul records.

Gramaphone LTD
663 N. Clark, 773/472-3683   N
Records, tapes, and CDs. Dance specialty plus pop and rock.

Great Scott Records & Tapes
9523 S. Jeffery, 773/734-5317   FSW
Records, tapes, and CDs. Oldies specialty, with R & B, pop, gospel, rap, and hiphop sections.

HiFi Records
2570 N. Clark, 773/880-1002   N
All styles, all vinyl: 12", 45s, and 78s.

Hot Jams
5012 S. Pulaski, 773/581-5267   **SW**
Tapes and CDs. Acid, hip-hop, house, jungle, rap, and techno.

House of Music
2057 W. 95th, 773/239-4114   **FSW**
Records, tapes, and CDs. Blues, jazz, oldies, soul, and rare finds.

The Interval
5905 W. Irving Park, 773/286-9272   **NW**
LPs, 45s, tapes, CDs of all stripes. Guitar and drum instruction available on
the premises.

Jazz Record Mart
444 N. Wabash, 312/222-1467   **C**
Records, tapes, and CDs. In business for over 40 years, **Jazz Record Mart**
boasts the largest jazz and blues collection in the world. Other musical styles
also available.

Laurie's Planet of Sound
4703 N. Lincoln, 773/271-3569   **N**
New and used records, CDs, and tapes. Plus, alternative videos and books,
'zines, posters, and other music paraphernalia.

Out of the Past Records
4407 W. Madison, 773/626-3878   **W**
LPs, 45s, and tapes. Dusties, jazz, R & B, and gospel.

The Quaker Goes Deaf
1937 W. North, 773/252-9334   **W**
Chicago's self-proclaimed "most dangerous record store" that carries "all
the strange stuff." Stock includes new and used imports and indie label
domestic releases, along with rare and collectible music and artifacts. Tapes,
CDs, and records, plus books, videos, and magazines.

Raffe's Record Riot
6714 N. Northwest Highway, 773/763-5075   **FN**
Tapes, CDs, and 100,000 records, as well as memorabilia and collectibles.

Reckless Records
3157 N. Broadway, 773/404-5080   **N**
2055 W. North, 773/235-3727   **W**
Records, tapes, CDs, videos, and laserdiscs. They carry "everything," which naturally includes the unusual, interesting, rare, and imported.

Record Dugout Used Records
4220 W. 63rd, 773/582-8080   **SW**
Records of the 50s, 60s, and 70s and...baseball cards.

Record Emporium
3346 N. Paulina, 773/248-1821   **N**
Records, tapes, CDs, and memorabilia. Alternative and mainstream rock, jazz, and blues.

Record Exchange
925 W. Belmont, 773/975-1904   **N**
1505 W. Morse, 773/973-0452   **FN**
Records, tapes, CDs, and videos. Large dance and techno selections.

2nd Hand Tunes
2602 N. Clark, 773/929-6325   **N**
2604 N. Clark, 773/281-8813   **N**
1377 E. 53rd, 773/684-3375   **S**
Chicago's oldest (22 years) and largest used record, tape, and CD chain with three city and three suburban stores. They specialize in the rare, out-of-print, and obscure.

Sound Booth
1151 W. Webster, 773/528-5156   **N**
CDs plus T-shirts and accessories.

Topper's Recordtown
4619 N. Broadway, 773/878-2032   **FN**
Tapes and CDs. 1000s of oldies: pop, rock, soul, R & B, jazz, blues, and gospel.

Video Beat
2616 N. Clark, 773/871-6667   **N**
Music videos, records, tapes, and CDs. Lots of rock, from vintage to alternative.

⇒ SPORTING GOODS

The Northcenter neighborhood sports two used athletic equipment stores where goods are bought, sold, consigned, and exchanged: **Play It Again Sports** (2101 W. Irving Park, 773/463-9900) and **Sports Exchange** (4159 N. Western, 773/583-7283). **Play It Again** is larger, cleaner, brighter, pricier, and more neatly organized. They also carry new items as well as providing a good-sized driving range for customers to test out golf clubs. Closer in spirit to the typical resale shop is the crammed **Sports Exchange**, where they just might let you wrangle over a price or two.

Several small neighborhood shops afford good deals on used bicycles. **Blackstone Bike Co-op** (6100 S. Blackstone, 773/241-5458) sells used bikes fixed up by neighborhood kids in an apprentice-type program. **Urban Bikes** (1026 W. Leland, 773/728-5212) similarly receives some help from young neighborhood residents in offering used bicycles, used bike parts, and low-cost repairs. **Recycle** (1255 S. Wabash, 312/987-1080) and **Upgrade Cycle Works** (1062 N. Milwaukee, 773/489-7228) should also be checked for low-priced used and new bicycles.

Where to go when you need a cocktail, Middle Eastern appetizers, and your bike repaired—at a bargain—all at the same time? The **Easy Rider Bike Shop** (4119 N. Lincoln, 773/549-1240) is your simple solution. After 24 years of running a neighborhood bike shop and after 12 years of operating its adjoining fast food grill, **Easy Rider**'s owners have upgraded their burger stand to a casual dining restaurant. So, while your two-wheeler is getting an expert tune-up, step next door for some expert renditions of hummus, tabouleh, and baba ganouj.

⇒ STEREOS AND ELECTRONICS

Stereo Exchange
4743 N. Western, 773/784-0004   **N**
Primarily a repair shop where electronics are sent from around the country to be fixed, **The Stereo Exchange** also buys, sells, trades, and installs stereos, amps, speakers, VCRs, car alarms, and other home and auto electronics.

Non-Profit Resale Stores

When you don't mind picking and hunting, when you want the real bargains, or when you have a pet cause you like to support, take your business to one of the following shops.

The Ark Thrift Shop
1302 N. Milwaukee, 773/862-5011   **W**
3345 N. Lincoln, 773/248-1117   **N**
Medical, dental, barber/beautician, and job counseling services are among the many free offerings that **The Ark**—a Jewish social welfare agency—provides its constituents. They also run the only Kosher food pantry in the city, deliver Kosher meals to seniors and people with disabilities, and assist Russian Jews trying to establish themselves in the United States. **The Ark** is well-known for the high-quality of their ever-changing stock, especially in the furniture and housewares departments.

Brown Elephant Resale
3651 N. Halsted, 773/549-5943   **N**
3939 N. Ashland, 773/244-2930   **N**
The **Brown Elephant** stores benefit the Howard Brown Health Center—a health and human services organization serving the gay and lesbian community and offers extensive programs for AIDS patients and those who are HIV+. The concept behind this pioneering resale shop which does well over $1 million in annual sales has since spread to other American cities.

National Council of Jewish Women's Thrift Shop
1524 W. Howard, 773/764-2364   **FN**
Monies from this shop provide non-sectarian help, primarily to local women and children, via support for battered women, children's scholarships, and more. Some funds are used for international women's causes.

Roseland Christian Community Thrift Store
10858 S. Michigan, 773/264-5665   **FSE**
This store's income benefits the surrounding community in many ways—through a food pantry, a homeless shelter, summer programs for kids, job opportunities and economic development, emergency funds, and Christian ministry.

REMAR (REhabilitation of people on the MARgin of society)
Second Chance Resale Shops
917 S. Western, 312/243-3304   **W**
1539 N. Milwaukee, 773/384-0819   **W**
REMAR's profits supports Christian outreach and drug and alcohol abuse rehabilitation programs.

Society of St. Vincent DePaul Resale Shops
1043 N. Keeler, 773/235-6505   **W**
4738 N. Western, 773/334-1004   **N**
5413 S. Kedzie, 773/434-0109   **SW**
9321 S. Western, 773/881-0600   **FSW**
The chain of St. Vincent DePaul resale stores serves the poor, low-income, and bargain-hunting members of the Chicago populace in a variety of ways. Each store employs nearly 75 people—including seniors and the mentally disabled—providing training, new job skills, and advancement opportunities. Individuals in need are given vouchers for clothing and household supplies, allowing them to shop with dignity in the stores. Revenue supports **S.V.D.P.** programs that help with utility, rent, clothing, and basic supplies for the homeless and those who need to "get back on their feet." Non-useable goods are recycled in a responsible manner.

White Elephant Shop of Children's Memorial Hospital
2380 N. Lincoln, 773/281-3747   **N**
Buying an $8,000 Bob Mackie dress for $135 was among the recent ways a resale shopper helped the Children's Memorial Hospital's **White Elephant Shop** assist low-income families pay their children's medical bills. Good finds at good prices are the norm here—look for designer clothing for women, men, and children, artwork, TVs, telephones, appliances, furniture, and more. Other programs the shop supports include assistance to families of children with catastrophic illnesses, temporary relocation for people who have been displaced from public housing for asbestos and lead removal, and organ transplant research.

Like most other cities, Chicago has several resale stores operated by the typical non-profit thrift store administrators:

Goodwill Industries
1001 W. Van Buren, 312/491-2900   **C**
3039 N. Pulaski, 773/286-4744   **NW**
7010 W. Grand, 773/745-3839   **NW**

Salvation Army

1515 N. Milwaukee, 773/489-5194	**W**
2270 N. Clybourn, 773/477-1300	**N**
3055 W. 63rd, 773/476-8718	**SW**
3301 W. Montrose, 773/588-7343	**NW**
3837 W. Fullerton, 773/276-1955	**NW**
3868 N. Lincoln, 773/528-8893	**N**
5112 S. Ashland, 773/737-3335	**SW**
5713 W. Chicago, 773/287-9774	**W**

VFW Thrift Store

2919 N. Harlem, 773/836-9380 **NW**

Other shops' causes can be determined from their self-explanatory names: **Council for Jewish Elderly Good Byes Resale Shop** (3503 W. Lawrence, 773/583-5118), **Mount Sinai Hospital Resale Shop** (814 W. Diversey, 773/935-1434), and **N.S.A.R. (Northwest Suburban Aid to the Retarded) Thrift Shoppe** (7710 W. Touhy, 773/631-6230).

The proceeds from the **Luther North High School Thrift Shop** (6059 W. Addison, 773/725-4406) go into the general school operating budget to help defray tuition costs. **The Right Place** (5219 N. Clark, 773/561-7757) raises scholarship funds for the B. Zell Anshe Emet Day School, a private Jewish grammar school.

The **Firman Community Services Thrift Shop** (120 E. Garfield, 773/373-1433), **St. Pius Parish Store** (1701 W. 18th Place, 312/226-6234), and **Our Lady of Sorrow Resale** (3149 W. Jackson, 773/722-0861) all support various local programs for the disadvantaged.

Other Resale Stores

Finally, the most complete list anywhere of Chicago's plethora of second-hand shops... Consult it when you need to find someplace close or when you feel like browsing in another part of town.

⇒ **FAR NORTH**

Almost New Resale   7758 W. Talcott, 773/792-3260
American Thrift Store   3125 N. Central, 773/685-5566
Antique and Resale Shop   7214 N. Harlem, 773/631-1151
Bargain Boutique   6238 N. Northwest Highway, 773/594-6930

Chicago Recycle Shop   5308 N. Clark, 773/878-8525
Economy Resale Furniture   6600 N. Clark, 773/338-6560
Extra Second Hand   7029 N. Clark, 773/274-3151
I Remember Mama   6122 N. Northwest Highway, 773/631-1301
Northeast Resale Shop   6634 N. Clark, 773/338-1136
Northwest Resale Shop   6221 N. Milwaukee, 773/631-0530
Norwood Park Home Thrift Shop   6019 N. Nina, 773/763-3775
Resale House   7129 N. Clark, 773/743-5616
Simply Seconds   6310 N. Milwaukee, 773/631-8742
Treasures for All   7536 N. Ashland, 773/764-3020
Vespucci Resale Store   5202 N. Sheridan, 773/769-2670
Village Discount Outlet   4898 N. Clark, (no phone)

⇒ NORTH

Best Thrift   3115 W. Irving Park, 773/583-2880

Crusaders of America
1217 W. Wilson, 773/275-5949
Gives away some free clothes to the homeless in the neighborhood.

Finders Keepers   2467 N. Lincoln, 773/525-1510
Hollywood Mirror   812 W. Belmont, 773/404-4510
Kay Fra Paas Resale Shop   3511 N. Lincoln, 773/868-4888

Land of the Lost
614 W. Belmont, 773/529-4966
Among their general stock of vintage and resale clothes and collectibles, **Land of the Lost** has special collections of casual clothes, games, signs, glassware, and clocks.

Something Old Something New   1056 W. Belmont, 773/271-1300
Twice Treasured   5424 N. Milwaukee, 773/631-3117
Ultimately Yours Resale Shop   2931 N. Broadway, 773/975-1581
Unique Thrift Store   4112 N. Lincoln, 773/281-1590
Unique Thrift Store   4445 N. Sheridan, 773/275-8623
Village Discount Outlet   2855 N. Halsted, (no phone)
Village Discount Outlet   2032 N. Milwaukee, (no phone)
Village Discount Outlet   2043 W. Roscoe, (no phone)

⇒ NORTHWEST

A Niche In Time 5758 W. Irving Park, 773/685-3988
All Saints Resale Shop 2816 N. Laramie, 773/545-6818
Amara's Resale Shop 4712 W. Diversey, 773/283-1862
Bargain Basket Thrift Shop 4740 N. Austin, 773/481-6965
Community Thrift Store 3012 N. Central, 773/237-1441
Deja Vu 5315 W. Lawrence, 773/282-1177
Everything Under the Sun 5122 W. Grand, 773/622-1181

Lidias Resale
4340 N. Central, 773/205-5939
Maybe the largest resale shop in the area, **Lidias Resale** does a booming trade in used computers, peripherals, and software. Amongst the general merchandise at this 11,000-ft.^{2} store is an ample supply of TVs, VCRs, and other electronics; musical instruments; and antiques.

Second Time Around 3250 W. Montrose, 773/866-1928
This N That Resale Shop 4041 N. Milwaukee, 773/286-4116
Three Sisters Resale Shop 3951 W. Irving Park, 773/478-0430
Unique Thrift Store 4441 W. Diversey, 773/227-2282
Village Discount Outlet 4635 N. Elston, (no phone)
Village Discount Outlet 3301 W. Lawrence, (no phone)

⇒ CENTRAL

Frank's Second Shop 547 W. Roosevelt, 312/733-7733
R Z's Resale 1531 W. 18th, 312/733-4265

⇒ WEST

A & A Resale 1314 N. Pulaski, 773/276-2024
African National Treasury Resale Shop 3814 W. Chicago, 773/862-5303
Ann's Thrift Store 5 N. Cicero, 773/378-6023
Backseat Betty's 2053 W. North, 773/227-2427
Cheryl's Thrift Shop 14 S. Kostner, 773/921-4438
Laboy Resale 2615 W. North, 773/384-1318
Let's Do It Again Resale Shop 651 N. Cicero, 773/378-1342
Mark's Resale Shop 4755 W. Madison, 773/626-4299

⇒ **SOUTH**

Make Us An Offer   6459 S. Cottage Grove, 773/667-1295

⇒ **SOUTHWEST**

Unique Thrift Store   2329 S. Kedzie, 773/762-7510
Unique Thrift Store   3224 S. Halsted, 312/842-8123
Unique Thrift Store   3542 S. Archer, 773/247-2599
Unique Thrift Store   5040 S. Kedzie, 773/434-4886
Victory Resale Center   1022 W. 63rd, 773/476-4812
Village Discount Outlet   6419 S. Kedzie, (no phone)
Village Discount Outlet   4020 W. 26th, (no phone)
Village Discount Outlet   2514 W. 47th, (no phone)

⇒ **FAR SOUTHEAST**

Alice & Shannon   724 E. 79th, 773/224-0599
Alice Johnson Resale   2122 E. 75th, 773/752-7519
Davis Resale   125 E. 69th, 773/874-8662
Jackson Resale   6756 S. Stony Island, 773/667-9189
Oh's First and Second Shop   519 E. 79th, 773/783-3984
Ron & Jan's Resale #2   8123 S. Cottage Grove, 773/994-3321
Second Hand Rose Thrift Store   9237 S. Commercial, 773/978-4080
South End Thrift Shop   8533 S. Cottage Grove, 773/873-0717

⇒ **FAR SOUTHWEST**

L & B Resale New & Used   11123 S. Kedzie, 773/445-2023
Paradise Resale Shop   7849 S. Ashland, 773/651-1689
Roberts Antiques & Resale Shop   918 W. 119th, 773/660-9449
Unique Thrift Store   9341 S. Ashland, 773/239-3127
Village Discount Outlet   7443 S. Racine   (no phone)

MARKETS AND BAZAARS

Flea markets and bazaars: an ideal leisurely weekend activity for browsing for your cheap buys and watching others browse for theirs...

Ashland Swap-O-Rama
4100 S. Ashland, 708/344-7300   **SW**
The owners of this 110,000-ft.^{2} flea market in the Back of the Yards
neighborhood like to brag that you can find "everything that's legal to sell"
here. Stadium-sized bathrooms, multi-ethnic concessions, and kiddie
distractions make it easy for shoppers to stay all day. Thur. 8am-8pm,
Sat.-Sun. 7am-4pm. $.50 admission fee.

Buyer's Flea Market
4545 W. Division, 773/227-1889   **W**
Year-round weekend flea market features hundreds of dealers indoors, with
more outdoors as the weather allows. Children's kiddieland and ample
parking on the premises. The CTA's Division Street bus will drop you off in
front of the place. Open Sat.-Sun. 8am-5pm.

Little Village Discount Mall
Little Village Plaza at about 3100 W. 26th   **SW**
Walk up and down the endless aisles of vendors at this indoor market and
you just might think you've been transported to Mexico. Find good bargains
on clothes (lots of dresswear), leather, jewelry, shoes, cowboy boots, music,
electronics, hardware, and toys. Refuel at the food booths.

Supermall of the Midway
52nd & Pulaski   **SW**
Take the Mexican atmosphere of the **Little Village Mall**, add a touch of
Korea, and you'll have the **Supermall of the Midway**. This cavernous
building, subdivided into 10' x 10' stalls, sells mostly clothing, but a bit of
everything else. Open seven days a week, 10am-7pm. Plan to bring cash;
very few of the vendors accept credit cards.

Similar malls in different neighborhoods are also popular with immigrants—
both as shoppers and vendors—and make great places to experience some of
Chicago's cultural diversity while bargain hunting: **The Clark Mall** (7212
N. Clark, 773/764-7091) and the **Logan Square Discount Mega Mall**
(2502 N. Milwaukee, 773/489-2525). The **Logan Square Mall** has a
particularly wide assortment of international food booths that serve up
endless American fast food favorites, Asian dishes, Mexican specialties, and
traditional Puerto Rican fare.

Maxwell Street Market
Canal Street between Roosevelt Road and 17th Street   **C**
Over one hundred years old, the **Maxwell Street Market** was at one time

the largest open-air market in the world. Some thought this bargain hunters' nirvana should have received landmark designation. Others with more power thought it was a dump and had been trying to shut it down or relocate it for years—especially because of the expanding University of Illinois. These folks succeeded a few years back. As of September 1994, the market has been located a few blocks east of its original location (Halsted & Maxwell St.) on Canal Street. This new site has room for only half of the regular Maxwell Street vendors, but retains much of the commotion of the original Maxwell Street Market, including nearly 500 vendors, musicians, food booths (particularly Mexican stands and carts), and serious haggling. Sundays 7am-3pm.

Morgan Street Market
375 N. Morgan, 312/455-8900   **C**
Weekend flea market in an old railroad building. Open Sat.-Sun. 8am-5pm.

PUBLIC AUCTIONS

Chicago Police Department's
Evidence and Recovered Property Auction
Washburne Trade School, 31st & Kedzie, 312/747-6224   **SW**
One Saturday a month, the **CPD's Evidence and Recovered Property Unit** auctions off a mountain of unclaimed merchandise from tools to bicycles to shoes to stereo equipment. The auction begins at 10am and ends when everything has been sold—usually about 3 or 4pm. Sale items can be viewed on the Friday afternoon before the auction from 1pm-3pm and on the morning of the auction from 8:30am-10am. Call the above number to get a list of upcoming auction dates, because the Saturday varies from month to month. No entrance fee.

9 KEEPING INFORMED

Though long past its railroad heyday, Chicago still supports
a bustling network of trains—a portion of which is seen here,
tucked between downtown and Grant Park.
(*Photo by Rames Shrestha.*)

KEEPING INFORMED

A *Native's Guide To Chicago* will help you navigate through permanent, or, at least, semi-permanent Chicago. To stay current, however, with the changing, developing, and fleeting Chicago requires additional and ongoing effort. The phone, radio, television, internet, and print resources listed in this chapter should keep you moving with the day-to-day news and events that enliven our city.

PHONE NUMBERS/HOTLINES TO KNOW

Basics

City Council Information	312/744-3081
Dental Referral Service	312/836-7305
Emergency	911
Fire Department (non-emergency)	312/744-6666
Library - Main Branch (Harold Washington)	312/747-4300
Mayor's Office of Inquiry and Information	312/744-5000
Medical Referral Service	312/670-2550
Police Department (non-emergency)	312/746-6000
Post Office (CustomerService Center)	312/765-4357
Time	312/976-8463
Weather	312/976-1212
Zip Code Information	312/765-3585

Cultural Events

Chicago Architecture Foundation	312/922-3432
Chicago Fine Arts Hotline	312/346-3278
Chicago Live Concerts (Popular Music)	312/666-6667

Chicago Music Alliance (Opera/Classical)	312/987-9296
Dance Hotline	312/419-8383
Dial-a-Poem	312/346-3478
Grant Park Music Festival	312/742-4763
Jazz Hotline	312/427-3300

Mayor's Office of Special Events
The place to call for info. on parades, summer festivals, art shows, concerts, etc.

⇒ **General**	312/744-3315
⇒ **24-Hour Hotline**	312/744-3370
⇒ **Film and Entertainment**	312/744-6415
⇒ **TDD**	312/744-2964
Movie Phone	312/444-3456

Dining

Illinois Restaurant Association	312/787-4000

Lodging

Hotel/Motel Association of Illinois	312/236-3473
Hot Rooms (Discount Rooms Downtown)	773/468-7666

Sports and Recreation

Chicago Park District	312/747-2200
Chicago Park District/TDD	312/986-0726
Sports Information	312/976-1313
Sports Scoreboard Recap	312/976-2525

Tickets

Hot Tix Hotline	312/977-1755
Ticket Master	312/559-1212

Tourist Information

Chicago Convention and Tourism Bureau	312/567-8500
Chicago Office of Tourism	312/744-2400
Chicago Office of Tourism/TDD	312/744-2947
City Information for the Hearing Impaired/TDD	312/744-8599

Illinois Bureau of Tourism	800-223-0121
Travelers and Immigrants Aid	773/489-7303

Transportation

American United Cab	773/248-7600
Amtrak Union Station	312/558-1075
Amtrak Fare & Scheduling Information	800/USA-RAIL
Yellow Cab	312/829-4222
Chicago Transit Authority (CTA)	312/836-7000
Route/schedule/fare information	
Flash Cab	773/561-1444
Greyhound Bus	800-231-2222
Illinois Department of Transportation	
312/DOT-INFO	
Automobile traffic information	
Meig's Field	312/744-4787
METRA (Regional Transit)	312/836-7000
Route/schedule/fare information	
Midway Airport	773/767-0500
O'Hare International Airport	773/686-2200
Pace (Suburban Buses)	312/836-7000
Route/schedule/fare information	
Skyway Information	312/747-8383
Tollroad Authority	773/242-3620

RADIO PROGRAMMING

Need some different music for your morning commute? News in Spanish or Polish? Want to comment on da Bulls or dem Bears? An intellectual analysis of a new city program? Consult the following list for your radio information and entertainment needs.

News/Talk

WBEZ (91.5 FM) Public radio, news, talk, jazz
WMAQ (670 AM) News, Bears and Blackawks games, old-time radio shows
WGN (720 AM) Chicago talk shows, Cubs games
WBBM (780 AM) News

WYPA (820 AM) Personal achievement radio
WLS (890 AM) Talk

> In a town of bigger and better boasts, even radio station call letters get into the act. **WLS**, once owned by Sears Roebuck, came from the department store's moniker, "World's Largest Store." (Speaking of superlatives, **WLS** is now owned by Disney.) The *Chicago Tribune*'s radio station, **WGN** (World's Greatest Newspaper), is equally prideful. Yet, neither can beat the claim of **WBBM**: We Broadcast Better Music.

Sports

WSCR (820 AM) Sports talk, "The Score"
WMVP (1000 AM) Chicago sports talk, White Sox games

Ethnic

WOJO (105.1 FM) Spanish
WIND (560 AM) Spanish
WSBC (1240 AM) Foreign language programming: Spanish, Polish, Greek Italian, Thai, Hindi, Gaelic, Russian, Ukrainian, and Latvian
WCEV (1450 AM) Chicago's Ethnic Voice—multi-ethnic local, religious, cultural, and news programming. Broadcasting in English, Polish, Croatian, Czech, Lithuanian, and Ukrainian.
WONX (1590 AM) Spanish

Music

WXRT (93.1 FM) Progressive and classic rock, blues, jazz
WLIT (93.9 FM) Light rock classics and contemporary
WCDX (94.7 FM) Classic rock
WNUA (95.5 FM) Smooth jazz, new age
WBBM (96.3 FM) Dance, pop, R & B
WNIB (97.1 FM) Classical
WLUP (97.9 FM) Rock
WFMT (98.7 FM) Classical, fine arts
WUSN (99.5 FM) Country
WNND (100.3 FM) Adult contemporary
WKQX (101 FM) Alternative, new rock

WTMX (101.9 FM) Adult contemporary
WVAZ (102.7 FM) Urban adult contemporary, dusties
WXXY (103.1 FM) R & B
WRCX (103.5 FM) Hard rock, alternative, metal
WJMK (104.3 FM) Oldies
WCKG (105.9 FM) Classic rock
WGCI (107.5 FM) Urban
WHN (1510 AM) Gospel

Chicago Radio on the Internet

Chicago Radio Online Watch
http://www.zecom.com/zecom/crow
Keep informed about the latest in Chicago radio. Site includes news and analysis.

Low End (Non-Commericial FM Radio in Chicagoland)
http://www.geocities.com/SunsetStrip/Alley/2246
Listing of all local high shool, college, and public radio sites in the Chicago area.

Broadcasting in Chicago: 1921-1989
http://www.mcs.net/~richsam
This beautiful page gives an in-depth history (with photos) of broadcasting in Chicago, with special emphasis on the NBC Studios in the Merchandise Mart.

TELEVISION

Network TV

ABC/WLS (Channel 7)
http://www.abcnews.com/local/wls

CBS/WBBM (Channel 2)
http://wbbm.cbsnow.com

NBC/WMAQ (Channel 5)
http://www.nbc5chi.com

FOX/WFLD (Channel 32)

⇒ **Fox Thing In The Morning** (Weekdays, 7-9am)
Many Chicagoans begin their day with the offbeat news show of anchors Bob Sirott and Marianne Murciano. Among their trademark segments are "Extremely Local News," "In Bed With..." celebrity interviews, and movie reviews by local personalities.

PBS/WTTW (Channel 11)
http://www.wttw.com

⇒ **Art Beat** (Wed. 7:30pm, re-broadcast Fri.10:30pm and Sat. 11pm)
Arts magazine showcases cultural and artistic events in the Chicago area.

⇒ **Chicago Matters** (Mon. 9pm)
The **Chicago Matters** series explores local issues around a new theme every year. This year, it's "Regionalism & Community." Past topics have been the environment, aging, childhood, race relations, violence, immigration, religion, and work.

⇒ **Chicago Tonight with John Callaway**
(Mon.-Thur. 7pm, re-broadcast at 10pm, 1am, and 5am)
John Callaway hosts one of the the only prime-time public TV news programs in the country. Four nights a week, he moderates a panel of various guests as they discuss and analyze Chicago politics, art, foreign affairs, consumer concerns, sports, and more.

⇒ **Chicago Week in Review** (Sat. 6pm, re-broadcast Sun. at 5am)
Emmy winning conversation show in it's 20th season brings together a new lineup of reporters, editors, columnists, and newscasters every week to examine the week's events. Hosted by Joel Weisman.

⇒ **Wild Chicago** (Sun. 10:30pm, re-broadcast Fri. 11:30pm)
Zany investigations into out-of-the-ordinary people, places, and things in Chicago and the surrounding area.

UPN/WPWR (Channel 50)

⇒ **Ben Loves Chicago** (Sundays, 10pm)
http://www.adscape.com/ben
Ben Hollis, one of the co-creators and original host of Emmy Award

winning *Wild Chicago,* continues his search for the interesting and unique things, places, and especially, people of Chicago. Two of his regular features, "Ben's Instant Talk Show" and his "Sleep Over" segments (he's slept over at a firehouse and in people's basements), bring to light the idiosynchracies of everyday Chicagoans.

WGN (Channel 9)
http://www.wgntv.com
One of the country's most popular local television stations and home of the Chicago Cubs games.

WYCC (Channel 20)
http://www.ccc.edu/wycc/home.htm
WYCC is the television station of Chicago's City Colleges.

⇒ **Absolute Artistry** (Sun. 7:30pm and Wed. 7pm)
Features and interviews focusing on the local theater and arts scenes.

⇒ **First From Chicago** (Sun. 7pm)
In-depth interviews with interesting Chicagoans by host Lowell Beck.

> TV soap operas originated in Chicago in 1949 with the airing of NBC's *These Are My Children.*

Cable TV

CLTV (Channel depends on cable service)
http://cltv.com
Chicago Land TV. 24-hour, all news cable channel for the Chicago area owned by the *Chicago Tribune.*

⇒ **Front & Center** (Thurs. 5:30pm)
Weekly forum allows viewers to speak to local lawmakers, celebrities, and major figures in Chicagoland news and air their thoughts on the latest issues of local and national importance.

Municipal Information Channel
(Channel depends on cable service)
The City of Chicago's cable channels offer continuous Chicago-oriented programming covering news, music, education, health, sports, politics,

social issues, and more. From 2am-Noon and in between regular shows, the station runs an informational bulletin board listing Chicago Park District and city job opportunities, an aldermanic directory, public service announcements, and upcoming community events.

INTERNET SITES

Chicago Area Statistics and General Facts

Chicago Fact Book
http://www.ci.chi.il.us/WorksMart/Planning/ChgoFacts/
Fun and sundry facts about Chicago, geography, climate, demographics, and statistics on conventions, education, business, housing, health care, and more.

Best Collection of Chicago History Links on the Web
http://www.suba.com/~scottn/explore/links/links2.htm
Scott Newman's massive list of Chicago history links covers general Chicago history, famous Chicagoans, major events, organizations & businesses, popular culture & fine arts, transportation, architecture, lost and existent landmarks, history-related museums, libraries & archives, and more!

Chicago Public Library Chicago Information
http://www.chipublib.org/004chicago/004chicago.html
Compiled by librarians from the Chicago Public Library and the Municipal Reference Library, this site gives oddball facts, municipal details, and historical information along with massive links to all things Chicago. Learn the city motto, charter, corporate seal, flower, and flag. Get bios and pics of past mayors, histories of the police and fire departments, and a master timeline of the Windy City's history.

Chicago Public Library's Frequently Requested Phone Number List
http://www.chipublib.org/004chicago/chicfreq.html
An extensive list of phone numbers most often requested from the Chicago Public Library: AIDS information and testing, Alcoholics Anonymous, contacting your alderman, the arson hotline, Better Business Bureau, CTA route info., grammar hotlines at local universities, homework hotline, legal services for low income families, passport information, and many more.

Directory of City Services and Departments
http://www.ci.chi.il.us/WorksMart
Links to the City Council, alderman & ward offices, and all city departments
& agencies.

Chicago Area Government Information Locator
http://www.chicagoinfo.fed.gov
Chicago area "information gateway" for federal, state, and local government
services. "A virtual file cabinet..." Information for individuals, business, and
non-profits.

Chicago Demographics
http://www.cagis.uic.edu/demographics/demographics_intro.html
UIC Geography Department spot provides Chicago area demographics;
statistical goodies like population, average income, and median age for
Chicago neighborhoods and suburbs; and transportation links like the CTA
subway map and an up-to-the-minute traffic congestion map for the
Milwaukee-Chicago-Gary area.

Metro Chicago Information Center
http://205.253.29.149
MCIC—a non-profit research organization supplying current Chicago data
for non-profits, government agencies, corporations, and research communities—has fascinating data on the metro Chicago area concerning health care,
personal finance, housing, poverty, employment, arts and culture, information technology, and more from their annual surveys.

Chicagoland Weather Report
http://iwin.nws.noaa.gov/iwin/il/local.html

Chicago Vocabulary Page
http://members.aol.com/mistamoose/vocab.html
A glossary of Chicago vernacular, shorthand, and "in the know" phrases—
useful for newcomers, enlightening for residents.

Chicago Newspapers and Magazines

Chicago Tribune
http://www.chicago.tribune.com

Chicago Sun-Times
http://www.suntimes.com/index

Chicago Magazine
http://www.chicagomag.com

Crain's Chicago Business
http://www.crainschicagobusiness.com

Chicago Reader
http://www.chireader.com

New City's Best of Chicago Issues, '93, '94, '95, '96, and '97
http://www.newcitychicago.com/boc.html

Lerner Community Newspapers
http://www.intheloop.com

Chicago Reporter
http://www.Chicagoreporter.com
Investigative reporting on race and poverty in Chicago since 1972.

Outlines
http://www.suba.com/~outlines/
Publications for Chicago's lesbian and gay community.

Comprehensive Chicago Pages

City of Chicago Page
http://www.ci.chi.il.us
The city of Chicago's Web site produced by the mayor's office contains a wealth of great Chicago info. both for tourists (interactive downtown map, electronic tour guide, information for student travellers, safety tips, current events, etc.) and residents (directory of city services, pubic school and public library info., date/time of next city council meeting, special events listings, and more).

Chicago Convention & Tourism Bureau
http://www.chicago.il.org
Some of the most current information on the internet about what's going on in Chicago—from theater and gallery offerings to specialty tours, events, and festivals. Also general info. on visiting the city, Navy Pier, and Mc-Cormick Place.

Chicago Tribune's Digital City
http://www.chicago.digitalcity.com
Encyclopedic collection of Chicago information and interactivity: virtual tours of the Chicago River and Chicago neighborhoods, how to find the lowest air fares from Chicago, extensive neighborhood information and statistics, city parking lot lowdown, series of "Best of Chicago" articles by *Tribune* staff, and more. Sections include news, sports, entertainment, visiting, and community.

Chicago Tribune's Metromix
http://www.metromix.com
The *Tribune*'s Chicago guide for the savvy urbanite. Massive searchable databases for nightclubs, film, art & culture, recreation, shopping, family, and more, plus several new feature articles a month in various departments—many on topics that would never appear in the *Trib* itself.

Chicago Web Guide to Chicago
http://www.chiweb.com
Gordon Lake's incredible Web page covers Chicago nightlife, hotels, restaurants, movies, events, sports, weather, transportation, family activities, and theater, as well as providing city maps, top Chicago Web sites, and local grocery store sales. Don't miss *Lake Shore Drive*, Chicago's first internet soap opera.

Chicgao Yahoo Homepage
http://www.yahoo.com/Regional/U_S__States/Illinois/Cities/
Chicago links to links. Major clearinghouse of Chicago information, particularly helpful for finding the more specialized, special interest pages.

Dive In Chicago
http://www.diveinchicago.com
Home of the Centerstage entertainment databases. Also get local news, movie & TV listings, traffic updates, customized maps, lottery results, and phone books here.

Chicago Page of CityNet
http://www.city.net/countries/united_states/illinois/chicago
Links to all the Chicago essentials: government, books & libraries, arts & entertainment, news & weather, food & drink, sports teams, and tour guides. Look for the lodging guides and restaurant reviews and guides.

Chicago First
http://www.chicagofirst.com
Community links (businesses, churches, schools, entertainment, events, lodging, organizations, restaurants, and shopping), recreation links (outdoors, sports, and state parks), and resource links (used car guides, government, health, kid stuff, maps, news, real estate, travel, and weather).

FREE PERIODICALS

A multitude of free publications connect Chicagoans with a range of communities and interest blocks. They're the perfect way to remain informed on a specific segment of Chicago society or learn more about one with which you're unfamiliar. Most can be found at a variety of stores, restaurants, coffeehouses, theaters, libraries, banks, or schools throughout the city. Contact the publishers of those that interest you to learn of a nearby drop-spot or how to be put on their mailing list. Try them all and walk the fine line between well-informed citizen and information junkie...

African-American Interest

N'DIGO
401 N. Wabash; Chicago, IL 60611; 312/822-0202
Biweekly newsmagazine for black Chicagoans.

Alternative Newspapers

New City
770 N. Halsted, Suite 208; Chicago, IL 60622; 312/243-8786
Weekly Chicago news and arts paper with extensive event listings.

Reader
11 E. Illinois; Chicago, IL 60611; 312/828-0350
Nearly the size of the Sunday paper, the *Reader* may be the largest free alternative weekly in the United States, noted for its in-depth cover stories; comprehensive coverage of art, movies, music and theatre goings-on; and an overwhelming classified section.

Bar Scene

Barfly
2821 N. Milwaukee; Chicago, IL 60618; 773/489-6890
Extensive monthly review of Chicago's bars and bar scene.

Chicago

Chicago Life
P.O. Box 11131; Chicago, IL 60611; 773/528-2737
Bimonthly Chicago edition of a national chain magazine, containing a few Chicago features among many general articles and lots of Chicago advertising.

Chicago Official Visitors Guide
Chicago Convention and Tourism Bureau, 312/567-8500
McCormick Place on the Lake; 2301 S. Lake Shore Drive; Chicago, IL 60616
Quarterly visitors' guide published by the Chicago Convention and Tourism Bureau.

Key Magazine
904 W. Blackhawk; Chicago, IL 60622; 312/943-0838
Weekly Chicago visitors' info. guide that has been around since 1920.

Premier Chicago
450 E. Ohio, Suite 500; Chicago, IL 60611; 312/664-7100
Monthly visitors' magazine distributed in premier hotels.

Spotlight Chicago
6008 W. Belmont; Chicago, IL 60634; 773/283-7900
Small, city-wide weekly, covering Chicago happenings.

WHERE Magazine
1165 N. Clark; Chicago, IL 60610; 312/642-1896
Monthly visitors' magazine covering shopping, theater, dining, nightlife, and events. Available mostly in hotels and tourism offices.

Children/Parents

Chicago Parent
Wednesday Journal
141 S. Oak Park Avenue; Oak Park, IL 60302; 708/386-5555
Hefty, all-purpose monthly newsmagazine aimed at Chicago parents and their children.

Cultural Centers/Museums

Chicago Cultural Center Calendar of Free Events
Chicago Cultural Center
78 E. Washington; Chicago, IL 60602; 312/744-6630
Monthly calendar of free events (concerts, films, lectures, exhibits, dances, etc.) at the Chicago Cultural Center.

Children's Programs at Harold Washington Library Center Calendar
HWLC; 400 S. State St.; Chicago, IL 60605; 312/747-4200
Monthly listing of programs for kids in the Thomas Hughes Children's Library of the Harold Washington Library Center.

Harold Washington Library Center Calendar of Events
HWLC; 400 S. State St.; Chicago, IL 60605; 312/747-4999
Monthly calendar of free events (concerts, plays, dances, exhibits, films, lectures, workshops, etc.) at the Harold Washington Library Center.

Past Times
Chicago Historical Society
1610 N. Clark; Chicago, IL 60614; 312/642-4600
Quarterly calendar and newsletter of The Chicago Historical Society.

Film

Chicago Filmmakers Schedule of Events
Chicago Filmmakers; 1543 W. Division; Chicago, IL 60622; 773/384-5533
Quarterly newsletter with articles, class/workshop/film schedules, and film festival listings.

Film Center Gazette
The Film Center; School of the Art Institute of Chicago
280 S. Columbus; Chicago, IL 60603; 312/443-3733

Monthly publication of the Film Center of the School of the Art Institute of Chicago, featuring articles, movie schedule, and membership information.

Films at Facets Schedule
Facets Multimedia; 1517 W. Fullerton; Chicago, IL 60614; 773/281-4114
Bimonthly schedule of films and classes.

Gay and Lesbian Interest

Gay Chicago
3121 N. Broadway; Chicago, IL 60657; 773/327-7271
20-year-old weekly newsmagazine for gay men filled with local and national news, theatre and restaurant reviews, columnists, events and nightlife calendar, and extensive classifieds.

Outlines
Lambda Publications; 1115 W. Belmont; Chicago, IL 60657; 773/871-7610
"The Voice of the Gay and Lesbian Community." Monthly newspaper covering local and national news. Also publishes *Nightlines*—a weekly publication devoted to gay nightlife and local events and *Blacklines* for the black gay and lesbian community.

Windy City Times
325 W. Huron Chicago, IL 60610; 312/397-0025
Lesbian and gay newsweekly covers local and national news, books, theatre, and events.

Jewish Interest

Chicago Jewish Star
Star Media Group, Inc.
P.O. Box 268; Skokie, IL 60076-0014; 847/674-STAR
Chicago's largest independent Jewish newspaper, published twice monthly, covers local, national, and international news and includes commentary and a calendar of events.

Literary

Strong Coffee
P.O. Box 1959; Evanston, IL 60204; 847/338-5383
Monthly collection of ideas, art, poetry, and fiction for the coffeehouse crowd.

Music

Illinois Entertainer
2250 E. Devon; Des Plaines, IL 60018; 708/298-9333
Music monthly with articles, interviews, schedules, local band directory, and classifieds for musicians.

Neighborhoods

Your local neighborhood papers, often found in banks, bars, libraries, restaurants, and stores are invaluable resources for keeping in touch with neighborhood and city happenings.

New Age

The Monthly Aspectarian
TMA Communications, Inc.
6407 W. Elm St.; Morton Grove, IL 60053; 847/966-1110
Chicago's monthly 100-page New Age magazine, with articles, resources, and calendars of events.

Over Fifty Interest

Vital Times
Chicagoland Seniors Communications; 847/498-4004
1500 Skokie Blvd.; Suite 330; Northbrook, IL 60062;
General monthly paper geared towards those over fifty.

Socially Conscious

Conscious Choice
920 N. Franklin; Suite 301; Chicago, IL 60610; 312/440-4373
Ample bimonthly covers ecology and natural living at local, regional, and national level.

Spanish Language

Exito!
820 N. Orleans; Chicago, IL 60610; 312/654-3000
Spanish weekly covers local, national, and international news, plus Chicago entertainment and special events. Can be found in special newsboxes in neighborhoods with high-concentrations of Spanish speakers.

Sports

Chicago Runner Magazine
1450 W. Randolph; Chicago, IL 60607;312/421-1551
Quarterly magazine of the Chicago Area Runners Association, with articles and race/event information.

Windy City Sports
1450 W. Randolph; Chicago, IL 60607; 312/421-1551
Monthly magazine for the Chicago athlete: articles, resources, and schedules of events.

Theater

PerformINK
3223 N. Sheffield; Chicago, IL 60657; 773/296-4600
Biweekly publication devoted to the Chicago theatre scene, focusing particularly on items of interest to actors and others in the business.

Women's Interest

Chicagoland's Healthy Woman
141 S. Oak Park; Oak Park, IL 60302; 708/386-5555
New quarterly magazine focuses on health topics of interest to women through articles and columns, many with a regional slant.

Today's Chicago Woman
Leigh Communications, Inc., 312/951-7600
233 E. Ontario Street, Suite 1300; Chicago, IL 60611;
Large monthly newspaper for women, with an emphasis on professional life, image, networking, etc.

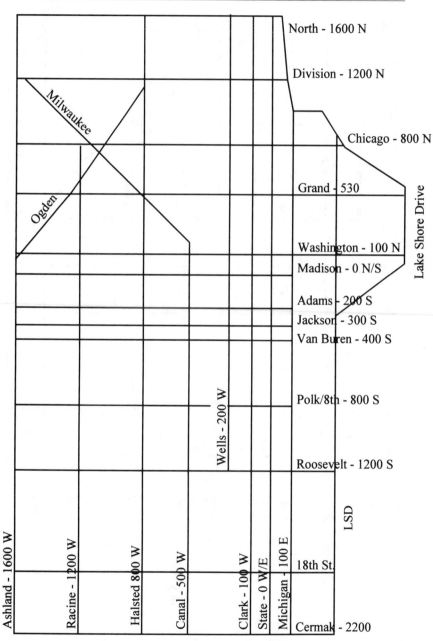

North - 1600 N

Division - 1200 N

Milwaukee

Chicago - 800 N

Grand - 530

Ogden

Lake Shore Drive

Washington - 100 N

Madison - 0 N/S

Adams - 200 S

Jackson - 300 S

Van Buren - 400 S

Polk/8th - 800 S

Wells - 200 W

Roosevelt - 1200 S

LSD

Ashland - 1600 W

Racine - 1200 W

Halsted 800 W

Canal - 500 W

Clark - 100 W

State - 0 W/E

Michigan - 100 E

18th St.

Cermak - 2200

CENTRAL

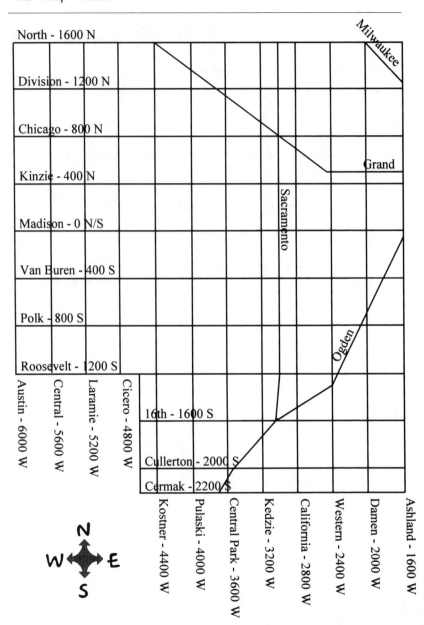

WEST

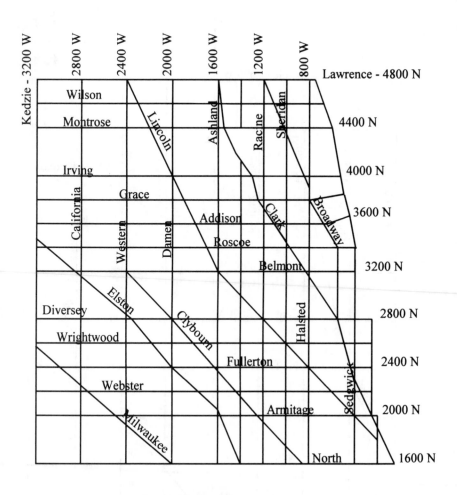

NORTH

Cumberland - 8400 W

Oriole - 7600 W

Harlem - 7200 W

W

S — N

E

Oak Park - 6800 W

North - 1600 N

Armitage - 2000 N

Fullerton - 2400 N

Diversey - 2800 N

Belmont - 3200 N

Addison - 3600 N

Narragansett - 6400 W

Irving Park - 4000 N

Montrose - 4400 N

Lawrence - 4800 N

Austin - 6000 W

Central - 5600 W

Laramie - 5200 W

Grand

Cicero - 4800 W

Kostner - 4400 W

Milwaukee

Pulaski - 4000 W

Elston

Central Park - 3600 W

Kedzie - 3200 W

NORTHWEST

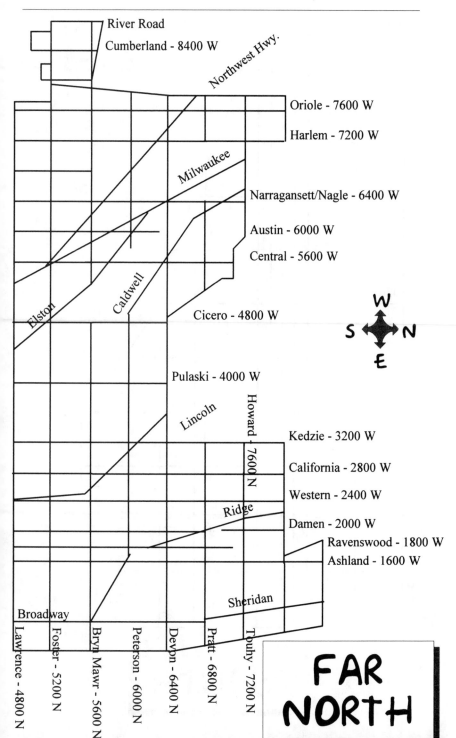

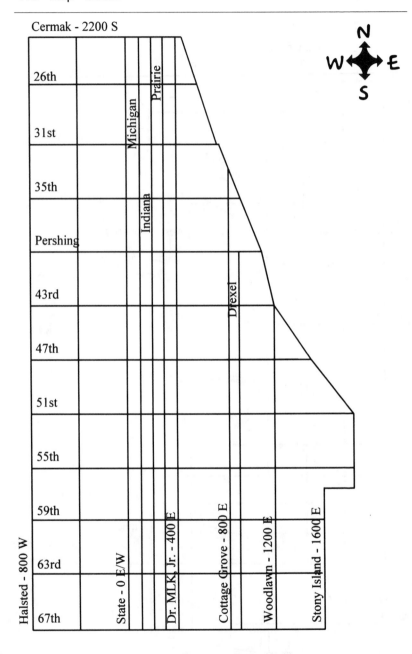

SOUTH

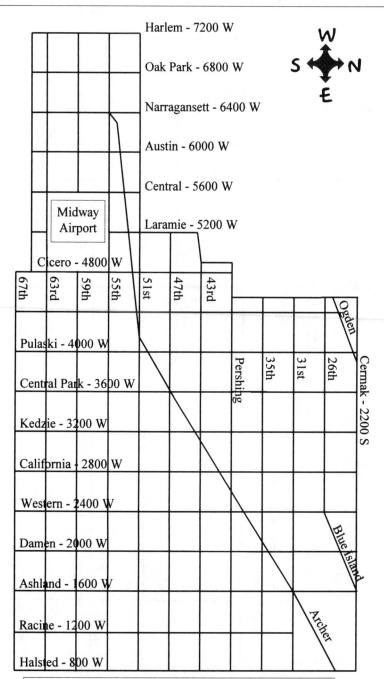

SOUTHWEST

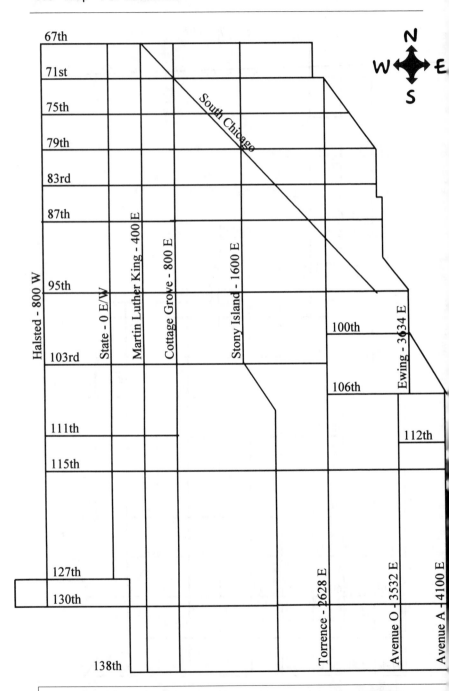

FAR SOUTHEAST

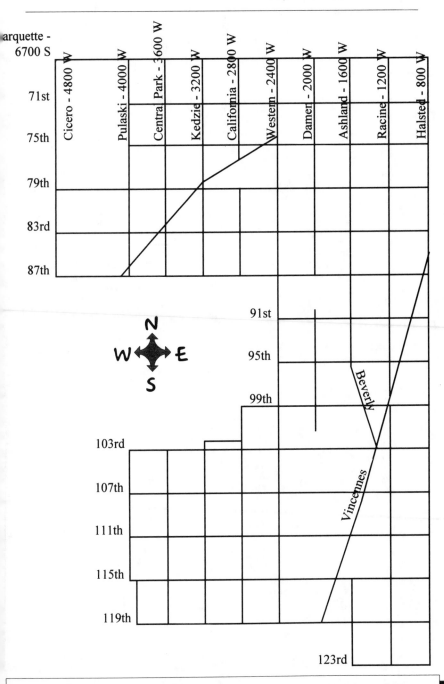

FAR SOUTHWEST

INDEX

B

E

F

M

U

Udupi Palace, 151
Ukrainian Institute of Modern Art, 58
Ukrainian National Museum, 58
Ukrainian Village, 58
ultimate frisbee, 107
Union Park, 101, 102, 105, 112
Union Stock Yards Gate, 26
unique browsing, 355
  alternative stuff, 355
  architecture and design stuff, 355
  art by locals, 356
  Austrian items, 361
  building parts, 357
  cookie jars, 357
  costumes, 357
  DJ equipment and accessories, 361
  hats, 358
  kites, 358
  magazines and newspapers, 358-359
  magic, 359, 361
  models, 359
  movie, radio, and TV memorabilia, 359
  paper, 360-361
  posters, 360
  spy stuff, 360
  surplus stuff, 360
  voodoo/hoodoo stuff, 361
University of Chicago, 26, 259, 287
  campus tour, 26
Uptown Poetry Slam, 252
Urban Market Cafe, 167, 204

V

Valley Forge Park, 94, 102, 115
Valois Cafeteria, 130
Vaughn's Pub, 219
Vee-Vee's African Restaurant and Cocktails, 199
Vegetarian Garden, 132
vegetarian dining, 132, 134, 138, 141, 151-153, 1158-160, 168-171, 175-179, 194, 199-203
Venice Cafe, 172
Veteran's Memorial Playground, 83
Viceroy of India, 152, 204
Victory Gardens Studios, 245
video horse racing, 98
video trivia, 98
Viceroy of India, 150
Vietnam Museum, 52
Vietnamese restaurants, 203
Villa de Marco, 155
Village Tap, 210, 235
Vittum Park, 94, 115
volleyball, 108
  indoor sand courts, 109

W

walking, 108, 275-326
  downtown, 300-325
  parks, 298-299
Walking chapter, 275-326
Walter Burley Griffin Prairie School Houses, 22
Warren Park, 80, 89, 94, 100, 102, 110
Washington Park, 93, 100, 103, 300, 105, 106, 114
waterfalls, 68-69

Z

y

ABOUT THE AUTHORS

Sharon Woodhouse

Sharon Woodhouse is a third-generation, lifelong Chicagoan. She began Lake Claremont Press, an independent publishing company specializing in unique books on the Chicago area and its history, in 1993, with the first edition of *A Native's Guide To Chicago*. In her free time she enjoys moviegoing, reading, traveling, and of course, appreciating Chicago and the many facets of urban living.

Mary McNulty

Mary McNulty was born in Baltimore but has lived in Chicago and its suburbs since 1975, when one look at the lakefront was all it took to keep her here. She has a bachelor's degree in sociology and has studied journalism at the graduate level. Working as a freelance writer and editor for the past 15 years, her byline has appeared in the *Chicago Tribune*, the *Daily Herald*, *Chicago Enterprise*, and *Catalyst*. In addition to Chicago, her passions include books, music, food, and her family.

OTHER CONTRIBUTORS

Brandon Zamora

Brandon Zamora helped with the fact-checking, proofreading, and indexing for *A Native's Guide To Chicago* and also did some research and writing for its "Food", "Entertainment", and "Walking" chapters. Cinephile, fiction writer, and balloon sculptor, Brandon is a native of Chicago. His writing has appeared in a number of fiction anthologies. He is currently working on a novel about the history of flatware and enjoys long nights of ballroom dancing.

Susan McNulty

Susan McNulty did extensive fact-checking for *A Native's Guide To Chicago* and assisted with the proofreading and indexing tasks. A native Chicagoan and a local actor who appeared most recently in *Tony and Tina's Wedding*, Susan is currently writing *The Chicago Resource Guide for the Chronically Ill and Disabled* for Lake Claremont Press. She is a fan of theater, movies, board games, and the Internet.

COMMENT CARD

Please help us with our continuous updates of *A Native's Guide To Chicago*. Let us know if you find typos, inaccuracies, or closed establishments within these pages. We would also appreciate your comments on this edition and suggestions for future editions.

_____

_____

_____

_____

_____

_____

_____

_____

We'll send a coupon for a 50% discount off the 4th edition to anyone who sends us their comments and suggestions—whether or not we are able to use them. Thanks for your help!

Name_____

Address_____

City_____**State**_____**Zip**_____

E-Mail Address_____

☐ Check here if you'd like to be added to our mailing list to receive information on future books and author events. We do not give out or sell our mailing list.

Lake Claremont Press
P.O. Box 25291
Chicago, IL 60625
773/784-7517
LakeClarPr@aol.com

OTHER TITLES FROM LAKE CLAREMONT PRESS

Hollywood on Lake Michigan:
100 Years of Chicago and the Movies
by Arnie Bernstein
This engaging history and street guide finally gives Chicago and Chicagoans their due for their prominent role in moviemaking history, from the silent era to the present. With trivia, special articles, historic and contemporary photos, film profiles, anecdotes, and exclusive interviews with dozens of personalities, including Studs Terkel, Roger Ebert, Gene Siskel, Dennis Franz, Harold Ramis, Joe Mantegna, Bill Kurtis, Irma Hall, and Tim Kazurinsky. Foreword by *Soul Food* writer/director, George Tillman, Jr.
0-9642426-2-1, softcover, over 80 photos and graphics, $15

Chicago Haunts: Ghostlore of the Windy City (Revised Edition)
by Ursula Bielski
From ruthless gangsters to restless mail order kings, from the Fort Dearborn Massacre to the St. Valentine's Day Massacre, the phantom remains of the passionate people and volatile events of Chicago history have made the Second City second to none in the annals of American ghostlore. Bielski captures over 160 years of this haunted history with her unique blend of lively storytelling, in-depth historical research, exlcusive interviews, and insights from parapsychology. Called "a masterpiece of the genre," "a must-read," and "an absolutely first-rate-book" by reviewers, *Chicago Haunts* continues to earn the praise of critics and readers alike.
0-9642426-7-2, softcover, 29 photos, $15

> **Insiders' Guides to Suburban Chicago**
> **for locals, visitors, and new residents!**

A Native's Guide To Chicago's South Suburbs
by Christina Bultinck and Christy Johnston-Czarnecki
0-9642426-1-3, softcover, photos, maps, $12.95 (Available Feb. 1998)

A Native's Guide To Chicago's Northern Suburbs
by Jason Fargo
0-9642426-8-0, softcover, photos, maps, $12.95 (Available Feb. 1998)

A Native's Guide To Chicago's Western Suburbs and **A Native's Guide to Chicago's Northwest Suburbs** will be also be released in 1999 to complete the series.

ORDER FORM

Please send me autographed copies of the following Lake Claremont Press titles:

A Native's Guide to Chicago, 3rd Ed. _____ @ $12.95 = _____

A Native's Guide To Chicago's
South Suburbs _____ @ $12.95 = _____

A Native's Guide To Chicago's
Northern Suburbs _____ @ $12.95 = _____

Chicago Haunts: Ghostlore of
the Windy City, Revised Ed. _____ @ $15.00 = _____

Hollywood on Lake Michigan:
100 Years of Chicago & The Movies _____ @ $15.00 = _____

Discounts when you order multiple copies!

2 books—10% off total
3-4 books —20% off total
5-9 books—25% off total
10+ books—40% off total

Subtotal: _____

Less Discount: _____

New Subtotal: _____

8.75% tax for
Illinois Residents: _____

Shipping Fees

$2 for the first book and
$.50 for each additional
book or a maximum of $5.

Shipping: _____

TOTAL: _____

Name_____

Address_____

City_____**STATE**_____**ZIP**_____

Enclose check, money order, or credit card number.

Visa/Mastercard#_____ **Exp.** _____

Signature_____

Lake Claremont Press
P.O. Box 25291
Chicago, IL 60625
773/784-7517
LakeClarPr@aol.com

Order by mail, phone, or e-mail.
All of our books have a no-hassles,
100% money back guarantee.